11\99

30
St. Louis

Before the Closet

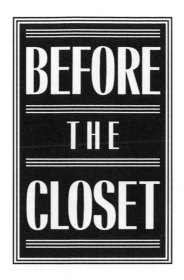

Same-Sex Love
from Beowulf *to*
Angels in America

Allen J. Frantzen

The University of Chicago Press
Chicago and London

Allen J. Frantzen is professor in the Department of English, Loyola University Chicago. He is the author of *The Literature of Penance in Anglo-Saxon England* (1983), *King Alfred* (1986), *Desire for Origins: New Language, Old English, and Teaching the Tradition* (1990), and *"Troilus and Criseyde": The Poem and the Frame* (1993); editor of *Speaking Two Languages: Traditional Disciplines and Contemporary Theory in Medieval Studies* (1991); and co-editor of *The Work of Work: Servitude, Slavery, and Labor in Medieval England* (1994) and *Anglo-Saxonism and the Construction of Social Identity* (1997).

The University of Chicago Press, Chicago 60637
The University of Chicago Press, Ltd., London
© 1998 by The University of Chicago
All rights reserved. Published 1998
Printed in the United States of America
07 06 05 04 03 02 01 00 99 98   1 2 3 4 5
ISBN: 0-226-26091-7 (cloth)

Library of Congress Cataloging-in-Publication Data

Frantzen, Allen J., 1947–
    Before the closet : same-sex love from Beowulf to Angels in
America / by Allen J. Frantzen.
        p.   cm.
    Includes bibliographical references and index.
    ISBN 0-226-26091-7 (acid-free paper)
    1. English literature—Old English, ca. 450–1100—History and
criticism.   2. Homosexuality and literature—England—History.
3. Kushner, Tony. Angels in America.   4. Anglo-Saxons in
literature.   5. Lesbians in literature.   6. Gay men in literature.
7. Love in literture.   8. Beowulf.   I. Title.
PR179.H66F73   1998
829'.09353—dc21   98-14935
                                                             CIP

For George

Contents

Acknowledgments

This book was a pleasure to write. I have many people to thank for encouragement, criticism, and assistance with it. The project began as a by-product of a hypertext edition of the Anglo-Saxon penitentials, sponsored by a fellowship from the John Simon Guggenheim Memorial Foundation. Work on this edition, which is still in progress, helped me see that there was more evidence of same-sex relations in Anglo-Saxon England than I had thought. I began to look for ways to integrate that data with larger questions about sexual codes and their role in shaping our ideas of early English culture. This book is the result. I am very grateful to the Guggenheim Foundation and to many people at Loyola University Chicago. I thank especially Timothy Austin, Suzanne Gossett, Kathleen McCourt, the Loyola Endowment for the Humanities Faculty Development Program, and Research Services for generous support of my requests for leaves of absence and research assistance.

I developed this study over several years and published some of my research in preliminary form during that time. Most of that material has since been substantially revised. The exception is the reading of *Angels in America* that forms part of chapter 7, which appears here in the form it takes in *Approaching the Millennium: Essays on Tony Kushner's Angels in America,* ed. Deborah A. Geis and Steven F. Kruger (1997). I thank the University of Michigan Press for permission to reprint the essay. Material expanded and extensively reworked for this book includes parts of the following essays: "When Women Aren't Enough," *Speculum* 68 (1993) (used in chapter 2) and "Between the Lines: Queer Theory, the History of Homosexuality, and the Anglo-Saxon Penitentials," *Journal of Medieval and Early Renaissance Studies* 26 (1996) (used in chapter 4). A small section of chapter 5 appeared as "Sodom and Gomorrah in Prose Works from Alfred's Reign," in *Alfred the Wise: Studies in Honour of Janet Bately,* ed. Jane Roberts and Janet

L. Nelson with Malcolm Godden (1997). Finally, material contained in "Bede and Bawdy Bale: Gregory the Great, Angels, and the 'Angli'," in *Anglo-Saxonism and the Construction of Social Identity,* which I co-edited with John D. Niles (1997), appears in condensed form in chapter 7.

For assistance in obtaining illustrations and permissions to use them, I am indebted to Eva Nichols of the Mark Morris Dance Group; to Frank-Rüdiger Berger of the Deutsche Staatsoper Berlin; to Robert Tuggle of the Archives Department of the Metropolitan Opera, New York; and to Alan Marshall of the British Library and to the Photographic Reproduction Department of the British Library.

Friends and colleagues who have offered comments and criticism are numerous. Among them I especially wish to thank Andrew Walters Cole and Christopher Castiglia, stimulating, patient, and perceptive readers both. I also thank Steven Kruger and two other (anonymous) readers for the University of Chicago Press for their challenging and helpful commentary and for guiding me to important corrections. Christina Heckman and Florentine Hoelker assisted the final phases of the project with efficiency and verve. Those who have helped me find my way as I wrote include David Aers, a formative influence on the project, Kimberly Bovee, Graham Caie, Mary Dockray-Miller, Michael Drout, Betty Ellzey, Bryon Grigsby, Scott Gwara, Charles Harmon, Joseph Harris, Stephen Harris, Antonette diPaolo Healey, Joseph Janangelo, Richard Lee, Karma Lochrie, Sally Metzler, Douglas Moffat, Kirk Ormond, Pierre Payer, Elizabeth Robinson, Barbara Rosenwein, John Ruffing, Nicholas Watson, Joyce Wexler, Jon Wilcox, and Benjamin Withers. I thank them all. I owe many thanks to my good friends in Germany, Lutz Haegert, Louise and Wolfgang Grandel, and especially Waldtraut Wollburg.

Matthew Howard from the University of Chicago Press proved a reliable consultant on editorial matters great and small. Doug Mitchell has been unfailingly enthusiastic and amazingly efficient in handling all aspects of this project, and I offer him warmest thanks. I will always regard him as the ideal editor.

The most important influence on this book has been George R. Paterson, and I am very pleased that it appears just in time to mark our twenty years together.

Introduction
Straightforward

I n this book I explore same-sex love in English culture of the early
Middle Ages, approximately AD 600 to 1200. Beyond these centuries
I examine the association of same-sex behavior with the Anglo-Saxons
in Chaucer's England, the Renaissance, and the gay world of *Angels in
America*. In the early Middle Ages, as now, same-sex love encompassed
a broad range of emotions and actions, ranging from gestures of affection to sexual intercourse. We are accustomed to thinking of sexual
behavior in one of three forms—straight, gay, or bisexual. This habit
has been reinforced by such important work as John Boswell's *Christianity, Social Tolerance, and Homosexuality: Gay People in Western Europe from the Beginning of the Christian Era to the Fourteenth Century*.[1]
But use of these categories has only recently become routine, and it is
not too late to check their power to reduce complex sexual experiences
to ironclad alternatives.

I call this a book about "same-sex love" because the obvious choice,
"homosexuality," is, for periods before the modern era, inaccurate.
"Homosexuality" and "homosexuals" were not recognized concepts in
the Middle Ages or in the Renaissance, although we can safely assume
that there were, then as always, men and women who preferred to be
intimate only with those of their own sex. Rather than try to establish
identities for medieval people, I describe "same-sex love" and "same-
sex relations" that range from sexual intercourse to expressions of nonsexual affection, acts seen not in isolation but as part of the "activity
and interactions" that make up a social world.[2] By "same-sex" I mean
no more, and no less, than that the partners involved in a given exchange are of the same biological sex, a determinant to which the gender roles assumed by either or both of the parties may or may not
correspond.

Many books have been written about the history of sex. Most of them discuss the early medieval evidence only briefly or omit it entirely. But that evidence plays an important part in these studies nonetheless. Richard Smith has described the history of homosexuality as "one big coming out story: after a polymorphous perverse infancy in antiquity we felt little, bar a few fumbles in our Renaissance adolescence. It was only this century that we came of age and burst triumphantly out of the closet."[3] In Smith's paradigm the medieval period constitutes the "childhood" of homosexuality, filling the crucial gap between infancy and adolescence. This symbolic position might seem suitable for the Middle Ages, a time often assumed to have been universally devout. But if current scholarship is to be believed, this "childhood" was permissive as well as pious. Boswell's book maintains that the early Middle Ages tolerated and even fostered homosexual relations. Only later, in the thirteenth century, did medieval people witness what Boswell describes as "the rise of intolerance."[4] Although there is good reason to believe that Boswell's portrayal seriously misrepresents the evidence (as others have shown and as I argue in chapters 3 and 5), his influence is far-reaching. For example, one reads in a recent study, "It is true, as the late John Boswell has amply demonstrated, that there was nothing inherently homophobic about medieval Christianity. Indeed, it was quite often tolerant, and occasionally even supportive of same-sex attachments, particularly in the period before the age of papal reforms" (i.e., the eleventh and twelfth centuries).[5] But many sources show that the early medieval Church overwhelmingly disapproved of same-sex relations. Whether that homophobia was "inherent" or whether it was contingent on particular agents and circumstances is not as important a distinction as it might at first seem to be, since disapproval of same-sex acts is not confined to particular centers of power. In the Boswell-influenced quotation above, the early Middle Ages are described as "particularly" tolerant and supportive of same-sex attachments. But by viewing the evidence less selectively than Boswell did, we can see that it is possible to reverse his now-standard paradigm and to argue that the early medieval period was actually less tolerant of same-sex relations than the later period. Instead of a "rise of intolerance" one could argue for a "rise of tolerance." Indeed, tolerance of same-sex relations is easier to hypothesize for the later Middle Ages than for the early period.

My aim is not to reverse Boswell's argument, however—we do not have enough information to decide the matter either way—but to argue against his analysis and work based on it and to make possible a new look at the early medieval evidence of sexual behavior. The first of four objectives for this book is to remedy some deficiencies in histo-

ries of same-sex relations by examining the categories operative in Anglo-Saxon England, an important and richly attested early medieval
culture whose extensive evidence Boswell's and other histories of sex
barely acknowledge.

My second objective is to show that by unfolding the subtleties of the
early medieval evidence we gain perspective on the discourse surrounding same-sex relations today, both as to its origins and as to the interplay
between same-sex and opposite-sex codes in that discourse. Of course,
many shifts in perceptions of sex took place between the early Middle
Ages and our own time. But I maintain that there are fundamental
similarities, if not continuities, between the Anglo-Saxons' experience
and the experience of men and women in western Europe and North
America, especially in rural and military cultures, up to and after the
middle of the twentieth century.

There are also many differences. The most important one, I believe,
concerns how we represent the place of same-sex love in relation to the
heterosexual or heteronormative social order that stigmatizes it. The
usual figure for this representation is that staple of modern gay and
lesbian criticism, the closet. Along with an attendant discourse of "open
secrets," the image of the closet is ubiquitous in the analysis of same-
sex relations. Although useful to understanding homosexual life today,
this figure is not always appropriate to same-sex evidence in premodern
(medieval) cultures. Like other familiar tags—"gay" and "straight,"
"homosexual" and "heterosexual," and newer terms, such as "transgendered" and "queer"—the language of closets and secrets can foreclose
discussion of the very questions we need to ask. Such terms as "closeted
relations" can be used to describe all forms of interaction between individuals and communities and to juxtapose private to public sins, in
the process unavoidably representing them not just as sexual but as
primarily sexual. Although such language might sometimes be appropriate to later medieval and Renaissance cultures, it is not, for many
reasons, appropriate to the period I discuss here.[6]

The thesis of this book is that the existence of the closet was not
recognized by the men and women of Anglo-Saxon England. Hence
I describe theirs as a culture "before the closet." Explaining the Anglo-
Saxon evidence as specific and straightforward rather than closeted and
queer is my third objective. According to Eve Kosofsky Sedgwick, the
closet is "the defining structure for gay oppression in this century," a
space wherein homosexual relations are tolerated only because they are
hidden from public view.[7] Gay men and women today can choose to
stay in the closet or come out of it, meaning that they can either continue to conceal their sexual identity (believing that it "belongs" in

a secret place) or express it (believing that their sexuality should be known to others—if it is not already).[8] Men and women in Anglo-Saxon England could not have made such a choice. They were without the apparatus of identity (gay, lesbian, straight, bisexual, transgendered) that automatically configures our discussion of sexual relations. There is very little evidence from this culture that sexual acts, with one's own or the opposite sex, constituted a distinctive behavioral trait. The early Middle Ages (the later Middle Ages, too, I would argue) lacked an identity that we might think of today as the "sexual subject" whose sexual practices and preferences inform, if they do not actually determine, both self-awareness and public identity. Anglo-Saxon culture, which was of course overwhelmingly Christian, did not attach special opprobrium to homosexual sins, although it did not tolerate them, either. Some sexual offenses (including homosexual acts) were included among those seen as especially grave and even sometimes regarded as unmentionable. But certain nonsexual sins were unmentionable, too. The evidence shows that *any* form of sexual behavior was harshly condemned if it exceeded the Church's view of what was necessary for procreation. A culture before the closet was not a culture before repression.

Given the lack of special status for same-sex offenses, it is difficult to see how those guilty of them could be said to occupy a closet, which would have to have been constructed by prohibitions against same-sex acts in particular. It might be said that the only closet or impermeable secret place known to the Anglo-Saxons was the sinner's conscience: that was the only space available for hiding one's sins, for concealing dark deeds one could not risk describing to others. Like other early and later medieval churches, the Anglo-Saxon church tirelessly warned that sins concealed in this life would be revealed in the next, and that whatever shame such exposure created here should be borne for two reasons: it would result in forgiveness and make salvation possible, and it would preclude unimaginable exposure at the Last Judgment. The earliest document expressing this idea was written by the Anglo-Saxon Boniface in the eighth century. A commonplace Old English version of it, quoted here from a handbook for the priest's use in confession, reads, "For it is better for you that you shame yourself now, here, before me alone, one of the miserable ones, than hereafter before God on the Day of Judgment, when the tribes of heaven, earth, and hell will be gathered together" ("Forðon betere þe is þæt ðe sceamige nu her beforan me anum yrmincge þonne eft on domes dæge beforan Gode, þær hefenwaru and eorðwaru and helwaru beoð ealle ætsomne").[9]

I would not claim that this motif is distinctively Anglo-Saxon, but I would argue that it bespeaks a religious culture in which there are no secrets particular to sexual sinners. Sexual sins, after all, are no easier to hide than others and could be more difficult to conceal (in case of pregnancy, for example). In Anglo-Saxon texts no special rhetoric is used to ferret out sexual sins as opposed to other kinds of sin. More-over, there was nothing to prevent Anglo-Saxon Christians from con-cealing some sins as they revealed others. Anyone could choose to hide sins, but to do so was not to occupy a "closet" or to act specifically to conceal sexual behavior.

Anglo-Saxon culture did not play a game of hide-and-seek with sexual relations. The same cannot be said for the later Middle Ages. The point at which secrecy and concealment became attached to same-sex acts, also the point at which same-sex acts became feared as espe-cially dangerous, is the mid–eleventh century, an important moment in the history of sex. As I will show in chapter 4, at this point the Church became increasingly concerned with standardizing penances for sexual sins and, at the same time, increasingly reluctant to describe them precisely. One reason that Church officials avoided explicit ref-erences to sexual acts is that by describing certain sins in detail they risked suggesting new sins to others. The fear of giving scandal and leading others into sin exercised considerable influence in the later Middle Ages. Preachers were warned not to use the word "sodomy" or discuss it, for fear that they would be encouraging one of the sins most hateful to God. Many Anglo-Saxon writers observed no such taboo, however. Some authorities believed that sodomy was a sin too foul to mention; in their writing we might be said to have the origins of the closet. Patristic authors who refused to discuss sodomy, or to name same-sex acts as the particular sins of the Sodomites, established the special seriousness of these sins by attempting to shield them from pub-lic discussion. But in Anglo-Saxon England this anxiety about same-sex acts was largely superfluous, since other voices in the culture, no less authoritative, discussed sodomy and related same-sex sins. It seems reasonable to suggest that sodomy itself was the first inhabitant of the closet, forced into hiding by some clerics in an effort to control it. That act, of course, acknowledged the power of sodomy to challenge and disrupt the social order. Then as now, nothing so greatly increased the attraction of a particular act as the decision to forbid it.

Some Anglo-Saxon writers, working in various genres, referred plainly to "sodomy" when they needed to do so and described other forms of sexual intercourse that they abominated. Their approach to same-sex sex was direct, frank, and open—in a word, straightforward. Straightforwardness is a principle that modern scholarship on same-sex relations both cherishes and shuns. On one hand, academic discussions of sex and sex acts are candid, even vivid, and long-standing taboos against certain once-forbidden words have disappeared (have these words thus lost their power?). Everyone agrees, I think, that frank and open discussion of sexual practices is much to be preferred to the coy and sometimes disingenuous discourse of the tradition. On the other hand, working in the opposite direction from straightforwardness—by a certain irony—is queer theory, which purportedly makes candor in sexual matters de rigueur. Queer theory is a collection of methods and perspectives that pursue an aggressive politics of gay and lesbian liberation. Now merrily sweeping all work on the history of sex into its domain—all gays, lesbians, bisexuals, and transsexuals are queer, any work on the history of same-sex relations is queer—this multifaceted movement seems to have become the age's dominant mode for writing about sex and gender. In my view, any juggernaut is worth resisting, especially one whose idol is Resistance. Queer theory is a sometimes useful strategy in the analysis of same-sex relations, but its limitations are as important as its advantages, and much less well understood. My fourth objective is not just to question the direction of queer medieval studies but to try to redirect their engagement with historical research and criticism. Not everybody who writes about homosexual issues in culture is satisfied with "queer" as a term for our work, and for good reasons. Some writers, including Terry Castle, have objected to the "sometimes dizzying" linguistic maneuvers of queer theorists, and others, myself included, have reservations about the way in which queer theorists occasionally treat complex historical evidence.[10]

Queer theorists have many differences among themselves but seem committed to a few agreed-on principles. One of them is that any text or cultural representation can be "queered," an operation that sometimes entails the disclosure of homoerotic content (i.e., same-sex acts) and sometimes, less specifically, the analysis of ways in which texts and cultures establish heterosexual standards or imperatives by excluding homosexual possibilities.[11] Queering seeks to reveal the dependence of the heterosexual order on a homosexual order by identifying rhetorical strategies that exclude same-sex relations, acts, and desires so that the world appears to be ordered along heterosexual lines. Thus gay and lesbian sexuality is seen not simply as transgressive or marginal, but rather fully engaged in a culture's sexual codes.[12] Queer theory struggles against the simple binarism of "homosexual" and "heterosexual" categories but dwells on the closet, a figure of speech created by a culture's gestures of exclusion that unfortunately reinforces binary points of view. Queer theory aims to break apart conventional patterns and ways of organizing thought, texts, and images, not to mention culture. Many queer critics are deeply invested in a deconstructive maneuver showing that the dominance of one group or idea always depends on the exclusion and subordination of a competing group or idea. Queer theory would have been impossible without postmodern notions of reality, including identity, as something produced by language rather than preexisting it, and as something therefore unavoidably difficult to define or locate (that, supposedly, is part of the "queerness" of the queer: it cannot be pinned down). The view that sexual identity is an effect of discourse might be said to be the most distinctive assumption of queer theory and the assumption that most sharply distinguishes it from other kinds of research in the history of sex and sexuality. But the extent to which previous inquiries assumed a stable or unproblematic sexual identity for medieval or early modern people is easily exaggerated. The value of histories of sex that do not engage queer theory, many of them studies of great merit, is, in my view, unchallenged. Indeed, those studies are even more valuable now that queer criticism has done so much to try to blur categories and obscure differences and create a critical culture of "messiness" liberated from the strictures of traditional social and academic discourse.[13]

FOUCAULT'S EFFECTS

Queer theory would also have been impossible without Michel Foucault, chief architect of the hide-and-seek economies on which queer theory depends. Foucault created an idea of history as a collection of discourses and truth effects, a collection of strategies and rules whereby power shapes its subjects and its subjects respond. Foucault's influence is prominently acknowledged in what is perhaps the formative work of queer theory, Sedgwick's *Epistemology of the Closet*.[14] Another seminal theorist in this field is Judith Butler, whose work analyzes gender performativity and problems of cultural determinism.[15] Of these three authorities, only Foucault was concerned with medieval culture, and his medievalism was remarkable only for its superficiality, lack of detail, and indifference to documents and their nuances. Butler does not write about literary texts, and Sedgwick does not write queer studies of premodern or early-modern material. The work of Foucault, Sedgwick, and Butler, seldom mediated with other commentary apart from feminist work, constitutes almost the entire theoretical basis of queer medieval studies. This, I believe, is a problem that queer medieval studies seldom acknowledge.

Foucault created a master narrative of hide-and-seek, of detection and evasion, a mechanism used to explain how the self was subjected (in every sense) to the truth-compelling apparatus of the medieval confessional. Through *The History of Sexuality,* Foucault has exercised an enormous influence on medieval studies and studies of sexuality.[16] But not everybody agrees that this influence has been benign. David M. Halperin has recanted his 1986 opinion that the first volume of *The History,* rich in "admittedly bright ideas," is also "full of hollow assertions, disdainful of historical documentation, and careless in its generalizations." Halperin has since decided that Foucault is a saint whose work is, apparently, above criticism, and has declared that he "would not write such a sentence today," manifesting in this move an appropriately medieval attitude toward authority. Halperin's initial characterization of Foucault's work strikes me as accurate.[17] Karma Lochrie has recently criticized Foucault's thinking on medieval topics, noting that his attitudes were contradictory. He viewed the Middle Ages both as "hegemonized medieval 'other,'" to quote Lochrie, and as host to a discourse of self-realization continuous with modern practices of avowal. He viewed confession both as a discourse of self-sacrifice and as a sinister exercise in social control.[18]

The greatest difficulty in Foucault's dominance in the study of medieval sexual practice, in my view, is not that his positions are contradictory; Foucault thrived on contradictions. Rather the problem is that he did not practice what he preached, or, in matters of medieval religion, even necessarily know much about it. Foucault's interest in the "techniques of the self" in classical cultures (especially clear in the second volume of *The History of Sexuality*) outstripped his interest in the historical analysis of sex acts.[19] He seems to have known almost nothing about either the theology or the social practice of penance and confession. The first volume of *The History of Sexuality* (the only one concerned with medieval perspectives) offers almost nothing beyond a superficial glance at confessional practice. The index entries under "penance" and "confession" are revealing: one reference to a manual of confession, two to confession in literature, three to confession "and the production of truth."[20]

Beyond a very brief analysis of confession as social practice, one finds in Foucault little more than fascination with a central mechanism uniting confessor and penitent in a discourse of power: "If I ask, you must tell." His view of sex in the Middle Ages as an "originary, natural, and unitary moment for sexuality and its discourses," to continue quoting

Lochrie, was not based on an analysis of the documents that describe medieval confession or penitential practice.[21] Medieval sexual practice is alluded to merely to illustrate distinctive ideas about history and discourse that Foucault had already developed. Leaving to one side his lack of concern for differences between early and late medieval traditions, it does not seem that his insights were either based on or tested against a broad field of documentary evidence. The standard apology for Foucault's antiempirical stance is that his example, in Halperin's words, "teaches us to analyze discourse strategically, not in terms of what it *says* but in terms of what it *does* and how it *works*." Halperin adds, "That does not mean that we learn from Foucault to treat the *content* of particular discourses as uninteresting or irrelevant (after all, one has to understand what discourses say in order to be able to analyze what they do and how they work)."[22] But Foucault himself seems to have treated the *content* of confessional discourses as both uninteresting and irrelevant, and too many writers ignore Halperin's warning and follow Foucault's lead. Foucault described a discursive strategy that seems to be automatically applied to any discussion of sex. But not all the evidence bears out the strategy Foucault outlined.

By disrupting the conceptual and political continuities that governed analysis of the past, Foucault made a valuable contribution to historiography, as Halperin and many others have acknowledged.[23] In the history of penance and confession Foucault's claim was specific and fundamental. He focused on the relationship between confession and sex, not only to reveal the power of confessional discourse over sex but to suggest how that discourse might be resisted. "[B]y making sex into that which, above all else, had to be confessed," Foucault wrote, "the Christian pastoral always presented it as the disquieting enigma: not a thing which stubbornly shows itself, but one which always hides, the insidious presence that speaks in a voice so muted and often disguised that one risks remaining deaf to it."[24] Sex "always hides," Foucault writes, meaning that it is always in the closet—and that the closet always already exists. But does sex hide, or is it hidden? To say that sex is hidden is contrary to Foucault's epistemology, which stresses the power of discourses rather than the agents through which discourses flow. But Foucault's discussion of sodomy, the hidden sin par excellence, suggests how an oppressive discourse can give rise to forces that resist it. Foucault memorably remarked that sodomy was an "utterly confused category," an observation that appears in *The History of Sexuality* in a discussion of detective strategies called "rule of the tactical polyvalence of discourses." Society manifested extreme reticence in regard to sodomy, and Foucault proposed that, because the term "sodomy" described many different kinds of sex acts (and eventually more than sex acts), it was never possible to define or control it completely. Punishments for sodomites were severe, but sentences for sodomites were rare. Confusion about the term—the confused discourse of sodomy—was in part created by the discourse's own silence, its reluctance to say too much. This reluctance not only weakened the power of social repression and frustrated attempts to punish sodomy but also created silences or gaps that undermined the discourse's power and rendered it "fragile" and liable to be thwarted.[25] Foucault argued that polyvalence (a term derived from chemistry and biology, meaning, roughly, that an element has the capacity to combine with or affect another element or elements) results from "a multiplicity of discursive elements that can come into play in various strategies." Polyvalence has significant "tactical" dimensions not only for the agents of enforcement but also for those subject to this control. Because it is polyvalent, "discourse can be both an instrument and an effect of power, but also a hindrance, a stumbling-block, a point of resistance and a starting point for an opposing strategy."[26] The more detailed prohibitions are, the more difficult they are to enforce and the more easily they give rise to exceptions.

Homosexuality, Foucault claims, spoke "in its own behalf" by using the language that spoke against it. Polyvalence here means that one set of statements about same-sex behavior can be taken two ways, seen as two different things. In Foucault's view, the two statements are opposite. But there is no need to limit polyvalence to a binary opposition. The concept of reverse discourses is useful in getting us to think about medieval sinners who failed to heed or defied the Church's demand that they confess. Told to speak about everything, some of them apparently chose to remain silent about a few things at least, and did so no doubt for many reasons, including fear and shame.

Foucault's analysis of the discourse of sodomy works reasonably well for later medieval evidence, but not for evidence from the earlier period. Late medieval confessional practice forbade the priest from inquiring too closely into the penitent's sexual behavior; within those constraints, it seems safe to say that sex did speak in a "muted" and "disguised" voice. In the early thirteenth century Robert of Flamborough advised priests how to inquire about "lust against nature." Robert asked "if he [the penitent] had sinned against nature at any other time and if he had sex with anyone in a particular way. If he should ask what is meant by a particular way, I would not answer him, for he would know. I never make mention of anything that might become an occasion for sinning, but rather speak of generalities that everyone knows are sins."[27] The Church required priests to clarify the sinner's sexual acts but also allowed confessors to assume that penitents were familiar with "generalities that everyone knows are sins." This language sets up a game of hide-and-seek; it creates a formal provision, should the confessor or the penitent care to exercise it, for not exploring certain sins. The confessor is told not to answer the penitent's question about "a particular way" of having sex with someone. It seems reasonable to assume that canny penitents could take advantage of this opportunity and not ask, thus making sure that their sins "against nature" or other "particular" sexual sins were referred to only as "generalities" and assigned lesser penances than they might have received had they been disclosed more fully. Confessors assumed that penitents knew everything about the categories of sexual sins that priests themselves had been taught, an assumption that enabled the penitent to manage the disclosure of sins if he or she chose to do so.

Robert's approach to confession reflects some well-documented tendencies of later medieval penitential practice, especially the desire to anatomize sins and distinguish their traits. Early handbooks of penance or penitentials seldom contain more than a few pages; penitentials from the later period are sometimes hundreds of pages in length, unfolding sins in elaborate schemata such as that of the seven "deadly sins," the structuring device of Chaucer's *Parson's Tale*.[28] It is useful to remember Foucault's concept of reverse discourse in relation to these immense texts. It is true that they located more places than before to look for sin, but it is also true that in doing so they created more places than before for sinners to hide. As Foucault's work suggests, detailed prohibitions are more difficult to enforce because they create more opportunities for evasion. In this sense we can argue, against Boswell, that the later period was more rather than less tolerant of same-sex sins.

Robert's tone is never less than very serious, but in this matter he might be said to wink at his readers and perhaps to advise his readers— confessors—to wink at their penitents, assuming that the penitents will wink back. In quite another context James Creech has written, "Rather than transmitting information from one who knows it to one who doesn't, the wink enacts a communion of those already presumed at least preconsciously to know the taboo secret. The confident hope for that communion, that sharing, is what a wink is."[29] A wink is an act that presumes a closet and creates a place to hide, for it is a "communion" enclosing two parties who think the same way and know the same things. What they know is not for everybody to know; that knowledge would, more widely dispersed, presumably be dangerous, scandalous. "Generalities that everyone knows are sins" can be de-scribed as a discourse "centrally representative of [a culture's] motivat-ing passions and contradictions, even while marginalized by its ortho-doxies," to paraphrase Sedgwick's description of the closet.[30] Robert's generalities are "centrally representative" of his culture's passion to con-trol sexual sins, but those "generalities" are also "marginalized by its [the culture's] orthodoxies." They cannot be acknowledged verbally even in the most private and remedial context.

In the early evidence no such closet-producing assumptions were made about "generalities that everyone knows are sins." Indeed, Anglo-Saxon confessional discourse did not consist of generalities. Priests were warned to suit their inquiries to the status of the person confess-ing. But if a confessor was not sure that his penitent knew what he meant, the confessor asked in order to be sure. "Did you take your wife or a serving girl from behind?" asks a ninth-century penitential. "If so, forty days of penance" ("Nupsisti cum uxore tua vel ancilla retro? XL dies poeniteas"). "Did you commit fornication as the Sodomites did, or with your brother or mother, or with an animal, or by some contriv-ance?" ("Fecisti fornicationem, sicut sodomitae fecerunt, vel cum fratre aut matre, vel cum pecoribus, vel ullo ingenio? XV vel XII vel VII vel I annum poeniteas"). Depending on the answer, the priest assigned a penance of fifteen, twelve, or seven years or one year.[31] How "mute" is the voice that responded to such questions? How would either priest or penitent have remained "deaf" to sex spoken about so bluntly? Mark D. Jordan claims that "references to Sodom or Sodomites" in the early penitentials both conceal and reveal. "They reveal to those who already know what the geographico-biblical reference means," he writes. "Otherwise they conceal."[32] But I think it is safe to say that confessors who asked about specific sexual positions were confident that their penitents understood the questions, and that the priests fol-lowed up with further questions or with explanations when they de-tected confusion or hesitancy. Confession in the early Middle Ages did not take place in a box, with the penitent hidden from view; rather these exchanges were face-to-face encounters that left little room for hiding the sinner's confusion or embarrassment.

Foucault's failure to explore this kind of evidence seems to me to undercut his analysis of medieval confessional practice. Rather than rely on an all-purpose mechanism of secrecy and discourse, I believe that historical inquiry into power relations should begin with the most powerful voices of a culture and should delineate their organization of the culture's dominant and dominated voices. Only then can resistance to the voices of power be imagined. I locate these voices in law codes, handbooks of penance, homilies, and other pastoral texts. From this perspective, there was no hidden terrain in the Anglo-Saxon landscape except that inhabited by recalcitrant sinners who thought that they could conceal their sins and thereby escape punishment. Those who did so, as I have already suggested, were not only those guilty of sexual offenses, same-sex or otherwise.

Anglo-Saxon authorities were remarkably clear about what they abominated, especially in the area of sexual relations, and very clear about what phenomena they feared, and why. The authorities never give the impression of not knowing what it is that sinners do or of hesitating to ask sinners to be clear about their actions. Their discourse about sexual sins is therefore much less polyvalent than the sexual discourse of the later medieval church. For this reason, the "epistemology of the closet," in Sedgwick's phrase, which is without doubt an ingenious device for reading texts and other cultural artefacts, is an inadequate device for historical analysis. It is a rhetorical convenience of modern subjectivity all too easily transferred to premodern cultures.

THE SHADOW

The closet is a metaphor of recent vintage, not used in the gay movement before the 1960s, according to George Chauncey.[33] The closet connects same-sex relations to heterosexual relations in a pattern of opposition and dominance. Rather than rely on the closet as a governing trope, I wish to use another, the shadow, itself already a minor metaphor in gay and lesbian criticism. The closet contains "a small, shadowily identified group," Sedgwick writes.[34] In a similar vein, Castle suggests that the lesbian "is never with us, it seems, but always somewhere else: in the shadows, in the margins, hidden from history, out of sight, out of mind, . . . a pale denizen of the night."[35] And Alexander Doty wants to remove "mass culture queerness from the shadowy realm of connotation to which much of it has been relegated."[36] Taking a clue from Sedgwick's "shadowily identified group," Castle's shadowy lesbian, and Doty's "shadowy realm of connotation," I propose to put the shadow in the spotlight, so to speak, and to treat the shadow not just as a place of obscured visibility but as a figure for the representation of same-sex love. In a sense partially compatible with that which I develop here, Alan Bray has used the shadow to figure the interrelation of homosexual and heterosexual orders. Commenting on the status of homosexual acts as "unnatural" and, in some poems, seen as "altogether outside the ordered world of Creation," Bray argues that sodomy and buggery in early modern England represented "the disorder in sexual relations that, in principle at least, could break out anywhere." Homosexuality was part of "a universal potential for disorder which lay alongside an equally universal order," adjacent to the ordered world and "part, in a word, of its shadow." [37] To see the world of same-sex relations as a "shadow" of universal order is to see the homosexual as secondary and insubstantial. In this sense, the shadow is an objectionable representation of same-sex desire or same-sex affection (of course, the closet is also secondary). But if the shadow denotes the obscure and secondary, it also fittingly registers the powerful role of same-sex relations in heteronormative culture, whether medieval or modern.

A shadow is more than a patch of darkness outlining an object. "Shadow: gloom, sadness, depression," insists a dictionary, as if to defeat my efforts to locate the positive qualities of the word. [38] A shadow is closely connected to the body whose shade it is, but it is also something else—something more—that belongs to the body but also stands apart from it. Shadows shape our field of vision. Objects not only cast shadows but serve as fields for them; shadows define the contours and planes of surfaces, creating variety, complexity, and depth. Shadows are instrumental in creating our perception of objects in three dimensions rather than two. It is because of shadows that we can see. One might object that an object is "real," while shadows are not. But only in the realm of pure ideas can we have an object without shadows on, around, and behind it; likewise, every object is a surface of shadows. Moreover, shadows have to be *made* to disappear—witness the machinations of photographers to banish or manipulate them. Shadows are naturally a part of all we see. I am quite happy with the shadow as a figure for same-sex love. Shadows cannot exist on their own, but nothing can be seen without them. Durable, adaptable, inescapable, they *define*.

If we imagine the heterosexual system ("the" sexual system) as a contoured field or ground, we can imagine same-sex relations as shadows on that field. Shadows help to elaborate the heterosexual world order, not simply complementing that order but completing it. The object and its shadow must be seen together. One of the goals of queer theory is to demonstrate that same-sex relations are not incidental to the heterosexual world order. Rather, queer theory seeks to consolidate homosexual relations as a presence in a culture and its history and uses them to reveal the extent to which power relations have been structured as heterosexual—frequently at the expense of the freedom of men and women who find pleasure, love, and happiness with those of their own sex, or with those of both sexes. The shadows I trace in this book consolidate same-sex relations and juxtapose them to the heterosexual patterns that organize narratives, texts, and whole cultures. I propose that same-sex relations are as closely attached to heterosexual relations as shadows are to their objects, and indeed that same-sex relations are indispensable to culture. I do not make this assertion merely to open a way to a deconstructive stance, claiming that homosexual relations, because they supplement heterosexual relations, can therefore be used to undo heterosexual claims to primacy; Lee Edelman has already done this.[39] The deconstruction of hegemonic heterosexuality, or heteronormativity, can endlessly manipulate historical conditions as rhetorical effects without approaching the reality of same-sex relations for the men and women who experienced them. My analysis attempts to see around the object of heterosexual relations to their homosexual shadow. If it is not always easy to find, it is almost always there.

I argue throughout this book that same-sex relations are never far from heterosexual relations. Bray advanced a similar point when he asserted that same-sex relations were tolerated in English Renaissance culture because they were usually constructed within patriarchal institutions and were never recognized in any distinctive way as "homosexual" or as any other uniquely identifiable form of social discourse. Renaissance homosexuality had no features "peculiar to it alone." Instead, it existed within institutionalized relationships that concealed same-sex activity, including the household, pedagogy, and prostitution.[40] Likewise, in Anglo-Saxon England same-sex relations had no features recognizably peculiar or particular to "homosexual" identity. But situated in various social institutions, especially those related to male-male friendship, they are detectable all the same. Although part of what I want to do is merely to point them out, I also want to analyze their relationship to the heterosexual world order, to the social and cultural objects whose shadows they are.

By preferring the shadow to the closet, I am doing more than substituting a Foucault-derived figure for one that is not. I am also seeking to differentiate my approach to the same-sex economies of medieval texts from the critical practices of queer theory as it has come to be known in medieval studies. Most of what has been done with queer theory in medieval cultural and literary criticism to date cannot really be called queer "theory." Exceptions are brief essays by Lochrie that question Foucault's dominance in studies of medieval sexuality and, from another perspective, a defense of the consistency of his political views by Carolyn Dinshaw.[41] Instead of querying the theoretical basis supplied by aggressively modernist and postmodernist writers and investigating the suitability of their ideas to inquiries into medieval culture, many critics seem content to borrow theoretical apparatus, make

some allowance for our lack of knowledge about medieval social categories and how they correspond to modern sexual typologies, and then
get to the business of reading texts. Many queer studies of medieval
texts and traditions do little more than use concepts derived from
Foucault, elaborated by Sedgwick or Butler, to launch closely textual
examinations that make glancing references to history but otherwise,
in their detailed and ingenious analysis, resemble nothing so much as
the version of formalism traditionally known in the academy as New
Criticism. Queer criticism of this sort shares no ideological or political
foundations with formalism, of course, but its accounts of medieval
cultures are often isolated from evidence offered by other kinds of
texts; although spiced with intertextual and deconstructive strategies,
they seem quite traditional.

In part as a result of Foucault's emphasis on the strategies rather
than the content of discourses (Foucault seldom quotes civil or ecclesiastical law or examines its documentary nuances), queer studies of medieval topics often pay only the most superficial attention to historical
evidence. They seem to operate within a concept of history designed to
place as few limitations as possible on the imaginings inspired by the
texts in question. Indeed, many of these studies manifest anxiety about
the "discipline" that history and philology bring to bear on the study of
same-sex relations as those can be imagined (or reimagined) within
medieval texts. Louise Fradenburg and Carla Freccero explain that "we
want history." They observe that "the joy of finding counterparts in the
past, for example, problematic though it may be, is not simply to be
dismissed as anachronism. While we do not want to talk naïvely about
fore-queers or fore-mothers, any more than we want to talk about forefathers, we also need to recognize how our scruples about doing so
might function as disciplinary." Their solution to this problem—how
to be historical without being "historical," or rather, how to avoid
"anachronism" while being anachronistic—is simply to redefine history as "an erogenous zone."[42] This explanation apparently suffices for
converts to queer theory, but it offers precious little assistance to anybody who wants to know what "history" means when it is redefined as
a queer figure of speech.

Fradenburg and Freccero's attempt to describe history as "an erogenous zone" underscores a characteristic preoccupation not just with the
physical but with the genital (other zones are erogenous, too, but they
all seek to arouse sexual desire). It is common now to find queer readings of medieval and Renaissance texts that seize on any form of intimacy between members of the same sex to ground a claim not just for
affection but for sexual acts. Jonathan Goldberg is foremost among

those concerned with sex acts, praising essays in a collection he edited for their shared "acute awareness of the multiplicities of acts that can be sexualized, the ever-shifting terrains between texts, across national and generic borders (to mix some more categories) that make available and opaque the sites upon which sexual possibilities fasten."[43] If the categories are suitably mixed, the language is tellingly vague. "Fasten" on "sites" within what sort of shifting terrains, to what effect, and with what authority or credibility? The critical ingenuity of such fastening cannot be doubted, but its historical value, to my mind, remains very much in doubt. As Bruce W. Holsinger comments, after quoting this passage, Goldberg fails to explain how "homoerotic desires and practices, despite their multiplicity, work to constitute human beings at specific historical moments."[44]

One explanation for this "sexualiz[ing]" of "multiplicities of acts" is that sex acts are extremely important now and therefore must have been extremely important then. What lies behind this concern with sexualizing "multiplicities of acts" is that nothing is really queer unless it is about genital sex. Holsinger has called attention to Caroline Walker Bynum's assertion, "convincingly argued," he notes, that "it may be a particularly modern fetishization of genital sexuality that has caused historians of the body"—we should include queer theorists here—"to focus such exclusive attention on the genitals as the privileged site of sexual definition and desire."[45] In order to read evidence in ways that support claims for ubiquitous "sexualization," queer theorists often eschew definitions and other critical protocols traditionally used to evaluate evidence. Those protocols are viewed with more than skepticism as "disciplinary" in two senses, of course, suppressing (or repressing) knowledge as well as structuring it according to traditional humanist patterns. At the same time, queer medievalists appeal to history in a quite ordinary sense, which they seem to realize is a necessary form for validating their textual speculations about both medieval and modern cultures.

Examples of queer studies in which analysis that is predominantly textual is presented as making historical claims are numerous. I look briefly at two, Holsinger's reading of *The Divine Comedy* and Dinshaw's commentary on the "General Prologue" to *The Canterbury Tales*. Both are detailed readings that exemplify the textual and theoretical sophistication—and, I think, the historical limitations—of queer analysis in medieval studies. Holsinger identifies Dante as a "subject of homoerotic desire" and seeks to analyze "Dante's own deep-seated homoeroticism" as it emerges in the poem "*despite* his love and desire for Beatrice and his lyrical nods to the tradition of courtly love" (emphasis in original).[46] Rightly wary of seeing the poem's homoeroticism "as a loose amalgamation of acts, pleasures, and desires," Holsinger reminds us that "we must never lose sight of Dante's own role as a subject of exile in fashioning a work as transgressive—politically, poetically, theologically, and, I hope to demonstrate, sexually—as the *Commedia* indisputably was" (247). Holsinger warns that "[h]istorical responsibility, moreover, demands that the analysis of the homoerotic subject in the Middle Ages work with medieval categories for identity and desire" (245). We should, then, expect him to discuss semantic and other categories for identity and desire as explicated in texts contemporary with Dante or in Dante's sources. But he does not do so. I would argue that the demonstration of medieval categories would require the critic to step outside the bounds of the text and its subject positions and turn to historical records that at least suggest the possibilities for Dante's homoerotic imagination. Likewise it does not seem satisfactory to me to assert that *The Divine Comedy,* often seen as a paradigm of Thomistic thought, can be seen as theologically or sexually "transgressive." Transgressive of what norms? one wants to ask. Holsinger's essay concludes with a triumphant, quite formalist juxtaposition of the smallest ring of the *Inferno,* inhabited by sodomites, with "the eternal ring of fire that is Christ." Dante "queers the very end of time," Holsinger claims, thus claiming Dante for queerdom. The plausibility of this sweeping move and its implications for what we know about Dante's life and work require both clarification and qualification (270).

Equally sweeping is Carolyn Dinshaw's queer reading of the opening lines of Chaucer's "General Prologue" to *The Canterbury Tales,* "Whan that Aprille with his shoures soote / the droghte of March hath perced to the roote." Focusing on "his shoures," Dinshaw notes that the poet "reverses the traditional gender of April, usually female." March is also traditionally male, so Chaucer's change "manifestly obviates— after it perhaps suggests—the potential for a representation of male-male sodomitical relations."[47] Dinshaw is fully Foucauldian in her analysis: the forbidden thing (sodomy) is neither said nor unsaid because the poet simultaneously obviates and suggests "sodomitical relations." I take this description of Chaucer's rhetoric to be the equivalent of a closet: "sodomitical relations" are both visible and invisible, *there* (a possibility in the culture) and out of sight (because they are in the closet). Once this point is established, the "General Prologue" can be seen as another text whose heteronormative order depends on an exclusion of the homosexual. Not only these lines but Chaucer's entire vision of nature, and all the interpretations built on it, are thereby queered. But what about the historical plausibility of this reading? Sodomy was not much discussed in the polite literature of the fourteenth century, and literary allusions to it are rare. How does this reading relate to the poet's acknowledged comments on sexual relations? And what of the fact that there is no linguistic basis for the claim in the first place? "His" would not necessarily have signaled "masculine" to Chaucer's audience, since in Middle English the neuter and masculine possessive took the same form in the third person singular. Only a modern reader, a queer one, could imagine the rhetorical strategy that Chaucer "manifestly obviates." [48] A queer reading requires us to seize a linguistic moment *after* April has been made masculine and *before* March is made feminine— Dinshaw refers to March's "feminine surface"—as the point at which male-male relations are suggested. Such a moment can barely be imagined for modern readers, much less for medieval readers, for whom "his" meant "its" as well as "his."

I have no objection to imagining the moment Dinshaw imagines here, or to Holsinger's vision of *The Divine Comedy* as a queer text (although I am not persuaded by their readings). As Holsinger has observed, queer theory is full of references to desires, fantasies, phantasms, borders, sites, and possibilities; these textual inquiries establish the ingenuity of the critics and the malleability of medieval texts. Moreover, the language of psychoanalysis and representation is as appropriate as any other to the study of medieval worlds. My reservations concern the extension of claims based on this language into the realm of medieval history and culture. Absent a definition of history as an "erogenous zone," how are we to assess these claims for Chaucer's or Dante's queerness? What do such claims tell us about the position of either author in his own time and about the relation of his thought to ecclesiastical orthodoxy? The failure to submit these queer moments to the sort of scrutiny that situates them in historical or philological contexts, or even, given the limitations of space, to acknowledge the need for that step, strikes me as crucial.

Such scrutiny, of course, "might function as disciplinary," to quote Fradenburg and Freccero again. But is that so terrible? Queer theory is already disciplined by Foucault, Sedgwick, and Butler. The prior communal agreements of historical discourse—the long conversation that is scholarship—constitute an old "discipline" that is still highly useful, for all its oversights and failures, as a set of statements about what is known about the past and about how the contingencies of certain procedures both produce and help to scrutinize that knowledge. It is difficult to know why untested claims should be regarded as serious attempts to understand medieval lives and cultures. Speculating on the future of "the term queer," Butler wonders how the term can continue to serve as a "point of departure for a set of historical reflections and futural imaginings."[49] The effect of queer theory on the study of medieval literature seems to be that the term has indeed become the point of departure—not for the historical reflections that Butler suggests, however, but rather for historical imaginings. They are, in my view, no substitute for rigorous inquiry into the thoughts, words, and actions of medieval people, phenomena that cannot be known through literary texts alone. These attempts to claim medieval authors and characters for queerness seem to me misguided. They rest almost entirely on the manipulation of language and categories outside the constraints of analysis that compares literary texts such as Dante's or Chaucer's to other sources contemporary with these authors. By appealing to canonical figures in various periods and cultures, such readings also reinforce the impression, which I would have thought was inimical to poststructuralist cultural criticism, that these works are more important and better registers of their cultures than less-studied sources contemporary with them. Furthermore, these readings continue to direct scholarship toward literary interpretation rather than research into still-unknown sources (manuals of preaching and handbooks of penance and clerical instruction, for example) and unexamined archives. At least in its early phases, queer criticism in medieval studies seems to me to replicate many of the features of literary analysis current thirty and forty years ago, when reading and rereading a handful of literary texts was almost all that literature departments did. This need to claim medieval figures for queerness, to argue that they queer narrative situations, that they create (only to obviate) queer possibilities, seems to me to be a misdirected search for origins. It is necessary to analyze historical conditions and unknown or undervalued sources. True enough, what they say about medieval attitudes toward same-sex love is rarely encouraging or affirmative, but what does that matter? It is more important to understand medieval attitudes as clearly as possible than it is to maneuver those attitudes into alignment with our own. I find it sad, and not a little pathetic, that so much energy should be expended by queer critics on reassuring each other (and their readers) that medieval people were, in some ways, as tolerant and queer as we could wish them to be. There is very, very little evidence to support such wishful thinking and a great deal that unambiguously contradicts it.

The critical prerogatives of queer theory as expressed outside medieval studies are weighty but vaguely defined. Lauren Berlant and Michael Warner have argued that queer theory should not be made to bear the burden of being "a theory" and should be known as "queer commentary" instead.[50] I agree. As I have suggested, too much of what passes for "queer theory" in medieval studies is derivative from a theoretical standpoint, although its commentary on medieval texts is at least interesting, if seldom, in my view, persuasive. In response to the common question, "What is queer theory?" Berlant and Warner reply, somewhat peevishly, "Why do people feel the need to introduce, anatomize, and theorize something that can barely be said to exist?" (343). But why should academics *not* want to pick apart the workings of the latest academic trend? We "feel the need to do this" because it is, quite simply, our job. Asserting that "[q]ueer commentary takes on varied shapes, risks, ambitions, and ambivalences in various contexts," Berlant and Warner insist that "queer" does not exist in a fixed context of "theory" in which the word will be forced to assume "a stable referential content and pragmatic force." They claim that "many queer and non-queer-identified humanists" regard "the multiple localities of queer theory and practice" with "panicky defensiveness" (344–45). But the defensiveness seems to be Berlant's and Warner's ("Why do people feel the need to introduce, anatomize, and theorize something that can barely be said to exist?"). To try to hold queer theory accountable for the historical claims queer theorists attach to fantasies, phantasms, trajectories, and textual sites is, it would seem, to oppose a struggle for social reform. To read queerly is a radical act. Because progressive politics are better than other politics, queer readings are better than other readings. Hence disciplined thinking is equated with oppression and the work of philologists with that of "phallologists."[51]

To express skepticism about the methods and claims of queer studies is to risk being seen as part of heteronormative hegemony. But not all gay men or lesbians see themselves as "queer," and not everyone who is skeptical about queer theory is a victim of internalized homophobia or other prejudice against efforts to establish sexual equality. Sometimes queer readings, like any readings, are poorly informed, inconsistent, and weak. These are drawbacks that political principles, however laudable, can scarcely overcome.

And what of the political principles themselves? What is the link between queer theory and queer politics more generally?

Queer theory is closely connected to gay, lesbian, and bisexual rights movements, from which the academic movement has derived some of its central objectives. One of these is the identity of queer theory as "anti-homophobic work."[52] Another is the emphasis of queer theory on sexual relations, often at expense of (if not to the exclusion of) other forms of same-sex affection. Especially given the extremes to which scholars once went to avoid discussing sex acts at all, openness about sex is important. But the focus on sex acts in queer theory is reductive and repetitive, and I regard it as a critical reflex based on a philosophy of gay liberation itself overly attentive to genital sex. It is one of the tenets of many gay, lesbian, and bisexual activists that sex is more important than anything else. The primacy of sex is seen as the most distinctive feature of homosexuality and, through the inevitable logic of binary thinking, a corresponding fear of sex is imagined as the most undesirable feature of heterosexuality. Thus liberating sex is seen to be the chief aim of gay liberation itself. "For academics, being interested in queer theory is a way to mess up the desexualized spaces of the academy, exude some rut, reimagine the publics from and for which academic intellectuals write, dress, and perform," writes Warner.[53] Exuding rut (animal sexual excitement, usually male) is certainly a way to sexualize academic space, but it is also a way to gratify professorial ego and remind the profession at large of who is a star with rights to act out, or up, and who is not.

Liberation is one strategy of the modern gay, lesbian, and bisexual rights movement. Another, as Urvashi Vaid points out, is legitimation. Vaid has neatly summarized the differences between these points of view. "Gay and lesbian legitimation seeks straight tolerance and acceptance of gay people," while "gay and lesbian liberation seeks nothing less than affirmation, represented in the acknowledgment that queer sexuality is morally equivalent to straight sexuality." The movement for liberation "focuses on the suppression of sexuality itself," Vaid writes, and seeks to "liberate an aspect of the personal lives of all people — sexual expression."[54]

This description raises two questions. What is "queer sexuality"? What is "moral equivalence"? If "queer sexuality" were to mean no more than preferring members of your own sex and identifying yourself as part of a community of others who do so, I would see no need to qualify Vaid's statement. However, there are reasons to think that "queer sexuality" means something more—specifically, that it means promiscuity, lots of sex with lots of people, either endorsed as one's own practice or recognized with approval as the preferred practice of one's community. Describing gay culture in New York in the 1970s, Michael Callen wrote that many then believed that "sex was inherently liberating," a proposition extended, he added, "by a curiously naive calculus" to mean "that more sex was more liberating."[55] In other words, as Callen seemed to be hinting, in order to prove that you were free, you had to behave as if you were compulsive. The return of promiscuity in the 1990s has been alternately welcomed and deplored.[56] But without regard to one's view of this development, it is safe to say that not all gay men or lesbians find it necessary to prove their freedom in this way.

And this raises the question about moral equivalence. Liberationists want to liberate sexuality in "all" people, putting pressure on hetero-sexual institutions and traditions, including marriage and monoga-mous relationships. Moral equivalence is to be pursued not by establish-ing common interests and similarities between the needs of gay and straight people but by reforming heterosexual institutions so that they look like queer ones.

Like liberationist thinking, queer theory maintains a "sex-positive" orientation. Liberating the sexual discourse of the past has become de-pendent on identifying modes of sexual intercourse, explicit or implicit, especially in literary texts, and "sexualizing" "multiple sites" in order to show that everything is about sex, same-sex sex in particular, espe-cially when it claims to be about something else. One means of real-izing this liberation is to blur the distinction between straight and gay. According to Vaid, liberationists pursue a radical social agenda of "alternative institutions and communities," extending to "a radically new relationship with the straight culture, one that saw gayness as an aspect of all straight people, not merely a genetically based queerness in some."[57] Gayness, by extension, becomes also "an aspect" of all texts.

But if gayness were an aspect of *all* straight people, surely it would be reasonable to argue that straightness also be recognized as "an as-pect" of *all* gay people. It is not clear, in the liberationist rhetoric of separation, that gay liberationists accept this proposition. But if we do grant it, agreeing on the mutuality of the liberationist proposition that all straights are somewhat gay, and all gays somewhat straight, then gay liberation and gay legitimation seem less far apart. Just as straights can be asked to acknowledge their gayness (i.e., to admit the extent to which they have same-sex desires), gays can be asked to acknowledge their straightness (i.e., to abandon claims of radical separateness and to own their own heterosexual desires). If gay men and lesbians cannot do this—cannot acknowledge their straightness, that is—why should heterosexuals be asked to acknowledge their gayness? Is the world, for so long said to have been heteronormative, in fact homonormative? Is it more "natural" to be gay than to be straight? The term "compulsory heterosexuality" has lately been used by queer theorists who seek to depathologize homosexuality.[58] But the term can also be used unwit-tingly (I think) to pathologize heterosexuality instead. Why should the alternative to "compulsory heterosexuality," a familiar enough regime to those of us who were not allowed to grow up gay, be "compulsory homosexuality"? Instead, I think it is better to propose that gays and lesbians share something important with straights (i.e., heterosexual desire), and that straights share something important with them (i.e., homosexual desire). Likewise, texts can be seen as expressing a mixture of same-sex and other-sex relations, just as a field of vision mixes shadow and light, with these tendencies coexisting with each other rather than radically opposed in discreet states as they are in the mechanism of the closet. A closet is made by somebody, usually for somebody else; a shadow simply is. Hence I use the figure of the shadow to suggest how same-sex implications can be seen to share textual and cultural surfaces with heterosexual desires.

I offer a version of queer theory—call it legitimist queer theory, if you will, to distinguish it from its liberationist kin—that tries to preserve some of the basic claims of queer commentary currently available in medieval studies while attending more closely to historical contingencies as they emerge in traditional documentary and social history. I draw my assertions from Foucault, but not from the mechanisms of hide-and-seek that work well for some readings of late medieval texts.[59] Rather, I adapt Foucault's concept of a reverse discourse and propose the shadow as an alternative figure, as a way of representing same-sex love in its relation to heteronormative discourse and social order. The shadow works better than the closet as a means of showing how, in the presence of a discourse that seeks to repress it, a secondary or counterdiscourse cannot only be detected but can be seen performing the indispensable role of defining or outlining the discourse that dominates it. It is always a problem to know where a closet is located, except on some metaphorical margin. It is never a problem to locate a shadow, since shadows are closely connected to objects in the way that I see same-sex relations connected to heterosexual institutions.

In the debate between liberationists and legitimists, my sympathies clearly stand with the latter. I endorse what Bruce Bawer calls a "general guiding philosophy . . . not of confrontation but of connection," a philosophy that holds, in other words, for common interests.[60] I do not believe that sex is more important to all gay men and lesbians than it is to all straight men and women, and I do not believe that sex acts are the sole barometers of a culture's expression of same-sex relations, some sort of litmus test of what is really queer. The assumption that same-sex relations can and should be measured by references to intercourse alone, and that these acts constitute the basis of communal identity, seems to me no more valid for the twentieth century than for the tenth. If same-sex relations in early cultures have been more extensive than traditional scholarship has acknowledged, same-sex love is also more varied and ambiguous, and less physically sexual, than some queer theorists are willing to believe. Taking this position is a provocation, I

realize. The gay press's reaction to Bawer's work or to Andrew Sullivan's *Virtually Normal* would give pause to anybody who shares some
of the views of either writer. Both Bawer and Sullivan are unquestionably effective advocates for social change. But they and others have
been attacked as homophobic, queer culture's stigma for those who
dare to question its political (or critical) assumptions.[61]

The study of same-sex relations is not synonymous with queer
theory. Just as many gay men, lesbians, and transsexuals do not see
themselves as "queer," not all writing about same-sex relations is queer
theory, although many queer studies claim the opposite. Unless an
author takes up the term or uses the label, I do not classify his or her
work as queer. To do so erases an important distinction between work
done before postmodernism became mainstream and work done after
that point, imparting assumptions to earlier work that its authors might
not want to accept or could not have anticipated. To do so also obscures
the still-important distinctions between the history of sex, a discipline
with a long tradition, and queer theory. Critical discourses are not
monoliths. Queer theorists demand tolerance of their views and are
therefore well-positioned to tolerate the views of gay and lesbian scholars who both believe in sexual equality and in the importance of examining sex and gender and want to exercise the freedom to explore
these goals and topics in discursive modes of their own choosing.

Although I dissent from queer theory's vague and indirect methods,
and its failure to face its historical responsibilities, I also acknowledge
that queer theory has helped to close the gap between personal and
professional styles in academic writing and helped make that writing
newly honest and engaging. Queer theory works to counter the widespread assumption that sexual definition and all it implies (e.g., categories of identity, sexual desire) are supposedly subjects of interest
only to homosexuals (just as women's studies supposedly interest only
women). That minoritizing perspective seeks to discourage scholarship
on same-sex relations and protects the claims of entrenched interests
from scrutiny. Queer theory has also served as a rallying point for gay,
lesbian, and gender studies and has generated much-needed discussion
about the place of such programs in the academic and publishing
world. This book is not a refutation of queer theory or a rebuttal of
queer readings of medieval texts. But it is a response to the lack of
critical rigor that obscures many queer readings. It is also an attempt
to show, in terms of the Anglo-Saxon evidence, why such readings, far
though they sometimes go, do not go far enough in what they tell us
about sexual behavior in premodern cultures.

This book is organized into three parts. In part 1, "Trouser Roles and Transvestites," I look at some moments in opera, dance, and Anglo-Saxon texts, and propose a variety of paradigms for sexualized relations that are not specific to genital sex. Chapter 1 examines an opera, Charles Gounod's *Faust,* through the framework of Edith Wharton's *Age of Innocence,* and then explores same-sex love as represented by the convention of the "trouser role," a male role written for a female voice, in Richard Strauss's *Der Rosenkavalier.* In two dances, *Dido and Aeneas* and *The Hard Nut,* choreographer Mark Morris reverses the convention of the trouser role by assigning parts written for women to men. I use the grand narratives of these works—their love stories, and their stories about the creation of art—to show how homosexual and heterosexual texts (and readings) can coexist within one work, and to explain why these perspectives are not mutually exclusive. In chapter 2 I look at some Anglo-Saxon texts in which homosexual and heterosexual meanings coexist under a rubric of same-sex love (rather than same-sex sex). I examine examples of cross-dressing—transvestite saints—and analyze some celebrated texts, including *Beowulf* and *The Wanderer,* in which men kiss and embrace and express physical affection for each other. These chapters establish some general similarities between modern and early medieval representations of same-sex relations. At some moments, I think readers will find the Anglo-Saxons surprisingly open to same-sex love.

The second part, "The Anglo-Saxons," analyzes the evidence of same-sex sex and presents a less encouraging impression of sexual tolerance in the culture. Chapter 3 argues that the early English evidence of same-sex relations is distinctive and examines how that evidence has been handled (or not handled, as the case may be) in a number of important surveys of the history of sexuality and of homosexuality. Chapter 4 focuses on the Anglo-Saxon and Anglo-Latin penitentials and on early English laws and compares the treatment of heterosexual and homosexual sins and offenses in these sources (appendices sum up and classify the evidence). Chapter 5 surveys Old English prose that discusses same-sex relations, especially homilies. I use references to Sodom as a way to identify texts that potentially refer to same-sex sex. This chapter includes a study of *Genesis A,* the only Anglo-Saxon poem to portray the fall of Sodom and Gomorrah.

Chapters 6 and 7 form part 3, "From Angles to *Angels.*" Chapter 6 traces developments in the discourse of sodomy after the Norman Conquest. In this period—and after—little remained of the Anglo-Saxons' treatment of sodomy as either penitentials or homilies represent it. A period of revival of Anglo-Saxon texts took place at Worcester in the thirteenth century, but elsewhere the memory of the Anglo-Saxons' achievement quickly faded. One aspect of Anglo-Saxon culture, however, struck many later medieval writers, including Chaucer and the heretical Lollards, and that was the strong tradition of vernacular preaching and teaching in the earlier period. I examine Chaucer's vision of early England in *The Man of Law's Tale,* a mix of myth and history with a same-sex love story at its heart, a narrative derived from a French chronicle and used by Chaucer to rewrite the story of the conversion of Anglo-Saxon England.

Chapter 7 supplies another rereading of Anglo-Saxon history, juxtaposing Bede's story about Gregory and Anglian boys he admired as "angels" to a bitter revision of the episode by John Bale, a sixteenth-century reformer for whom the history of sodomy and the history of the Roman Church were inseparable. I conclude the chapter with a more familiar account of angels, Anglo-Saxons (white Anglo-Saxon Protestants, that is), and Normans, offered in Tony Kushner's *Angels in America,* only the most recent in a long series of works that contrast Norman and Anglo-Saxon virtues. WASP and other nationalistic, even racialistic, constructions of Anglo-Saxon culture, including that implicit in Kushner's drama, are possible only for those who know little about the culture and the sources, few though they are, that describe the sexual practices of the Anglo-Saxon for us. In this case, as in so many others when cultures are adopted for reasons of identity politics, the utility of Anglo-Saxon culture is inversely proportionate to what is known about it.

The afterword is about my own shadows, or, more precisely, my experiences in three worlds in which same-sex relations still bore some resemblance to same-sex relations in premodern Europe. These include the rural Midwest, where I grew up in the 1950s and 1960s, the U.S. Army, in which I served in the early 1970s, and the Republic of Korea in 1971, where I was stationed as a GI. My experiences suggest to me, in retrospect, patterns that the Kinsey studies were proposing to the American public while I was growing up: that most people fall somewhere between what we think of as "gay" and "straight," that people see themselves and their sexual practices differently at different times of their lives, and that environment (the military, the convent, the monastery) has a great deal to do with their sexual behavior.[62] I have organized the chapters with different readers in mind. Anglo-Saxon literature and history are discussed in detail in chapters 2 through 6. Chapters closely related to the tradition of gay and lesbian studies include the first and third, the appendix to chapter 4, and the seventh chapter. I hope everybody will read the afterword (and everything else, of course).

I have not been concerned with affirming same-sex relations in my arguments, since it seems to me that neither gay, lesbian, bisexual, nor sympathetic straight readers need that reassurance. Nor have I argued that the Latin and Old English materials discussed here present same-sex relations in affirmative ways, since they do not, although sufficient expenditure of critical ingenuity could guarantee that they did. Queer theory gets along by suggesting the existence of "something queer" or finding "queerish effects" instead of distinguishing its agenda from other kinds of inquiry into sexual practices and problems. It would be easy enough to find some "queerish effects" in Anglo-Saxon texts and argue that the Anglo-Saxons tolerated same-sex sex even though their culture's official voices denounced it. But another exercise in critical ingenuity based on literary texts is not what is needed, and the sense of queer community and commonality that it strives to create (forefathers, foremothers, fore-queers) is, in my view, largely illusory.

I wish to make a broader claim. The evidence shows that some men and women in the Anglo-Saxon period indulged their same-sex preferences in spite of the culture's prohibitions. In a queer reading, the evidence would be used to identify these men and women as part of a queer resistance and to suggest that queer Anglo-Saxons were like us. We have the advantage of a discourse of identity politics; they did not. According to Barry Adam, "What distinguishes the modern lesbian and gay world from anthropological and historical examples of homosexuality is the development of social networks founded on the homosexual interests of their members."[63] The existence of such communities in the Middle Ages is very difficult to demonstrate. So too is the concomitant assumption that people who engaged in same-sex acts in the Middle Ages thought of themselves as defined by that behavior. Not all men and women who loved their own kind in Anglo-Saxon England acted in the full knowledge that their culture condemned their behavior.

Is this so strange? In my own lifetime it has been possible to find people who do not know what homosexuality is. But educated Anglo-Saxon men and women who preferred to have sex with their own kind did know, just as we do, what the culture at large thought of them. A 1994 study conducted at the University of Minnesota showed that 70 percent of those surveyed thought that homosexuality was wrong. Period. Nonetheless, gay men and lesbians do what they want to do when it comes to sex, and many others who are neither gay nor lesbian, and perhaps not bisexual either, experiment with homosexual acts. I believe that the Anglo-Saxons probably behaved in a similar way, made their choices and took their chances—and their lumps—not as queers defying heteronormative regimes, however much "joy" it might give us to imagine them as "fore-queers," but as men and women who experienced their desires in the shadow of the social and moral monoliths that supposedly embodied the desires of all men and women. I see all these desires moving together, the heterosexual orders of church and state shadowed by same-sex love, sex, and eroticism, often denounced but never left behind, an ever-present reminder that love and sex are not the exclusive rights of the majority who mate with the opposite sex. Same-sex relations in the period, despite their remoteness, resemble same-sex relations in the recent past, and even, in some places, same-sex relations today. I hope that readers will come to share my conviction that this evidence speaks to the current concerns of gay men, lesbians, and bisexuals, and to all those who want to see a more equitable world for everybody in it.

PART

1

*Trouser
Roles
and
Transvestites*

What's Love Got to Do with It?

In a few paragraphs at the start of *The Age of Innocence,* published in 1920, Edith Wharton examines opera and its audience.

> On a January evening of the early seventies, Christine Nilsson was singing in *Faust* at the Academy of Music in New York.
>
> Though there was already talk of the erection, in remote metropolitan distances "above the Forties," of a new Opera House which should compete in costliness and splendor with those of the great European capitals, the world of fashion was still content to reassemble every winter in the shabby red and gold boxes of the sociable old Academy. Conservatives cherished it for being small and inconvenient, and thus keeping out the "new people" whom New York was beginning to dread and yet be drawn to; and the sentimental clung to it for its historic associations, and the musical for its excellent acoustics, always so problematic a quality in halls built for the hearing of music.[1]

So at home at the Academy are New York's "old people" that they wander in whenever they please. One of them, Newland Archer, has "dawdled over his cigar" because it is "not the thing" to be early (that is, on time) for the opera and because he is a connoisseur of Charles Gounod's *Faust,* or at least a small part of it.

> [T]hinking over a pleasure to come often gave him a subtler satisfaction than its realization. This was especially the case when the pleasure was a delicate one, as his pleasures mostly were; and on this occasion the moment he looked forward to was so rare and exquisite in quality that—well, if he had timed his arrival in accord with the prima donna's stage-manager he could not have entered the Academy at a more significant moment than just as she was singing: "He loves me—he loves me not—*he loves me!*" and sprinkling the falling daisy petals with notes as clear as dew.

She sang, of course, "*M'ama!*" and not "He loves me," since an un-
alterable and unquestioned law of the musical world required that the
German text of French operas sung by Swedish artists should be translated into Italian for the clearer understanding of English-speaking audiences. This seemed as natural to Newland Archer as all the other
conventions on which his life was moulded. (4–5)[2]

During the scene, as he watches Marguerite's declaration, Newland
directs his glance across the house to a young woman who only that
afternoon had made a declaration of her own. Using "New York's consecrated phrase of maiden avowal," May had indicated that she "cared"
for him (7).

Directly facing him was the box of old Mrs. Manson Mingott, whose
monstrous obesity had long since made it impossible for her to attend
the Opera, but who was always represented on fashionable nights by
some of the younger members of the family. On this occasion, the front
of the box was filled by her daughter-in-law, Mrs. Lovell Mingott, and
her daughter, Mrs. Welland; and slightly withdrawn behind these bro-
caded matrons sat a young girl in white with eyes ecstatically fixed on
the stage-lovers. As Madame Nilsson's *"M'ama"* thrilled out above the
silent house (the boxes always stopped talking during the Daisy Song) a
warm pink mounted to the girl's cheek, mantled her brow to the roots
of her fair braids, and suffused the young slope of her breast to the line
where it met a modest tulle tucker fastened with a single gardenia. She
dropped her eyes to the immense bouquet of lilies-of-the-valley on her
knee, and Newland Archer saw her white-gloved finger tips touch the
flowers softly. He drew a breath of satisfied vanity and his eyes returned
to the stage. (5–6)

There he observes Faust gazing in rapture at Marguerite, a beautiful
but simple young woman who has captivated him. They speak tenderly
to each other ("Il se fait tard, adieu!", 148).[3] Marguerite asks Faust to
look away as she picks a marguerite—a daisy—and plays a "simple
game" with it, picking petals as she sings "He loves me—he loves me
not—*he loves me!*" Delighted, Faust exclaims that she has heard "the
voice of heaven" ("Oui, crois en cette fleur," 150); together they contem-
plate the joy of eternal love. During this scene, Newland shows himself
to be both patronizing and proprietary.

"The darling!" thought Newland Archer, his glance flitting back to the
young girl with the lilies-of-the-valley. "She doesn't even guess what
it's all about." And he contemplated her absorbed young face with a

thrill of possessorship in which pride in his own masculine initiation was mingled with a tender reverence for her abysmal purity. "We'll read *Faust* together . . . by the Italian lakes . . ." he thought, somewhat hazily confusing the scene of his projected honeymoon with the masterpieces of literature which it would be his manly privilege to reveal to his bride. (7)

Newland is pleased that May "doesn't even guess what it's all about," since "it" here is seduction. Although it begins with great tenderness, the music between Faust and Marguerite becomes increasingly passionate as their sexual desires become more and more insistent. Faust is sung by Capoul, a tenor absurdly got up in "a tight purple velvet doublet and plumed cap" who tries "to look as pure and true as his artless victim" (5).[4] He gestures "by word or glance" toward a window in Marguerite's house, presumably her bedchamber, as Marguerite affects "a guileless incomprehension of his designs" (6). She refuses his requests to hold her hand and gaze on her face and tells him to leave. But she promises to see him the next day. When Faust turns to rush out, Méphistophélès, who has witnessed the scene, blocks his way and ridicules him for giving up so easily. Marguerite enters the house. Thinking that Faust has left, she stands at the window and sings of her desire to see him again, reprising the "Daisy Song": "He loves me! . . . My love! ah, do not linger long so far away! Come! Ah!" ("Il m'aime!" 156). Faust runs back to her, and Marguerite embraces him and admits him to the house. "[T]he music that follows depicts a substantial discharge of sexual energy that finally merges into gentle exhaustion," writes Hans-Christian Schmidt. "The ear is permitted to hear what the eye is not allowed to see."[5]

The ear also hears the hideous laughter of Méphistophélès, not noted by Wharton but surely heard by Newland and his companions. Newland had, no doubt, seen *Faust* often since its premiere at the Academy of Music in 1863 and knows that this laughter portends the seduction of Marguerite.[6] Even May, innocent though she is, might at this point have begun at least to "guess" what "it" was all about. At the start of the next act, no doubt about Marguerite's fate can remain. She has been abandoned by Faust and shamed. "In my turn I must suffer too," she laments, "He does not return." The chorus mocks her ("Elles ne sont plus là," 158); society anticipates the fall of the pious, the better to enjoy their repentance. Later Marguerite kills the child she bears Faust, is imprisoned for this act, and dies in her cell, calling on angels to save her. And in the end, of course, they do ("Anges purs! Anges radieux!" 218).

The enormous popularity of *Faust* in Wharton's time and before suggests that society found this drama of sin and forgiveness especially significant.[7] But sin and forgiveness are not the themes that draw Newland to the performance, as we know from the moment he chooses for his entrance. He relishes the spectacle of unresisting love and the contrast between innocence and experience. May's innocence, and her ignorance, are figured in Marguerite's. Surrounded by a garish production, the soprano can only affect the chaste beauty of youth. But she and May resemble each other anyway, dressed in white, hair braided, flowers in hand, each believing, for the moment, that she understands her fate.

Newland does not enter the box until the middle of the opera's third act. What he misses in the performance is even more important than what he sees. With Newland, we witness the effects of Faust's seduction, but not its cause, and we hear nothing of the opera's other lover, Siébel, a young student described as "a simple soul with a big heart," "altruistic and unselfish," who adores Marguerite.[8] Chaste and idealistic, Siébel is no match for the charms of Faust, much less for the sinister powers of Méphistophélès. "Lovely flowers," the young man implores of a bouquet he has gathered in Marguerite's garden, "be kind and speak for me!" ("Faites-lui mes aveux," 112). The flower he holds withers at Méphistophélès' command, but the young man dips his hands in holy water and the next flower he picks remains fresh. He leaves the bouquet for Marguerite, saying that he will return in the morning to declare his love to her, words overheard by Méphistophélès and Faust. Warning that the young man is Faust's rival, Méphistophélès places a box of jewels and a mirror next to the bouquet. When Marguerite enters the garden, thinking of Faust, the noble lord who has been admiring her ("un grand seigneur," 122), she sees the flowers. They are from Siébel, she knows, "the poor boy" ("Un bouquet . . . C'est de Siébel, sans doute! Pauvre garçon," 124). But when she discovers the jewels she sings rapturously about them (the "Jewel Song," another aria, one feels sure, that brought the audience to a respectful silence, "Ah! je ris, de me voir," 126) and completely forgets Siébel's offering. Faust and Méphistophélès join her, Méphistophélès dedicating his energy to distracting Marguerite's friend Martha while Faust woos Marguerite. Siébel returns but is whisked away by Martha, who claims that his presence there would scandalize the neighbors ("Du courage!" 144). Then, just before the exchange between Faust and Marguerite that precedes the "Daisy Song," Méphistophélès commands the flowers to waft their "haunting perfume" so that they might "succeed in seducing the heart of Marguerite" ("Il était temps!" 146).

That is precisely what happens in the duet that follows, which New-land also missed, when Marguerite tells Faust, "By your spell I am bound" ("O silence!" 148).

Faust seduces the maid, Siébel protects her. After Marguerite has been deserted and her disgrace made public, he claims to cherish her like a sister with love that is chaste, pure, and fraternal ("Si le bonheur à sourire t'invite," 164). At her death, as a condition of her salvation, Marguerite is returned to a pure, contrite state worthy of his love. When she dies, the prison's rear wall opens and angels are seen bearing her to heaven. Trumpets blast, the organ soars, and an angelic chorus proclaims that "Christ the redeemer lives! Christ is born again! Peace and goodwill on earth!" ("Christ est ressuscité! Christ vient de re-naître! Paix et félicité!" 222). All this to welcome the reformed sinner into heaven! It is an unlikely (but magnificent) conclusion to a sordid tale, worthy of the best Christmas-card art, piety so routine that it evokes either a sentimental response or none at all.[9] This grim then glorious moment is not foreseen in Wharton's account of *Faust,* which we witness entirely through Newland's entertained and knowing gaze.

Had he come in a few moments earlier, Newland might have attached less benign significance to the flowers May holds in her lap. He would also have understood that Marguerite's playful game with her namesake flower is not a game of chance. For as she destroys the flower, she destroys herself; she thinks that she is deciding her fate, but it is already out of her hands. Just as surely as Méphistophélès guides Marguerite's decision, the social world of New York conspires to su-pervise May's future. This too is something that "the darling" "doesn't even guess." But how much does Newland guess? He prides himself on understanding what transpires between Faust and Marguerite and between men and women generally. A connoisseur, he recognizes and savors conventions, which seem "natural" to him; indeed, his world is "moulded" by them. Conventions are agreements without which soci-ety could not function at the superficial levels its survival requires. But conventions are also artistic traditions of obscure origin, and although it is easy to dismiss them, they are—like operas—seldom so irrelevant as they seem.

"[O]peras are not pale copies of 'real' social attitudes," Ralph P. Locke writes. Instead, "they are active units of cultural discourse, con-tributing materially to the ways we understand and respond to issues of gender, race, and social class, constructing images for us of what the individual owes to the larger community (and vice versa), and so on."[10] Few people, in Wharton's time or our own, seem to share this view. But I admit that I do. Wharton makes fun of the irrelevance of opera to its audience, whose talk during all but the best-known music demonstrates how little the events on stage mean to them. In opera, conventional wisdom has it, plots are always ridiculous because their conventions are outdated. The singers, often too old or too large, do not look the parts they play, and, as is the case in this production of *Faust,* the spectacle itself is often not much to look at. But opera thrives nonetheless, and for one reason above all, which is the convention that one does not go to the opera to see a performance but to be part of one. For gays and lesbians, I mean this in a very specific sense.

The Metropolitan Opera house, whose advent is heralded in Wharton's first paragraphs, was described when it opened in 1883 as a "semicircle of boxes with an opera house built around them, a private club to which the general public was somewhat grudgingly admitted."[11] By juxtaposing the conventions of opera to those of operagoers, Wharton compares the plots enacted in the boxes to those played out on the stage. When Marguerite and Faust embrace, the music says "sexual union" because the singers and the action cannot. Newland cannot say "sexual union" either, but Wharton makes it clear that he is thinking of it. The work of certain conventions in both locations, as Newland's attentive behavior demonstrates, is to disguise a subtext of sexual intrigue. I want to argue that in some cases—*Faust* is one—another subtext coexists with, and shadows, the sexual dynamic of the plot.

During the love music, Newland observes May's blush, which suffuses not only her brow but also "the young slope of her breast to the line where it met a modest tulle tucker." Newland's thoughts are not innocent. They lead beyond May's tucker to the lower parts of his own anatomy as well as hers. He takes "pride in his own masculine initiation," which he contrasts to May's "abysmal purity." Like Marguerite, May remains unaware of what is taking place around her. Her ignorance, or, at best, her superficial awareness, is something Newland counts on, another of his "delicate" pleasures. He treasures his superior knowledge of art (opera and literature), his sexual experience, and his "manly privilege" of revealing both (and himself, of course) to May once they are married. But like Faust, he is a seducer who has already been seduced. Standing over Newland is a social world whose claims on his perceptions and his choices are stronger than he realizes. When he visits May in the Mingott box, he encounters Madame Olenska, a worldly woman who will awaken him to passions that he has never expected to know and that he will ultimately be unable to reciprocate.

An acute observer of both the operatic stage and the opera box, Newland takes pleasure not only in the maiden's purity but also in its impending sacrifice. Unlike May, whose eyes are "ecstatically fixed" on the stage, signaling that she is in the thrall of the illusion, his eyes, those of the connoisseur, shift from stage to box and back. His plan to explain *Faust* to May by the lakes in Italy associates him more closely with Méphistophélès, who possesses knowledge, than with Faust, who acquires it. Up to a point, he identifies with Faust; up to a point, I identify with him, at least when I go to the opera (although I take pains never to be late). Newland enjoys *Faust* because it represents social and sexual truths that confirm his sense of himself. This particular performance is not the first time he has so carefully timed his own entrance into this or any other opera. "[T]hinking over a pleasure to come often gave him a subtler satisfaction than its realization," Wharton tells us. He prolongs his gratification (which is private and quite different in character from that of others in the audience) by not getting to the opera on time. This is perhaps another of Wharton's little jokes: nothing is more likely to kill one's keenly anticipated pleasures at the opera than opera itself. Once he arrives, he knows what to watch for. In this way he is a model reader for the kinds of texts I write about here. Making a crucial point about the audiences of another medium, Arthur Laurents says, "All minority audiences watch movies with hope. They hope they will see what they want to see." [12] Newland Archer is a member of the social majority, but as an attentive operagoer, he is in a minority at the performance Wharton describes. He sees and hears more than others because he brings to the opera not only the hope that he might see what he wants to see but the assurance, based on experience, that he will.

When I watch or listen to *Faust* I attach my hopes to the other side of the opera's sad love triangle, not to Faust and Marguerite, but to Marguerite and Siébel, whose part is sung by a woman. The side of the triangle that fascinates me is, on one level—*not* the first level of the plot—about love between two women, one of them in trousers. If the mezzo-soprano in the role is lithe and a good actress, Siébel might look like a young man. But he never sounds like one. Instead, his ardent declaration of love for Marguerite sounds for all the world like one woman singing passionately about her love for another.

Neither Wharton nor Newland, of course, comments on the "trouser role," sung by a woman who takes a part that the plot assigns to a man. There are many trouser roles in the opera repertory, some of them quite unknown. The trouser role has its origins in a rule that required women's silence in church (1 Corinthians 14:34) and that led to the formation of boys' choirs. These choirs in turn promoted the place of the castrati, young men castrated so that they would retain their high voices as they matured. For much of the Middle Ages and Renaissance, women's parts were generally taken by boys, because women were not permitted on the stage.[13] In the eighteenth century, most heroic male roles were written high and were sung by a castrato or by a woman. After the demand for castrati passed, these roles fell to a prima donna contralto known as the "musico."[14] Then composers began to write men's roles for women's voices, "especially when the impression of youth was crucial," Cori Ellison notes—for pages, shepherds, and other nonadult roles.[15] The development came full circle, from boys imitating women to women imitating boys. By the end of the nineteenth century, trouser roles were seldom created, and they now strike us as great curiosities. Interest in the dynamics of same-sex love, fortunately, puts them in a new perspective. Same-sex love stories will never be plentiful in opera, but within a limited repertoire they are, in one important sense, hardly rare.[16]

As she is in *Faust,* the trouser role is sometimes a romantic interest for the soprano who is the opera's central character. Corinne E. Blackmer and Patricia Juliana Smith argue that the trouser role developed, in part, as a response to changes in women's status in nineteenth-century opera, when the heroine became "less likely to experience anything resembling friendship, much less love, for another woman." Instead, "the isolated woman among men" was typical (Violetta in *La Traviata* is an example). "Consequently, when an operatic scenario featured more than one woman, the *secunda donna,* if not merely the maid or slave of her more prominent counterpart, functioned primarily as the antagonist in a romantic triangle."[17] As we see in *Faust,* the *secunda donna* could also become a male antagonist in such a triangle—but not just any male. Ellison suggests that, in adult roles, mezzo-sopranos don britches for an "obvious" reason. "[T]heir deliciously androgynous vocal range and timbre provocatively toes the line between youth and experience, light and dark, anima and animus."[18] Ellison does not mention the line between man and woman or male and female, but that line too is "provocatively toe[d]" by the role.

The trouser role's love for the leading woman is, as is Siébel's, idealized rather than sexual. The role of Siébel is meant, in part, to show that young and innocent males, like some females, maintain a pure and sexless idea of love. Like Faust, Newland is neither young nor innocent. Idealized love, ardent but pure, is not an option for either of them. If it is socially desirable that a "man" like Siébel be sexually moderate and restrained—and in this sense not a "real man" at all—the trouser role aptly illustrates how that role should be realized: such a man should be played by a woman. In a triangular love plot—the plot of *Faust*—the trouser role juxtaposes sexual innocence to sexual knowledge. The opera uses that juxtaposition to separate men from boys and to affiliate boys with a standard of female virtue. But in the shadow of this convention stands another one, somewhat more complex, which is that people of the same sex can declare their love in traditional theater so long as one of them is dressed as a member of the opposite sex.

Opera conventions no longer seem "natural" to anybody, but they still speak to those who, like Newland, go to the opera with hope. Among the vital social truths established by the shadow is one about the inevitability, and near invisibility, of same-sex love. "You can't keep gay life—gay behavior—out of the movies," Paul Rudnick has said. "It's like keeping it out of life in general." [19] I substitute other terms for "gay life" and "gay behavior," including "same-sex love," "intramale" and "intrafemale" sex. With Rudnick, I believe that we cannot keep them out of opera or dance or the study of premodern English culture. [20] But you do not necessarily have to see them. Indeed, their function is as easy to miss as the role of shadows in defining the objects around us. In what follows I examine conventions that encode same-sex relations in opera and dance and use the figure of the shadow to explain how it is that same-sex love, a proverbially marginal topic, can be found at (or near) the heart of social and cultural institutions, modern and medieval.

Rudnick's truism about "gay life" in the movies, and in "life in general," is appealing and optimistic. But even in much modern art and literature, same-sex love is seldom overt. Anglo-Saxon sources, narrative and otherwise, rarely discuss same-sex relations, and when they do, almost invariably frame them in damning contexts. Such contexts are not unique to ancient representations of same-sex love. Until a few years ago there were almost no love stories about gay men or lesbians, and same-sex relations either figured furtively in narrative contexts or were banned altogether. Moreover, especially in cinema, the few stories that were told invariably framed gay or lesbian characters as victims, finally, of their own despair. In every way their stories were unhappy ones; shadows are particularly appropriate images for them. [21] Today "gay life" and "gay behavior" are regularly and often affirmatively portrayed in theater, dance, and cinema, representations that can be called "homosexual" without reservation. But these narratives too, as Steven F. Kruger has shown, seldom end well. [22]

I want to analyze works in which the homosexual shadow is not a dark pall cast over life and hope but rather a presence that animates and extends them. In the examples from opera and dance I now turn to, same-sex relations shadow heterosexual partnerships in a sometimes playful, sometimes tragic fashion, as they do in *Faust*. If a focus on same-sex relations darkens the work in question, that is partly because the more closely heterosexual stories are examined, the more clearly we see how they can be and have been used to diminish same-sex love. In these examples, same-sex relations also expand and broaden the work by extending the range of its statements about love—and sex—beyond the expected heterosexual content (the object, so to speak) to same-sex or homosexual meanings (the object's shadow).

I turn to narratives drawn from opera and dance because these works readily accommodate gay and lesbian forms of the beauty, romance, and passion that heterosexual readers are used to seeing only in their own image. The operas and dances I examine represent same-sex love in different ways. Opera makes use of the trouser role, a convention indispensable to some works; dance lacks a comparable tradition, and in the works I examine same-sex dynamics must be created through intervention. I hope to show that same-sex relations can usually be found in Anglo-Saxon texts, just as they appear in opera and dance, in the shadows. As shadows do, they help define the object—the heterosexual system—that stands between them and the light. In the next chapter I look at some Anglo-Saxon texts that accommodate same-sex relations in a similar fashion, as incidental to the plot as it is usually seen, yet essential to the work's sexual politics.

My first example is one of the greatest love stories in opera, *Der Rosenkavalier,* by Richard Strauss (1864–1949). Based on a text by Hugo von Hofmannsthal (1874–1929) and sometimes described as "a comedy for music," *Der Rosenkavalier* is set in eighteenth-century Vienna. The work premiered in Dresden in 1911 and has remained one of the most popular operas in the repertory. By 1913 it had already been performed at the Metropolitan Opera, and in 1926 it debuted as a film in London *(The Rose Cavalier)* with a special score later recorded by Strauss.[23] In the opera, the Marschallin, thirty-two years old, very beautiful yet much neglected by her husband, has taken a young man named Octavian as her lover, not her first. In the course of the day in which the opera takes place, the Marschallin loses him to Sophie, a young woman about his own age, nearly eighteen. As the Marschallin once was, Sophie is soon to be married to a man she does not even know, much less love, a fate from which Octavian rescues her.

I will also examine same-sex relations in two dances by Mark Morris, both based on well-known musical works. The first is *Dido and Aeneas,* danced to the opera by Henry Purcell (1658–95), with text by Nahum Tate (1652–1715). This is also a story about a woman abandoned by her lover, not for another woman but for duty. The opera, which contains its own dances, premiered in London in 1689 and was first performed in the United States in New York in 1923. Morris's *Dido and Aeneas* premiered in Brussels in 1989. The second work by Morris that I discuss is *The Hard Nut,* which premiered in 1991, again in Brussels. This work is a revision of *The Nutcracker* (1892), the ballet set to music by Pyotr Ilich Tchaikovsky (1840–93) and based on "The Nutcracker and the Mouse King," by E. T. A. Hoffmann (1776–1822). This too is a love story and a story of abandonment—a young girl's fantasy about a toy transformed by its maker into a handsome prince who is only as real as the dream that brings him to her. None of these works is about the Middle Ages or premodern England or tells a story that is homosexual—"gay"—in any sense. But they are works in which the surface of the heterosexual world is made more complex, more beautiful, by a shadow of same-sex love whose ramifications are sometimes as compelling as those of the plot they comment on.

THE BOY IN *DER ROSENKAVALIER*

If Newland Archer were interested in same-sex love, he would never have arrived late for a performance of Strauss's *Der Rosenkavalier* and risked missing the scene on which the curtain rises. The Marschallin is lying in bed, her head turned from the audience. Her lover, Octavian, kneels at her side. She repeatedly calls Octavian a "boy," or "Bub," and uses his nickname, "Quinquin," as he uses hers, "Bichette."[24] The impression of youth is important. Soprano Lotte Lehmann, who performed all three leading roles in this opera during her career (the Marschallin, Octavian, and Sophie), once asked Strauss why Octavian's part was written for a woman's voice. His answer combines an appeal to common sense with a hint of defensiveness. "Have you ever seen a man young enough to play Octavian and at the same time experienced enough to be an accomplished actor?" Strauss asked. "Where would you find someone like that? Besides, writing for three sopranos was a challenge. I think I did the right thing."[25]

Der Rosenkavalier contains some of the greatest vocal writing of the twentieth century, all of it involving two and sometimes three women who sing about falling in and out of love. Three long scenes are devoted to this combination of female voices: the bedchamber sequence that opens the opera; the presentation of the rose in act 2, when Octavian meets Sophie; and a trio in which the Marschallin bids farewell to Octavian at the end of the opera, followed by a duet between the ecstatic lovers she leaves behind. Many more people hear this opera than see it, and for those who listen only, Octavian's costume is irrelevant. Octavian is one of the most famous and least typical trouser roles in all opera, and in a way his trousers are always irrelevant. Like Siébel,

Octavian is supposed to look like a young man but unmistakably is, and sounds like, a woman. The listener must constantly work to align the aural image of two or three women singing together with the visual—and psychological—image of one or two women singing with a man. In *Faust* the trouser role represents chaste, brotherly love, but not in *Der Rosenkavalier.* Octavian has just spent the night with the Marschallin, and the sexual nature of their relationship is never in doubt. Strauss's score, according to Lehmann and others, offers a musical clue to the lovemaking that has gone on before. "After a riotous prelude that describes with truly remarkable lack of reticence the pleasures of a night of love, the curtain rises upon a scene of peaceful intimacy: Marie Theres', the Marschallin, is reclining upon a couch in serene repose. Octavian, her lover, kneels by her side, his head in her lap while her hands gently stroke his hair."[26]

This is how Hofmannsthal planned the scene. But before the premiere in Dresden, the imperial court ordered "a thoroughly 'decent' staging of the opera." Thus the prominently displayed bed was replaced by what Lehmann scoffingly calls a "so-much-more-'moral' couch." "The music of the prelude, of course, also should have been suppressed or expurgated to conform to Imperial standards of decency," Lehmann adds. "[F]ortunately the Emperor and his moralistic censors appear to have been deaf to its brash implications."[27] *Kobbé's Complete Opera Book,* a venerable source, notes that the "impassioned orchestral introduction" is "explicitly supposed to represent the lovemaking which immediately precedes the audience's first view of the stage." The prelude "begins with the excitement of the love-making very much in mind."[28] Gary Schmidgall claims that the prelude to the opera portrays a "sexual climax,"[29] and the score supports this view. The pattern in which leaping ascending notes (Octavian) meet with graceful, descending notes (the Marschallin) can be read as an exchange between male and female in musical language. Strauss's markings in the score are also revealing: "The whole from here [measure 21] till the climax is reached, with strongly parodied expression," Strauss wrote. Twice notes in this passage are marked "seufzend," sobbing.[30]

A staging at the Metropolitan Opera in 1949–50 seems to approximate the original scheme (figure 1). But the scene set to this music can be staged in a way that undermines the heterosexual moment that the libretto imagines. In the 1995 production from the Deutsche Staatsoper Berlin, Octavian is not wearing trousers (figure 2). The Marschallin is sitting on the floor, wrapped in a sheet, resting against a settee (a "moral couch"). Octavian kneels nearby, wearing a shift with a bed

Fig. 1. *Der Rosenkavalier,* act 1. In a conventional arrangement of the opening scene, the Marschallin (Eleanor Steber) wears a low-cut, lacy gown. She embraces Octavian (Risë Stevens), who wears satin trousers. From a 1949–50 production of the Metropolitan Opera directed by Herbert Graf, with musical direction by Fritz Reiner. Photo: Louis Mélançon, provided by the Metropolitan Opera Archives. Reproduced with permission.

Fig. 2. *Der Rosenkavalier,* act 1. The Marschallin (Ashley Putnam) and Octavian (Iris Vermillion) awake after their night of revels. The women's costumes and unbound hair provocatively emphasize their femininity; in most productions Octavian has donned trousers before the curtain rises. From a 1995 production of the Deutsche Staatsoper Berlin directed by Raimund Bauer; with sets by Nicolas Brieger, costumes by Joachim Herzog, and musical direction by Donald C. Runnicles. Photo: Marion Schöne, Deutsche Staatsoper Berlin. Reproduced with permission.

sheet over his shoulders, looking as much like a woman as the Marschallin. Surprise and some confusion rippled through the audience as the implications of this staging took hold, and a certain anxious suspense lingered until Octavian followed the rules of the convention and donned his britches. Only then was it clear that the production was going to explore the "male" and "female" roles the opera was about.

The ambiguity of Octavian's gender might be described as a shadow. I describe the trouser role itself as a shadow rather than a closet, for there is nothing hidden either about his gender (Octavian's or Siébel's) or the singer's: we know that the role is male and the singer is female. There is nothing closeted about the gender of the woman singing

Octavian's (or Siébel's) part because her voice is supposed to be a woman's. However, Octavian and Siébel are shadowed by the singer's identity as a woman. What fascinates me is the interplay between the singers' gender and the gender of the sopranos with whom Siébel and Octavian have fallen in love. No matter how convincing the mezzo is as an actress, I have never seen a trouser role who did not seem to be a woman, if only because the sound of her voice constantly undoes the illusion that her costume is supposed to create.

Octavian's relations with the Marschallin emphasize his youth and her experience, while his relations with Sophie emphasize his experience and her youth. Schooled in some of the finer aspects of love by the Marschallin, who herself has presumably had many teachers, Octavian leaves her to teach an innocent woman some of what he has learned. An analogy that comes to mind is the institution of man-boy love in ancient Greece, in which an adult male, often married, took a young boy as his lover and then, as he neared maturity, released him so that the boy could marry and, presumably, repeat as an adult the cycle he experienced as a child.[31] Octavian has, I believe, learned more about sex than about love (this is not uncommon). At the end of the opera it is clear that, unlike the Marschallin, he is no teacher but is instead still an eager and short-sighted pupil. For him, love and sex seem to be the same; he experiences them and leaves them behind with obvious ease, a stereotypical male response that contrasts to that of the Marschallin, who continues to cherish her man after she relinquishes him to another.

As a same-sex drama, *Der Rosenkavalier* is about an older woman who loves a younger one, who leaves her for a woman younger still. The opera, seen in this way, is a lesbian triangle. It offers both straight and gay versions of a familiar (and depressing) paradigm. The bitterness of the Marschallin's loss is offset partly by her own magnificent resignation, partly by the naïve sweetness with which Octavian and Sophie greet a future for whose horizons neither has much thought. Since this paradigm in which the young desert the old is so familiar, does it matter that *Der Rosenkavalier* yields both homosexual and heterosexual versions of it? I think that it does matter, for it reminds us that the experience of love can be the same in either configuration— a point that needs to be reinforced more for the heterosexuals in the audience than for the gay men, lesbians, and bisexuals around them.

These same-sex dynamics play to stereotypical female-female relations in which one woman is "manly" and the other "feminine," heterosexual and hierarchized stereotypes that have drawn responses from lesbian critics.[32] Blackmer and Smith note that Strauss's trouser roles

"oscillate between signifying male and female and are represented
more distinctly as lesbian."[33] Curiously, it is precisely Octavian's sexual
manliness that creates the character's potential as a lesbian figure. In
one sense, he is more womanly (to lesbians at least) because he is more
manly (to everybody else). Trouser roles explore same-sex relationships
both openly and covertly. The explicit sexual context of Octavian's role
intensifies this dual function. In an essay about her admiration for
mezzo-soprano Brigitte Fassbänder, a celebrated interpreter of Octavian, Terry Castle writes,

> When Fassbänder-as-Octavian, singing of her passion for the Marschal-
> lin, takes her fellow diva in her arms, I find it difficult not to take *her*
> literally—to read "past" the narrative fiction toward what I am actually
> seeing: a woman embracing a lover, even as she pantomimes the part of
> an impetuous boy. The very deftness of the pantomime prompts a kind
> of lesbian chauvinism: this is a woman (we are invited to imagine) who
> is as good as, if not better than, any man.[34]

And when the older woman embraces Octavian, we can take that literally too. The Marschallin finds love not in a man (she has not found
it in her husband) but in a woman who loves and tries to understand
her.[35] This woman (the actress playing Octavian) is only imperfectly
seen, of course, because she must remain in the shadow of the trouser role.

But in *Der Rosenkavalier* there is also a clearly homophobic dimension to cross-dressing, seen in the relation of Octavian to another man,
and this is an aspect of the same-sex shadow that is truly dark and
oppressive, surrounded though it is with laughter. The opera establishes the contrast between Octavian and the absent Field Marshall, the
Marschallin's husband, who prefers hunting to keeping his wife company. Octavian indelicately, naïvely, disparages him: "The Field Mar-
shal sits in the Croatian forest and hunts bear and lynx. And I, I sit
here, young as I am, and hunt what? I am in luck! I am in luck!" (47).[36]
It is, Lehmann notes, "exceedingly bad form to mention the husband
while making love to the wife."[37] The Marschallin reproves Octavian
and says that she has dreamed about her husband. When the lovers
are interrupted a few moments later, both fear that he has in fact returned ("Lass' Er den Feldmarschall in Ruh!" 47). It is not the Field
Marshall who arrives, however, but Baron Ochs, the Marschallin's
country cousin, and this creates a second, much more awkward juxtaposition. In order to escape detection by Ochs and by the servants
who enter with him, Octavian hides, only to reappear disguised as

Mariandel, supposedly one of the Marschallin's maids. Owen Jander comments that "the comedy and eroticism inherent in the convention are intensified when the 'male' character is induced to don female costume," as Octavian does here.[38] Ochs leers and paws at the "maid" and jokes about his sexual experiences, including "vivid instructions on the conquest of bashful dairymaids," remarks usually cut from performances on the grounds that they are tedious, not that they are smutty ("Wo nicht dem Knaben Cupido," 81).[39] In figure 3, as Ochs possessively clasps the maid's hand, Octavian's exaggerated awkwardness conveys the difficulty this "man" has in pretending to be a "woman," the shadow incidentally useful in obscuring the mezzo's feminine features. Later, in act 3, the scene of Ochs's intended seduction of Mariandel/Octavian, the opera again features a bed, this time intended for two men (Ochs and Octavian), nicely balancing the bed in the first scene, which was occupied by two women (the Marschallin and Octavian). When Ochs is involved, but not otherwise, cross-dressing is played for laughs, a homophobic joke. At the same time, of course, Octavian's costume as Mariandel reassures us that what is taking place is all right, since the "man's" part is being sung by a woman.

We choose to remain blind to the biological role of the singer who takes Octavian's part and claim to "believe" that she is a man. However, we regard it as a sign of stupidity when Ochs imitates our blindness and takes Octavian for a woman. How can Ochs fail to notice that Octavian is a man? Obviously he is a dunce. How can we fail to notice that Octavian is a woman? We cannot. But, duncelike, we observe the convention all the same. When a man dresses up like a woman, we laugh at the suggestion of weakness and effeminacy (especially when the man has just left a satisfied woman's bed). The humor acquires a certain homophobic cast when that "woman" is sexually pursued by another man and Ochs gropes Mariandel/Octavian. But when a woman dresses like a man, we are not supposed to laugh, or even to question the appearance of a woman in a man's place. Instead, taking our clue from the composer (and tradition), we overlook the awkwardness, accept the convention, and assess how well the actress imitates masculine behavior—in everything, of course, but her voice, which in opera matters most of all. The situation closely parallels the humor that Bruce R. Smith describes in Renaissance plays in which boys taking women's parts imitate women imitating men. "A woman disguised as a man is full of suggestive power," he writes, while "a man disguised as a woman is ridiculous."[40] In *Der Rosenkavalier* we have both disguises simultaneously: a woman dressed as a man (the singer portraying

Fig. 3. *Der Rosenkavalier,* act 1. Octavian, an awkward chambermaid (Iris Vermillion), reluctantly serves chocolate to Baron Ochs (Gunter von Kannen). From the 1995 production by the Deutsche Staatsoper Berlin, directed by Raimund Bauer. Photo: Marion Schöne, Deutsche Staatsoper Berlin. Reproduced with permission.

Octavian) and a man dressed as a woman (Octavian in disguise). The homophobic humor emerges when another man tries to make love to the man dressed as a woman, thus doubling the ridicule.

The convention of the trouser role allows for the representation of same-sex musical drama between women, one of whom is disguised as a man. Whether it is justified on the grounds of plausibility or aesthetics—and Strauss's comment to Lehmann offers both rationales—the convention shows that a female-female pairing is sometimes a better vehicle for expressing romance and even sexual passion than a pairing of opposite sexes. The trouser role affirms Strauss's "love affair" with the female voice. He could not imagine this music for a man and a woman; he could not imagine that different genders could do justice to his vision of love and to the music that conveyed it. If, when we see the trouser role and the soprano, we do not think of two women in love—indeed, of two sets of women in love, the Marschallin and Octavian, and Octavian and Sophie—that is only because we have not learned to see beyond, or around, the representational convention to the shadow where other narratives of desire live. Marjorie Garber suggests that it is important to look at the transvestite as well as through her, but it is traditional to look *at* the trouser role and uncommon to look *through* him to the woman wearing the trousers.[41] Nonetheless, a vision of love reserved to two, or three, women's voices, must, at some level, express a vision of same-sex love, of love shared by the voices of one sex, not two.

I propose that we take Strauss's use of the trouser role straightforwardly and value the beautiful music in *Der Rosenkavalier* for what, on one level, it undeniably is: exquisite love music for women. It is not, admittedly, music about one woman's desire for another woman, but it is often the case that words and music in opera, no matter how well they are paired, can be experienced and understood separately. I do not recommend this separation exclusively as a mode of appreciating opera, needless to say, especially in an age in which many critics have argued that operatic texts have been unjustly neglected and ignored.[42] Thanks to the trouser role, a "queer" reading of *Der Rosenkavalier* is unavoidable; its representation of male-female relations simultaneously encodes expressions of intrafemale desire. This queerness—this shadow created by the sound of Octavian's voice in every important scene in the work—cannot be separated from the desire of woman for man and man for woman articulated by all of the opera's other conventions, including the presentation of the silver rose, Ochs's boasting about his conquests, the betrothal of Sophie by her father, his financial and social ambitions, and others. But the libretto itself sometimes emphasizes the opera's same-sex subtext. Two comments made when the Marschallin and Octavian think that the Field Marshall is approaching stand for many. When a servant rings a small bell, Octavian is furious at the interruption. "I'll have no one in here," he says (preposterously), "I am master here." ("Hier bin ich der Herr!" 41), a line that might suggest a stereotypical butch-fem pattern of dominance. Later, when Ochs approaches, Octavian slips through curtains behind the bed; in some productions this is, of course, a closet ("Dort hinters Bett! Dort in die Vorhäng'," 51). Such readings might make the opera fit contemporary ideas of intrafemale sexual relations. But they merely elaborate rather than establish the opera's same-sex content, which is figured as a companion to its heterosexual culture, rather than as an intervention into it. Intrafemale desires cannot be isolated from heterosexual desire in *Der Rosenkavalier*. Neither can the opera's representation of heterosexual desire be entirely isolated from them. *Der Rosenkavalier* gives gays and lesbians in the audience more than something to hope for: it offers them an extended exposition of love and its volatility so rich in same-sex desire that we need only close our eyes to imagine that it is after all an opera about people like us.

Close your eyes at the opera? Is sensory deprivation necessary in order to experience opera as a text about same-sex love? It might seem an extreme recourse, but not to people like me whose first acquaintance of opera came through Saturday afternoon radio broadcasts from the Metropolitan Opera and whose eyes were, in a sense, always closed to the goings-on on stage anyway. In order to grasp the connection between radio broadcasts and sightlessness, one has only to attend the Grand Ole Opry and experience the frustration of having to watch a program designed to be heard rather than seen.[43] Wayne Koestenbaum thinks about closing his eyes "to hear better" at the opera. He quotes an opera magazine in which, "[i]n preparation for the broadcast, the listener is advised to 'study the pictures of the settings in *Opera News,* shut your eyes and try to visualize them.' To be passionate, must I deprive myself of sight?" he asks.[44] In order to be passionate and to have a gay experience at the opera, the answer, Koestenbaum surely knows, is often yes. But closing one's eyes is not always sensory deprivation. And even if it were, it is a small sacrifice, since closing one's eyes at the opera is itself a convention. Straight or gay, we do it for several reasons—to escape the incongruity of a beautiful voice coming from a body that does not suit a role, or to eliminate the distractions of an ugly set or one's neighbors. But most of all, we do it to permit the ear to hear what the eye is not allowed to see.

THE MAN IN *DIDO AND AENEAS*

Closing one's eyes at the ballet would not be an effective way to experience choreographed narratives of same-sex desire. But dances by Mark Morris require no such compromises. Lacking queer conventions in ballet, Morris has transformed standard heterosexual narratives into homosexual ones. He does not "queer" the content of the original text. Instead, he queers the performance, substituting male performers in female roles. Through this ingenious strategy the works become simultaneous narratives of heterosexual and homosexual love. I discuss two examples: women's roles he himself takes in a dance performed to Purcell's *Dido and Aeneas* and a gender reversal featured in *The Hard Nut,* a work in which Morris revises the grand pas de deux from *The Nutcracker* into a dance between two men.

Purcell's *Dido and Aeneas* is loosely based on book 4 of the *Aeneid.* The single known contemporary performance of *Dido* took place at a girls' school, although the opera was probably not written for that venue.[45] The widow of Sychaeus and not a naïve maiden, Dido was the founder and ruler of Carthage. Robert Worth Frank writes that Dido "was for the Middle Ages *the* heroine from the classical past," her passion celebrated first by Virgil and then by Ovid.[46] In Purcell's opera, Aeneas, his ship wrecked nearby, enters Dido's court to woo her, asking, "When royal fair shall I be bless'd, / With cares of love, and state distress'd?" (1:43–44).[47] Dido replies, "Fate forbids what you pursue" (1:45), but Aeneas is not deterred. "Aeneas has no fate but you," he replies. "Let Dido smile, and I'll defy / The feeble stroke of Destiny" (1:46–48). Dido overcomes her reluctance and becomes Aeneas's lover. Her happiness enrages her enemy, the Sorceress, who swears to destroy this union.

> The Queen of Carthage, whom we hate,
> As we do all in prosperous state[,]
> Ere sun-set shall most wretched prove,
> Deprived of fame, of life and love. (2:9–12)

Dido accepts Aeneas. They set off on a hunt which leads them to a grove where Dido has often retired to bathe. "So fair the game, so rich the sport," sings Belinda, Dido's companion, "Diana's self might to these woods resort" (2:33–34). In this dangerous grove, where Acteon was destroyed by his own hounds, "Dido and Aeneas make love," according to the synopsis of the plot (Morris's own). "Another triumph for the hero."[48] Immediately after the consummation, enacted in what

Joan Acocella describes as "one brief spasm,"[49] Aeneas celebrates his success in the hunt in plainly sexual language.

> Behold upon my bending spear
> A monster's head stands bleeding,
> With tushes [tusks] far exceeding
> Those did Venus' huntsmen tear. (2:41–44)

Dido returns to town with her court to escape a storm conjured by the witches; at this point the spirit commands Aeneas to return to Rome. He is stricken.

> But ah! What language can I try,
> My injured Queen to pacify?
> No sooner she resigns her heart
> But from her arms I'm forced to part.
> How can so hard a fate be took,
> One night enjoyed, the next forsook? (2:61–66)

When Dido learns that Aeneas will leave her, she calls him a hypocrite and orders him to leave her to die. "For 'tis enough, whate'er you now decree, / That you had once a thought of leaving me" (3:47–48).

It is not much of a love story, really: seduction and abandonment, a familiar tale of sailors and the broken hearts they leave behind. What is gained by recasting it as a story of intramale sexual conquest? Morris provides the answer by dancing both Dido's role and that of the Sorceress and intensifying the opera's focus on seduction and betrayal. As Dido, Morris reminds the audience that men don't just seduce and betray women. They also seduce and betray other men, routine treachery seldom witnessed outside the genres of explicitly gay film, theater, and fiction. It has been suggested that Purcell's opera commented on a king who did indeed abandon his queen, although few scholars seem willing to press the opera too far as allegory.[50] The opera also suggests that duty seduces (and perhaps abandons) men. Aeneas assumes that his recall to Rome is a genuine one, and it clearly means more to him than love. Dido, once abandoned, proves to be neither a Marschallin—no philosopher—nor a Marguerite—no repentant fallen woman. Her unredeemed suffering is an unhappy fact piously, and tersely, summed up in the opera's conclusion. "Remember me," she sighs, "But ah! forget my fate" (3:62). Why should we do that? Remembering her fate is the one thing that could save us from it.

Morris seems to have realized that the opera's themes of abandonment are secondary. His version suggests that Purcell was more interested in the intrafemale tension between Dido and the Sorceress, not found in the *Aeneid* but introduced by Tate. In a lesbian commentary on the two worlds of these two women, Judith A. Periano writes, "*Dido and Aeneas* presents the audience with a glimpse of two societies: the natural world driven by economics and politics, and a supernatural utopia, driven by pleasure and passion. Ironically, it is the witches' utopia that receives endorsement—from destiny, and from Purcell."[51] Both Purcell and Morris exploit the tension between Dido and the Sorceress brilliantly. Purcell used it to transform the love story between man and woman into a hate story between two women. By dancing both women's parts, Morris goes the composer one better, transforming the plot into a conflict not only between two women or between men but also between two sides of one man, Morris himself.

Morris is a large man, not svelte. He danced Dido opposite the Aeneas of Guillermo Resto. Figure 4 shows them in a pose typical of the Carthagian court's abstract, friezelike gestures, hands touching hands and thighs. For once, there is nothing funny about a man dressed as a woman. This dance language was inspired, Morris has said, by sign language for the deaf, suggesting that both the words to this music and the music itself are secondary to the visual images; a reviewer called the dancers' bodies "sung speech."[52] The deceptive relation of what is seen to what is heard—and the power of sight to suggest what one *wants* to hear or think is true—is a motif of the work. We find it in Belinda, who promotes Aeneas's cause. Near the end of act 1 she sings, "Pursue thy conquest, Love—her Eyes / Confess the flame her tongue denies" (1:56–57). After Aeneas's betrayal, in act 3, Belinda urges Dido to excuse him: "See, madam, where the Prince appears, / Such sorrow in his looks he bears, / As would convince you still he's true" (3:26–28). While she sings, convinced herself, apparently, that Aeneas is true, he enters for his final scene with Dido. Duped by the messenger sent by the Sorceress, he too believes what he sees.

Morris's manly appearance (his five o'clock shadow, one could say), ever in tension with his artful interpretation of the women's actions, constantly asserts as a visual fact that this is a love story between two men. The sexual dynamic here reverses what we see in *Der Rosenkavalier*. In the opera the shadow that partners the Marschallin is a female presence around a women dressed as a man; in the dance the leading female role has been turned into the shadow of a man dressed as a woman. A soprano sings the role offstage, so Morris's version of the love story is effectively bisexual, simultaneously male-male and therefore transgressive, and male-female and therefore normative. Yet

Fig. 4. *Dido and Aeneas,* act 1. Dido (Mark Morris) and Aeneas (Guillermo Resto) mirror each other's positions. Staged and choreographed by Mark Morris (1989), with costumes by Christine van Loon. Photo: The Mark Morris Dance Group. Reproduced with permission.

actions speak louder than words, especially words that are sung. In Morris's *Dido and Aeneas* the same-sex relation between men can be said to *over*shadow the primary romantic relationship in the opera. For as we watch Morris dance the part of Dido, we cannot forget that he is a man. Dido is "the largest and greatest role of his career," according to Acocella. "In it he does not show himself to us as a double exposure of male and female, as he did in *Deck of Cards.* Instead, he is unequivocally a man . . . playing what is unequivocally a woman," and his "big male body," not at all a woman's body, is "essential to [Dido's] pathos." [53] The same-sex statement is underscored by the history of the dance Morris created. Resto, a heterosexual member of the Mark Morris Dance Group, is "the person Morris fell in love with in 1984." They lived together for three years in Brussels and, according to Acocella, had a "passionate friendship" which had "no easy resolution." Morris wrote the role of Aeneas for Resto upon his return to the company after an injury (110).

Morris ingeniously complicated the gender ambiguity he introduced into the dance by also dancing the Sorceress's role, which some believe Purcell wrote for a male singer.[54] Hence both of the opera's key female roles were interpreted by a man who is, alternately, a woman reluctantly accepting a man's love and a woman jealous of that sexual fulfillment. Dancing both roles, Morris invites us to see two sides of one sexual psyche at war: Dido's reluctant surrender to manly charms sends her alter ego into a frenzy of mockery and destruction. By casting another man—or woman—in the Sorceress's role, Morris would have altered the conflict and simplified it into a paradigm of sexual jealousy. Seeing the same man dance these roles, however, we are invited to read them as two sides of one woman's—one man's—response to love and sexual fulfillment. The Sorceress and Dido "are the same woman," says Acocella, but in fact, in Morris's body, they are the same man, and they exhibit two different attitudes toward sex (100).

In her reading of this dance, Acocella argues that Morris emphasizes and even exaggerates the role of sexual intercourse and sexual desire in the story. As we will see in reference to Old English saints' lives in the next chapter, an act of gender-crossing seems to have this effect on the narrative in which it takes place. Dido becomes "profoundly sexual" in Morris's hands, a picture of dignified sexual awareness. The Sorceress becomes the opposite—vulgarly and obscenely sexual. As Aeneas boasts of his success in the hunt (and in having intercourse with Dido), he turns his back to the audience and opens his tunic. The members of the chorus (the court) avert their eyes, and only Dido sees his exposed penis. "She stares at it with stony dignity, as if she were gazing at her death," Acocella writes, "which she is" (101). In an earlier scene, the Sorceress shows her coven how Dido will die: she pulls a sword "straight up from her crotch to her gullet, in one stroke going from sex to death," which is precisely what Dido's path will be. Then she masturbates—her own version of sex, without death. Since the Sorceress is also Dido, their gestures and their overt responses to sexual knowledge are strikingly opposed. Dido's "queenliness dignifies sex," says Acocella.

> Seeing it in her, we see that it is not just the black joke the witches make of it (though it is that too) but a monumental human fact, a crucible of the soul. This meaning is not there on the surface of Tate's script—as befits a girls' school play, the libretto is more assured on the subject of

how unmarried women should treat men's advances—but it is there in
the music, and it is the reason this opera has lasted. (100)

Acocella argues that the "violation of sexual identity depersonalizes
the portrait," and suggests that Dido is "[r]aised above the wall of gender." Morris's performance, in this view, is neither masculine nor feminine and is instead a "poetic strategy" that creates "a new strangeness"
in which "[p]olitics and psychology have become art" (101). But what
Acocella calls Morris's "gender-testing" also asserts that whatever *Dido
and Aeneas* says about women's sexuality can also be said about men's
(104). Morris's "gender-testing" is "not there on the surface of Tate's
script," either, any more than is Dido's queenly dignifying of sex. But
it is no less apparent, no less powerful, no less true.

In Morris's hands, *Dido and Aeneas* becomes a love story between two
men in which homosexuality is not *the* issue, or even *an* issue. A dance
about two men or two women who loved each other today would unavoidably be a dance about homosexuality, but a dance about two men
or women who loved each other three hundred years ago, before homosexuality became a "lifestyle," cannot be made simply into a tale
about homosexuality. Instead the dance is also about intramale love, a
form of same-sex relation more complex and nebulous—and more
common—than a sexual union. Likewise, through the trouser role,
Der Rosenkavalier becomes a tale about intrafemale sexuality as well as
a conventional story about romantic love. Tate's story, as queered by
Morris, becomes, on one level, a story about a man who loves a man.
This level is visual, and hence paramount for our perceptions of dance,
but like the musical level of opera, it is a level inseparable from the
opposite-sex pairing that Purcell had in mind—he might have cast a
man in the role of the Sorceress—and that the voices of the singers
and the voice of history constantly reassert.

Morris's gender-crossing dance supplies a contemporary version of
a warning that some think was an important aim of Purcell's work.
The idea that the opera was written for a girls' school has long been
discounted. According to *The Grove Dictionary of Opera,* the oldest version of the score calls for a baritone and male chorus parts, roles beyond
girls' vocal capacities. But recent arguments suggest that the work
might have been written for this venue after all.[55] The opera might, as
Acocella suggests, illustrate how unmarried women should regard
men's advances; Dido's history shows that the reward of unbridled passion is death. Perhaps Purcell saw the work as a sort of textbook for
the virginal; he certainly did not see it as a textbook about same-sex
relations. Morris's performance informs *Dido and Aeneas* with a mod-

ern argument for sexual restraint. A man can seduce and abandon another man. A man can stare at another man's penis and see death. Sex with a man leads to death. Sex with yourself does not.

In Morris's dances after *Dido,* according to Acocella, "romantic love has resolved itself into something less romantic." Acocella does not see a vision of same-sex love emerging from Morris's *Dido.* She also de-emphasizes the same-sex content of *The Hard Nut.* This work, she writes, "is of course about love—Marie finds love with her Nutcracker, just as in other *Nutcrackers*—but this is treated as puppy love, and aside from his pleasure in showing the brave Marie's triumph, Morris does not seem deeply engaged with it" (111).[56] Much in this dance is a campy recapitulation of *The Nutcracker,* but Morris also beautifully transforms the romantic and sexual subject of the original. Morris features several men in roles the ballet traditionally assigns to women, notably the Maid and the Mother. But the transformation of gender in this work is nowhere clearer than in Morris's revision of the grand pas de deux for Marie and the Nutcracker, who changes into a handsome prince just before the dance begins.[57]

Everyone knows the story of Clara's magic nutcracker (Clara is known as Marie in Morris's source), broken by her infamously jealous brother and magically repaired by Drosselmeier, an uncle who has given the doll to Clara. After he mends the toy, Drosselmeier dances with Clara, showing her how to comfort the toy as if it were an injured baby. It grows late. Clara reluctantly goes to bed, forced to leave the toy behind, but then she sneaks out to finds that the Nutcracker has come to life. He fights off invading mice but is felled in the combat. Drosselmeier revives the Nutcracker a second time, and now also transforms him into a handsome prince who awakens to kiss Clara's hand and lead her in a pas de deux. The pas de deux, Acocella says, is nothing less than the organizing principle of ballet. It tells a three-phase story about "man and woman": they need each other (the adagio—thesis), they are apart (solo variations—antithesis), they come together (the pas de deux—synthesis). Morris avoids this form of partnering (it is rarely used in modern dance) because he is seldom interested in its limited commentary on relations between the sexes.[58]

One of Morris's striking innovations in this convention was to reposition the pas de deux between the young man and Marie and to reassign its gender roles. The pas de deux takes place after the battle with the mice, in which Marie, not the young man, is felled. However, in Morris's version, Marie is overcome not by the mice but by a scrim that falls as the battle ends. She lies prone, most of her body behind the scrim but her feet sticking out, shod in pink bunny slippers, a telling sign of her childhood and her innocence. Two attendants remove the Nutcracker's ugly mechanical jaw. Suddenly transformed into a handsome young man—Drosselmeier's nephew—he starts to dance. At the same moment we see someone, partly obscured by the scrim, moving parallel to the young man. It is Drosselmeier, whose costume resembles the young man's uniform. At first Drosselmeier appears to be repeating the younger man's movements, but soon it seems that Drosselmeier is actually controlling them. They are apart at first—the first stage of the pas de deux—and then they draw together, just as the form requires. All the conventional gestures that articulate the man's and woman's responses are there—he leads, and his nephew, in her place, follows—but the meaning of that power relationship changes completely. It is not only a single-sex partnership but, more suggestively, a partnership between one man and another, a younger one, although not quite a boy.

At points the dance is clearly romantic. Drosselmeier puts his hand on the young man's heart, a gesture that is later reciprocated. Then Drosselmeier lifts his partner, at one point touching the boy's rapt face with his hand in a gesture of great intimacy (figure 5). During this extended and intimate dance, Marie does not move. Her presence on stage—registered by her bunny-slippered feet—makes the dance seem even more dangerously erotic. Marie represents the feminine in a passive, indifferent state—as if the men's dance could not take place if she were awake. Like Dido, she has been reduced to a shadowed role, her place taken by a man. There's something clandestine, secretive about this sequence, a forbidden, stolen moment; I always want it to last longer. At the end Drosselmeier and the young man together pick up Marie, place her on a sofa, and whisk her offstage.

Later in *The Hard Nut,* a version of the grand pas de deux is danced—parodied, really—not by the young man and Marie but by the whole company. The young man and Marie have a long dance immediately afterward, but, as Acocella notes, "it is not a very interesting dance." Indeed, much of it is "openly copied" from the "earlier and far more moving *pas de deux*" between the young man and Drosselmeier—"far more moving," perhaps, but for Acocella of uncertain effect:

> The latter dance, Morris's only sustained male-male *pas de deux,* is not a romantic number. Its character is heroic and tender; it is about family love and growing up. In any case, the fact that the most poignant duet in this boy-meets-girl ballet is a duet for the boy and his uncle—and that when the boy and girl are finally allowed to dance together, their

Fig. 5. *The Hard Nut,* act 2, pas de deux, Drosselmeier (Rob Besserer) and the trans-
formed Nutcracker (Jean-Guillaume Weis). From the 1991 production at Théâtre
Royal de la Monnaie, Brussels. Staged and choreographed by Mark Morris. Photo by
Tom Brazil. Reproduced with permission.

steps (and so, by extension, their feelings) are borrowed from that earlier
family-love dance—is a sign of something. (112)

In this reading, even an inverted convention is a convention still. I find
the dance between Drosselmeier and his nephew unavoidably romantic, in part because like many viewers, I remember the "original" form
of this dance between the handsome prince and the young woman
when I see it danced by two men. I respond to the moving sweep of
music which "everyone knows" and to the intimate (if not sexual) gestures that accompany it. This is, after all, "one of the most famous *pas
de deux* numbers in ballet history" (103). Why is a dance "about family
love and growing up" necessarily any different from a dance about an
older man initiating a younger one into emotional expression and intimacy? Acocella seems to have some doubts herself, as her syntax indicates. She begins her last sentence with an equivocal "In any case" and
ends it with an even vaguer "sign of something." It seems that she
might not quite believe what she wrote. What are the other cases?
What might the dance be a sign of? I think I know.

I see the nephew as a boy prince, even a toy prince. In *The Hard
Nut,* when the nutcracker breaks and Drosselmeier fixes it, he cradles
the toy tenderly, like a father (or a mother). Later, their pas de deux,
with its intimate gestures, is unmistakably an initiation into Eros.
But Morris curbs the risks in this bold innovation. In the end the
dance seems to show that the older man teaches the younger one
what the young man himself wants to know. When the dance is enacted by the young man and Marie, heteronormative perspective is restored. The young man's dance with one of his own sex is rendered
acceptable, and perhaps made to seem necessary, because it is only a
step leading to his dance with her. As the love expressed in the male-
male dance is recuperated, normalized, by the dance between the boy
and the girl, we can see the powerful outlines of the same-sex shadow
shrink and all but disappear. The constant role is the young man's; it is
his partners who change, and whom we have to consider more closely.
His new and former loves might have something in common.

Der Rosenkavalier forces us to examine exactly the same principle.
Octavian exchanges the Marschallin for Sophie, just as the young man
exchanges Drosselmeier for Marie. But Octavian and Marie's young
man seem destined to break more hearts. Sophie seems to know this:
"It is a dream, it cannot be real," she sings, "that we two are together,
together for all time and eternity." In his half of this duet, Octavian
offers little reassurance: "I feel you and only you and that we are to-

gether! All else passes like a dream before my senses" ("Spür nur dich" . . . "Ist ein Traum," 319). They do not notice that the Marschallin has left, her last line, "In God's name" ("In Gottes Namen," 319), part blessing, part discreet exclamation at the boy's faithlessness and short memory. Should we expect that Sophie has captured his heart for all time?

Although I disagree with Acocella's interpretation of the same-sex relations in Morris's works, I have found her commentary immensely insightful. Morris's "message of gender-breaching," she writes, is inclusive. "Having discovered masculine and feminine aspects of himself, he must have imagined that everyone had more aspects than gender could explain. That, after all, is the message of gender-breaching: not that everybody should be homosexual, but that most people have larger inner lives than sexual definition will allow them to draw upon" (105). I believe that most people *do* have "larger inner lives than sexual definition will allow them to draw upon." This, I suggest, is the tough nut to crack in *The Hard Nut. The Nutcracker* is a title that suits a charming but simple romance: the fictional shell is cracked, the kernel easily extracted. *The Hard Nut*—also a tough nut as a title, both sexy and slightly obscene—suggests that the gender code is not easy to break. A raunchy send-up of the primness of *The Nutcracker, The Hard Nut* is full of sexual innuendo. But it is mostly heterosexual innuendo. Sexual definition is one of the conventions that Morris plays with. He shows how gender testing negates the power of that convention to obscure same-sex relations. Finally the nut is too tough: Drosselmeier does not run off with his nephew but hands him off to Marie. We do not know how long her triumph—"the brave Marie's triumph," Acocella calls it, with which Morris (understandably) "does not seem deeply engaged"—will last. Maybe Marie will keep her catch; maybe not. Who knows who else, male or female, might be interested in him?

The operas and dances I have discussed are filled with representations of love that are romantic in a traditional, conventional sense but that are also openly suggestive of the connection of romance to sex. In a comment on "the absence of romantic love, that expectable and venerable outlet," in Morris's works, Acocella says that this absence "made way in his imagination for the hatching of other ideas of love. . . . Dog love, vampire love, uncle love, angel love, doll love— they have no name, but they are all part of the psychology of love . . . and it is very interesting to see them in a dance" (112). What is left out here but the love that dare not speak its name? Acocella says nothing about homosexual, gay, lesbian, or same-sex loves. But surely they are more important than vampire love or dog love, and surely they should be added to this list as alternatives to the "expectable and venerable outlet" of heterosexual romance.

The sexual side of the operas is more for the ears than for the eyes (the overture to *Der Rosenkavalier,* the sexual consummation hinted in the music at the end of act 3 of *Faust*). The sexual side of the dances is more for the eyes than for the ears (Morris and Resto in sexual confrontation, Drosselmeier caressing his nephew's face). But as Wharton's exploration of *Faust* suggests, the forbidden sexual subtext makes its presence felt, as Newland and no doubt at least a few others in the audience know. Like Newland, some people look to the opera for confirmation of their own desires. They—we—go to the opera filled with hope, alert to ways in which, through cross-dressing and gender-crossing conventions, the same-sex shadows of these works might stand out—to us, if to nobody else. Romantic love is always a primary theme, but all the works I have discussed—*Faust, Der Rosenkavalier, Dido and Aeneas, The Hard Nut*—also show that, even in traditional forms from the tradition of high culture, art is close to sex. And where there is sex, there is same-sex, its shadow. As I have suggested, the trouser role creates a same-sex shadow adjacent to the opera's heterosexual dynamics, waiting to be observed, commenting on those conventions, extending them, queering them, if you will, by reminding us that what is true for man and woman is also true for man and man, and for woman and woman. By underscoring the sexual subtext to the familiar romantic plots of dance and opera, we expand romantic conventions to include everybody who sees them, not just the heterosexual majority for whom they were (presumably) written.

Morris and Strauss—and others—offer gay people entertainment and affirmation of the highest order, year in, year out. Theirs is art filled with politics, sexual and otherwise; they tell great stories of betrayal and seduction, and these are stories that can involve homosexual passion as effectively as the heterosexual passions they are always taken as commenting on. It is also art that meets basic emotional and aesthetic needs of homosexuals without addressing them—the basic needs *or* the homosexuals—as such. These works and productions get to what Andrew Sullivan describes as "the deepest desires of the human heart," feelings that are frustrated for gay people by the impossibility of public declarations of love. "To reach puberty and find oneself falling in love with members of one's own sex is to experience a mixture of self-discovery and self-disgust that never leaves a human consciousness," Sullivan writes. That shame attaches to "the very heart of what makes a human being human: the ability to love and be loved."[59] Everybody is supposed to respond when performers of *opposite* sexes sing about being in love, something that happens in opera all the time. When two members of the *same* sex sing about their love for each other, with one of them cross-dressed, we are supposed to have the same reaction. But for some of us, such declarations of same-sex affection are—dare I say it?—liberating, not merely legitimating. There it is, before the whole (opera-going) world, two people of the same sex avowing their love. When the conventions of opera betray the restrictions of society, something like 5 percent of the population—and, by no accident, a far higher percentage of most opera and dance audiences—gets to enjoy something that, from our earliest years, art, culture, and society have denied us.

Our neighbors in the audience can learn something, too, about the varieties of human love and passion. I heartily agree with Locke, who, referring to Koestenbaum's well-known work, writes, "That this kind of cross-gender identification can be particularly intense or treasurable for gay men, as some recent writings suggest, should not lead us to think that it is inaccessible to or even particularly unusual among other operagoers, whether female or male."[60] This, one could say, is art that is both "virtually normal" (to adapt Sullivan's phrase) and "virtually queer," by which I mean that it appears straight to straight people and gay to gay people.[61] As Urvashi Vaid has reminded gays and lesbians, in a work published before Sullivan's, "virtual equality" is not something to be desired, and the kind of mainstreaming of gay and lesbian life that Sullivan and others advocate has its costs.[62] But I believe that a little mainstreaming of same-sex relations in prestigious cultural forms such as opera and dance benefits the case for sexual diversity and creates some needed common ground. After all, same-sex relations are already represented—mainstreamed—in opera, a notoriously conservative art form. What gay men and lesbians need to do is to exercise critical power, to put some light on the convention's sexual meaning, to bring life to its shadows, and to bring its shadows to life.

On the surface the trouser role reinforces a heterosexual social order. But gays, lesbians, and anyone who wants to can use the convention against that order. Indeed, the trouser role, like Mark Morris's gender switching, forces heterosexuality to assert itself—for once—and puts heterosexual viewers in the position in which most art puts its homosexual audiences. When same-sex relations are straightforwardly represented, heterosexuality has to go on the defensive. Seeing two women embrace on stage, the audience has to remind itself, as did the audience of the Berlin production I have referred to, that this scene of homosexual passion is permissible because one of the women is supposed to be a man. In these moments the heterosexual audience occupies a place of unknowing. Gays and lesbians, on the other hand, know—whether or not they believe it—what is transpiring on stage. Behind the trouser role lies not only the potential for same-sex relations but a same-sex reality, openly expressed through the women's voices. The convention attempts to disguise women's appearance, not their sounds. Because it is written for a woman, the trouser role is, in one sense, no disguise at all. And when Mark Morris assigns roles created for women to men, the male dancer's disguise is equally transparent (although we look at him as well as through him). *Through* him we are meant to experience the role's (and the dancer's) capacity to express a man's thoughts and feelings for another man—Dido (Morris) loving Aeneas (Resto), and dying because he has been duped by yet another man (Morris again).

The same-sex stories I have traced in opera and dance are elusive, as shadows tend to be. I have not outlined these shadows as places of oppression (as closets), limited spaces to which heterosexual hegemony confines the homosexual, because I am concerned with demonstrating the coexistence of these orders (and what lies between them) rather than their mutual exclusivity. I do not see the homosexual as needing defense or liberation (uncloseting), for I think that it can often be seen on its own, just as shadows are, although they are seldom noticed. In the next chapter, I explore some same-sex shadows in Anglo-Saxon texts. We may treat these texts either like Strauss's opera or like Mark Morris's dances. Some of these texts encode same-sex relations in ways that are obvious and largely unambiguous, even though historians of sexuality have chosen not to see them. Most texts are like Strauss's opera in that they use conventions to neutralize the same-sex content of the exchange, desexing same-sex exchanges. Thus gestures of affection between men, especially between lords and retainers—although in Anglo-Saxon texts these are few indeed—can be read as no more overtly sexual than the hugs and chummy ass-pats that padded football players bestow on each other during games. Some Anglo-Saxon texts yield same-sex meaning only through a transgressive reading. One could queer almost any Anglo-Saxon text in which two members of the same sex speak or interact. I do not propose to do so. My preference for writing about same-sex *love* rather than same-sex *desire* is a preference for writing about what texts say rather than what they might, under certain conditions, be made to say. This preference is part of the rhetoric of straightforwardness.

In Anglo-Saxon texts, as I have suggested, such desires are rarely articulated. Smith distinguishes various discourses about homosexuality, arguing that most of them—legal, medical, moral—are concerned with deeds, while poetic discourse alone is also concerned with desire. "[O]nly poetic discourse can address homosexual *desire*," he writes. Sex acts can be observed; they are deeds that can be known "from the outside." Desire, on the other hand, cannot be observed. Because it is a feeling, "it needs to be talked about, not simply named." [63] The Anglo-Saxons named same-sex acts and desires but did not otherwise "talk about" either one, unfortunately. My use of the shadow is an attempt to elaborate and refine our perceptions of their discourse about sex.

The Anglo-Saxons knew few of the romantic conventions, which, in modern texts, have the power to obscure same-sex relations and claim love as the exclusive right of male-female pairs. Love, it turns out, has everything to do with it—everything to do with the capacity of opera and dance to cast a same-sex shadow. Romance is the framework for all the representations of same-sex relations in the works just examined. Rich and varied though those representations are, they are limited by that fact. When they show us love between two women, or love between two men, they do so only because their primary object is romantic love between a woman and a man. Yet only a small adjustment, a tilt, if you will, offsets the mystique of romantic love and makes the shadow stand out. In the works I have examined, we only have to hope for and believe in the possibility of same-sex love in order to find it. Hope and belief are not so readily rewarded in the case of Anglo-Saxon texts, but they too cast shadows where same-sex love dwells.

Kiss and Tell

Anglo-Saxon Tales of Manly Men and Women

When nineteenth-century operatic romance went beyond love to sex, the conventions of decency forced composers to say with music what they could not portray in words or actions. But other conventions put the trouser role at the composers' disposal, and the trouser role inadvertently enabled them to represent something more daring than sex—that is, same-sex—on stage, spiking opera with scenes in which two women sang of their love for each other. The dampening force of history and repetition has succeeded in persuading both ear and eye that there is nothing unusual in such scenes. In order to grasp the same-sex content of the operas and dances I have written about, it seems, it helps to be queer and to be willing to adopt an overtly political stance toward the performance. You have to go to the opera or dance filled with hope that you will see what you want to see; chances are good that you will. Or you can do as Mark Morris has done with *Dido and Aeneas* and *The Nutcracker* and make the work into what you want it to be.

These are two models for criticism that correspond to two approaches to gay and lesbian life outlined in my introduction—liberationist or legitimist. Readers who take a liberationist perspective emphasize the sexual content of texts, overt or covert, and queer it when they can, making it into what they want it to be—not just finding same-sex relations but finding them affirmed. Throughout this book, I favor a legitimist approach. I argue that the same-sex valences of Anglo-Saxon texts coexist, if not always peaceably, with heterosexual culture. They are incidental to that culture but essential to it, always present but seldom obvious, seldom represented except as shadows, or in shadows. If same-sex relations are not restricted to sexual intercourse but are broadened to include a range of expressions of affection and social gestures that bring two or more members of the same sex into intimate proximity, the shadow of same-sex relations—the shadow of the queer—becomes more visible. Although my aim is to redirect some energies within queer theory rather than to argue against it, I differentiate my approach from queer criticism on three grounds: I am not concerned with affirmation or normalization of same-sex relations; I do not restrict them to genital sex; and I do not represent them as closeted.

Most of the evidence of same-sex love in the Anglo-Saxon period comes from the discourses of church law and ecclesiastical instruction, especially homilies. Consequently, most of my analysis is devoted to these sources. In the language of Bruce R. Smith, I focus on deeds rather than desires, on evidence that can be seen from the outside, and that sees same-sex relations from the outside, rather than on that which can be seen only from the inside and which therefore has to be described.[1] No one, so far as anybody knows, wrote an Anglo-Saxon poem about same-sex love that corresponds to the Latin literature celebrating same-sex affection.[2] The poetic discourse in Old English that deals with same-sex love is very small; if we add narrative texts, saints' lives in particular, the corpus grows only slightly but at least begins to include more material involving women (but usually crossed-dressed as men). Because these sources are especially revealing, I examine them first. In chapter 4 I examine the legal discourse affecting same-sex relations, and in chapter 5 I explore poetic, narrative, and didactic texts in which Sodom and Gomorrah sometimes refer to same-sex love.

My approach is straightforward, as I have said, and so too are the Anglo-Saxon sources. No critical manipulation, whether deconstructive or queer, is needed to explain what most Old English texts say about same-sex relations. Where same-sex contact is explicitly sexual, Anglo-Saxon sources invariably condemn it. What the eye is permitted to see—images of sodomites pitched into a stinking, fiery hell— merely underscores the denunciation that the ear is forced to hear. But when sex acts are not explicit, and when other social forms and conventions are involved—that is, male camaraderie, familial bonds, religious devotion—a number of celebrated texts display surprising latitude in expressing male-male affection. Expressions of affection between women are rare and only once, in a case of mistaken identity, is sex explicitly involved. In all these texts, Anglo-Saxon authors write about same-sex relations as a consequence of narrating the life of a transvestite saint or describing social gestures, such as kissing and embracing between men. Those gestures have sexual resonance. To us, although probably not to an Anglo-Saxon audience, their same-sex shadows are especially prominent.

These texts sometimes affirm rather than disparage same-sex contact. They do so because affection and love, although not sex or romance, have everything to do with the social worlds of their plots. It is possible to reimagine both the worlds and the texts queerly, so that the reader will find what he or she hopes to find. But the more sexually explicit one's interpretation of the shadow becomes, in my view, the less likely it is to correspond to Anglo-Saxon social codes. Sooner or later we have to open our eyes at the opera. Sooner or later we must yield our vision of *Der Rosenkavalier* as a love story about three women to Strauss's vision of it as a love story about two women and a man.

I begin with saints' lives in which women, sometimes called "manly," don men's clothing, and with poetry and prose that describe men who kiss and embrace in same-sex pairings. The texts I discuss represent a cross-section of the literary forms known to the Anglo-Saxons, although I have not chosen them because they are representative. Included are homiletic saints' lives, epic and elegiac poetry, a history of the world, and a philosophical dialogue. The earliest of these texts were written at the end of the ninth century, during the reign of King Alfred (d. 899); the latest of them were written by the abbot Ælfric (d. c. 1010). This literature offers a fair cross-sample of what learned circles in the tenth and eleventh centuries read and listened to, although other genres, including handbooks of penance, homilies, and pastoral letters, arguably exercised greater influence over the Anglo-Saxons' conduct. I describe some narratives about both love and sex, and men and women, although not in equal measure. The stories of women are not, in the main, stories about the Anglo-Saxons and their social and sexual codes but rather about women from Rome and Egypt in the early Christian period. They offer a chance to examine early Christian attitudes toward homoeroticism, whether male or female, and they invite us to wonder how women in Anglo-Saxon England responded to such narratives, especially since violence toward women (torture, martyrdom) is prominently featured in them. The stories about men, however, are largely about the Anglo-Saxons and their ancestors. We may suppose that the Anglo-Saxons regarded these tales in something like the way we regard what is conventionally thought of as history: not as entertainment, but as stories about their predecessors and, in a sense, also stories about themselves. Violence is prominent in these texts, too, but this was violence that conformed to the Anglo-Saxons' social and legal codes and that was therefore unobjectionable.

Narratives change in the telling, of course; they never represent only the past but also represent the present in which they are retold. So it is reasonable to conclude that texts about early Christian culture eventually did become stories about the Anglo-Saxons or about people not too different from them. It is reasonable to imagine these texts being read and listened to by men and women who assumed that the writings were authoritative and who perhaps made less of the cultural foreignness of this material, and more of its Christian imperatives, than we are inclined to. Regardless of the origins of these texts, we can be certain that they were seen as exemplary. Their work in the culture was not only to celebrate great deeds of bravery and holiness but also to inspire their audiences to better behavior.

Although not representative of Anglo-Saxon literature, these texts are representations of Anglo-Saxon culture. Clare A. Lees has drawn some important connections between regulatory literature, especially Anglo-Saxon laws and penitentials, and texts that represent cultural codes. She positions both kinds of texts within a "complex cultural matrix of the body" governed by "the doctrines of chastity and sin." Anglo-Saxon texts, whether representational (i.e., predominantly narrative) or regulatory (administrative, legal), repress sexual pleasure (of any sort, not just same-sex pleasure) but also, as Lees points out, permit expressions of pleasure so long as they are reconciled to a Christian perspective, or, in Lees's terms, "cathected to Christian desire."[3] Because they imagine an interior world even as they describe a world from the outside, representational texts are more complex and subtle registers of a culture's structure of gender relations than regulatory texts.

We are likely to use regulatory texts to read representational texts, assuming that the former had greater authority in the culture or even that they tell us what life was really like, while representational texts tell us how life was imagined. This is an understandable tendency, and I am not sure that it is entirely unwise, although its assumptions about the closeness of regulatory texts to daily life cannot be validated. It is also important to remember that regulatory texts are themselves representational—they use categories and employ rhetorical effects— and that representational texts are regulatory, since their sometimes graphic images of sexual violence (to take one example) could easily have played on fears of authority. Both regulatory and representational texts contribute to what we might call the culture's ethic of restraint, a virtue, as Lees notes, prized in both secular and Christian Anglo-Saxon culture.[4] Both kinds of text promote a social vision with a public outside and a private inside. They focus on deeds as seen from the outside and only rarely describe them from the inside, from a personal, private perspective (as in poetic elegies). Even then, private recollections are likely to involve witnesses to the actions recalled. The social vision of the Anglo-Saxons, as seen in either representational or regulatory evidence, was dominated by disciplined loyalty in men's relations with each other and by women's loyalty to men within marriage. Pleasure, even eroticism, was permitted within these bounds, provided that the public nature of the bonds was respected. Nothing sexual, secret, or shameful could be allowed to taint a man's relation to his lord; nothing secret or shameful could be allowed to alienate a married couple's bond from the larger social structure to which it conformed. The culture seemed to permit certain kinds of intimacy so long as no private meanings—that is, unique meanings—were attached to them. Intimate social gestures such as embraces and kisses were permitted (and still are), and could be described, so long as their meaning was apparent to everyone who witnessed them, so long as they were seen from the outside.

Love between man and woman appears in all the texts I examine here in some form, sometimes expressed as the illicit desire of a wicked man for a virtuous woman, and sometimes unobtrusively as a marriage that operates quietly in the background of a narrative, determining its patterns of inheritance and political allegiance. Other forms of male-female friendship appear, too, involving eunuchs and unmarried women, and fathers and daughters. Same-sex love appears in both male and female forms, although instances of the latter are greatly outnumbered by the former. In heroic genres (epic and elegy), the primary male bond is that between lord and retainer; bonds between fathers or uncles and sons and between abbots and monks, especially novices, appear in monastic literature and didactic texts. Female bonds are confined to those between mothers and daughters and women within monastic communities; a notable exception is a woman sexually attracted to a man who turns out to be a woman in disguise. In the saints' lives we find a third form of love that supplies the standard against which all other forms are measured, and that is the Christian's love of God. Human affection and desire not only pale in comparison to love of God but are routinely sacrificed to it. However inclusive they seem to be, these texts do not portray a complete sex-gender system or claim to report how real men and women lived. They have almost nothing to do with sex, but they have at least a little to do with love, and they outline some possibilities for the expression of same-sex relations. They make a good beginning.

MANLY WOMEN

I will look first at saints' lives in which women hide their female identity, an act that was as close as Anglo-Saxon culture, lacking a Joan of

Arc, came to a trouser role. Narratives about transvestite saints are not exactly commonplace in the Middle Ages, but neither are they rare. Although scholars dispute the idea that the hagiographical convention owes its origins to pagan antiquity, cross-dressing among the gods seems to set a precedent for it. The roots of transvestism in the saints' lives cannot be completely disentangled from earlier manifestations of the phenomenon in antiquity.[5] The term "transvestism" seems to imply a desire to dress in the clothes and to imitate the behavior of the oppo-site sex, but the desire operative in these lives is spiritual. These women believe that they save themselves and escape the desires of men only by dressing as men and joining male religious orders.

The convention of the transvestite saint cannot recapitulate the ef-fect of the trouser role, but there are important similarities. First, be-ing a woman is not enough: a man's appearance is essential to her mis-sion. Second, the woman cannot be too manly. The trouser role cannot be overly sexual; the love he expresses is often chaste and fraternal (Octavian is a rare and daring exception). Likewise, the cross-dressed saint must be shielded from sexual encounters, although her disguise may be so effective that unwanted sexual attention is invited anyway. Neither the trouser role nor the cross-dressed saint is allowed to ap-proach the status of a fully functioning, fully sexualized male—that is, a man with a wife, mistress, lover, or children. Such men—Faust, Baron Ochs, the Field Marshall—stand directly opposite to the trouser role, and comparable figures of commanding authority are juxtaposed to the cross-dressed female saint to show that, however manly, she is nothing like a "real" man.

What motivates the use of cross-dressing in medieval narratives is, in part, the traditional assumption of the superiority of the male, domi-nated by reason, to the female, dominated by passion, and of the pos-sibility of passing from the latter to the former position. "The easiest way for women to approach the male level of rationality was for them to deny their sexuality," Vern L. Bullough writes, not only by remain-ing virginal but also by adopting a man's role. This convention, there-fore, is partly about power relations. What was a step up for women was, of course, a step down for men. "It would seem logical then," Bullough adds, "to argue that the female who wore male clothes and adopted the role of the male would be trying to imitate the superior sex, to become more rational, while the man who wore women's clothes, who tried to take on the gender attributes of the female, would be losing status, becoming less rational."[6] Gender-crossing in some saints' lives raises other considerations, however. The woman's denial of her sexuality is a response to demands made on her by the sex-gender system, either through sexual aggression by a man or by familial pressures to take a husband against her will. Two women portray themselves as eunuchs, as desexed males; they aspire to male status without sex—not to status that is ambiguously gendered, but to a male role that is conspicuously absent sexual functions.

The crossed-dress female saint is much more plainly involved in power relations than her trousered operatic counterpart. The saint occupies an inferior position, subject to her father or to a man who wants to possess her. To escape these men's desires, the women dress as men. Cross-dressing is not a way to *become* rational (or more rational), for the decision to wear men's clothing is itself a shrewd one and displays a highly rational approach to oppression (at least in imaginative literature). It is an attempt to gain the status needed to speak with a man's authority and without the burden of marriage. Womanliness offers inadequate protection, or no protection at all, for a woman's spiritual self.

Women who wear men's clothing are called both "manly" and "womanly" in the saints' lives. In Old English, words for "like a man" ("manlice," "werlice") are common; their feminine counterparts ("wyflice," "fæmnenlic") occur less often.[7] The adjective "werlic" designates the masculine gender in the grammatical sense, the advent of manhood, and a husband's status; the adverb "werlice" describes behavior "after the manner of a male" and "like a man, manfully." The adjective "wiflic" designates the feminine gender (although "wif," "woman" or "female," is neuter in Old English), feminine, female, and matronly; the adverb "wiflice" means "like a woman," "womanly," and "fæmnenlic" means "maidenly."[8] The application of either word to a person of the opposite sex is of exceptional interest. Not surprisingly, we do not find men called "womanly"; when a man is condemned, he is said to be "soft" or "wanton," but not "womanly." "Womanly" is an attribute applied to women, often—but not only—to identify their weakness. For example, St. Mary of Egypt speaks to a monk who seeks spiritual renewal and who has pursued her in the desert. "I am a woman," she says, and the Old English registers the secondary nature of her identity: "Ic eom wif-hades mann," literally, a person of womanhood, of female sex (206–7).[9] Seen by the monk from afar, she seems to have a human or "man-like bodily appearance" ("mennisce gelicnysse on lichaman," 168). But when she stands naked before him, she asks for his mantle to cover her "womanly weakness," her body ("wiflican tyddernysse," 211). As if to explain that this weakness is not simply her naked body but the body itself, Mary says that her "womanly weakness" ("þære wiflican unmihte," 411) once kept her physically from entering a church. Mary's life illustrates another important point about the straightforwardness of Anglo-Saxon discussions of sex. She repeatedly tells the monk that her sins are unmentionable, even though she refers to them often. At one point she claims that there is no description of lewdness, mentionable or unmentionable, that she has not taught to others or performed ("Nis nan asecgendlic oððe unasecgendlic fracodlicnysse hiwung þæs ic ne sih tihtende and lærende and fruma gefremed," 382–84; see also 311–12, 327–28, 361–62).

The story of Mary of Egypt appears in Ælfric's *Lives of Saints,* although it was not written by Ælfric, who was one of the best-known prose authors of the late Old English period. *Lives of Saints* was written for a lay audience rather than a monastic one.[10] Addressing his patrons, Æthelred and Æthelmær, Ælfric observes that his previous collections concerned saints honored by the "English nation" generally; this collection, in contrast, dealt with saints honored by the monks themselves.[11] Ælfric's lay audience held monastic communities in high regard and saw them as spiritual models. The collection was presumably read aloud among a circle of the wellborn who "emulated in secular and vernacular ways the pious life of a reformed monastery."[12] Compared at least to such famous poems as *Beowulf* and *The Wanderer,* which we traditionally assume to have had broad appeal, these lives probably reached a small audience. But it is wholly possible that they reached the same audience as the poems did—that is, educated and pious laymen and -women interested in ideals of conduct from bygone eras.

The collection includes stories of three women, two of them martyred during the persecution of Christians in early Rome. Two women, Eugenia and Euphrosyne, were transvestite saints; the third, Agatha, was subjected to torture that temporarily refigured her bodily gender.[13] Agatha's mutilation demonstrates why women are sometimes made to seem manlike in saints' lives. Like many other early saints, Agatha is the daughter of a wealthy family (an appeal to status probably not lost on Ælfric's audience); unlike most of them, however, she has no father or other male protector. She is desired by the cruel minion of the emperor, a governor named Quintianus. He attempts to corrupt Agatha through a woman, Aphrodosia, who reports that Agatha's womanly mind, her "femnan mod," cannot be bent ("gebigan ne mihte," 26–27). This remark shows a "womanly" trait to be a sign of strength—in contrast to most uses of the term—and introduces the transformative theme of this narrative. "Stones may soften," Aphrodosia says, "and hard iron become like lead before the faith can be extinguished in Agatha's breast" ("Stanas magon hnexian and þæt starce isen on leades gelicnysse ærðan þe se geleafa mæge of agathes breoste beon æfre adwæsced," 29–31). Quintianus then threatens Agatha with brutal torture; unfazed, she dismisses him as the "servant of sin and stones" ("þeowan synne and stanum," 52) and dismisses his gods as devils imaged in brass and stone (60–61) and wood (109). Infuriated, Quintianus directs his rage at Agatha's body, ordering that she be tortured on the breast and the breast be cut off.

Agatha is a virgin, but her reply to this assault both invokes and supersedes motherhood. "Oh, you merciless one," she cries, "are you not ashamed to cut off that which you yourself sucked?" Then, as if indicating that this organ is superfluous, she adds, "But I have my breast safe in my soul, with which I shall feed my understanding entirely" ("Eala ðu arleasosta, ne sceamode þe to ceorfanne þæt þæt ðu sylf suce; ac ic habbe mine breost on minre sawle ansunde, mid þam ðe ic min andgit eallunga afede," 124–27). Her breast is later miraculously restored by a messenger from God, and her other wounds are also healed (145–46). Imprisoned, Agatha dies amid burning coals, calling out to God who created her "in human form" ("to menn gesceope,"185). At her funeral, an angel carries a stone to her tomb, walking like a human being ("gangende swa swa mann," 199). The angel demonstrates that the Old English "man" can mean either "male person" or "human being." I take him or her to define "man" as "human" rather than "of or pertaining to a man opposed to a woman." Agatha's life shows not only what she is made of—the strong stuff of a death-embracing martyr—but suggests that the stuff of sanctity cannot be captured within the boundaries of either gender. The governor disfigures her womanhood but leaves her spiritual identity untouched, for the true nature of her faith does not reside in her outer breast but rather in her inner breast, her soul. Nonetheless, because her body is restored to its natural condition after it is disfigured, Agatha dies as a complete women as well as a holy one.

The breast is a marker of the female, the beard of the male. Before examining the lives of the cross-dressing saints, I turn briefly to the story of Galla, daughter of Symmachus the Roman consul, whose life is included in the *Dialogues* of Gregory the Great, a text translated into Old English during Alfred's reign. Galla is one of a number of female saints who grew beards in order to avoid marriage (Paula and Wilgefortis are others).[14] Galla's husband died one year after their marriage; thereupon she decided on a spiritual marriage to Christ. But her passionate nature wars against this decision.

> Soþlice þysum wife wæs inne swyðe fyrenu **7** hat gecynde þæs lichaman, **7** þa ongunnon wise læcas **7** hire magas hire secgan, þæt gif heo ne gecyrde to hwylces weres lufan, þæt hire þonne wolden beardas

weaxan on þam andwlitan for þære swiþlican hæte hyre gecyndes, ⁊
þæt þonne wære wifmen sceamu ⁊ ungerysnu eallum hire freondum.[15]

Truly this woman was very fiery inside and hot in the nature of the
body (i.e., bodily temperament), and the wise physicians and her kin
began to tell her that if she did not turn herself to the love of a man, she
would grow a beard on her beautiful countenance because of the great
heat of her nature, and that would be a disgrace to the woman and
unbecoming to all her friends.

Galla's unfulfilled sexual nature increases her bodily heat; this is a man-
nish quality and it takes the form of a beard.[16] But she accepts this
disfigurement and concentrates instead on the face of Christ, her heavenly bridegroom. She retires to a convent (no one mistakes her for a
man) and there performs good works. The excess of Galla's feminine
nature, denied the release of intercourse with a man, produced a beard,
both a sign of manly identity and of womanly disgrace. In this case, a
marked contrast from the saints whose lives I turn to next, a woman
who does not have a man is made to look like one. But Galla is twice
deformed, for she dies of breast cancer, receiving a vision of St. Peter
to assure her that her sins are forgiven when she dies. Her life is a good
example of the regulatory function of representational texts. The excesses of her body's desires are independent of her control over them.
Denied sex with a man, her body gives the woman a face that resembles
that which she will not have, a man. The saint overlooks this sign of
shame and disgrace to her family, but how would a woman consider-
ing to refuse men and choose virginity respond to such a text? Would
she wonder if she too might grow a beard as a sign of her "bodily
heat"? Would her breasts betray her too? Was a vision of St. Peter
worth it?

The breast is a crucial and concealed marker of womanly identity
in the life of Eugenia, one of two women saints who dress in men's
clothing. Eugenia is the daughter of the governor of Alexandria and
has been sent to school with her brothers; even her servants, Protus
and Jacinctus, are educated in Greek philosophy and Latin rhetoric
(20–21, 44–45).[17] Both servants, significantly, are eunuchs, and their
sexlessness is an important indicator of how gender ultimately works
in this narrative. When she learns about the Gospels, Eugenia and her
servants seek Christian instruction. Calling the eunuchs her "brothers,"
she cuts her hair "after the fashion of men" ("on wæpmonna wysan,"
50), and dresses as if she were a boy ("swylce heo cniht wære," 51).
Presumably she now looks like Protus and Jacinctus, and in this
disguise she presents herself to the bishop Helenus, who says that he

has already learned in a vision that "she is no man" ("heo man ne wæs," 78). He warns that she will suffer terribly when her virginity is tested but that she will triumph. Thereafter Eugenia lives with a man's mind, although she is a woman ("mid wærlicum mode þeah þe heo mæden wære," 93), and is elected abbot of the monastery (116–20). The account of her transformation repeatedly points to the contradiction between her masculine disguise and her biological identity as a woman.

Eugenia works many miracles and becomes a famous healer. She cures a widow named Melantia, who continues to visit the abbot afterwards, offering lavish gifts, believing the abbot to be a handsome youth—that is, that "she was a young man" ("heo cniht wære," 146). The confusion is understandable, for although Eugenia has a "man's mind" ("wærlicum mode," 93), she does indeed look like a boy ("cniht," 51). What she does *not* resemble is what she is: a woman. When her attempt at seduction fails, Melantia feigns illness and sends for the abbot. When he comes to her, she boasts of her property and, although a widow, claims to be a virgin because she and her husband did not have sexual relations (literally, "we two were not a common or single one in this life," "unc næs gemæne man on ðysum lyfe," 157). "Now is my mind greatly inclined to you," she tells the abbot, "so that you might be master of these goods and of me" ("Nu is min mod awend mycclum to ðe, þæt þu hlaford beo þæra æhta and min," 158–59). Eugenia responds that worldly desires are full of deceit, but her instruction has little effect, for Melantia then embraces her and attempts to fornicate with her: "the wanton woman embraced the pure maiden and wanted to persuade her to shameful fornication" ("beclypte seo myltestre þæt clæne mæden and wolde hi gebygan to bismorlicum hæmede," 169–70).[18]

This attempted rape mirrors those moments in *Der Rosenkavalier* when Baron Ochs gropes Octavian, the young man (really a woman) disguised as a chambermaid. The male homophobia of the opera—a man's desire for a woman misdirected at another man—appears in the saint's life as female homophobia. Like Ochs, Melantia forgets who she is; although she is a widow, a fact probably meant to indicate she has reached a certain age, she claims to be a virgin—that is, a young woman; like Ochs', her riches are a compensation for her undesirable features. When her advances are repelled, Melantia becomes greatly ashamed ("micclum ofsceamod," 178) and fears that the abbot will make known what she has said ("hyre word ameldian," 179). In a preemptive strike, she goes to the city's ruler to claim that the young man tried to rape her. But the man to whom she must bring her complaint is Philip, Eugenia's father, the center of patriarchal authority in the text.

The irony intensifies when Melantia testifies that "he" (i.e., Eugenia) came to her dressed as a physician ("on læces hiwe," 186), a disguise appropriate for one famous for healing, as Eugenia is, and wanted to fornicate with her.[19] Philip imprisons Eugenia, whom he does not recognize as his daughter, along with her servants.

Only when she is about to be tortured does Eugenia declare that she hid her identity in order to keep herself pure for Christ, live as a virgin, and remain unknown to man ("mannum uncuð," 230); that, she says, is why she put on a man's garments ("wærlices hades," 232). Then she bares her breast to her father and to the bystanders, who include her two brothers, and announces that she is his daughter and that her companions are his servants (she calls them young men, however, "cnihtas," 242). In response, Philip and the rest of the family promptly convert to Christianity. Ever merciful, Eugenia intercedes for Melantia, but the widow is not permitted to escape the exposure and shame she feared. Christ himself sends a rushing fire witnessed by all ("swægende fyr ufan of heofonum þæt menn onhawoden") and utterly destroys her house, so that she has nothing left ("swa þæt ðær næs to lafe nanðing þe hyre wæs," 260–63). Both the widow and her household are annihilated, a devastation as fiery and complete as that visited on the Sodomites and mentioned in many other Anglo-Saxon sources. The tale of her misdirected desire for a man who is really a woman has taken up nearly a third of Ælfric's text; its violent—indeed, apocalyptic—conclusion underscores the episode's importance. A briefer, more pointed account of Eugenia and Melantia is offered in Aldhelm's De virginitate, an eighth-century poem on virginity. Aldhelm briefly acknowledges the same-sex nature of Melantia's desire for Eugenia, invoking the standard of "nature" that was to become fundamental in the history of sex. The matron, he writes, "sought to dishonour the servant of Christ by wanton words, disregarding the laws of nature." As punishment, Melantia endured "the great mockery of laughing words" of the bystanders.[20]

Eugenia deliberately uses the disguise of a man to transcend a woman's body and a woman's fate. Eugenia bares her breast not only to escape torture but to protect and to save her spiritual family—herself and her eunuchs. She has used her manly status to become holy and no longer needs a disguise. But what has her cross-dressing gained her? Once she is returned to a woman's garb, Eugenia—formerly the "abbot" of a monastery—founds a female monastery ("mynecena mynster," 311). Thereafter conversions seem to be coordinated with gender and status is organized within gender categories. Eugenia and the virgin Basilla are maidens who convert other maidens (343); Eugenia's mother Claudia converts other widows (345); and the eunuchs

convert other young men ("fæla cnihta," 347–48). Notably absent in
this mix of eunuchs, widows, and maidens is a strongly sexed male
figure—a husband, a father, a patriarch. Philip, who, once converted,
became a bishop, is murdered by agents of the governor (300–305), and
the others are executed by the Roman emperor (Basilla when she refuses to marry; Eugenia, Protus, and Jacinctus when they refuse to
worship false gods). Up to the end, the community remains firmly segregated, both by sex and by gender. The eunuchs' purity is singled out
for praise: they were never "defiled by women" while alive ("næfre on
life þurh wif besmytene," 380–81). The praise of the eunuchs' purity
indicates that the text retains its monastic perspective, even though it
was directed at lay patrons; the model males, it seems, are those who
are sexless. Furthermore, the sexual segregation of these holy martyrs
makes a point that would not have been lost on the Anglo-Saxons of
Ælfric's time. In the early Anglo-Saxon period some spiritual communities were double monasteries, although segregated by sex. In the later
Anglo-Saxon period double monasteries disappeared, and men's and
women's communities were no longer proximate.[21]

The life of another transvestite saint, Euphrosyne, also emphasizes
the segregation of women and men but grants its women characters
far less freedom. This text is included in *Lives of Saints* and is often
paired with the life of Eugenia, although Euphrosyne's life was not
written by Ælfric.[22] Euphrosyne's father, a prominent benefactor of the
monastery where he and his wife pray, teaches the young girl and has
her baptized. When she is going to be married, he takes her to a monastery to be blessed and given special instruction from the abbot (41).
Enamored of the faith, she exclaims that the monks are like angels
("englum gelice," 46) and desires their life for herself. A monk who
visits her home urges her to remain a virgin, secretly go to a monastery,
and take the monastic habit (77–82). Another monk reminds Euphrosyne of the Gospel, which says, "Whoever will not forsake father
and mother and all his kindred, and moreover his own soul, he cannot
be my disciple" ("Drihten cwæð on his godspelle swa hwa swa ne
wiþsæcð fæder and meder and eallum his magum and þærtoeacan his
agenre sawle ne mæg he beon min leorningman," 112–14). He cuts her
hair, puts her in a habit, and leaves. Euphrosyne then decides to enter
a male monastery, reasoning that if she goes to a woman's monastery
she will be found; she therefore doffs her womanly clothes ("wiflican
gegyrlan," 130–31), changes into a man's clothes ("gescrydde mid wer-
licum," 131), and presents herself as a eunuch from the king's household ("an eunuchus of cinges hirede," 137–38). Euphrosyne does not

merely conceal her female identity but acquires a male identity devoid of sexual potential. The eunuch's status, here and in the life of Eugenia, is symbolic, male but not masculine; like the trouser role, it is not a position for a man but for a woman pretending to be one.

The abbot welcomes the newcomer, who says his name is Smaragdus, and assigns him to a senior monk for instruction. But complications ensue.

> Ða forþam se sylfe Smaragdus wæs wlitig on ansyne swa oft swa ða broðra comon to cyrcan, þonne besende se awyrgeda gast mænigfealde geþohtas on heora mod and wurdon þearle gecostnode þurh his fæger-nysse. And hi þa æt nyxtan ealle wurdon astyrode wið þone abbod for-þam swa wlitigne man into heora mynstre gelædde and he þa gecigde Smaragdum to him and cwæð: "Min bearn þiu ansyn is wlitig and þis-sum broþrum cymð micel hryre for heora tyddernyssum. Nu wille ic þæt þu sitte þe sylf on þire cytan and singe þær þine tida and þe þær-inne gereorde. Nelle ic þeh þæt þu ahwider elles ga." (159–69)

Because this same Smaragdus was beautiful in appearance, the cursed spirit sent many thoughts into the brothers' minds as often as they came to church and they were very tempted by his fairness. And eventually the brothers became angry with the abbot because he had brought such a beautiful man into their monastery. And the abbot called Smaragdus to him and said, "My son, your face is beautiful, and great destruction is befalling the brothers because of their weakness. Now I want you to sit by yourself in your cell and sing the hours there and eat there; and I do not want you to go anywhere else."

"The cursed spirit" uses Euphrosyne's fairness to tempt the brothers "as often as they came to church," a place where sexual temptation could be especially strong. Eventually ("æt nyxtan") they protest, giving no indication that they enjoy this temptation. Monastic rules and Anglo-Saxon penitentials provide penances for clerics who experienced nocturnal emission or had sex in church.[23] The brothers are susceptible to temptation because of "their weakness" ("heora tyddernyssum," 166–67)—a manly weakness for a pretty face, apparently, the only part of Smaragdus that is not covered and the feature singled out by the abbot when he decided to sequester the novice.

Distraught at his daughter's disappearance, Paphnutius comes to the monastery and asks the brothers to pray that he will find her; alone in her cell, Euphrosyne prays that he will not (214–15). The abbot consoles Paphnutius, assuring him that no harm will have come to his daughter. On another visit Paphnutius is sent to see Smaragdus, who is said to be the holiest of the brothers. Smaragdus recognizes her father, but she has been so greatly transformed by ascetic practices that he does not recognize her. She teaches him, among other things, that "a man should not love father and mother and other worldly things before God" ("man ne sceolde fæder and modor and oþre woruldlice þing lufian toforan gode," 241–43), thus reproducing the doctrine she herself was taught when she was about to leave her family. Her father is so pleased that he tells the abbot, "I am as happy *as if* I had found my daughter" ("ic eom *swa bliðe swilce* ic mine dohtor funden hæbbe," 258, emphasis added). This irony requires some comment. The truth that the daughter teaches makes her father as happy as she would herself, were he to find her again. By taking on a man's form, Euphrosyne not only enters into a world of prayer and spiritual authority otherwise denied her but becomes an agent who exchanges her own presence for wisdom: seeking his daughter, her father finds instead a truth which satisfies his need for her.

Thirty-eight years later, Paphnutius, now nearing death, returns to the monastery and spends three days with Smaragdus. At the end of that time she reveals herself to him as his daughter but insists that he tell no one. And then, saying that God has fulfilled her desire to "manfully end the course of my life" ("ryne mines lifes werlice ge-endian," 287), *she* dies (290–92). Her father takes her place as a supplicant; she had already taken his place as teacher, and now she leaves him her "house," her cell, to occupy. Her monastic teacher unknowingly echoes her final words, praying that through her powers the other brothers will come manfully to safe harbor ("werlice becuman to hælo hyðe," 315–16). Euphrosyne lived a holy life, for many years as a man and only for a few moments as a woman. But it is as a female that she is remembered. When the monks learn that Smaragdus was a woman, they give glory to God, "who works such wonders in a womanly and weak nature" ("se þe on þam wiflican and tydran hade swilce wundra wyrcað," 320). Skeat diplomatically translates "tydran hade" as "tender nature," but we have seen forms of the word "tydernes," "weakness," used to describe Mary of Egypt's weakness and the weakness of the monks attracted to Smaragdus.[24] Now it is Euphrosyne's own weakness—womanly weakness—that is the source of their amazed reverence.

The Old English saints' lives do not comment on the intended significance of cross-dressing, but Ælfric's Latin source for the life of Eugenia includes a revealing explanation of the phenomenon.

So great indeed is the power of [Christ's] name that even a woman standing in fear of it may obtain a manly dignity *(virilem dignitatem)*. Nor can a difference in sex be considered superiority in faith, when blessed Paul the Apostle, the master of all Christians, says that before God there will be no distinction between masculine and feminine, for we are "all indeed one in Christ." Therefore, his precept I have followed with a burning heart, and from the firm trust which I have had in Christ, I have not wanted to be a woman, but preserving a spotless virginity with a total effort of the soul, I have acted consistently as a man in Christ. I have not put on a senseless pretense of respectability so that as a man I might imitate a woman, but I, a woman, have acted as a man by doing as a man, by boldly embracing a virginity, which is in Christ.[25]

This comment, as Paul E. Szarmach notes, derives its "moral explanation" for the saint's cross-dressing from St. Paul's letter to the Galatians, which deals with the need of Gentiles to become Jews before they can be saved. "There is no longer Jew or Greek, there is no longer slave or free, there is no longer male and female; for all of you are one in Christ Jesus," Paul wrote (Galatians 3:28).[26] Paul's letter argues that faith is the ground of one's true identity—as Agatha has demonstrated—and that, like ritual observances dividing sects, gender roles are secondary.

But Eugenia's explanation also points out that gender roles for the faithful on earth do matter and that it is not just better but necessary to be a man. "I have not wanted to be a woman," Eugenia says, "but preserving a spotless virginity with a total effort of the soul, I have acted consistently as a man in Christ"—a man, that is, free of any sexual demands, whether from women or other men. Eugenia acknowledges that cross-dressing works two ways. "For I consider the pretence by which a woman pretends to be a man not to be injurious of honour," she says, adding, "[b]ut this is rightly to be punished if, with a desire for vices, a man feigns (to be) a woman."[27] Gopa Roy notes that St. Jerome considered women who gave up sex to be manly. A woman imitating a man "acts as a man by doing as a man" and embraces virginity in Christ.[28]

As Szarmach notes, Ælfric omitted this speech and other details from his source that "advance the theme of sexuality."[29] Eugenia's explanation might also have been omitted because, at least in regard to its comment on men who dress as women, it is not clear. Moreover, the speech plainly contravenes a central point in the lives of Eugenia and Euphrosyne. Eugenia claims that "a difference in sex [cannot] be considered superiority in faith." This is a point Ælfric and his contemporaries would probably have refuted, for the lives of Eugenia and Euphrosyne clearly demonstrate that "a difference in sex" does indeed matter where faith is in question, in at least two senses. First, in order to be able to profess her faith—and, in Euphrosyne's case, escape an undesired marriage—the woman must pretend to be a man. Second, religious communities are segregated by sex; once she is no longer cross-dressed, Eugenia obviously loses her right to preach to males, who are better proselytized by other men. The secondary status of the holy woman is reinforced in another text by Ælfric about the miracle of the loaves and fishes, an event that appeared to exclude women from those who were fed.

> Ðær wæron getealde æt ðam gereorde fíf ðusend wera; forðon þe ða menn, þe to ðam gastlican gereorde belimpað, sceolon beon werlice geworhte, swa swa se apostol cwæð; he cwæð, "Beoð wacole, and standað on geleafan, and onginnað werlice, and beoð gehyrte. Ðeah gif wifmann bið werlice geworht, and strang to Godes willan, heo bið þonne geteald to ðam werum þe æt Godes mysan sittað." [30]

> There were numbered at that meal five thousand males, because those people who belong to the spiritual banquet should be manfully made, as the apostle said. He said, "Be watchful, and stand on faith, and undertake manfully, and be bold. Though if a woman is manly by nature and strong to God's will [i.e., strong in serving God's will], she will be counted among the men who sit at the table of God."

"Werlice" here translates Latin "viriliter," meaning "courageously" but also "manfully." In the Latin source for this text, Bishop Helenus echoes this pun from Paul (1 Corinthians 16:13): "Rightly you are called Eugenius, because by doing manfully, you have offered yourself [as] a perfect man in the Lord's contest" ("Recte, inquit, vocaris Eugenius, quia viriliter agendo, virum perfectum in agone te dominico obtulisti").[31] A woman earns salvation by acquiring a man's nature. Eugenia and Euphrosyne first acquire and then relinquish a manly appearance, a temporary transformation made permanent in life everlasting.

Both lives depend on a shadowy male gender category, the eunuch, the sexless male. Both women disguise themselves as men in order to protect their virginity, but each simultaneously creates a threat to sexual purity in doing so, Euphrosyne with the monks, Eugenia with Melantia. It is not only men and women who attract each other: those who occupy an undefined middle ground attract men and women alike. Male honor is saved from potential embarrassment when the monks are disturbed by Euphrosyne's beauty. They seem to be exposed as weak and vulnerable to a man's—a eunuch's—beauty. Their discomfort reminds us that homosexual acts in the monastery were a serious and persistent problem, as medieval handbooks of penance and other sources tell us, and not a subject suitable for the monks' sacred reading, much less the laity's.[32]

But the story of Euphrosyne both curbs and disguises the risk. First, the source of the temptation to the homosexually vulnerable men (all of them, apparently) is a beautiful woman. They do not know this, of course, but we do, and so did Ælfric's audience. The monks' attraction to the beautiful eunuch can be compared to intimacy between the Marschallin and Octavian in *Der Rosenkavalier:* it is surprising, even shocking (as it was in the Berlin performance in which Octavian was not dressed as a man; see figure 2, chapter 1), but, in the end, it is all right because we *know* that Octavian is supposed to be a man (so the opera is heterosexual). Just so, we know that Euphrosyne is a woman, so the monks' attraction to her, although fully revealing their susceptibility to same-sex desires, is likewise, in the end, all right: the eunuch really is a she, and the sexual attraction is, ultimately, a heterosexual one. Commenting on a later version of this story, Simon Gaunt argues that the Old French text manifests "casual treatment of transvestism and homosexuality" and claims that, rather than posing a risk, as I see it, "homosexual activity is taken for granted as a danger against which the monks should be vigilant." It is noteworthy that in the Old French version the monks "look at [the saint] as if she were a wild beast" and insist that the stranger is "not a eunuch, but jealous Satan himself."[33] I do not find this a particularly "casual" treatment of either transvestism or "homosexuality." Gaunt's views express "queer wishes" that tell us what Gaunt wants to see (or hopes to see) in Euphrosyne's life, and I have no objection to his reading so long as it is not used as a basis for a historical commentary on same-sex relations in either medieval France or England.[34] The Old English life does not suggest that "homosexual activity" is a routine danger, either. The point seems to be that Euphrosyne is extraordinarily beautiful and that her beauty compels the monks to desire her. She is obviously the most beautiful novice they have ever seen. But are we to imagine that there were no other good-looking men in the monastery? I would suppose that there were. Euphrosyne's beauty and the danger it creates are extraordinary, not routine.

The episode presents a risk to Ælfric as a reflection on the problem of same-sex sins in the monastery. The scandal of such acts would complicate the monks' need to recruit novices, would alarm donors, and would demonstrate the monks' failure to observe their vows of chastity.

Thus Ælfric undercuts the potential power of this manifestation of same-sex desire (that is, he curbs its risk) by showing that monks respond to their desires with fear. They "became angry with the abbot because he had brought such a beautiful man into their monastery" ("wurdon astyrode wið þone abbod forþam swa wlitigne man into heora mynstre gelædde"). The abbot sees that "great destruction" is befalling the monks because of their weakness ("micel hryre for heora tyddernyssum") and protects them by isolating Smaragdus, thus precluding any possibility of same-sex contact. The monks make no secret of their aroused desires, and the abbot (only he is immune, apparently) does not hesitate to tell Smaragdus about the turmoil his arrival has created. The only secret in the community is kept by Smaragdus herself. The power of temptation is subordinate to their determination to prevent it. What might have been a scandalous episode is, in the telling, exemplary. The monks' discipline forms a sharp contrast to the deviousness of Melantia, who foolishly, unknowingly desires one of her own sex and who is humiliated—and annihilated—because of her lust. The lay women in Ælfric's audience could take heed of the fate awaiting evil females who try to exploit saintly, sexless men. Everybody hearing this narrative could admire such men and their determination to resist temptation.

Szarmach observes that the life of Eugenia is "an erotic story with no erotic content."[35] I would revise this to say that the story contains "almost no erotic content," for Melantia's desire for Eugenia, like the monks' desire for Smaragdus, is specifically erotic. The prominence of eunuchs—either castrated males or males born without male genitalia—registers the erotic by repressing physical signs of gender. Lees has stressed the role of bodily sexuality in saints' lives, in women's lives especially, but some commentators regard a focus on the body as inappropriate to this material.[36] Michael Lapidge asserts that it is a violation of "hagiographical intentions" to see anything individual in these narratives, whose representational power lies in their collectivity. Ælfric "regarded himself as the apologist of the universal church," Lapidge writes, "and it would have been no compliment to him to tell him that his hagiography had imparted individual characteristics to individual saints. . . . The saint's power of intercession was the hagiographer's uppermost concern, and hence it did not matter whether the saint was tall or short, fair or bald, fat or thin, blond or brunette."[37] What Lapidge says about Ælfric's stance in relation to the universal church is certainly true. At the same time, the lives of Agatha, Eugenia, and Euphrosyne also show that physical beauty and fairness, always the property of the saint, are fundamental to hagiographic plots. These saints are not short, fat, or ugly. Their bodies, instruments that simultaneously invoke and repress the sexual, are, in a sense, as exemplary as their souls. But these bodies are troubled signs. They wander among categories of gender assigned to both males and females—the same territory occupied by the trouser role.

The aim of the trouser role is to assign an awkward male position in the gender system to a woman because of acting experience, voice, and other dramatic considerations, but also because conventions of gender militate against men taking roles that compromise masculine behavior. If Octavian were a man, could he also be Bichette's "Bub," her boy? The trouser role is a secondary figure both to the woman he loves and to his male competitors, who are manly—that is, mature—men. The transvestite saint also defines an awkward gender space, awkward at least in terms of an asymmetrical gender hierarchy such as that recently outlined for the early Christian world—the world of hagiographic narratives—by Bernadette J. Brooten. In that system, manly men come first, then womanly women (i.e., women who are passive); they are followed by passive (homoerotic) men, passive homoerotic women, and last, active homoerotic women.[38] It is not possible to be an independent woman in this system. A heterosexual woman must be subordinate to a male, and a homoerotic woman, whether active or passive, ranks lower still, inferior to women who know their proper place.

This system derives from the writings of the second-century exegete Clement of Alexandria, who described both passive and active female homoerotic partners as acting "contrary to nature" and "behaving like men" because they did not take the proper woman's role with a man.[39] In Clement's terms, "behaving like a man" means that such women "do not assume the female role with a man" and are not passive with men. In the saints' lives, fathers and aggressive males occupy the most powerful positions: it is at their will that women and other men, such as eunuchs, act. All the women, wives and maidens, are next. The monks who are disturbed by Smaragdus stand lower in the system than the abbot to whom they report their dangerous desires. Below them is Melantia, ironically portrayed as an active homoerotic woman, who retains the least status and acquires the most shame. Within this system, we can see how the transvestite saint functions. Were Eugenia to follow her father's wishes, she would retain her status as a passive female. Quintianus tries to force Agatha into a similar position. Instead, like Euphrosyne, Eugenia takes the place of the passive male (although obviously not also homoerotic), thus escaping the sexual pressure placed on women by the demand that they marry and have intercourse with men. This position was the only option in a man's world available to women who sought freedom from sexual subordination and who also wanted, as did Euphrosyne, to avoid detection by living in a female community. This is, in the system Brooten outlined, a step down for the woman. But each returns to a higher female status at the end of her life. Women dressing as men are comparatively common in medieval texts; their threat to the gender hierarchy, sometimes explicitly sexual, is neutralized when the woman is revealed for what she is and returned to a position appropriate to her. Women's or men's cross-dressing is seldom mentioned in Continental penitentials, and no English penitentials punish transvestism. Men dressing as women are rare, and it is significant that men who dressed as women were not described as misbehaving sexually. Rather their transvestism is associated with witchcraft and pagan observances and is assigned penances of one to three years (it was the same for a man who dressed as a woman as for a woman who dressed as a man).[40]

Cross-dressing in saints' lives demonstrates three points at which same-sex relations intersect with heteronormative social order. First, cross-dressing exposes the inferiority of woman's position and its vulnerability to the operations of patriarchy (marriage, sexual subordination). Second, cross-dressing reveals the possibility of foiling these operations, if only insofar as they would have compromised the saint's ministry. Third, the turmoil that cross-dressing produces ultimately underscores the necessity of restoring social order, including gender hierarchy within patriarchy, when the saint's mission is accomplished and no threat of sexual violation, sanctioned or otherwise, is possible.

"Culturally," writes Brooten, "a woman in man's clothing is neither a woman, nor a man, but can rather signify a countercultural challenge."[41] Brooten's comment concerns modern rather than ancient culture, but in the lives of Eugenia and Euphrosyne it is exactly the case that the cross-dressed woman signifies "a countercultural challenge." The countercultural movement is, in all three lives I have discussed here, Christian conversion and its heroic demands on women who wish to escape patriarchal claims on their bodies and commit themselves to spiritual and physical unions with Christ rather than with men. In order to accomplish this aim, they must cease to be either women or men, as sexual behavior defines those categories, and pursue a life without sex. Their mobility is perfectly represented by the eunuch, the male who stands outside the patriarchal system constituted by marriage and sexual custom. The gender of the eunuch is ambiguous. As these lives show, the eunuch is a possible sexual partner for a woman (Melantia's advances to Eugenia) or a man (the monks' attraction to Euphrosyne). These possibilities are not merely modern projections of the saints' lives but are indeed their same-sex shadows.

The trouser role can make same-sex sparks fly. No such sparks surround the transvestite saint, needless to say, and gay or lesbian readers of these works find little in them to regard with hope—hope that we will see what we want to see, that is. Gay or lesbian readers are likely to sympathize with Melantia and, up to a point, the monks who are attracted to Smaragdus, but there is no possibility of closing one's eyes to the fate of their same-sex desires. Melantia is exposed as worse than a lusty woman. Failing to realize that Eugenia's sex is the same as her own, she is a fool who cannot tell a woman from a man. The monks' desires are treated more gently. They think they desire a beautiful man, a shameful and socially unacceptable wish. But the audience knows better and so understands that their desires are not in fact aberrant. Although they do not know it, they are manly men in that they desire what all men should want: a woman. But these monks are also exemplary in another sense. They not only monitor their desire but understand that it endangers their vows of celibacy, which constitute their real manhood, their virginity in Christ. They recognize and police their own deviance.

MANLY MEN

Time, then, for a man who indulges his excesses, even though he pays for them in the end. He is the only cross-dressed male I know of in Anglo-Saxon literature, and like his female counterparts, he entered the world of premodern England through the channels of late antiquity. His name is Sardanapallus, the last of the Assyrian kings. His escapades are recounted in the Old English translation of the *Historiarum adversum Paganos Libri Septem,* or *The Seven Books of History against the Pagans,* which was written by Orosius at the behest of Augustine of Hippo and completed in 418. The Old English translation was completed during the reign of Alfred (d. 899). Augustine wished to augment his assertion, in the third book of *The City of God,* that the fall of Rome was not caused by the city's conversion to Christianity. He enlisted Orosius to demonstrate that the city had suffered disasters before the conversion, as well as after.[42] Orosius chronicles events in relation to the founding of the city of Rome.

> In the sixty-fourth year before the founding of the City, Sardanapallus, the last of the Assyrian kings, ruled, a man more corrupt than any woman. While he was wearing purple cloth in the garb of a female in

the midst of a flock of harlots, he was seen by his prefect, Arbatus, who was then in command of the Medes and he was cursed by him. Soon also, when the people of the Medes rose in revolt, he was called forth to war and when conquered cast himself upon a burning pyre. Then, the kingdom of the Assyrians yielded to the Medes.[43]

The Old English version is altered in revealing ways.

Ær þæm þe Romeburg getimbred wære lxiiiigum wintra, ricsade Sardanopolus se cyning in Asiria, þær Ninus se cyning ærest ricsade. 7 Sardanopolus wæs se siðmesta cyning þe on ðæm londe ricsade. He wæs swiþe furþumlic mon, 7 hnesclic 7 swiþe wræne, swa þæt he swiðor lufade wifa gebæro þonne wæpnedmonna. Þæt þa onfunde Arbatus his ealdormon, þe he gesett hæfde ofer Meðas ðæt lond. He angan sierwan mid þæm folce þe he ofer wæs, hu he hiene beswican mehte, 7 aspon him from ealle þa þe he ondred ðæt him on fylste beon woldon. Þa se cyning ðæt anfunde, þæt him mon geswicen hæfde, he ða hiene selfne forbærnde, 7 siþþan hæfdon Mæðe onwald ofer Asirie.[44]

Sixty-four years before Rome was founded, Sardanapallus reigned as king in Assyria, where Ninus first reigned. Sardanapallus was the last king who ruled that land. He was a very corrupt man, wanton [or "soft"] and very licentious, in that he better loved the conduct of women than of men. That was discovered by his alderman, Arbatus, whom he had set over the Medes in that land. He began to plot with the people whom he governed, how he (Arbatus) might betray him (Sardanapallus), and he (Arbatus) persuaded to (his side) all those whom he feared would be of assistance to him (Sardanapallus). When the king discovered that (that he had been betrayed), he burned himself, and afterwards the Medes had control of Assyria.

Sardanapallus is excessively fond of women and imitates their behavior. This definition of effeminacy has nothing to do with same-sex behavior. In the Renaissance, effeminacy was a charge usually brought against men who paid too much attention to women. Neither then nor in the Middle Ages, early or late, was effeminacy an invariable sign of a man who had sexual intercourse with other men.[45] Instead effeminacy was a sign of weakness, a moral defect; it might lead to further deviance, but it was in itself already corrupt. Given that Sardanapallus appears to be the sole male cross-dresser in the literature, we should take care not to misread his conduct. It is possible that the king dressed himself as a woman only because he would rather have been a woman in women's company. But both the Latin and Old English claim that he is wanton and licentious, charges that suggest more than effeminacy. And the scandal his conduct gives when Arbatus sees him, and the king's subsequent military defeat and suicide, carry further implications. It is possible that Sardanapallus consorted with harlots in order to consort with manly men—with the kind of men who keep harlots company.

The Old English translator dilutes some of the sexual implications of Sardanapallus's behavior. The gaudy trappings—the king's purple robe and the flock of harlots—vanish. We are told only that Sardanapallus was so indulgent ("furþumlic")[46] and wanton ("wræne") that he preferred the conduct of women to that of men, and perhaps—although this point is only implied—that he preferred women's company to men's. Another word that characterizes Sardanapallus is "hnesclice," which means "soft," "wanton," or "weak." It is a term also used in an Anglo-Saxon penitential to describe men who have sex with other men.[47]

Women's dress figures prominently in a later episode as a sign of their courage. Many years later the Medes fought the Persians, who were overwhelmed and who took flight. In retreat, the Persians were confronted by their wives and mothers, who lifted their skirts and asked if the men wished to escape into their wombs. Shamed by this taunt, the Persians returned to rout the Medes.[48] The example of the Persian women helps us understand a principal objective of the text, which was not to comment on same-sex relations but to sustain the imperatives that distinguished manly and womanly behavior. These imperatives, as Carol Clover and others have argued from Icelandic sources, were presumably used to shame men who fell short of the masculine standards they were expected to uphold (it is not clear that women were shamed in the same way).[49] Sardanapallus reveals his unmanliness in his womanly attire; as they lift their skirts to reveal womanly vulnerability, the Persian women shame their unmanly defenders. The Anglo-Saxon translator avoids the unsavory implications of the Latin text. Merely by mentioning the king's and the warriors' bad example, however, the author invokes a standard of male conduct if not specific homosexual acts that violate it. Members of the audience familiar with the penitentials—certainly members of the higher clergy, and some monks—might well have thought of this ancient and corrupt king as one of those men who had sex with their own kind.

The gender crossing of Sardanapallus shows that the Anglo-Saxons were aware that men could be womanly and women manly. Such examples are very rare in the literature, but we can learn at least a little more about men's behavior toward other men from the word "manly" as it is applied to men. I wish to consider three accounts of men who embrace and kiss other men and another episode in which an Anglo-Saxon hero is possibly accused of effeminate behavior. Even traditional commentaries sometimes note the erotic overtones of the first three of these passages, each of which invokes a convention of male friendship, usually structured within the bonds joining a retainer to his lord. Two of these encounters take place within the "duguð," the Anglo-Saxon word for a community centered around a lord and his hall, an all-male world that is as strongly same-sexed as the monastery.[50] Same-sex shadows play over each of these three episodes. Each is erotic, but each contains erotic expression within the boundaries of a male-centered, patriarchal system that frustrates a specifically sexual construction of the text. The fourth episode is not erotic but may describe an insult hurled at an Anglo-Saxon warrior that causes him to make a fatal error in battle. If this construction of the episode is valid, it would constitute a unique example in Anglo-Saxon of a tradition of male-to-male insult that is richly attested in Norse and Icelandic sources.

Beowulf describes two of the most manly men in Old English literature—Hrothgar, the aged Danish king whose kingdom is collapsing, and Beowulf, the young hero who rescues it. Having heard of Hrothgar's powerlessness before a monster who ransacks Hrothgar's hall, Beowulf appears to fight and kill Grendel. The deed done, Hrothgar fittingly rewards the hero, and the narrator approves.

> Swa manlice   mære þeoden,
> hordweard hæleþa   heaþoræsas geald
> mearum ond madmum,   swa hy næfre man lyhð. (1046–48)

> So manfully did the glorious prince, hoard-guard of heroes, repay the battle-rush with steeds and treasure that no man will ever find fault with them.[51]

"Manlice" is translated as "nobly" and "generously" as well as "manfully" in standard editions and translations of the poem.[52] These choices come as no surprise to anyone familiar with the ways in which Anglo-Saxon scholars have used glossaries to shape translations produced from their editions, and used translations to shape readers' ideas of the culture. Is it the poet or the editors or translators who valorize "manfully" as that which is "generous" and "noble" in this passage? Hrothgar seems to define the word "manfully" rather than to be described by it: the word need not mean "generous" or "noble" here, but instead "that which is an appropriate human response to the situation," that which is fully in accord with what a good person would do, the fullest human response. The *Oxford English Dictionary* defines "manly" as "belonging to human beings, human" (obsolete) and "possessing the virtues proper to a man as distinquished from a woman or child."[53] The *OED* also uses the word to describe a woman who possesses "qualities or attributes regarded as characteristic of a man." The poet claims that this generosity is so appropriate to human nature that no one—that is, no "man"—could fault it, although presumably someone less than a man—a monster, perhaps, one of Grendel's kin, or a coward—might want to. The translation silently appropriates attributes of generosity and nobility to a word that need indicate no more than Hrothgar's exercise of a man's judgment. He behaves suitably and without reproach. His gifts, offered in a spirit as manly as that in which the deeds they reward were accomplished, repay Beowulf's victory in battle. No man among the witnesses should have any criticism of this exchange. The poet seems to be assuring the audience that Hrothgar, whom we have come to see as weak and ineffective, is as much a man as the young hero who has just killed Grendel. The audience is implicitly challenged to affirm its manliness—its humanity, but also its sense of what is appropriate—by approving of Hrothgar's gesture.

Hrothgar's manliness becomes an issue during his farewell to Beowulf. The young man, highly honored for his triumphs, is eager to depart. But Hrothgar is not eager to see him go. As he sends Beowulf back to his people, Hrothgar gives him twelve treasures and asks that he return again soon. The poet lavishes sentiment and emotion rare in Old English verse on their parting.

> Gecyste þa   cyning æþelum god,
> þeoden Scyldinga,   ðegn betstan
> ond be healse genam;   hruron him tearas,
> blondenfeaxum.   Him wæs bega wen,
> ealdum infrodum,   oþres swiðor,
> þæt h[i]e seoðða(n) [no]   geseon moston,
> modige on meþle.   Wæs him se man to þon leof,
> þæt he þone breostwylm   forberan ne mehte;
> ac him on hreþre   hygebendum fæst
> æfter deorum men   dyrne langað
> beorn wið blode.   Him Beowulf þanan,
> guðrinc goldwlanc   græsmoldan træd
> since hremig. (1870–82)

Then the good king, of noble race, the great Scylding prince, kissed the best of thegns and grasped him around the neck. Tears flowed from him, the gray-haired one. In the wisdom of his age, he expected two

things, and one more than the other—that they would never see each
other again as in this brave meeting. That man [Beowulf] was so dear
to him [Hrothgar] that he could not restrain surging breast-sorrow. In
his heart, fixed by the bonds of thought, a secret longing for the beloved
man burned in his blood. Then Beowulf left him, marched over the
grass-earth, a gold-proud warrior rejoicing in treasure.[54]

Hrothgar's behavior has not gone unnoticed. Howell D. Chickering
comments extensively on Hrothgar's display of emotion as part of a
scene that disrupts a father-son relationship, a connection, he observes,
emphasized elsewhere in the poem. Chickering adds, "It almost seems
as though the language of erotic poetry were being misapplied to a
father's love for a son."[55] Chickering's reading is unusual in admitting
the erotic element into the verse. More typical is John M. Hill's comment that the parting scene offers "a contrast of two worlds within the
embrace of the same values: the young man's in which the loss of dear
ones is relatively unknown; and the old man's in which loss is a part of
one's lot on this middle earth."[56] In Hill's reading, the scene does not
seem to be an erotic gesture at all but rather a nostalgic one that extends
leave-taking to thoughts of separation at death.

I wish to examine briefly the elements of the "language of erotic
poetry" that seem to echo in Chickering's reading of these lines, and to
see what Anglo-Saxon literature in *Beowulf* and elsewhere tells us
about affection or displays of emotion between men, especially between
fathers and sons. The key elements in the passage include tears, the
kiss, the embrace that follows, and especially the old king's "secret
longing for the dear man" ("æfter deorum men dyrne langað"). What
is the nature of this longing, and why does Hrothgar keep his longing
secret? Does he in fact do so? A secret longing—a longing for Beowulf
that "burn[s]" in Hrothgar's blood but that the king cannot acknowledge—might well be sexual. It might well be something else, however,
something more probable. We have already learned that Hrothgar
wanted Beowulf to succeed him. It seems likely that this secret longing
is for a son, or rather for another son, rather than a sexual passion for
Beowulf. I cannot deny that a secret longing suggests a hidden sexual
desire. But absent any other suggestion of a sexual attraction for the
hero on Hrothgar's part, that "something" is sexual only by fiat. On the
other hand, the embrace and kiss the men share is one of the most
impressive and moving displays of same-sex love in Anglo-Saxon literature, and for me the fact that it unites two men, at least one of whom
deeply loves the other, is quite enough.

Hrothgar's tears, examined in the context of ancient heroic literature, are not quite so unusual as they seem to be. David M. Halperin
has written about "heroes and their pals," describing intimate but not
sexual relations between an older and a younger man, in the *Iliad,* the
Gilgamesh epic, and the books of Samuel.[57] Achilles' tears at the death
of Patroclus are often taken as a sign of homosexual love between
them, a speech best remembered from Christopher Marlowe's famous
line from *Edward II:* "And for Patroclus sterne Achillis droopt."[58] Halperin points out that Homer never comments on sexual relations between the two men and that even readers from subsequent periods in
Greek history disagreed about the erotic ties between them. "Modern
readers may reasonably feel amused at the difficulties the classical
Greeks confronted when trying to map their own sexual categories
onto the Homeric texts and onto the erotic and emotional patterns contained in them," Halperin remarks. "But those difficulties remain in-
structive for us as well."[59]

Beowulf and Hrothgar do not qualify as heroic "pals," to use Halperin's phrase. Halperin's pairs live in a "micropolitical" world of asymmetrical relations (one is older, one is more prominent, socially and
narratologically, etc.). Patroclus, for example, older and wiser, is also
subordinate to the young and impetuous Achilles, who has "narrato-
logical precedence."[60] Beowulf is socially subordinate, but he dominates the narrative. In the *Iliad,* the older partner weeps at the wrath
of the younger man. Hrothgar's tears mourn Beowulf's departure, not
his rash actions. There is no conjugal language used to describe their
relationship, no domestic details—one partner preparing food and
serving it to the other, for example—and the language of kinship
that connects them is carefully limited. Hrothgar's implicit attempt to
"adopt" Beowulf is thwarted by Hrothgar's wife, Wealhtheow, in a famous defense of her sons and their rights (1175–91). No women are
associated with Beowulf, but his manliness is never in doubt.[61] His
comments on relations between men and women are incidental, such
as his prediction that the warrior Ingeld's "wiflufan" ("woman-love")
will be cooled by hatred for his enemies (2063–66).[62] Hrothgar's marriage, by contrast, is prominent. There is no point at which he and his
young hero constitute a closed, exclusive, and intense or heroic pair.

All the same, it is important that Hrothgar's blood burns with "secret longing." Longing in Old English poetry is seldom a feeling one
man has for another. In *The Wife's Lament* "longing" expresses a
woman's feelings for a man four times: longing seizes her (14), she is
oppressed by intense longing (29), and she fears she will never escape

it (41). "Woe is it for him (or her) who must wait for his (or her) loved one in longing," she concludes ("Wa bið þam þe sceal / of langoþe leofes abidan," 52–53).[63] This poem is a *Frauenlied,* a rarity on several counts. It expresses a woman's point of view and refers to the sexual side of relations between lovers, candor quite out of keeping with the rest of the literature. *Wulf and Eadwacer* is another poem of longing, even shorter and more enigmatic. In both poems, as Marilyn Desmond has written, female speakers are defined by their marriages.[64] The Wife's exile stems from political and social complications that are none too clear. With refreshing if bitter directness, she describes the domestic, private consequences of the political context created by her marriage, a matter routinely viewed by most Anglo-Saxon poets at the level of kinship, feud, and tribe but otherwise swept from view. Secrecy, as well as longing, is part of the Wife's experience, although in this case it was a secret kept from her. The kin of her husband—women and men— plotted with secret thought ("þurh dyrne geþoht," 12) to separate the couple and succeeded, leaving the Wife "seized with longing" ("mec longade," 14). Alone, she contrasts her isolation to the warmth enjoyed by others.

> Frynd sind on eorþan,
> leofe lifgende,   leger weardiað,
> þonne ic on uhtan   ana gonge
> under actreo   geond þas eorðscrafu. (33–36)

There are friends on the earth, lovers living, lying in bed, while I go alone at daybreak under an oak tree through these earthcaves.

It is rare to find an Old English poem representing lovers in bed, as well as to find a reference that could include various constructions of who these lovers are; we assume that they are a heterosexual pair, but that is not a necessary assumption.[65] Significantly the Wife sees herself as an exile from a lover's bed, while famous Anglo-Saxon males in exile—the Wanderer, the Seafarer—see themselves in exile from the great hall of the men.[66] She imagines an audience of one for her description of inner turmoil, a man waiting for her in her bed, while the men imagine a much larger audience, many men who go on without them. *The Wife's Lament* recalls another Old English poem that counsels secrecy for women who do not want to be married off by their kin. *Maxims II* cautions:

> Ides sceal dyrne cræfte,
> fæmne hire freond gesecean,   gif heo nelle on folce geþeon
> þæt hi man beagum gebicge. (43–45)[67]

> A woman [ides], a girl [fæmne] must through secret skill (clandestinely)
> chose her lover if, while among her people, she does not want it to come
> about that someone buys her (from her father) with rings.

Here is advice that the Wife should perhaps have heeded, for it cautions that women can get their way in matters of the heart only if they operate in secret. This passage is tainted by the maxim that comes immediately before it: "A thief must go forth in murky weather. The monster must dwell in the fen, alone in his realm." Secret desires are outside what the social will permit: what is public must be for the public good (as the marriage of the woman at her people's wish). To contravene this wish, as the Wife and her husband both have done in *The Wife's Lament,* is to invite expulsion, disaster, and death. Secret longing and tears seem to belong to a woman's world, not to a man's—to the Wife, not to Hrothgar. Such longing is socially dangerous only when it contradicts what is expected of one, compromising one's social position. Hrothgar's secret longing does not do so. Rather, it seems to intensify our awareness of his admiration and love for the young man who is about to leave him.

Old English texts that discuss relations between fathers and sons offer no models for Hrothgar's response. Affection between fathers and sons is not commonplace in Old English verse. The one poem given to father-son relations, *Precepts* (sometimes called *A Father's Advice to His Son*), is singularly devoid of expressions of sentiment or longing.[68] A father's response to his son's death is the subject of a later episode in *Beowulf.* Beowulf's grandfather and foster father from age seven, King Hrethel, had three sons. One of them, Herebeald, was accidentally killed by another, Hæthcyn, and since the death was caused by a member of the victim's own family, it could not be avenged. Old and wise ("eald ond infrod," 2449) Hrethel is "heart-sorrowful" ("sorhcearig," 2455), like a father whose son has been hanged for a crime. He sings of his grief, takes to his bed, thinks of the empty, wind-swept bed of his son ("windge reste," 2456), and dies. It is easy to pass over the references to the beds, but we should not, for they offer a rare glimpse of a father's thoughts about the domestic, private side of the man's world his son once inhabited.

Chickering argues effectively for the association of the scene of Hrothgar's tears with other scenes in which fathers mourn their sons, with other ruptures in father-son relations.[69] Beowulf matters more to Hrothgar than the old man expected. Who has not been surprised, at a death or a farewell, to be experiencing greater grief than was expected? Chickering suggests that "one must have sustained the losses of middle life to understand the poet's violent psychological language" at this point.[70] I agree with him, but I also think that Hrothgar's secret longing for Beowulf might have more to do with Hrothgar himself than with the young man. As he says farewell to the hero, Hrothgar is forced to realize that he long ago bade farewell to the young hero within. It is not just Beowulf's departure that grieves him (we must remember that he long ago said goodbye to Beowulf's father) but the passing of his younger and more valorous—may I say more manly?—self.

My second example of male friendship and intimacy comes from *The Wanderer*. Alone at sea, the Wanderer dreams of his life before his exile from lord and hall.

> Forþon wat se þe sceal   his winedryhtnes
> leofes larcwidum   longe forþolian,
> ðonne sorg ond slæp   somod ætgædre
> earmne anhogan   oft gebindað.
> Þinceð him on mode   þæt he his mondryhten
> clyppe ond cysse,   ond on cneo lecge
> honda ond heafod,   swa he hwilum ær
> in geardagum   giefstolas breac.
> Ðonne onwæcneð eft   wineleas guma,
> gesihð him biforan   fealwe wegas,
> baþian brimfuglas,   brædan feþra,
> hreosan hrim ond snaw,   hagle gemenged. (37–48)[71]

For he who must for a long time be deprived of advice from his beloved lord understands, when sorrow and sleep together often grip the miserable wanderer. It seems to him that he clasps and kisses his lord, and lays his hands and head upon his knee, just as when previously he enjoyed the gift throne. Then the friendless man awakes again and sees the dark waves before him, the seabirds bathing, spreading their feathers, falling frost and snow, mingled with hail.

Regarding the gesture of the warrior's head in his lord's lap, T. P. Dunning and A. J. Bliss comment, "It is generally agreed that lines 41b–43a refer to some kind of act of homage paid by the retainer to his lord, a supposition confirmed by the use of the technical term *mondryhten* 'liege lord.'"[72] Such acts needed to be public—needed to be witnessed—and could not have been private. This gesture of loyalty is both erotic—the kiss and the clasp—and courtly; that it takes place in a dream might intensify its fleeting but moving sexual resonance, its sexual same-sex shadow.[73] In an analysis of Geoffrey of Monmouth's

Historia Regum Britanniae, J. S. P. Tatlock cited many examples of men sleeping with their heads in other men's laps, "usually for protection against the perils of the wilderness, and to prevent desertion by the companion without the sleeper waking, also (I regret to say) for the protector to rid the sleeper's head of its habitual vermin."[74] According to the early-twelfth-century laws of Henry I, a change in status from slave to freeman was symbolized when the freed man "place[d] his hands and head in the hands of his lord."[75] I cite Tatlock's commentary not to suggest that the Wanderer and his like suffered from "habitual vermin" (although there is no good reason to suppose that they did not), but to show that what strikes us as a gesture of erotic intimacy may indeed be intimate but not erotic. Alone, cold, and in the grip of sorrow and sleep, the Wanderer recalls the gift throne, the hall, the companionship of his fellows, bleakly reflected in the cry of the seabirds, and a moment of acceptance and protection now long past. Such allegiance was signaled by a clasp and a kiss; what the two men involved in those actions thought, or where such actions might have led, we do not know. It was a public gesture, however, not a private one, and part of what eroticizes the moment for us is the suppression of an audience for the act—onlookers in the hall, others about to make or having just made the same gesture, the same commitment. The gesture must be allowed an erotic, even sexual aura, if only for a moment; it is a kiss, after all, and a clasp. But thoughts of the lord's embrace quickly yield to the grip of sorrow; the pillow of the lord's lap (so to speak) contrasts with whatever hard and cold surface the Wanderer finds for his weary head, vermin and all.

The third example is probably the most intimate moment of intramale sexual contact in Old English. It appears in one of the most unusual texts from the period, a translation of St. Augustine's *Soliloquies* attributed to King Alfred. The Old English text, a dialogue between Augustine and Reason, survives only in one twelfth-century manuscript. The original Latin text is at best a work of minor importance in Augustine's canon, and the translation, its language corrupt and its manuscript defective, constitutes an imperfect and often confusing revision of it. Alfred often added to and changed the meaning of his presumed Latin original. In one of those moments he supplied the following description of the pleasures of caressing an unclothed rather than a clothed body. For reasons I explain below, I have offered two translations, treating Old English "man" both as "male person" and simply as "person," and translating pronouns referring to Wisdom, a masculine noun, as either "he" or, more conventionally, "it."[76] Reason speaks to Alfred's Augustine:

Hu ne wost ðu nu þæt ælc þara manna þe oðerne swiðe lufað, þæt
hine lyst bet þaccian and cyssan ðone oðerne on bær lic, þonne þer þær
claðas beotweona beoð? Ic ongyte nu þæt (þu) lufast þone wisdom swa
swiðe, and þe lyst hine swa wel nacode ongitan and gefredan þæt þu
noldest þæt ænig clað betweuh were. Ac he hine wyle swiðe seldon
ænegum mæn swa openlice ge(e)awian. On ðam timum þe he ænig lim
swa bær eowian wile, þonne eowað he hyt swiðe feawum mannum. Ac
ic nat hu þu hym onfon mage mid geglofedum handum. Ðu scealt æac
don bær lic ongean, gyf ðu hine gefredan wilt. Ac sege me nu gyf ðu
hwilc ænlic wif lofodest swiðe ungemetlice ofer æalle oððer þing, and
heo ðonne þe fluge and nolde þe lufian on nan oðer gerað butan (þæt)
þu woldest ælce oðer lufe aletan for hyre anre lufe, woldest þu þonne
swa don swa heo wylnode? (75.20–76.8)[77]

How do you not now know that, [for] each of those men [persons] who
greatly loves another [man, or person], it pleases him better to stroke
and kiss the other [man, or person] on the bare body than where there
are clothes between [them]? I now see that you love Wisdom very much
and that you so wish to see and feel him [or it, i.e., Wisdom] naked that
you do not want any cloth between [you and him, or it]. But he [it] will
seldom reveal himself [itself] so openly to any man [person]. In those
times when he [it] will reveal any limb so bare, then he [it] reveals it
[i.e., the limb] to very few men [persons]. But I do not know how you
can grasp him [it] with gloved hands. You must also place your bare
body against [him, or it] if you will touch him [it]. But tell me now if
you loved a certain woman so immoderately and above all other things,
and she fled from you and would not love you on any other condition
except that you would forgo all other love for her love alone, would you
then do as she wished?

A few lines later Reason returns to this point, stressing that "he who
would feel the bare body must feel it with bare hands" ("se se þe bær
lic gefreddan wolde, þæt he hyt scolde myd barum [handum] gefredan," 76.25–26).

The passage strikes us as remarkable because the first sentence describes physical contact between two men, stroking and kissing rather
than kissing and clasping, that could either lead to or be part of sexual
play. The following sentences, with their description of revealing bare
limbs, also seem to invite an erotic reading. The text offers the image
of one man caressing and kissing the bare body of another as an analogy for direct as opposed to unmediated contact with wisdom, which
is seldom experienced unclothed; a gloved hand cannot touch it. An
analogy so homoerotic may seem both inappropriate and unlikely. But

the grammar of the passage cannot be denied. As Ruth Waterhouse observes, "the distinctive masculine [oðerne, twice] endings are noteworthy."[78] We can defuse this possibility by translating "man" as "person," including both male and female, which is also correct. However, contact between a man and a woman would very likely have been read in a sexual register, so if we insist that Old English "man" means "person" (male or female) we unavoidably intensify the sexual resonance of the passage. If the strokes and kissing *are* sexual (if "man" means "person," so that a man strokes and kisses a woman, or a woman a man), then the text more readily accommodates a shadow in which same-sex eroticism is clearly sexual too. The alternate approach—the Mark Morris approach, as I identified it in chapter 1, the approach I prefer— is to assume that "man" refers to "male person" and to allow the male to displace the female in what we expect to be a heterosexual scene, as Morris does when he dances women's parts in *Dido and Aeneas.*

These are, however, not the only noteworthy masculine signs in the passage's grammar. I have toyed with this passage in my translation by taking a literal approach to the Old English, in which "Wisdom" is a masculine noun and by referring to Wisdom throughout as "he." This is not an accepted practice. Henry Lee Hargrove's translation uses the traditional neuter pronoun for Wisdom ("to know and feel it naked").[79] But, given the striking same-sex analogy that goes before, Hargrove's is not the only translation possible. Without doing violence to the grammar and indeed in following it closely, one can extend the same-sex language and the same-sex analogy. My case is strengthened by Alfred's introduction of the immoderately loved "certain" woman at the end of the passage. It seems that Alfred intends a contrast between the desire for Wisdom (seen as a man, especially if "man" is translated as "male person") and desire for this woman. To see Wisdom as "male" merely reverses the Modern English practice, which routinely refers to Wisdom as female, a tradition including such figures as Lady Philosophy.

The significance of this same-sex intimacy becomes clear in the context of Alfred's statement, a discussion about the importance of friendship to the pursuit of wisdom. Alfred's original—we do not know exactly what it was—read something like this (note that Wisdom, in this translation from the Latin, is feminine):

> But now what kind of man are you to be Wisdom's lover, desirous of seeing and embracing her, as it were, without any covering garment but yet most chastely. That privilege she allows only to a very few chosen lovers. If you burned with love for some beautiful woman, she would

not rightly give herself to you if she found you loved anything else besides. So that most chaste beauty, Wisdom, will not show herself to you
unless you burn for her alone.[80]

At this point in the *Soliloquies,* friendship is denounced as one of the
earthly attachments that impedes the search for wisdom. At Reason's insistence, Augustine somewhat reluctantly agrees that he will "wish and
strive" to separate himself from friends who do not wish to search for
wisdom, for whatever reason.[81] In Alfred's version Augustine makes
no such denial and indeed pointedly and repeatedly asserts the very
opposite. Reason reminds Alfred's Augustine that he has renounced
excesses in wealth, honor, and luxurious living and wants to know
whether he will take up these things (these weaknesses) and, in the
process, take up his friends again. "I heard before that you said that
you loved your friends, after God and after your own *gewitte* [under-
standing], above all other things," Reason says. "I wish now to know
whether you would for love of them receive these things again" ("Ic
gehe[r]de ær þæt þu sedest þæt þu þine freond lufodest, æfter gode and
æfter þinum agnum gewitte, ofer ælle oðð re þing. [Ic] nu wolde witan
hweðer þu for heora lufum woldest ðas þing eft underfon," 73.25–
74.3). Alfred's Augustine replies that he will take hold of his friends
again, if that is the only way he can have the companionship they offer;
however, as if sensing that he is giving the wrong answer, he adds that
it does not please him to do so ("þeah hys me for wel ne lyste," 74.4–
5). Reason takes this to mean that worldly desires ("worlde-lustas,"
74.7) are not yet uprooted in his mind. But because it is better to love
friendship than power, honor, and luxury, Reason does not criticize the
choice Alfred's Augustine makes. Still, she ("heo") asks why he loves
his friends so much, whether it is for their own sake or for some other
reason—which might, plausibly, be excessive desire of some kind. Alfred's Augustine replies:

> Ic hi lufige for freondscype and for geferædenne, and þa þeah ofer
> ælle oðre, þe me mæstne fultum doð to ongyttanne and to witanne
> gesceadwisnesse and wisdom, ælra mæst be gode and beo urum sau-
> lum. Forðam ic wot þæt ic mæg æð myd heora fultume æfter spurian
> þonne ic butan mæge. (74.14–18)

> I love them for friendship and companionship, and above all others I
> love those who most help me to understand and to know reason and
> wisdom, most of all about God and about our souls. For I know that I
> can more easily seek after Him with their help than I can without it.

Reason persists. What if they don't help him find God? Alfred's Augustine replies that in that case he will teach them to search for him. But what if they love other things more than God and the search for wisdom, and won't cooperate? Alfred's Augustine is undaunted: "I will have them anyway," he says ("Ic hi wylle þeah habban," 74.24). Then (in a section missing from the Old English manuscript, partially reconstructed by editors from the presumed Latin source), Reason adds bodily infirmities ("lichoman mettrimnysse," 74.27) to the list of impediments to Wisdom.[82] Reason then introduces the analogy of direct bodily contact—a bodily pleasure, that is—as an analogue to direct knowledge.

The passage is cleverly managed on Alfred's part. His persona in the dialogue (i.e., Augustine) stoutly defends the merits of friendship; Reason stresses the weaknesses that friendship can lead to. Yet it is not Alfred's Augustine, the strong defender of friendship, who uses the erotic analogy but instead Reason who does so. Alfred's Augustine has made a case for continuing to value friends even if they impede his search for wisdom, but it is Reason herself who reveals, through the analogy between Wisdom and the naked body, one way among others in which such distractions might occur. The switch to the case of "a certain woman" near the end of the passage seems sudden; the analogy is no longer governed by the gender of "Wisdom," and at that point a new, heterosexual analogy takes over. One can almost hear a sigh of relief when this woman appears—a sigh of relief, I like to think, from a heterosexual position, which has been forced to assert itself, put on the defensive, by the same-sex erotics of Alfred's translation. Augustine's Latin not only proposes a female analogy—Wisdom is a woman—but insists that the contact between Augustine and wisdom be chaste. Alfred's text, by comparison, is not just sexed but same-sexed; whether we place the same-sex analogy in the text (as Mark Morris would) or in the shadow, it is undeniably there. Only a belief that such analogies are queer—that is, inappropriate—keeps translators from acknowledging the power of this small verbal gesture to create a moment of same-sex affection and Eros in our image of Anglo-Saxon England.

A translation that portrays Wisdom as "he" queers this part of the passage but also does some unqueering work and perhaps suggests why Alfred used a male-male illustration. Augustine's text insists that one's experience of Wisdom be pure and chaste. She seeks lovers "with whom intercourse is truly chaste and without defilement."[83] Yet Augustine used a sexual analogy—"embracing her, as it were, without any clothing"—for this rare, direct experience of wisdom. It is worth noting that the trope of the "naked" or plain meaning of a text was known in Anglo-Saxon England.[84]

Although Alfred introduced a same-sex analogy at this point, there is every reason to believe that he too endorsed a pure and chaste experience of wisdom and sought to preserve, or even elevate and intensify, the ideal of learning as it is characterized in his source. Any specifically sexual overtones to the analogy, any suggestion that it was about sexual intercourse, would have made the analogy unacceptable, just as such a suggestion would have made Hrothgar's demonstration of affection for Beowulf unacceptable. Nowhere in Anglo-Saxon literature is sexual contact between men spoken of with approval. Intimate contact between men is, in modern registers, unavoidably sexual, and there is no reason why we cannot *imagine* that it was also sexual in the Anglo-Saxon period. Although that act of imagination reveals our wishes and hopes, it also points to a possibility that most of the evidence contemporary with the text flatly contradicts. The Anglo-Saxon source refers to intramale contact that is intimate and even erotic but not a sex act. Alfred's presumed original not only used a heterosexual model but specifically lauds chastity, as does the king's translation. There is no narrative context for the same-sex gesture in the *Soliloquies,* no farewell between two manly heroes, no thegn paying allegiance to his lord. In the absence of such a story, we are tempted to introduce a story that begins when one man strokes and kisses another's naked body. But the only readers, or writers, who can continue the story in this enticing direction are those of us who live hundreds of years after Alfred wrote. I believe that most (but not all) medieval readers would have strenuously objected to such a tale, had it been suggested to them. It would have been a story almost unimaginably out of keeping with any others that their culture had preserved. If we are culturally straightforward, we must contrast our awareness of same-sex possibilities with the disapproval of same-sex sexuality that other sources, literary and non-literary, manifest. Thus I read the scene as one driven by a social convention whose sexual qualities are implicit in the text but which appear fully only in its shadow. I regard this as a straightforward approach: the text is not about sex, but its shadow might be.

The Soliloquies follows a sexual analogy introduced by Augustine and comes, as do the saints' lives already considered, from a Latin culture in which the social gesture of the kiss is far more common. *Beowulf* and *The Wanderer* offer evidence of gestures of kissing and embracing—social rather than sexual—that are rare in heroic and elegiac Old English verse. Later medieval ecclesiastical authorities, including

Thomas Aquinas and Peter Damian, interpreted any form of kissing as a prelude to sexual temptation, as Carolyn Dinshaw has noted.[85] In the earlier period, however, kissing is rarely mentioned. The only penitentials that discuss same-sex kissing are early Irish documents (from the sixth and seventh centuries) that are concerned with kisses between boys. Monastic rules also prohibit kissing between boys and older monks.[86] Heterosexual kissing between a priest and a woman is forbidden in some Anglo-Saxon handbooks of penance, which list sins and appropriate penances and contain the most explicit discussions of same-sex contact to be found in any Anglo-Saxon sources. They warn that priests are not to kiss laywomen,[87] and one warns a man doing penance that he is to seek holy places but is not to kiss anyone.[88]

There are many kisses recorded in Old English literature, but few appear in poetry. Elsewhere, kisses between men are as common as kisses between men and women. Most of these references come from texts translated from Latin, from saints' lives especially, and pertain to the cultural milieu of late antiquity or scripture rather than to contemporary Anglo-Saxon or Germanic life. (Other references to kissing imply a liturgical or ceremonial context, such as kissing the cross or a bowl or a horn.)[89] In *Andreas,* a poetic life of Andrew, the saint finds Matthew in prison and the two embrace and kiss, one of many similar examples.[90] We must ask about our reconstruction of these kisses, just as later Greek readers asked about Patroclus and Achilles. There is no indication in any of this evidence that the physical contact between men is regarded as in any way weakening or shaming either of them; nothing about it seems out of the ordinary or sinful. Old English sources are unambiguous about the shame brought on by same-sex relations that are sexual, and such relations are not likely to be found in heroic, elegiac, or moral-philosophical literature that so patently seeks to ennoble its audiences.

The fourth example I will discuss seems to contain the only known reference to one man shaming another's sexual conduct in Anglo-Saxon poetry. *The Battle of Maldon* recounts a famous episode in which Byrhtnoth, ealdorman of Essex, unwisely allows his Danish enemies to cross the river Blackwater at low tide, using a ford. Byrhtnoth inexplicably breaks formation and is killed, leading to both the desertion of some of his men and the defeat of the others. Critics have debated the meaning of the poet's statement that Byrhtnoth yielded to the Danes' request to cross the river because of his "ofermod," his pride or excessive confidence. Richard North has argued that this statement is the poet's attempt to deflect attention from the warrior's greater error in breaking formation and stepping forth to fight alone.[91]

Wod þa wiges heard,   wæpen up ahof,
bord to gebeorge,   and wið þæs beornes stop.
Eode swa anræd   eorl to þam ceorle,
ægþer hyra oðrum   yfeles hogode. (130–33) [92]

Then the one fierce in battle [the Dane] advanced, raised his weapon, his shield as defense, and stepped toward the soldier [Byrhtnoth]. Just as resolutely the earl went toward the yeoman. Each of them intended evil to the other.

North suggests that Byrhtnoth has been taunted by a charge of cowardice, the Old English *earg,* defined by the *Dictionary of Old English* as "cowardly, craven, timid."[93] North argues that *earg* is cognate with Norse *argr,* a term used to indicate the passive partner in male homosexual intercourse, and claims that the term was regularly used by Icelanders to insult Christians. He speculates that in the poem the Danes engage in the tradition of *nið* or sexual defamation found in Old Norse sagas and analyzed by Clover.[94] In *The Battle of Maldon,* however, *earg* is not applied to the hero but to one of the traitors, Godric, a son of Odda, who is the first to flee the scene. Offa, one of Byrhtnoth's followers, denounces Godric as a "cowardly son of Odda" ("earh Oddan bearn," 238). Thus North's argument would suggest that the "nið" tradition was being used by one Christian against another (not impossible, of course). But other uses of "earg" do not suggest that the word had strong sexual connotations for the Anglo-Saxons; it glosses "adulter," meaning "wicked," "peccatrix," "sinful," and even "luxuriosus," "excessive," but uses of *earg* to denote timidity and cowardice are much more frequent.[95] Although North's argument is not strong, the example is useful all the same. It is possible that the Danes used sexual taunts of effeminacy against Christians, just as Icelanders did, and it is possible that such an accusation prompted the Anglo-Saxon leader to disregard his own advice, break formation, and die. At the same time, this example, the only one of its kind known to me, suggests how rare sexual accusations are in the Anglo-Saxons' heroic literature. Sardanapallus would seem to be an excellent target for such an insult, but we do not find such accusations made in Old English texts, even though they were recorded in the literatures of contact cultures.

If not homosexuality, what sort of same-sex system do the documents I have discussed reveal, and how can we relate such a system to relations between men and women? The intimate exchanges between men discussed above can be situated between the extreme ends of a polar structure, but it is not a polarity of homosexual and heterosexual, or even of women and men. It is, rather, a continuum between the manly and the unmanly, between the strong and the weak, between that which conforms to what men should be and all that which is its antithesis.

The intramale exchanges I have described would be "deviant" if they included sexual intercourse. But if they did so, they would deviate from the "manly" ideal that—to recapitulate the gender hierarchy of the saints' lives—governs all men, including weak, effeminate, and sexually passive men, and all women, including strong, sexually aggressive women. Anglo-Saxon authorities knew very well what sexual behavior they loathed and feared. As I will show in chapter 4, they specified the acts and even named the actors and sanctioned them severely. Nonsexual intramale acts, including embraces and kisses, took place within an institution of male friendship, defined by the bonds between a lord and his retainer, that the culture authorized and indeed valorized. Intramale relations are powerful, suggestive, intimate, socially, even sexually, charged (one man is dominant, the other subordinate, one sitting, one kneeling, and so forth), but not necessarily about sexual intercourse. And so long as sexual intercourse is not involved, the acts cannot be considered deviant. But neither are they meaningless, or without erotic significance.

I have said that I want to see what is in the shadows, to bring same-sex relations out of the shadows of early medieval English culture, not out of a closet constructed by modern criticism, and to show that shadows, far from being secondary or illusionary, define the planes and contours of all that we see. What hides same-sex love is not a dead trope or an archaic convention like the trouser role, but rather a variety of unhelpful ideas about medieval culture: it was prudish; it suppressed any discussion of sex; such things as same-sex or homosexual relations could not have existed then; and so forth. Stereotypical ideals of manliness and masculinity as emotionally and physically repressed are part of this limited and limiting perspective. Same-sex relations are also obscured by homophobia. But homophobia must share the blame with homophilia. Same-sex relations have been disguised by scholarship that greatly overestimates tolerance of this conduct and in the process discounts the power of disparaging references. In this chapter I have examined a few Old English texts enlivened and deepened by same-sex shadows. Before I look at further Old English evidence of same-sex love in the context of Anglo-Saxon social structures, I will review what has been said about the history of same-sex acts in the early Middle Ages.

PART

2

The Anglo-Saxons

Surveying Same-Sex Relations
in the Early Middle Ages

Comparisons between manly men and women, and between trousered women in opera and cross-dressed women in Old English saints' lives, can suggest the nature and variety but not the extent of Anglo-Saxon evidence of same-sex behavior. Before I analyze this evidence more fully, I wish to discuss some of its distinctive features and review its treatment in some recent histories of medieval sex and sexuality. Almost all commentary on sex in the Anglo-Saxon period occurs in large-scale surveys of sexual behavior. They are all indispensable. But each has its own limitations, and one limitation is common to them all—a failure to assess the particular qualities of the early medieval evidence, Old English sources especially.

Three characteristics of the early English evidence are distinctive. First, English and Irish texts from AD 700 onward contain the earliest medieval evidence of official attitudes concerning same-sex relations. In England and Ireland, but nowhere else during the early Middle Ages, this literature was propagated in two languages, not one. Latin regulations governing sexual conduct were translated into vernacular penitentials, or handbooks of penance, and were incorporated into homilies, pastoral letters, and other kinds of texts concerned with the education and regulation of clerical and lay spirituality. Anglo-Saxon England produced a corpus of vernacular pastoral materials without parallel in the early Middle Ages of western Europe.[1] Surveys that deal with the Anglo-Saxon period (c. AD 600–1100) focus almost exclusively on texts in Latin. The vernacular texts, I believe, are especially important, since they are not mere translations of the Latin, any more than the Anglo-Latin versions are exact transcriptions of earlier texts.

A second reason to explore evidence from the Anglo-Saxon period is that later English evidence has figured prominently in pioneering work in the history of sex and sexuality. Texts from the Middle English period, those by Chaucer especially, have been studied by Glenn Burger, Carolyn Dinshaw, Steven Kruger, and others who view same-sex relations with attitudes ranging from the mildly apologetic to the aggressively queer.[2] A rare nonliterary text, a court record pertaining to John Rykener, a male transvestite prostitute in late-fourteenth-century London, has been analyzed by Ruth Mazo Karras and David Lorenzo Boyd.[3] Thanks in large part to Alan Bray's *Homosexuality in Renaissance England* (1982), the study of same-sex relations in the Renaissance has long been on solid historical footing.[4] Bray gives due credit to the tradition inaugurated by Havelock Ellis's 1897 study, *Sexual Inversion,* an early work by a sexual radical that made implausible and sweeping claims for the acceptance of homosexuality in the Renaissance.[5] Homosexual themes figure prominently in English Renaissance studies since Bray, whose work exerts strong influence on queer scholarship. Prominent studies of Renaissance same-sex relations include Jonathan Goldberg's *Sodometries* (1992) and *Queering the Renaissance* (1994) and Gregory Bredbeck's study of sodomy (1991).[6] The best of these books seems to me to be Bruce R. Smith's *Homosexual Desire in Shakespeare's England: A Cultural Poetics,* a 1991 study.[7] Smith's emphasis on imaginative literature complements Bray's emphasis on social history, adding the category of "desire" to Bray's category of "deeds." Smith does not hesitate to describe his work as "a political tract" that seeks to consolidate gay identity for Smith's own time (27). But in marked contrast to queer theorists (Goldberg, Bredbeck, and others whose work is included in *Queering the Renaissance*), Smith always works within the language and the cultural contexts of a wide array of Renaissance texts. Historical periods subsequent to the Renaissance have been studied by John C. Fout, Randolph Trumbach, and others.[8] In the modern period the English tradition in queer autobiography seems to be particularly strong, as witnessed by Paul Hallam's *Book of Sodom* and Derek Jarman's *At Your Own Risk,* both of which incorporate historical perspectives on homosexual issues (Jarman's are similar to Ellis's views) into their personal accounts of gay life.[9] There is, then, an extensive body of scholarship concentrating on English texts and traditions, starting with the fourteenth century. But the origins of this venerable and distinctive tradition have never been explored.

The third and most compelling reason to examine the early English evidence of same-sex behavior reaches beyond its date and the extensive body of scholarship that has accumulated around it. The Anglo-Saxon evidence needs to be examined because it is straightforward, a characteristic that subsequently became very rare. Anglo-Latin and Anglo-

Saxon handbooks of penance, like contemporary texts on the Continent, catalogued children's same-sex acts and provided penances for active and passive male partners in homosexual intercourse, for same-sex relations between adult laywomen and nuns, and for intercourse between children and adults. Other sources, including homilies and catechetical dialogues, reviled Sodom and sodomites. There was no ambiguity in the attitudes expressed toward the city, its citizens, or their supposed descendants, and Sodom was sometimes specifically associated with same-sex relations. With a specificity that cannot be matched in later sources, the Anglo-Saxon texts named and sometimes described same-sex acts, not just in intimate forms of discourse, such as handbooks of penance, meant for confessors and penitents, but in homilies and even in poetry. This evidence identifies same-sex relations of many kinds and unambiguously condemns them. That is what I mean when I argue that there was no closet—no sexual closet, at least—in this culture. I do not want to argue that the Anglo-Saxons possessed a consciousness in which there was no repression or that Anglo-Saxons who wished to conceal sins from confessors did not do so. Such secrecy might constitute a closet, but only on the level of the individual's conscience.

The candor of the Anglo-Saxon sources, especially as attested by handbooks of penance and by references to sodomy in other sources, began to disappear in the twelfth century. Pastoral sources from the twelfth century and after avoided the word "sodomy," which encompassed diverse acts sharing a single common denominator: all thwarted conception. In the later medieval period, beginning in the eleventh century, sodomy was a name for anal intercourse, both homosexual and heterosexual, any form of male homosexual intercourse, masturbation, and other sexual offenses. In early Irish, Latin, and Anglo-Saxon sources, sodomy is a more limited term. The *Preface of Gildas on Penance,* written in Wales, possibly in the sixth century, equated sodomy with "natural fornication" (heterosexual vaginal intercourse), and assigned these acts equal penances: "A presbyter or a deacon committing natural fornication or sodomy who has previously taken the monastic vow shall do penance for three years" ("Praesbiter aut diaconus faciens fornicationem naturalem siue sodomitam praelato ante monachi uoto .iii. annis peniteat").[10] The *Penitential* of Cummean, perhaps a century later, required "those who commit sodomy" ("qui faciunt scelus uirile ut Sodomite") to do seven years of penance and, in a canon concerning "the playing of boys," described sodomy as fornication in the rear or backside ("in terga") and assigned penances from two to seven years for it.[11] The late-seventh-century *Penitential* of Theodore,

written in England, rendered the categories more complexly, but still
concretely: penances for male homosexual acts range from fifteen years
for habitual sodomy to two years for boys who did it only once.[12] These
references are translated, with few changes, into the Old English penitential texts I will examine in chapter 4.

Candid references to sexual acts in some early penitentials were incorporated into later collections of canons.[13] The most important such
collection is the *Decretum* of Burchard of Worms, especially its nineteenth book, known as the *Corrector et medicus* (c. 1018). Burchard
treated sodomy and all sexual sins in great detail and drew on Theodore's *Penitential* for some of his penances for male homosexual acts.[14]
Burchard was more explicit than any previous author in describing
sexual sins and gave sodomy its widest definition to date, making the
sin a compendium of all sexual acts "against nature." Burchard also
had more to say about sexual sins than did the authors of later penitential manuals, including those whose work was important to the post-
Anglo-Saxon tradition in England.[15]

In the mid–eleventh century the Church's attitude toward penitential manuals began to change. In his *Book of Gomorrah* (c. 1050), which
Mark D. Jordan claims as the first work to use the term "sodomy,"[16]
Peter Damian urged the standardization of penances for sexual sins.
He mocked the penitentials, with their inconsistent tariffs, as "mon-
sters" that had been "made by human industry, some of which begin
with horses' heads and end with goats' hooves."[17] At the end of the
eleventh century, Ivo of Chartres avoided Burchard's detailed lists but
included the vast majority of Burchard's decisions in his *Decretum*.
Ivo was the first to group all forbidden sexual sins into one category,
the sins "against nature."[18] His work was the chief conduit of earlier
standards concerning sexual sins into later penitentials, including those
written in England. Subsequent developments in canon law, especially
by Peter Lombard (c. 1100–1160), elaborated the theological error of
the sin "against nature" without distinguishing precisely between this
sin and sodomy. About the time Peter was writing, Gratian formu-
lated his *Concordia discordantium canonum* (c. 1140). Gratian's compendium followed Ivo's categories and established the sin "against nature"
as the gravest of sexual offenses. But as Vern L. Bullough demonstrates,
"Gratian raised more problems about sexual sins than he answered,"
for he failed to describe precisely what was involved in the sexual sins
he named. The sin "against nature" was one of the sins of Sodom (suggesting any form of sex that frustrated reproduction, including intramale sex), but it could take place between married couples (suggesting

anal sex or coitus interruptus in particular). After Gratian, Bullough notes, "the law came increasingly to use euphemisms to deal with forbidden sexual activities." Subsequent councils, including the Third Lateran Council of 1179, also failed to define either the sins of Sodom or the sin "against nature."[19] Other discourses, including medical tracts, were also reticent about explaining sexual sins as references to sexual conduct became increasingly codified.[20] For example, a fifteenth-century commentator on Avicenna decided against relating "several types of sodomite coitus, which men and women abusively indulge in," thinking it "better to keep silence, so that human nature, inclined towards evil and towards the exercise of new lusts, may not attempt, on hearing about them, to put them into practice and thus prejudice one's honour and one's soul."[21]

English penitentials incorporating the new codifications include those by Bartholomew of Exeter, written c. 1150, and by Robert of Flamborough, written in the early thirteenth century.[22] Both Bartholomew and Robert draw substantial provisions from Burchard's collection, including many sections on sexual sins. Robert's material on sodomy, however, is taken from Ivo's work. Robert's chapter on fornication begins with a section entitled "De fornicantibus sodomitice vel cum brutis" that indicates the encompassing nature of "sodomitical fornication": it included homosexual acts of laywomen and nuns, mixing of semen in food to make a love potion, and male homosexual intercourse of various kinds (men, boys, clerics, laymen).[23] The immense *Summa confessorum* of Thomas de Chobham, written in England c. 1216, repeats the penances and categories of sodomy prescribed by Robert and Bartholomew, prefacing them with scriptural references and quotations from Augustine.[24]

After the eleventh century, references to sodomy manifested both a confusion of categories and something else—the reticence notable in Ivo's work, Gratian's, and others'. On the subject of sodomy, sources from the twelfth to the fifteenth century are terse. The *Summa de poenitentia* (c. 1222–29) of Raymond of Peñafort regarded sodomy as a worse sin than incest and warned, in a statement already then dogmatic, that even hearing about it could be the occasion of sin.[25] Raymond's work is one of the sources of Chaucer's *Parson's Tale* (1390s), where the confessor's diffidence wavers slightly. Sodomy is "thilke abhomynable synne, of which that no man unnethe oghte speke ne write." However, the Parson adds, "it is openly reherced in holy writ," and "though that hooly writ speke of horrible synne, certes hooly writ may nat been defouled, namoore than the sonne that shyneth on the mixne" (i.e., the Bible is not fouled by mentioning horrible sins, any more than the sun is by shining on a dunghill).[26] A contemporary fourteenth-century text, *The Book of Vices and Virtues,* based on a thirteenth-century French original, says that the "synne aȝens kynde" is "so foule and so hidous þat [it] scholde not be nempned." Although the narrator cannot say what this sin is, he nonetheless insists that guilty men and women "telle it openly in his schrifte to þe prest as it was y-don." God so abominated this sin that he sent fire and stinking brimstone upon the cities of Sodom and Gomorrah where it was committed. Stink is still associated with the sin; even the devil who induces this foul deed is "squeymous þer-of whan any doþ it" ("offended by it when anyone commits it").[27] In the mid–fifteenth century John Mirk instructed priests not even to mention the "synne aȝeynes kynde" and to say only that for any man to "do hys kynde other way, / þat ys gret synne wyþowte nay."[28]

These Middle English sources (even Chaucer, it would seem, since he too remains reticent) reflect a concern that the confession of sins could, paradoxically, itself become the occasion for sin. Early Irish and Anglo-Saxon penitentials warned confessors to use discretion, to avoid scandalizing penitents by asking inappropriate questions that might suggest sins, and to protect their own purity.[29] These warnings are reminders that questions about sexual sins, if too explicit, might lead penitents to commit sins they had not previously known about. "The need to be specific[,] coupled with ignorance among ordinary people of specific differences[,] required the priest to question penitents so as to ensure a true confession," Pierre J. Payer writes. "Although priests are encouraged to ask questions, they are to begin with the common or usual sins. They are not to descend to the unusual such as sodomy or deviant sexual positions unless the context warrants."[30] As definitions of sodomy became more complex and inclusive, a development recently traced by Jordan, it became increasingly important to inquire about sexual sins.[31] Hence a paradox developed. The sin of sodomy could not be named, but priests were nonetheless forced to ask questions about it.

In his *Penitential,* Robert of Flamborough suggests how these contradictory impulses created a closet for same-sex acts. When asking about "lust against nature," specifically if a man "had sex with anyone in a particular way," Robert refused to explain what "a particular way" meant, saying, "I never make mention of anything that might become an occasion for sinning, but rather speak of generalities that everyone knows are sins."[32] But in Anglo-Saxon confessional discourse, nobody spoke in generalities. If a confessor could not assume that his penitent knew what he meant, the confessor was required to ask in order to be sure. Because the distinctive qualities of the Anglo-Saxon evidence are clearest in the handbooks of penance, I note the significance of the penitentials in the following overview of histories of sex and sexual behavior.

The early English evidence has played a small but sometimes significant part in many histories of sex and accounts of ecclesiastical regulations governing sexual conduct in the Middle Ages. The works I discuss here include the wide-ranging surveys by Havelock Ellis (1897), Derrick Sherwin Bailey (1955), Vern L. Bullough (1976), Michael Goodich (1979), John Boswell (1980), James A. Brundage (1987), and David F. Greenberg (1988), and inquiries into specific topics within sexuality by John T. Noonan, Jr. (1965), Pierre J. Payer (1984), and Mark D. Jordan (1997). Noonan and Brundage do not focus on same-sex relations exclusively but discuss homosexual acts as they relate to contraception (the subject of Noonan's work) and attitudes toward all sexual behavior. I treat these studies chronologically, paying particular attention to their relation of homosexual and heterosexual acts and their treatment of early medieval—and especially English—evidence.

Havelock Ellis, *Sexual Inversion*

Havelock Ellis's *Sexual Inversion* sought to present the Renaissance as an atmosphere of intellectual and social freedom, a time when homosexuality burst into view. "Brilliant propaganda," Bray writes, "but it was not sober history."[33] But, as Bray acknowledges, Ellis's work deserves credit on several counts, chiefly for producing an extended discussion of same-sex relations and attempting to create a historical narrative documenting the existence of same-sex attraction in a wide variety of cultures and ages. Ellis was—and, unfortunately, still is— highly unusual in attending to very early English evidence, citing the association of "natural fornication and sodomy" in the penitentials.[34] Bray locates Ellis in a circle of turn-of-the-century "sexual radicals" who "succeeded in demonstrating, often in the teeth of opposition and at considerable personal cost . . . that there was a historical dimension to homosexuality: it had a history."[35] Ellis made a strong case for seeing same-sex attraction as an inborn rather than an acquired trait; indeed, that argument was the aim of his historical survey.[36] But his views are dated. For example, he criticized lesbianism as weakening the institution of marriage (although he provided a full commentary on lesbianism, which is rare), and he reinforced gender stereotypes that do little today to draw scholars to his work.[37]

Derrick Sherwin Bailey, *Homosexuality and the Western Christian Tradition*

Scholars of homosexuality in early modern periods often cite John Boswell's *Christianity, Social Tolerance, and Homosexuality* as a source for the medieval background of sexual practices in later periods. Bray's and Smith's studies are important examples.[38] But they would do much better to begin with Bailey's thorough and reliable guide to the development of antihomosexual attitudes in the early Church. Boswell, who was not noted for generous views of the scholarship of those with whom he differed, said that Bailey's book gave a "wholly misleading picture of medieval practice" because it ignored "all positive evidence on the subject." Nonetheless Boswell regarded *Homosexuality and the Western Christian Tradition* as a "pioneering" study and "the best single work on the subject in print."[39] In many ways Boswell's evaluation still holds. Bailey belonged to an informal group of Anglican clergymen who issued a report called *The Problem of Homosexuality*.[40] He subsequently investigated the scriptural and historical background to this report and focused on male homosexuality (presumably because the evidence overwhelmingly concerns the sex acts of men). Bailey sought to counteract a tendency on the part of "those who demand justice and sympathy for the homosexual" to blame the Church for antihomosexual attitudes (viii). While making no attempt to excuse the Church from responsibility for shaping negative attitudes toward homosexuals, he nonetheless pointed out that homosexual acts were traditionally denounced because they were believed to provoke God's wrath, as they did in Sodom and Gomorrah. Fear of further such reprisals, Bailey argued, was understandable if misguided justification for society's attempts to discipline homosexual conduct (ix). Bailey did more than defend the church. He also argued that "there is much to indicate that by retaining in its hand the spiritual punishment of the sodomist, the Church actually shielded him from the penalties of the secular power" (x). That is, since the Church punished homosexual acts, secular authorities did not need to do so. His book is less an apology for homosexuality than an apology for the Church's treatment of homosexual acts. (Boswell, we shall see, took the same approach.)

Bailey sought to separate the category of "sodomite," which has a long history as a term of abuse, from the sins of Sodom and Gomorrah, arguing that the cities were destroyed for acts other than, or in addition to, homosexual offenses. He tried to break the connection between homosexual conduct and more general categories of wicked acts that had provoked God's wrath, so that those who engaged in same-sex intercourse would not be seen as solely responsible for God's vengeance. Bailey demonstrated that biblical denunciations of same-sex relations do not mention Sodom and Gomorrah (11) and, conversely, that there is no clear mention of specifically homosexual relations in the description of the cities' destruction (although illicit sex is clearly associated with the cities). He argued that the link between the cities and same-sex immorality was made in the first century, in the commentaries of Philo, who claimed that the verb for "to know" in the famous scene in which the men of Sodom assert their right "to know" Lot's visitors (Genesis 19:5), meant "unseemly and male pederasty," a reference Bailey claims to be "the first instance of the express attribution of a homosexual coital connotation to the word 'know' in this text" (21). In *De Abrahamo,* Philo also described Sodom as a place where "men mounted males without respect for the sex nature which the active partner shares with the passive" (22). "Here at last," wrote Bailey, "we have the Sodom of nameless and unmentionable vices which has obsessed the mind of the theologian and the legislator for so many centuries; but it is not the Sodom of the Bible, wicked though that city was, by the general consent of the Scriptures" (22). Subsequent rabbinic writing did not associate Sodom with homosexual sins, but Bailey demonstrates that patristic authorities (Clement of Alexandria, John Chrysostom, Augustine, and others) "entertained no doubt whatsoever that the Sodomites were peculiarly and inordinately addicted to homosexual practices" (25).

Bailey's treatment of evidence from Anglo-Saxon England and contemporary Continental cultures is less thorough than his work with biblical and patristic commentaries. He discussed in detail Carolingian statutes against homosexual acts and eighth-century Latin handbooks of penance thought to have been written in England (100–110). But his overview of sources then moves to 1107 and after (111), not dealing with English evidence again until the post-Conquest period. Furthermore, Bailey's discussion of English law begins with late-thirteenth-century codes (145), omitting both the legal and the ecclesiastical evidence from Anglo-Saxon England.

Bailey followed his survey of ecclesiastical legislation with an apology for Christianity's role in repressing same-sex acts. He believed that regulations against homosexual practices occupied only a small place in conciliar and synodal proceedings, comprising merely "some one hundred items of legislation . . . during a period of more than a thousand years." He argued, quite implausibly, that the evidence does not constitute "convincing proof of an implacable ecclesiastical animus against the sodomist" (99). Attempting to qualify assertions of that animus,

Bailey showed that the penitentials also punished other sins, including perjury and homicide, as severely as homosexual practices (106). But he did not make more relevant comparisons that showed that both Latin and Anglo-Saxon texts sometimes punished intramale sex acts more severely than heterosexual acts (I give examples in chapter 4).

The lasting value of Bailey's survey is his demonstration that traditional concepts of homosexuality and its textual origins had been grossly misconceived and that they could not be "regarded as an adequate guide by the theologian, the legislator, the sociologist, and the magistrate." The tradition unjustifiably saw homosexual offenses as "intrinsically and socially more serious than heterosexual offences" and punished them with disproportionate penalties. Female homosexuality was routinely ignored, and "sodomy" was used as an inclusive but poorly defined category (173). This catalogue of defects accurately described work in the history of sex for decades both before and after Bailey wrote. Scholars no longer choose to accept Bailey's categories of the "invert" and the "pervert" or other limitations of his study, but *Homosexuality and the Western Christian Tradition* retains an important place in the history of homosexuality.

John T. Noonan, Jr., *Contraception: A History of Its Treatment by the Catholic Theologians and Canonists*

Noonan's history of contraception treats same-sex acts in relation to other sexual practices denounced by the Church because they prevented procreation. Noonan too was an apologist for the Church, seeking to justify the modern church's position by showing how narrowly the case against contraception had been constructed. "The recorded statements of Christian doctrine on contraception did not have to be read in a way requiring an absolute prohibition," he wrote.[41] Noonan treated the penitentials as "testimony to the dominant ecclesiastical opinion" from 500 to 1100, and believed they constituted a reliable index to what was taught and believed. "The penitentials are most clearly a witness to the moral judgments of the monastic writers"; the monks were "the chief expositors of the moral ideas of this period," and their views "helped shape the mentality, the ethic, of western Europe" (153; see 152–70 for Noonan's description of how the penitentials taught "the lessons of the monks"). Noonan read the evidence carefully. He noted that medieval authors sometimes described sins in "evocative" and confusing ways, especially where marital intercourse was concerned. For example, he pointed out that a penitential (falsely) attributed to Bede (d. 735) "classifies [heterosexual] anal intercourse as 'sodomitic crime'" (166). This canon, which is found in a series concerning heterosexual intercourse, specifies that "[w]hoever fornicates in the rear, which is a sodomitical sin, [shall perform] a penance of four years."[42] This evidence attaches a heterosexual rather than a homosexual practice to the celebrated Cities of the Plain. One little-appreciated contribution of Noonan's book was his realization that inquiry—the interrogation of sins in confession—was itself a sanction.

> In a secular legal system, inquiry would usually be considered only a prelude to sanction, although even secular interrogations have sometimes appeared punitive in themselves. In a spiritual system, it seems proper to understand inquiry as itself a sanction: deterrence of sin is aimed at when a potential sin is asked about; and actual sin receives a preliminary punishment in being the subject of inquiry. The use of inquiry as this sort of spiritual sanction becomes common only with the growth of private confession and penance in the West. (166)

This understanding of confession itself as a penance is a reminder that fear of a severe penance was not the only discouragement confronting medieval penitents who confessed homosexual acts. They could also expect to endure a searching interrogation itself intended to punish them with embarrassment and, it is fair to say, shame. This too suggests the absence of a "closet" for unorthodox sexual behavior in this period, an assumption that those who confessed were guilty and began their reformation with the act of confessing. The only way one could avoid the sanction of inquiry was to avoid confession, and among communities of the faithful and pious that believed in the universality of sinful behavior, such avoidance was a public declaration—paradoxically—of one's guilt.

Vern L. Bullough, *Sexual Variance in Society and History*

Bullough's work was the first full-scale investigation of homosexuality to encompass a wide range of "deviant" sexual behavior and to survey attitudes toward such behavior in non-Western as well as Western cultures. His analysis of sexual behavior in the medieval Christian world is exemplary. Bullough was and is all but alone among historians of sexuality in separating early from late medieval evidence (dividing the fifth to the tenth centuries from the eleventh to fifteenth).[43] Bullough analyzed the penitentials' statements on homosexual acts, noting that in these sources "homosexual and homoerotic activity is often spelled out in more detail than heterosexual activity" (361), although not suggesting why. Payer has argued that the vocabulary for same-sex acts was not well-developed, lacking common nouns in particular, and that as a result these acts had to be described in detail.[44] Bullough firmly

established the hostility of the early Church to all forms of nonreproductive sex and stressed the opposition to homosexual acts in particular,
especially in monastic contexts.

Bullough balanced prescriptive evidence from penitentials and other
forms of ecclesiastical legislation with narrative sources, saints' lives in
particular. It was in this context that he analyzed cross-dressing, showing that the practice was permitted for women but not for men, a policy
that reflected the general assumption that the female was inferior and
that when she dressed as a man she was imitating the superior sex
(364–69). Bullough surveyed some of the epistolary evidence that was
later to play an important part in Boswell's study, although, in marked
contrast to Boswell, Bullough was reluctant to overemphasize the positive view of male-male friendships found in these sources. Bullough
drew sharp distinctions between the early and later medieval period,
emphasizing the growing influence of the Church in centralizing and
standardizing Christian teachings. Bullough's analysis of later medieval attitudes included a number of literary sources, including Dante,
Chaucer, the author of *Sir Gawain and the Green Knight* (also called the
Pearl-Poet), and William Langland (385–89). Bullough concluded his
analysis of medieval traditions of same-sex relations by exploring the
connection between sexual acts and heresy or other unorthodox religious conduct. He argued that sexual "deviation" eventually became
"a way of denying the validity of current societal standards," probably
because "the heretic was both more sexual than the orthodox, and the
orthodox attributed greater sexuality to the heretic than he or she had"
(390). Bullough made this comment about medieval dualists, panthe-
ists, Albigensians, and Waldensians, but it would seem to apply to
queer theorists, too, many of whom insist that homosexual acts are
means of criticizing social standards and want to be seen as "more
sexual than the orthodox" by orthodox and unorthodox alike.

Michael Goodich, *The Unmentionable Vice*

Michael Goodich's analysis of "the unmentionable vice" contrasts both
to the broad scope of Bailey's and Noonan's studies, and to these scholars' apologetic stance toward Christianity's role in governing sexual
conduct. Goodich concentrated on late medieval evidence, but some
attention to sources from earlier periods would have improved the perspective of his survey. For example, Goodich claimed that "[t]he first
testimony to the existence of homosexuality in Europe in the Middle
Ages appeared in the late tenth and early eleventh centuries." "In this
period," he wrote, "deviant sex was not yet regarded as a serious threat

to Christian morality" (3). He acknowledged that the Church condemned same-sex relations earlier, but argued that "it was not until the Gregorian reform movement that a determined effort was made to impose the canons of Catholic sexual morality on an often indifferent public" (xv). Goodich claimed that opposition to homosexual acts was not organized until the eleventh century, that the lines of polemic that eventually became standard emerged then and in the twelfth century, that militant antihomosexual reform swelled in the thirteenth century, and that persecution of homosexuals became evident only a century later (xv).

The reformers to whom Goodich referred include Regino of Prüm (d. 915), Burchard of Worms (d. 1008), and other tenth- and eleventh-century figures who consolidated and revised the standards enforced by penitential texts. However, these authors and others like them did not discard handbooks of penance but often recommended their use. Goodich's chronology creates the impression that before the late tenth and early eleventh centuries the Church did not oppose homosexual acts or try to legislate against "deviant sex." The penitentials, however, show that legislation against homosexual acts had been in progress since the sixth century in monastic environments and since the seventh in the lay Christian world. One of the texts cited by Goodich, Regino's *Libri duo de synodalibus causis et disciplinis ecclesiasticis* (906), illustrates the continuity between the new wave of reform and earlier documents. Goodich noted that Regino was clearly indebted to earlier handbooks of penance and that he drew on penitentials attributed to Theodore of Canterbury and to Bede (26). What Goodich described as "deviant sex" was considered a "serious threat" to Christian morality in both texts, which show in detail how ecclesiastical authorities sought to repress and obliterate it. By suggesting that opposition to same-sex acts was new, Goodich portrayed the earlier periods as tolerant—they were not—and discounted the most significant feature of the reforms of the eleventh century and after, which was an attempt to regularize and standardize the often arbitrary ancient penitentials.

Goodich's study of medieval homosexuality grew out of a study of the saints' lives, which were rich in details describing "the lusts which tempted these pious men and women, all the better to illustrate the saints' skill in driving way the minions of Satan." According to Goodich, "In the Middle Ages, therefore, although sex was regarded as a necessary evil at best, its importance was at least recognized, and even emphasized, as an expression of human weakness" (vii). Church historians, however, whom Goodich described as "mainly ecclesiastics, or believers," chose "not to emphasize the church's repressive role in the history of sexuality in the light of more liberal attitudes prevalent today." As a corrective to their apologetic stance, Goodich cited the work of several scholars, including Bailey (curiously enough, since Bailey seems quite apologetic), Vern Bullough, Arno Karlen, A. L. Rowse, and others, as "dispassionate and scholarly" (vii). Goodich was right to point out that much scholarship in the history of same-sex relations sought to minimize the Church's responsibility for antihomosexual attitudes, a tendency that Jordan's book, which is openly critical of the Church's position, fully reverses.

John Boswell, *Christianity, Social Tolerance, and Homosexuality*

Scholarship and passion, as Bailey showed, do not have to be antithetical, and both qualities can be found in abundance in a book published shortly after Goodich's that exemplifies the apologist stance he criticizes. This is Boswell's *Christianity, Social Tolerance, and Homosexuality: Gay People in Western Europe from the Beginning of the Christian Era to the Fourteenth Century,* a turning point in the history of homosexuality. Boswell sought to analyze a much broader spectrum of evidence than the predominantly legal and ecclesiastical sources central to Bailey's study (Noonan's work, however, was no less sweeping than Boswell's). The pointed difference between his work and Bailey's, Boswell noted, was that Bailey concentrated on negative evidence, while Boswell stressed what he regarded as "positive" evidence (4 note 3). In fact, it is often the case that these scholars consider the same evidence, Boswell affirmatively, Bailey negatively. On several counts, including access to original manuscripts and use of ancient languages, Boswell claimed superiority of method. But nearly twenty years later the scholarly reception of his book does not suggest that many historians were persuaded by his claims.[45] In some regards, Boswell's aim did not much differ from Bailey's. Boswell too sought to refute "the common idea that religious belief—Christian or other—has been the *cause* of intolerance in regard to gay people." Such beliefs might "cloak or incorporate intolerance," he wrote, but "careful analysis can almost always differentiate between conscientious application of religious ethics and the use of religious precepts as justification for personal animosity or prejudice" (6–7). This is not a proposition I would care to defend, since the use of religion for "personal animosity or prejudice" is not, after all, so easy to distinguish from "conscientious application of religious ethics." Most medieval authorities, I believe, thought they conscientiously applied religious ethics when they attacked same-sex acts. Few of them would have been able to separate those ethics from "personal prejudice," a term whose valence today cannot be automatically transferred to cultures of an earlier millennium.

Boswell sought to show that "the hostility of the Christian Scriptures to homosexuality" is no more pronounced than hostility to hypocrisy, and that prostitution is denounced more frequently than homosexual acts (7). He believed that something "other than religious belief" motivated the oppression of same-sex acts. This view taints Boswell's interpretation of the early medieval evidence. Ecclesiastical authorities in that period vigorously opposed prostitution (and hypocrisy too, no doubt equally in vain) and denounced same-sex acts between both men and women. That Scripture itself does not clearly justify those prohibitions is, ultimately, irrelevant. What matters is that medieval authorities who drew up and enforced ecclesiastical standards were convinced that Scripture did so.

Boswell himself illustrated the importance of this difference. Discussing a quotation from Paul's first letter to the Corinthians (6:9) often thought to deal with homosexual acts, Boswell argued that Paul was concerned with male prostitution and masturbation, not with homosexuality (106–7). Later, however, Boswell showed that Bishop Hincmar of Reims (845–82) "cited 1 Corinthians 6:9 in a context suggesting both homosexuality and prostitution" (205). Boswell's quarrel with the meaning of Paul's letter, recently examined by Bernadette J. Brooten,[46] has no bearing on medieval understandings of the text. Hincmar's interpretation of Scripture was different from the one Boswell considered correct or accurate. But other medieval ecclesiastical figures drew the same meaning from this quotation that Hincmar did, and that—and not Boswell's view on the "correct" meaning of the text—is what matters for the history of same-sex relations. Boswell also claimed that Hincmar demoted homosexuality to "the ranks of common failings with which almost anyone could empathize" (204). As evidence for this claim (the only evidence offered), Boswell merely noted that Hincmar listed homosexual acts *among* the sins of the Sodomites, rather than as their sole crime, the latter being a claim no one had made (204–5). Demonstration of such tolerance was necessary for Boswell's thesis about the development of the antihomosexual attitudes in the later Middle Ages, but such tolerance does not exist in the early medieval sources where Boswell claimed to find it.

At nearly every turn, Boswell produced similar, remarkably sanguine evaluations of social tolerance of same-sex relations. For example, he claimed to find "relative indifference" to homosexual behavior in early medieval Europe and argued that the intellectual climate was "ambivalent" toward gay people (200). Boswell arrived at his position by reading at least some of the evidence very selectively. He concluded his discussion of the Frankish evidence with this remark: "The correspondence between the relatively mild attitude of Carolingian theologians toward homosexuality and the notable restraint of contemporary legal enactments—indeed the virtual absence of civil statutes regarding it—argues very strongly that the Christian hierarchy in the seventh through the tenth centuries considered homosexual behavior no more (and probably less) reprehensible than comparable heterosexual behavior (i.e., extramarital)" (179). The notion that church officials regarded homosexual behavior as "probably less" reprehensible than heterosexual offenses contradicts almost everything that the early medieval evidence states. Some heterosexual offenses (e.g., anal intercourse) were considered worse than others because they prevented conception. But *all* same-sex intercourse took place outside the context of procreation, and all of it was abominated. Boswell's claim would be valid only if evidence from handbooks of penance and other pastoral texts could be ignored and the antihomosexual testimony from other sources, such as correspondence, diluted.

Boswell frequently sought to document church officials' restraint by recruiting certain figures among them into the ranks of "gay people," a category Boswell defined to mean "persons who are conscious of erotic preference for their own gender" (43).[47] An example is Alcuin (d. 804), the English monk who was one of Charlemagne's teachers and who helped to draft an important document called the *Admonitio generalis,* which was published in 789. Boswell characterized the *Admonitio generalis* as merely "an ecclesiastical admonishment" (178), an example of how he sought to dilute antihomosexual evidence. Rosamond McKitterick, a leading historian of the Frankish church, called it "the most complete statement of all the proposals for the reform of the church and its ministers and for the education of the people" and noted that it was issued by Charlemagne "at the height of his conquests."[48] This text ordered strict penances for those who fornicated with animals or "with men, against nature," and instructed priests and bishops to "attempt in every way to prohibit and eradicate this evil." Boswell discounts the effect of the edict by arguing that the sin indicated in the *source* of the canon in question is not a sex act but rather the loss of reason, although the meaning of the *source* is surely irrelevant to the meaning of the canon itself. He also argued that the supposed leniency of the canon regarding homosexual acts was due to Alcuin: "it is conceivable that his own inclinations disposed him to treat homosexuality leniently" (178 note 3).[49]

Also lenient was Regino, who, like "most of his contemporaries," is credited with a "largely gender blind" approach to sexual sins, a pointed anachronism, however flattering to Regino and his contemporaries. Regino is said to have punished heterosexual fornication with the same penance given for male homosexual intercourse and to have been "somewhat more sympathetic" in his approach to the latter (183).[50] Boswell emphasized that Regino's own prescriptions were not as harsh as those in his sources. The point would seem to be that, since the severity of the earlier canons was still in effect, Regino's own canons governing other matters could be more relaxed. But they were not. As Payer has shown, Regino repeatedly specified punishment for same-sex acts, with penances extending to ten years, more severe than those for heterosexual sins.[51]

As his treatment of Regino's work indicates, one of the most notable weaknesses of Boswell's survey is its treatment of handbooks of penance. These sources present evidence that consistently contradicts and never supports his thesis. Yet he chose in the main to ignore it, even though it had been fully and helpfully discussed by Noonan and Bailey before him. Significantly, Boswell accused Bailey of relying too heavily on the penitentials, English handbooks in particular.[52] These penitentials show that homosexual acts were severely punished over a period of some six hundred years leading up to what Boswell, unpersuasively, characterized as "the rise of intolerance" in the thirteenth century (269–70). Boswell's view of the penitentials forms a pointed contrast with Bailey's and Noonan's. Boswell argued that confession was irregularly heard, that handbooks of penance enforced different standards, and that in some places church officials objected to them. None of this has ever been disputed. He also argued that the penitentials "reached a rather small audience and hardly constitute an index of medieval morality" (182); both of these assertions are debatable. Boswell also offered a gratuitous insult to those who had consulted the penitentials. "Their extensive use by some scholars [he cites Bailey] results not so much from their importance as from their accessibility: they are among the very few medieval works generally organized topically and hence relatively easy to consult on a particular subject such as sex" (182).

Boswell can have read few penitentials! Many of them are chaotic, even contradictory; some of them place sex acts under several different categories. Until recently, many of these texts were not available in good editions; more than a few have not been edited for a hundred years. Boswell claimed that "many penitentials" contained "heretical" provisions and that "the church officially discouraged their use at least from the ninth century" (182), a view that applies only to the unique opposition to the handbooks mounted at Frankish synods. The eighth-century *Penitential* of Theodore attacked heresy, and no penitential known to me contains anything like "heretical" views.[53] Comparable objections to the handbooks were not raised in other regions where the handbooks were known (i.e., Ireland, England, Italy). Frankish bishops denounced the penitentials because their errors were certain and authors uncertain, as one council put it.[54] The bishops' concern was not heresy, however, but the proliferation of anonymous texts. The penitentials continued to be copied and used in the Frankish and later churches. Charlemagne's own *capitula* required priests to own and know how to use penitentials, as did statutes issued in Liége, Basel, Freising, and Vesoul in the late eighth and early ninth centuries.[55] These authorities were not urging their pastors to use heretical texts but rather insisting that confessors choose penitentials carefully and use them with discretion. The Church in England and Ireland expressed no reservations about them, and even Boswell admitted that when the Council of Paris prohibited priests from consulting the handbooks, it was "probably in the hope of instituting greater severity of punishment" for homosexual acts (182). The objection, in other words, was that the handbooks were not severe enough in their treatment of same-sex sins. The bishops did not want to eliminate penalties for same-sex acts, therefore, but to increase them.[56]

Because Boswell underrepresented the opposition to same-sex behavior in early sources, he was able to use them to construct the historical development required by his thesis, showing that an early tolerance for same-sex behavior gradually gave way to oppression of homosexual acts and that this "rise of intolerance" was the result of political and social conditions rather than an animus toward same-sex relations in Christianity itself. Does English evidence demonstrate an ongoing tolerance for same-sex behavior? Boswell claimed that such authorities of the English church as Bede, Boniface, Alcuin, Anselm, Aelred, and others denounced sexual immorality in general but expressed no opposition to same-sex behavior. He used these sources to show that attitudes toward homosexuality grew "steadily more tolerant" in the early Middle Ages (206). The twelfth century, according to Boswell, was a time when "gay love was by no means limited to the ranks of the ordained" (228). It was widespread among the laity, too (232), and "numerous" English manuscripts of the period "contain gay literature" (235).

English records are in fact a particularly useful register of such tolerance, since they provide a steady production of texts from the seventh century forward, a chain of evidence from the earliest periods of the Church in England up to the early thirteenth century, when Anglo-Saxon penitentials, long since out of date, were still being glossed by a scholar interested in penitential discipline.[57] But what this evidence demonstrates is the opposite of what Boswell claimed for it. "Intolerance" of same-sex acts is steadily manifest in English and Continental evidence throughout the early medieval period. The so-called rise of intolerance in the later period is nothing more than more systematic and thorough control of the laity's and the clergy's sexual behavior by an augmented ecclesiastical bureaucracy. The early evidence demonstrates that there was no period of "tolerance" such as that Boswell describes, and it powerfully undermines the central premises of his highly influential study.

Despite my criticism of it, Boswell's book made important contributions to the historical study of same-sex relations. It examined an enormous range of evidence and drew attention to the need to reread many tired sources. It is surely the first serious historical inquiry to try to put same-sex relations in a perspective that affirms them in both modern and premodern terms. The book's greatest contribution is that it fostered an atmosphere in which same-sex relations could be studied as the stuff of serious scholarly inquiry rather than as a small area of interest to only a few—to a homosexual few. In trying to see same-sex relations as so thoroughly acceptable as to be inconspicuous, if not normal, Boswell grossly exaggerated the tolerance he claimed to find in medieval sources. But he succeeded in drawing serious attention to the subject by mainstream academia for the first time.

Pierre J. Payer, *Sex and the Penitentials*

Boswell's interpretation of the early medieval evidence, the penitentials in particular, was swiftly corrected by Payer's *Sex and the Penitentials*. This book benefits greatly from Payer's decision to limit analysis to texts written between the mid–sixth and mid–eleventh century. Like Noonan, Payer situated same-sex acts in the context of a comprehensive survey of sexual behavior as the penitentials organize it, with marriage in a central position. Responding to Boswell's wholesale dismissal of the penitentials, Payer demonstrated that all the penitentials that he himself surveyed contained at least one provision against homosexual acts and that some treated the topic extensively. He distinguished general references to same-sex acts from mentions of sodomites as a category and from references to anal and interfemoral intercourse. Within the category of same-sex acts, he further identified oral sex acts, forcible sex with young boys, and others (135–39).

Payer noted that, concerning developments prior to the tenth century, penitentials not only form an important evidentiary base but in fact constitute "the sole tradition of a comprehensive sexual code" independent of conciliar literature, diocesan status, and early canonical collections. These two streams, penitential texts and conciliar decrees, did not come together until Regino and Burchard of Worms, both of whom draw substantially from handbooks of penance (116). The strategy of playing the penitentials off against conciliar texts to contrast unofficial or "heretical" (according to Boswell) views with the position of the official Church—a strategy used by both Bailey and Boswell— is thus exposed as ill-founded. These two traditions do not, in the early period, significantly overlap. Elsewhere, in his translation of the *Liber Gomorrhianus* of Peter Damian, Payer summed up censures of homosexual acts before the mid–eleventh century and concluded that "prior to 1048 the church displayed a consistent and uninterrupted pastoral concern with homosexuality."[58] *Sex and the Penitentials* omits the Anglo-Saxon vernacular penitentials and does not incorporate same-sex relations as fully as it might have in regard to same-sex conduct, resulting in the segregation of "homosexuality and the penitentials" in an appendix (135–39). Nonetheless, Payer's book offers the most complete guide to early medieval sexual regulations yet written; his categories shape part of my analysis in chapter 4.

James A. Brundage, *Law, Sex, and Christian Society in Medieval Europe*

Another scholar who examined same-sex behavior within a heteronormative context, and who shares Payer's penchant for codification of the evidence, is James A. Brundage. Although Brundage did not discuss English evidence at any one point in *Law, Sex, and Christian Society in Medieval Europe,* he explained and illustrated the role of handbooks of penance in regulating same-sex relations accurately and in detail. He also showed how later handbooks of penance correlate with canonical and other texts that governed sexual conduct (152–69).[59] Brundage's survey is divided into large chronological periods. The early medieval evidence is surveyed in a chapter ranging from the sixth to the eleventh century (124–75). Subsequent periods of reform in the canonical tradition, 1000–1140 and 1140–90, are analyzed more fully (176–255, 256–324), and the second half of the thirteenth century is singled out as a period of "sharp growth of legislation about homosexual relationships" (472). Within each period Brundage treated the same set of topics—marriage, prostitution, "deviant" or homosexual behavior, and others.

Like Payer, Brundage elaborated the central place of marriage in the Church's supervision of lay sexual behavior and stressed that sex within marriage was treated as a concession rather than as a right (154). The negative view of heterosexual relations in marriage necessarily meant that the Church viewed same-sex relations and other forms of "deviant" conduct with extreme disapproval. In this book and elsewhere Brundage took the lead in quantifying and codifying the Church's regulation of sexual acts. Tables in his appendices illustrate comparable penances for sexual offenses, periods of abstinence, and other matters; they are a compendium of medieval attitudes toward sex. One table illustrates penances for selected sexual offenses, ranging from adultery to bestiality and oral sex (600, table 4.3). Anal sex is one of these categories, but unfortunately Brundage did not include same-sex relations so that readers could compare penances for them to those meted out for heterosexual sins; nor are the vernacular Anglo-Saxon penitentials included in this table. The table shows that the *Penitential* of Columbanus assigned a penance of either seven or ten years for this act, the same penances as those assigned for homosexual intercourse. The *Penitential* of Theodore assigned penances ranging from seven to ten to fifteen years for both categories. As I demonstrate in chapter 4, penalties for same-sex acts equal those for all but the gravest heterosexual offenses and generally match penances assigned for anal sex.

David F. Greenberg, *The Construction of Homosexuality*

Brundage's attention to quantifiable data and method resembles that found in David F. Greenberg's immense *The Construction of Homosexuality*. Greenberg set out to create a "phenomenology of homosexuality for different cultures" (3–4). In pursuit of this aim, he gave equal attention to evidence from Eastern as well as Western cultures and juxtaposed patterns of behavior from remote civilizations with those found in the records of Western Christianity. Greenberg paid more attention to methodology than many of his predecessors; his perspective as a sociologist helped him maintain a useful distance from the defensive rhetoric that dominates some other discussions of homosexuality in history. Greenberg considered and set aside a number of explanations for the origin of deviance-making regulations, including group conflict, functionalism, cultural transmission, psychoanalysis, and others, which he criticized as "state-focused" explanations of particular legislative acts (17). He focused instead on social change and preferred a conceptual framework that explained how "[e]volving social structures and ideologies" transformed sexual practices (18). Such analysis is possible only in the context of concrete data that indicate which aspects of human social behavior are relevant to sexual practices, a context not easily created out of the histories of Anglo-Saxon England and other pre-modern societies. All the problems of evidence Greenberg cited—the preponderance of evidence pertaining to social elites, the loss or destruction of evidence, gaps in our knowledge of women's lives, and others—are manifest in the Anglo-Saxon records that discuss same-sex relations (19–20).

Although Greenberg included the early English data in a chapter that deals with "feudalism," a concept unknown in the Anglo-Saxon period, he made excellent use of early penitentials in his survey of early Germanic attitudes toward same-sex relations (242–98). He stressed the impact of male virtue and personal valor in combat as an example of how a particular political formation could affect sexual categories. He suggested that "heterosexual deprivation" in military culture could create intense emotional bonds between men that could have sexual significance (257–60), a point repeatedly stressed by Allan Bérubé in *Coming Out under Fire* and highly relevant to the male, military ethos of Anglo-Saxon society.[60] Greenberg made a similar—and similarly sound—suggestion about the need for shared intimacy and its possible homosexual consequences in monasteries (285).

Like Payer, Greenberg argued that the penitentials were created for practical rather than theoretical purposes but also accepted Boswell's point that during the early medieval period in particular confession was not regular or necessarily widely observed (263–64). Greenberg described the handbooks as "'grassroots' sentiment of the priesthood," although they are more likely to represent the collective sentiment of bishops and abbots (264). He pointed out that same-sex behavior was "a subsidiary category of nonreproductive sex" (265; see also 277). His conclusion that the medieval Church lacked the will or the capacity to "deploy punitive measures effectively enough to destroy the social world of medieval male homosexuality" remains slightly ambiguous (268). It would be safer to say that the Church lacked the means; it is difficult to read Greenberg's summary of the evidence, or that offered in other studies surveyed here, and believe that what was lacking was will. A corrective to such views is found in Jeffrey Richards's *Sex, Dissidence, and Damnation: Minority Groups in the Middle Ages,* a book that makes good use of penitentials (from the later Middle Ages only, however), in its analysis of homosexual relations (132–49).

Mark D. Jordan, *The Invention of Sodomy in Christian Theology*

The contemporary feature of Greenberg's book, like Brundage's, is its interest in quantifiable data. Jordan's work, *The Invention of Sodomy in*

Christian Theology, is contemporary for another reason. The first book on this subject by an openly gay author since Boswell's, it is also the first written after "queer theory" became an academic trend. Jordan's comments on queer theory seem to me to strike exactly the right balance between a commitment to historical particularity and the protocols of a politically engaged approach to texts and culture. Jordan acknowledged his debt to the work of Sedgwick, David M. Halperin, and others, and then added,

> But I do not think that these writers give or mean to give a completed science of queerness that can be applied as a cookie cutter to any possible historical dough. On the contrary, what is so admirable in the writing of Foucault, Halperin, and Sedgwick is precisely the refusal to take the question of same-sex desire as settled, as captured by theory. I myself tend to think that we have barely begun to gather evidence of same-sex desire. We are thus very far from being able to imagine having a finished theory. (5)

Just as he made no attempt to queer his sources, being content instead to analyze their linguistic detail, Jordan refused to organize texts and events into the narrative structures common in the traditional history of ideas, emphasizing cause and effect and chronological developments. Jordan made no attempt to construct a continuous genealogy of sodomy but set out instead to represent "the shapes, the voices" that narrative history can conceal (2). He focused, in general to great advantage, on close readings of key texts, beginning with Peter Damian's *Book of Gomorrah* and works by Alan of Lille, Paul of Hungary, Robert of Flamborough, William Peraldus, Albertus Magnus, and Thomas Aquinas. His analysis of these sources forms a powerful response to Boswell's claims about them, although Jordan avoided taking issue with anything Boswell said.[61] Jordan did not construct a narrative to counter Boswell's narrative of progress; instead he showed that fierce and studied opposition to same-sex acts was part of the Church's orthodoxy not only when Peter Damian invented "sodomy" but for centuries before, when references to same-sex acts were less systematic but more explicit.

Jordan construed the verbal evidence of same-sex behavior narrowly around the word "sodomia" (sodomy) and did not give the same weight to words related to it, even "sodomitic." The most frequent expressions used to identify and condemn homosexual intercourse in the centuries before Damian are combinations of references to "sodomites" and to fornication "in terga" (in the backside). Although this evidence was sufficient to persuade Bailey, Payer, and others, that medieval authorities often if not invariably associated anal intercourse with Sodom, Jordan argued that the advent of the word "sodomia" had special significance. "The prescriptions against Sodomitic intercourse are not the same as the construction of the category *sodomia,* for which the appearance of the abstract noun serves as an important index," he wrote (42). "To abstract an essence from a proper name is to reduce the person named to a single quality," so that "[a] term like Sodomy suggests, by its very grammatical form, that it is possible to reduce persons to a single essence, which can then be found in other persons, remote from them in time or place" (42).

All this is true. Absent the category of "sodomia," which, Jordan argues, was invented by Peter Damian (45–58), we cannot claim that medieval authorities distilled references to homosexual acts into a single category. Nor did these authorities seek to reduce persons to essences. I would argue that they did not have to do so. The most important fact about early penitential discourse on same-sex acts is that references to Sodom, "sodomitic," and others like them, for example, "in the manner of a Sodomite," clearly involve male homosexual acts, and almost always anal intercourse. Where other sexual sins, such as fellatio, interfemoral intercourse, and masturbation are concerned, they are named. Where words related to Sodom are applied to heterosexual rather than homosexual intercourse, they again almost always refer to anal intercourse. In chapter 4 I will examine the extent to which the penitentials sanctioned same-sex relations at least four hundred years before the "invention of sodomy." The early sources seem to have settled on a working definition of sodomy as anal intercourse between two men. I would argue that it was only after Burchard collapsed these forms of sin under the category of "sins against nature," an umbrella term rarely used in the penitentials, that the category of "sodomy" became necessary and that the term was invented. Earlier sources link the city and the act of anal intercourse many times. Jordan makes the familiar point that names for acts and ideas matter, as linguistic, textual, and social events. But a name does not necessarily matter more than the act described by some other set of words that, on their own, could be used to regulate same-sex acts.

Nor did the discourse surrounding sodomy change greatly because Peter Damian invented the category and the word. What was unclear and imprecisely known before Damian continued to be unclear and imprecisely known after him. Indeed, numerous later injunctions forbad confessors to use the word, as we have seen above—the early authorities, as we have also seen, had no such scruples—and this tended to make things even more confused than they were before. The word "sodomia" took its time to appear in theological discourse. Jordan rightly did not consider penitentials to be part of such discourse and called them instead "samples of theological speech about same-sex acts" (41). It is useful to recall Payer's distinction between conciliar and penitential texts at this point, and to note that both textual streams exercised authority over medieval sexual practices before the development of scholastic theology.[62] The very fact that dozens of penitential manuals exist and were copied and recopied from century to century argues strongly for their continued use. So too does the fact that Peter Damian attacked the penitentials with numerous arguments, including one— that their authors were "unknown or uncertain"—first made by the Frankish bishops over two hundred years earlier. Damian outdid the bishops, claiming that the penitentials were, in Jordan's words, "as unnatural, as unconvincing, as the crimes they condone" (54). On a soberer note, Jordan himself claimed that these texts "need to be read with an eye to ritual functions as much as to juridical or descriptive ones," which seems to be an attempt to diminish their significance (41). One of the most important "ritual functions"of the handbook was to sustain, over centuries, a particular textual form of ecclesiastical discipline. To separate their "ritual" from their "juridical" function seems to argue, unnecessarily, that these categories were distinct and exclusive. Juridical functions may well be ritualistic, but they are judgments all the same.

Jordan argued that the penitentials "are noted for their blunt speaking about sexual matters," but that in these texts "references to Sodom or Sodomites are used both to conceal and to reveal" (42). Those who know what the reference means—that is, that it refers to same-sex intercourse—are the only ones to whom these regulations speak. If Jordan is right, then the early medieval penitentials play the same game of hide-and-seek that later handbooks, such as that by Robert of Flamborough, do. But I think it can be demonstrated that the penitentials' references to "Sodomites" and to acts committed "according to the sodomitical custom" are, in context, not ambiguous, and that they indicate a particular form of male homosexual intercourse, anal intercourse. These references are much more explicit than those to be found in later penitentials. The textual references do not stand on their own, needless to say, but they are—as Jordan pointed out—part of a ritual that also included interrogation and clarification. Robert of Flamborough would not have answered his penitent's questions about "unnatural sins," but Cummean or priests using other early handbooks were never instructed to dodge their penitents' questions.

No common thread unites all the works I have surveyed in this chapter, but some important features can be observed. First, it is routine to begin the history of the church's opposition to same-sex relations—conceptualized at different levels of discourse—in the later Middle Ages, starting with Peter Damian (Jordan), the Gregorian reforms (Goodich), and the thirteenth century (Boswell). Unlike Goodich and Boswell, Jordan made no attempt to deny or minimize the existence of antihomosexual regulations in the early medieval period. Second, little of this work declares its own political interest in the questions at hand. Bailey, Noonan, and Boswell adopted an apologetic stance concerning Christianity's influence on the regulation of sexual behavior. Jordan's vigorous criticism of such authors as Peter Damian is an important exception to the studied neutrality maintained by most authors. Third, studies that take up sexuality in general terms (i.e., those by Noonan, Payer, and Brundage) isolate same-sex behavior rather than compare it to regulations governing heterosexual acts, while studies of homosexuality tend to make few references to heterosexual standards (Goodich, Boswell, Jordan). Greenberg is an exception to this pattern of segregating rather than integrating homosexual and heterosexual norms.

My approach is to see same-sex relations coexisting with heterosexual relations, always there, always present, if sometimes only as a shadowy trace. When same-sex relations fit social structures—codes of heroic or kingly behavior, for example—they are tolerated, even valorized. These relations express social ideals that have nothing to do with sex; hence they pose no threat to social order. When same-sex relations deviate from social structures and infringe on protected territory, however, such as the sexualization of young men, or suggest sexual intercourse rather than a social idea of friendship, they are severely censured because they menace heterosexual order with a threat of the moral chaos of unnatural acts. That is, they cast a shadow such as that described by Bray, who writes that homosexuality was adjacent to the ordered world and "was part, in a word, of its shadow."[63] That is not the only kind of shadow same-sex acts create, however, as we have already seen.

The texts I survey in the next two chapters tell us about Anglo-Saxon society as church officials saw it and addressed it. First I discuss the handbooks used when priests heard the confessions of laymen and -women. What the laity understood by references to Sodom and acts performed "according to sodomitical custom" cannot be deduced only from the handbooks, however. The Anglo-Saxon laity formed its knowledge of sexual standards not just from penitentials but from other sources, including homilies that referred to Sodom and Gomorrah. These texts supported and explained the standards that the handbooks enforced. In what follows I will attempt to show what it means that these texts treat sexual morality, homosexual and heterosexual, in a straightforward manner.

The Sociology of Sex in Anglo-Saxon
Laws and Penitentials

This and the following chapter examine evidence of same-sex behavior in Anglo-Saxon England found in a variety of vernacular
texts, beginning with the law codes and the penitentials. A model for
the kind of study required by the medieval English evidence is available in John W. Baldwin's *Language of Sex,* which describes "a sociology
of those who were depicted as sexually active" in a variety of sources
written in France around 1200. Baldwin examines the "physiological,
social, marital, and marginal configurations" of the men and women
he studies.[1] A similar "sociology of those who were depicted as sexually
active" would greatly assist an attempt to understand the place of same-
sex relations in the sex-gender system of Anglo-Saxon England. But
the narrative sources frustrate that aim. They seldom explore the dynamics of male-female relations, such as those discussed in *The Wife's
Lament,* and they do not make explicit references to sexual practices.
Indeed, if the Anglo-Saxon texts were as forthcoming as Baldwin's fab-
liaux and romances, both they and the period they represent would be
much better known.

We might hope to supplement the deficiencies of the narrative
sources with administrative texts, especially texts associated with secular or ecclesiastical discipline. David F. Greenberg describes a "phenomenology of homosexuality" that requires us to "reconstruct, to the
limited degree possible, the patterns of actual sexual behavior associated
with perceptions of it."[2] Unfortunately, administrative sources do not
describe "actual sexual behavior" in the premodern period in England,
as they do in some later periods. The relevant Anglo-Saxon texts are
neither biographical nor autobiographical, and none of them concerns
the actual same-sex experiences of men and women. Nor are there
court records or other accounts of individual behavior. Administrative sources supply the views of ecclesiastical and secular authorities,
but not the views of those whom they governed, which, if available,

would offer researchers the opportunity to offset one kind of bias with another.

Instead, the texts concerning same-sex relations served a purpose that has been called "deviance-defining." According to Howard Becker, deviance "is not a quality of the act a person commits, but rather a consequence of the application by others of rules and sanctions to an 'offender.'" Before anyone can be classified as deviant, "someone must have made the rule which defines the act as deviant."[3] A sociology based on these rules can accurately describe certain influential perceptions of behavior but cannot get beyond them to the actual deeds, much less the desires, of Anglo-Saxon women and men.

Both the laws and the handbooks of penance used to govern Anglo-Saxon England are "deviance-defining" sources. They were carefully coordinated. From very early in the Anglo-Saxon period, the Church worked closely with secular authorities; even the oldest Anglo-Saxon law codes show traces of ecclesiastical influence. The Kentish code of King Æthelberht, who died in 616, begins, "[Theft of] God's property and the Church's shall be compensated twelve fold" ("Godes feoh 7 ciricean XII gylde").[4] The *Penitential* attributed to Theodore of Canterbury, dated to the early eighth century, requires a less severe penance, specifying that someone who takes money from a church must repay the amount fourfold.[5] The interaction of these two kinds of legislation became increasingly apparent in the tenth and eleventh centuries, when large parts of the secular codes were devoted to matters that were primarily of ecclesiastical concern. The code known as V Æthelred, for example (c. 1008), manifests a preoccupation with clerical celibacy.[6]

Pastoral texts, especially penitentials, were more varied and abundant than the laws; they explain how priests and other officials were to regard all sexual relations, including intramale and intrafemale sex. Like the laws, the ecclesiastical sources are straightforward. They do not attempt to conceal information or details about sexual crimes or sins. Some of the texts, handbooks of penance in particular, seem oblique or cryptic—not because the authorities were coy, however, as they were in the later Middle Ages, but because the penitentials, like the laws, depended on a context of oral performance, memory, and custom that cannot be reconstructed simply by reading these texts today.

A schematic representation of homosexual and heterosexual acts and their moral and social consequences in Anglo-Saxon culture is a tool much to be desired. But modern editions offer a poor beginning for such an instrument. Although editions are usually based on several different manuscript versions of a single text, the editor usually selects the form of the text considered to be the earliest and closest to the original version, or perhaps the most complete and correct, and reduces other copies to the status of variants of that version. This procedure is adequate for certain kinds of documents. But for others, including handbooks of penance, which were subject to considerable structural variation from manuscript to manuscript, such an approach creates serious distortions. Penitentials originally circulated as small booklets, frequently recopied. Even those copies containing important errors or omissions, no matter how far they stray from the original or "best" version of the text, might well have been used in hearing confession and assigning penance. If we assume that these texts were used in confession, we must also assume that any form of one particular text could have been used to interpret the Church's standards and to govern the lives of devout Anglo-Saxons.

In some cases, different manuscript copies present quite different versions of the text. The manuscripts of a vernacular Anglo-Saxon penitential called the *Scriftboc* are cases in point. The manuscript selected by the editor as the "base" or primary form of the text is approximately 20 percent longer than the other two versions, which also differ from each other in their arrangement of the material. One of the shorter versions omits parts or all of several chapters involving adultery and sex acts in marriage.[7] These omissions are noted in the editor's critical apparatus, but readers must be closely attentive to the fine print in order to reconstruct the version of the *Scriftboc* in which these omissions occur. Editorial methods can also obscure variation in penances for individual sins. According to the editor's base manuscript, those who failed to refrain from intercourse after conception and after childbirth received a penance of six months, meaning that they had to fast during this period, the standard form of doing penance. (Fasting required following a special diet, often without meat, and eating fewer meals on certain days, and sometimes every day, for periods ranging from a week to several years.) But the other two manuscripts agree on a penance of seven months. In this case, the editor rejected readings from *all* the manuscripts in favor of a penance of three months, basing his correction on the penance supplied in the presumed Latin source of this canon.[8] It is not sufficient, in such cases, to refer to an edited or reconstructed text; the manuscript evidence shows that standards differed, whether intentionally or accidentally.

Electronic research tools will make it possible to navigate large databases that contain all manuscript versions of these texts and even to analyze conditions within the specific region where each copy circulated.[9] Lacking such tools, however, it is necessary to survey the evidence in the more general terms in which current editions (most of them quite old) present it. Where it is possible to point out manuscript variations without greatly encumbering the argument, I will do so. But the reader should be warned that variations within the conclusions offered below are possible and even likely. In what follows I will outline the sexual system of the Anglo-Saxons in three areas. The first concerns adultery, as treated in the laws and penitentials. The second area, the largest, comprises male and female homosexual acts, including sex between boys and men. The third area includes other sex acts. I have organized the relevant canons from the Latin and Old English documents into appendices (where they are translated) and summarized some statistical information (e.g., the proportion of sexual offenses to other sins, the proportion of heterosexual to homosexual acts) in tables in this chapter.

Law and the Codification of Sex

The Anglo-Saxon legal system is far older than our most ancient textual witnesses to it. Laws were recorded in writing only after Christianity was adopted in England, in the late sixth century. The oldest codes date from the early seventh century but exist only in much later copies. Old laws were transcribed for various reasons, not merely to preserve an archive but to supply points of reference for new laws. Sometimes the old laws were revised when they were recopied, but the evidence also shows that transcribers usually were careful to preserve the language of the original text. "[I]t must not be assumed that there was a widespread practice of modernisation," wrote Dorothy Whitelock, "for the presence of much archaic diction and syntax proves that in general the text was rendered much as it stood."[10]

Until recently scholars assumed that the laws were historical documents and, when editing the texts, organized them in chronological order. However, as Whitelock's remark indicates, and as recent work by Mary P. Richards has shown, the laws were not transcribed in neat patterns. According to Richards, the laws "are never arranged chronologically in the manuscripts, nor do they retain a fixed shape through successive additions and recopyings." More recent codes take priority in the manuscripts, and older collections are included as supplements to them.[11] The laws of Ine (who reigned from 688 to 726) form part of the laws of King Alfred (d. 899) but have traditionally been extracted from Alfred's collection—the only context in which they survive—and edited as a separate code, a form of the text for which there is no manuscript authority. As this example shows, the body of early English law is cumulative. Anglo-Saxons in the tenth and eleventh centuries followed codes written by their own kings as well as codes written by their ancestors.

Adultery in the Laws

The Anglo-Saxon laws deal with sexual behavior almost entirely within the context of marriage and adultery. They are generally consistent with Germanic codes, which, according to Vern L. Bullough, ignore almost all sexual activities except adultery. Because adultery was considered to be a crime against property, it was much more than a sexual offense.[12] James A. Brundage argued that Germanic societies regarded adultery as "an exclusively female crime." Sometimes men were punished for it as well, but in Roman law only a woman could commit adultery.[13] The importance of the offense is obvious. The adulteress "cast doubt upon the legitimacy of her husband's descendants as well as offending his honor and pride."[14] Anglo-Saxon law codes also treat adultery as a question of property; women are seen as belonging to husbands or fathers, and the laws protect men's rights over wives, daughters, and female servants.[15] The laws also protect women in various ways, ensuring that they were not held responsible for their husband's misdeeds, that widows were not forced into second marriages or into the convent, and that women were compensated for sexual assault. But Brundage's description of the regulation of sexual conduct in the Germanic kingdoms of the ninth century also suits the Anglo-Saxon legal evidence. So long as men's sexual adventures did not compromise the rights of other men, they had little consequence. "Women, however, were heavily penalized, even for minor sexual peccadillos, partly because of the danger of pregnancy, partly because female chastity had an appreciable market value. Sexual misbehavior by a woman not only constituted a moral offense, but also diminished her desirability, either as a wife or concubine."[16]

Particularly important codes for the study of sexual standards in the period are those of Æthelberht, Alfred, and Cnut (d. 1035). These collections reveal how sexual acts were regulated by laws in the seventh, ninth, and eleventh centuries respectively. The laws of Æthelberht include several dealing with adultery. The penalty for a "freeman," "frigman," or simply a "man" of undefined marital status (but presumably married), varied with the status of the woman involved. He was fined 50 shillings if he lay with a maiden belonging to the king, 25 shillings if she were a "grinding slave," and 12 shillings if she were a serving maid.[17] If a freeman lay with another freeman's wife, he paid him wergeld, procured a second wife for him, and delivered her to the man he wronged (apparently the adulterer was free to chose any woman he wished, without consulting the man he had offended).[18] If he lay with a servant's wife, he paid double compensation as long as the servant lived.[19] Some idea of the relative values involved can be had from Alfred's laws. Anyone who lay with the wife of a man whose wergeld was 1,200 shillings paid the man 120 shillings in compensation; if the husband's wergeld was 600 shillings, the fine was 100 shillings; a commoner whose wife was taken in adultery received 40 shillings in compensation.[20]

Later laws do not rely only on the wergeld system of compensation for adultery; other penalties were also used. Adultery, according to one of the laws of Cnut, was an act committed by a married man who fornicated with an unmarried woman, with another man's wife, or with a nun. Cnut's second code specifies that one who commits adultery is to "make amends according to the nature of the offence" ("gebete þæt be ðam þe seo dæd sy"), language that suggests ecclesiastical penance as well as secular penalties ("betan" means "to do penance") and that shows the hand of Archbishop Wulfstan, one of Cnut's advisers.[21] If a married man committed adultery with his own slave, he had to free her and "make amends for himself both to God and to men" ("bete for hine sylfne wiþ Godd [7] wið men"). The woman was not so lucky. If she was found guilty of adultery, her ears and nose were cut off and she lost all her property.[22] This harsh penalty was new to the Anglo-Saxon laws in the eleventh century; other evidence, including that from charters that record ownership of estates, suggest that financial penalties were the standard punishment for adultery.[23]

Sex acts other than those construed as adultery were prohibited but less systematically and less specifically. Cnut's laws are unusually attentive to sexual conduct, forbidding fornication and prostitution among exhortations to Christians to avoid all forms of sexual excess.[24] Several laws prohibit the abduction of nuns from convents and sexual assault on nuns.[25] Cnut's laws also forbid sexual intercourse during Lent and urge Christians to confess and to learn prayers.[26] Cnut's codes sometimes borrow language from the penitentials about adjusting punishments to correspond to the social circumstances of the offender.[27]

Marriage, as the laws make clear, was the normative condition for adult Anglo-Saxons; laws for children concern their readiness for marriage. Most matters of inheritance and many matters of one's rights before the law depended on bloodlines, which in turn depended on sexual union. According to the laws of Wihtred, those who refused to "regularize" their unions were to be excluded from the Church. If they were foreigners, they were to be driven out of the land "with their possessions and with their sins" ("of lande mid hiora æhtum ⁊ mid synnum gewiten").[28] Laws about sexual offenses outside of marriage, including abduction, rape, sexual assault, and incest, reflect a concern with a man's rights over a woman and with legitimacy of offspring. Abduction or *raptus,* the crime of carrying a woman off by force, did not necessarily include sexual intercourse. But it did violate the father's rights over his daughter.[29] Sexual assault was punished separately and took the harm to the woman into account. Alfred's laws require that compensation be paid to a young girl if she were sexually assaulted: 5 shillings if a man touched her breast, 10 shillings if he threw her down, and 60 shillings if he had intercourse with her (reduced by half if she were not a virgin; she could contest her status before wergeld was reduced).[30] A girl not of age was compensated for her rape as if she were an adult; rape of a commoner's slave was punished by a fine of 60 shillings and a payment of 5 shillings to her owner; but if a slave raped a slave, he was castrated.[31] Incest required payment of wergeld based on the degree of relationship between the parties involved; forfeiture of all possessions was a possible penalty.[32] No penalties for men who consorted with prostitutes are specified, but the laws require that such women be "driven from the land." [33]

Homosexual offenses are never mentioned in the laws. Within a system designed to define and maintain property rights and patterns of inheritance, these acts apparently had no consequence. Engaging in homosexual acts evidently did not compromise one's status before the law. With two possible exceptions in the thirteenth century, both of them disputed, there were no secular laws against same-sex relations in England until 1533, when statutes of Henry VIII for the first time punished the "vice of buggery" and superseded the Church's jurisdiction over this offense.[34]

Adultery in Latin Penitentials

Unlike the laws, both Latin and vernacular penitentials treat sexual acts exhaustively. The penitentials are worth analyzing because they are abundantly attested in the early Middle Ages from the seventh century onward.[35] Their close alignment with secular law on most issues and the frequency of calls for confession and penance in such sources as homilies and vernacular poetry support the argument that the penitentials were, in some form, connected to social practice. As we saw in chapter 3, scholars do not agree on the penitentials' value as evidence of medieval sexual standards. Greenberg, Pierre J. Payer, and John T. Noonan, Jr., among others, accepted these texts as an index to sexual standards; John Boswell, who did not, was in an extreme minority. I agree with Payer's assumption that penitentials "were actually used in the pastoral ministry and that they reflect what people were doing sexually." As evidence he noted the persistence of certain regulations, selective borrowing and modifications of canons, and additions that show the penitentials to be "living documents used for the practical ends which they frequently claim for themselves."[36] In other words, they are the best material available for constructing a "sociology of sex" in the early medieval period.

I will deal with the Latin texts selectively, surveying those thought to have been of English provenance or claiming English authorship. These handbooks most frequently served as sources for the vernacular handbooks. I will then discuss the penitentials in Old English. The *Penitential* attributed to Theodore of Canterbury, the most important of the Latin documents, is thought to be a collection of decisions authorized by Theodore and issued under his name. Also important are two related texts: the *Penitential* attributed to Bede but not written by him (hereafter "Bede"), a collection based on Theodore's work and on Irish penitentials and circulated on the Continent and in England in the eighth and ninth centuries; and the *Penitential* of Egbert, possibly authorized by Egbert of York, Bede's pupil, who died in 766.[37] The penitentials attributed to "Bede" and Egbert are closely associated and were combined in some manuscripts to form what is called a "pseudo-Bede" penitential; the authorship of these texts remains unknown.[38] The other Latin document important as a source for the Old English handbooks is the *Penitential* of Halitgar of Cambrai, written in the first quarter of the ninth century.[39] Each of these documents has an extensive and largely Continental manuscript tradition; they form the immediate textual background to the Anglo-Saxon sources. The Latin texts coexisted with the vernacular handbooks and were presumably used in conjunction with them; a number of Latin penitentials are found in English manuscripts of the tenth and eleventh centuries.[40] The Anglo-Saxon penitentials draw most of the canons with which I am concerned from only two sources, Theodore's *Penitential* (which was known in several versions) and the *Penitential* of Halitgar.

The sexual offense most thoroughly discussed in the penitentials, as in the laws, is adultery. The penitentials extend the term "adultery" beyond the simplest formulation—sex between two people, at least one of whom is married—to include sexual relationships involving those who had taken religious vows. Sex between an unmarried man and a nun was considered adultery because the woman was "married" to God. A man who had been married before he became a cleric and who then returned to his wife was also guilty of adultery.[41] Penances for this sin prescribed by the handbooks were added to penalties assessed by the laws. A man's punishment for adultery, for example, would include not only a heavy fine but a penance ranging from three to ten years.

The *Penitential* of Theodore contains the most complete set of statements about adultery in all the English penitentials. The most general and the most severe penance was reserved for the man who committed "many evil deeds" ("multa mala"), including "adultery with a woman and with a beast" ("adulterium cum muliere et cum pecude"). In this case the man was required to go to a monastery and do penance until he died.[42] Most penances were less severe and were assessed for more specific acts.

The penance for a man who committed adultery depended on the woman's status. According to Theodore's *Penitential,* if a married man defiled a virgin, his penance was one year (1.2.1, *CED* 3:178; see also 1.14.10, p. 188). If she were a married woman, his penance was four years (1.2.1, p. 178), but if she were his neighbor's wife, the penance was three years (1.14.9, p. 188); if she were a slave, his penance was only six months (he also had to free her; 1.14.12, p. 188). An adulterous woman, however, did penance for seven years (1.14.14, p. 188). If she were guilty of adultery, her husband could dismiss her and marry again, if she were his first wife; if she accepted penance for her sin, she too was allowed to remarry after five years (2.12.5, p. 199). A man who did not send away his wife but continued to have sex with her, knowing that she was an adulteress, did penance for two years and had to refrain from having intercourse with her so long as she did penance herself (1.14.4, p. 188). If she committed adultery and her husband did not choose to remain with her, she could keep one-fourth of her inheritance only if she entered a monastery (2.12.10, p. 199). A priest who committed adultery was thrown out of the church and did penance among the laity for the rest of his life (1.9.5, p. 185). The lay adulterer's penance was equal to the adulteress's (i.e., seven years) only if he put away his wife and remarried (and, presumably, the wife was not guilty of adultery); he had the option of accepting a lighter penance for fifteen years (1.14.8, p. 188). The asymmetry of the power relations is obvious in every canon. The husband could dismiss an adulterous wife (2.12.5, p. 199), but a wife could not get rid of an adulterous husband unless she wanted to join a monastery (2.12.6, p. 199). "Any woman who commits adultery is in the power of her husband if he wishes to be reconciled to an adulterous woman," Theodore declared. "If he makes a reconciliation, her punishment does not concern the clergy: it belongs to her own husband" (2.12.11, p. 200).[43]

The penitentials of "Bede" and Egbert provide extensive penances for the sexual offenses of the clergy but treat adultery much less thoroughly than Theodore's *Penitential*. "Bede's" *Penitential* does not always follow the standards of Theodore's penitential where penances for adultery are provided. "Bede" assigns a penance of seven years for a man who defiled a virgin (3.12), compared to one year in Theodore (1.2.1); two years for an unmarried man who fornicated with another man's wife (3.13); and three years for the act if he had a wife of his own (3.14; all references from "Bede," *CED* 3:328). Sex with a serving woman required a penance of one year and subsequent fasts ("Bede," 3.15), compared to six months in Theodore (1.14.12); if she bore a child he had to free her ("Bede," 3.16). Egbert's *Penitential* says little about adultery but does require the man who dismisses his wife to do penance for seven years (4.9, *CED* 3:420). The priest who committed adultery was expelled from the church and required to do a lifetime of penance as a layman, a point on which Egbert's text matches Theodore's (Egbert 4.8, p. 420; Theodore 1.9.5, p. 185).

Adultery in the Anglo-Saxon Penitentials

The Latin penitentials are found in numerous copies. The four Anglo-Saxon handbooks are less well attested. The texts were very likely composed starting in the mid–tenth century; their sources are as old as the eighth century, and all the Old English handbooks are found in eleventh-century manuscripts. They are the *Confessionale Pseudo-Egberti,* which I have renamed *Scriftboc;* the *Poenitentiale Pseudo-Ecgberti,* hereafter the *Old English Penitential;*[44] the *Old English Handbook;*[45] the *Canons of Theodore* and the *Canons of Theodore, Supplement.*[46] I have listed the first three documents in the chronological order suggested by their source relationships. The *Old English Penitential* translates three books of Halitgar's *Penitential* and borrows from the *Scriftboc*. All of the canons of the *Old English Handbook* are taken from the *Old English Penitential.*[47] The *Canons of Theodore,* which is derived from the Latin penitential attributed to Theodore, is possibly contemporary with the first, the *Scriftboc*. These two texts are independent translations of parts of the *Penitential* of Theodore; the *Scriftboc* has additional sources, including the penitentials attributed to Egbert and "Bede" and Irish handbooks.

The vernacular penitentials include only a few of the regulations in the Latin texts concerning adultery and do not always correspond closely to the standards of the older documents. For example, the *Scriftboc* assigns a penance of one year to a married layman who defiled another man's wife *or* a virgin; Theodore (1.2.1, 1.14.10, *CED* 3:178,

188) also requires a penance of one year, but "Bede" sets a penance of seven years (3.12, *CED* 3:328). If she had a child, the *Scriftboc* increases the penance to three years (6ab, *DAB* 177). If a bachelor ("hægsteald") committed this sin, however, he did penance for seven years, and "some wish[ed] (it to be) ten" (6c, *DAB* 177).[48] Theodore's *Penitential* allows the woman who committed adultery to keep one-fourth of her inheritance only if she went into the monastery (in which case she would not retain it, obviously) and deprived her of her wealth if she did not do so. The Old English translator was unintentionally generous, permitting her to enter a monastery if she wished or to take one-fourth of her inheritance and leave her husband (19zγ, *DAB* 185).[49] The *Scriftboc* says that a woman cannot leave a husband who is a fornicator (19u *DAB* 185); a canon in the following chapter allows the husband to send the adulterous woman away (19zδ, *DAB* 185–86). Both canons are derived from Theodore (1.14.4 and 2.12.6, respectively, *CED* 3:188, 199). In the *Scriftboc*, as in Theodore's *Penitential*, the man's penance equaled the woman's only if he sent away one wife and took another, in which case he did a strict penance for seven years or a lighter one for fifteen (15e, *DAB* 181). Again repeating Theodore, the *Scriftboc* declared that the punishment of the adulteress was not merely the Church's responsibility; rather, her punishment is "in hyre weres handum," in her husband's hands (19zδ, *DAB* 185–86).

The *Canons of Theodore* follow Theodore's *Penitential* closely in most matters. A man who had sex with his neighbor's wife was given a penance of three years and had to abstain from intercourse with his own wife (188, Mone 525). A man could dismiss an adulterous wife, but she could not dismiss him (106–7, Mone 518). Like the *Scriftboc*, the *Old English Penitential* required a penance of seven years for adultery but also denied the adulterer the Eucharist and Christian burial unless he repented (2.8, 2.10, *DAV* 20–22). The *Old English Handbook* repeats these provisions (p. 22, lines 173–86).

Canons for adultery implicitly concerned liaisons between married people not married to each other and between married men and women and unmarried women and men. There are few penances for any heterosexual misconduct between unmarried laypersons. Incest was an exception. Sexual intercourse with one's sister required seven or twelve years of penance; intercourse between sisters is not mentioned, but sex between brothers brought a penance of fifteen years.[50] The *Scriftboc*, translating canons from the *Penitential* of "Bede," requires partners in fornication outside of marriage to fast for one year. The penance was reduced if the sin was committed only once; the penance for unmarried partners who began the act but did not consummate it was to fast during the three fasting periods and on Wednesdays and Fridays for a year (39c–39e, *DAB* 194).[51] This suggests that fornication outside of marriage was not considered a serious offense. Payer notes that canons concerning these relations are miscellaneous in nature (unlike those governing adultery, for example), and suggests that such relations were probably infrequent.[52] If the man were unmarried and if the woman or girl were not socially significant—that is, if she was a servant or slave, or could not be promised to another, or was a prostitute or otherwise "fallen"—such relations involved no significant *social* issues. But the number of women whose social standing was insignificant was small, since women were, in the main, seen either as virgin daughters or as wives.

HOMOSEXUAL ACTS IN THE PENITENTIALS

Heterosexual acts that had an impact on marriage in some way were the concern of both church and state in Anglo-Saxon England. The secular government seems to have been indifferent to homosexual acts. The Anglo-Saxon laws, as we have seen, contain no provisions for sex between men or between women. The church was intensely concerned with the regulation of same-sex behavior, however, and dealt with it within the framework of the penitentials, showing considerable thoroughness and never manifesting anything like tolerance, much less approbation, for same-sex acts.

Payer organized his survey of homosexual acts in the early medieval penitentials into nine categories, a comprehensive list that I have divided into three groups. The first division contains sex between adult males or females. Canons in the second division concern sex between boys or between a boy and a man. The third division contains references to specific sex acts: mutual masturbation, fellatio, anal intercourse ("in terga"), and interfemoral intercourse.[53] Within each group I will first survey references in the Latin texts and then those in the Old English penitentials. I will pay special attention to references to Sodom and sodomite as terms designating same-sex sins. For ease of reference, Latin texts are supplied in appendix 1, Old English texts in appendix 2 (both follow this chapter, as do tables 1–3). Summaries of penances for homosexual acts are given in table 1 (Latin texts) and table 2 (vernacular texts). Table 3 shows the number of canons in each text and the number of canons dealing with heterosexual and homosexual acts.

Sex Acts between Adult Females

Bernadette J. Brooten has shown that a "focus on penetration as the principal sexual image" in ancient Rome "led to a simplistic view of female erotic choices and a complex view of the erotic choices of free men."[54] The same dichotomy is apparent in the penitentials. Only a few general references pertain to female homosexual acts, six canons out of a total of forty-six that concern same-sex acts (13 percent). According to the *Penitential* of Theodore, "If a woman fornicates with a woman, she shall do penance for three years" (1.2.12, *CED* 3:178). In some manuscripts there is a second canon assigning the same penance to women who have sex with other women.[55] The *Penitential* of "Bede" contains the same canon and adds another: "If a nun fornicates with a nun by means of a device, she is to do penance for seven years" (3.24, *CED* 3:328).[56]

One manuscript of the *Scriftboc* incorporates Theodore's canon without change: "If a woman has intercourse with another woman, she is to fast three years" (19q, *DAB* 185). Two manuscripts, however, indicate a penance of ten years—a case in which one hopes, for the woman's sake, that confessors were aware of custom and even other authorities.[57] The *Canons of Theodore, Supplement* says the same, although it omits the reference to sex between nuns; it retains the reference to use of an artificial phallus (68.8, *ALI* 2:228). A related canon of the *Scriftboc* forbidding female masturbation shows a concern with female sex acts. But since no partner is mentioned—also the case with some references to male masturbation—the canon does not pertain to same-sex behavior: "If a woman in any way touch herself sexually so that she knows herself (she does it), she is to fast for two years, because that is a defilement to her" (19r, *DAB* 185).[58] This is a good example of the straightforwardness of the Anglo-Saxon penitentials in sexual matters: the confessor apparently asked not only if the woman touched herself but if she excited herself deliberately ("so that she knows herself").

Female homosexuality is also included in a general canon that seems to pertain to homosexual intercourse; although the gender of the offenders is not specified, Anglo-Saxon grammar permits an interpretation that includes women. "If anyone foully through unnatural things soils himself [or herself] against God's creation in any way, he [or she] is to repent that forever while he [or she] lives, until he or she be dead" (Additamenta 1, *DAV* 69). This canon is repeated in the *Old English Handbook* (p. 25, lines 275–78; appendix 2, example B). The word "unnatural" does not occur elsewhere in the penitentials, but it is found in related pastoral literature (surveyed in chapter 5). Bullough has suggested that the man who acted like a woman behaved "contrary to nature," meaning that he took the passive role in sexual intercourse; "contrary to nature" later became a term that described all acts that prevented procreation.[59] Taking into account a gender hierarchy such as that outlined by Brooten and discussed in chapter 2, which ranks, in descending order, dominant men, passive women, passive men, and dominant women, it would also seem reasonable that a woman who took the active or dominant role in intercourse with another woman would be seen as acting "against nature."[60] Thus the reference to "unnatural things against God's creation" ("ungecyndelicum ðingum ongean godes gesceafte") might well pertain to *any*one, man or woman, who sinned with his or her own sex.

Sex Acts between Adult Males in Latin Penitentials

In contrast to this scant attention to intrafemale sex acts, all penitentials, Latin and Old English, deal with intramale sex in numerous canons. The *Penitential* of Theodore includes the largest number of these canons. Three general references in Theodore's text refer to intramale intercourse and two refer to Sodom (one by implication, since it begins "Item," "likewise").

The first canon (1.2.2, *CED* 3:178) requires a penance of ten years for one who "often" fornicates with a man or beast. Another canon increases the penance to fifteen years if the offender is older than twenty (1.2.4, *CED* 3:178) but says nothing about the age of his partner. The following canon (1.2.5, *CED* 3:178) confuses matters by requiring a ten-year penance without mentioning either the frequency of the sin or the age of the sinner. Two canons referring to Sodom add further complexities. The "sodomite" receives a penance of seven years; the "mollis" receives the same penance as an adulteress (1.2.6, *CED* 3:178). Lesser penances are also specified in the continuation of this canon (1.2.7, *CED* 3:178): four years if sodomy is committed only once; fifteen years if the act is habitual; and one year less, "as a woman," if the act is not habitual.

The "mollis" is given a woman's penance, not only to intensify the shame of the penance, it would seem, but perhaps to make another point. The adulteress, as we have seen, violated a social contract between men; when she committed adultery she received a greater penance than her spouse received when he committed adultery, because they did not, in fact, do the same thing. He violated an agreement he had made with her; she violated an agreement she had made with her husband and also abrogated an agreement between her husband and her father, as well as her husband's rights over her. The "mollis" might have been like the adulteress in three respects. First, he might have taken the passive role in sexual intercourse and been "like a woman" in that sense. Second, like the adulteress, he betrayed a contract between men—not a marriage contract, but a more important one, a social, gender-based contract among manly men. The "mollis" is not merely like a woman but like a particular kind of woman—an adulteress, a woman who got out of line. Third, the adulteress's crime was public knowledge and punished by the secular government, not just the church, and this fact might well have intensified the shame visited on the "mollis" as an implicit part of his penance.

Three categories of male offender seem to be named in the *Penitential* of Theodore: "sodomite," "molles," and "masculus." The first canon, which assigns the sodomite a penance of seven years, is surprising, since it requires a lesser penance for the sodomite than for the "masculus." The "masculus" is a man who fornicates with another man ("masculus cum masculo"), and his penance is ten or fifteen years (1.2.2, 1.2.4, 1.2.5). The "mollis" is punished "as an adulteress"; according to Theodore the adulteress's penance is seven years (1.14.14, *CED* 3:188), and this is the same penance that the sodomite receives. The author does not say that the sodomite is also punished as an adulteress—that is, with a penance of seven years—although this was the case. Neither partner, apparently, was regarded as more responsible than the other; the "mollis" was associated with a woman; the other, the sodomite, was not. It would seem fair to say that the "mollis," who was perhaps the passive partner in the act, was meant to be shamed by this association with the adulteress.

The second canon dealing with the sodomite (1.2.7) is cryptic. A man who is full-grown ("virile") receives a penance of four years for performing "this wicked deed" once, that deed ("hoc scelus") being what sodomites, named in the preceding canon, do (Theodore 1.2.6). But the habitual offender receives a penance of fifteen years, a penance much greater than the seven years given to the "sodomite" (1.2.6). The next provision suggests a penance "one year less" if the sin is not habitual. This statement is very unclear. Does it mean three years, one year less than four (which was the penance if the act was committed only once), or fourteen years? John T. McNeill and Helena M. Gamer (*MHP* 185 note 47) suggest that the former was the case and that a penance of three years matches that assigned to a woman who fornicated with another woman, a penance specified in a canon that follows shortly in the text (1.2.12, *CED* 3:178). The details are confusing and, finally, undecidable, but we can see that, three times in two canons concerning the sodomite and the "molles" (1.2.6, 1.2.7), the penances for men who engage in sex with other men are compared to penances for women. (I am reminded of Mae West's "quaintly sexist" belief, recounted by Vito Russo, that New York police should not beat up on homosexuals because "a homosexual is a female soul in a male body. 'You're hitting a woman, I says.'")[61]

Two points seem clear. First, even within a single text, there were multiple and sometimes contradictory options for assigning penances for homosexual acts and other sins. Confessors seem to have had considerable leeway, which suggests that they asked detailed questions about the habits of those who confessed to them in order to determine which of the available penances would be appropriate. Second, the use of penances for women and women's status in canons pertaining to male homosexual acts indicates that homosexual intercourse was thought of as a perversion of heterosexual coupling. When two Anglo-Saxon men had sex, ecclesiastical authorities not only thought of one of them as a woman but treated him like one.

Two of five canons concerning adult male homosexual acts in Theodore's *Penitential* make reference to Sodom. "Bede's" *Penitential* also refers to Sodom and shows that this word was a touchstone for a specific manner of intercourse. A penance of four years is assigned to the sodomite (3.19, *CED* 3:328) and seven years if the sin is habitual (matching Theodore 1.2.6) or if the offender is a monk (3.20, *CED* 3: 328). The first of these canons is a reference point for a later canon assessing a penance of four years for anal intercourse between husband and wife ("in terga nupserit"), which is called "a sodomitical sin" ("quia sodomiticum scelus est," 3.39, *CED* 3:329). The four-year penance matches both Theodore's penance for a man who commits the sin of the sodomites only once and "Bede's" penance for the sodomite (3.19). The penance concerning heterosexual anal intercourse should be compared to the one immediately before it, which sets a penance of forty days for the man who fornicates with his wife "from behind" ("retro," 3.38, *CED* 3:329). Mark D. Jordan has argued that references connecting sodomy to male anal sex "are not easy to find," and this is true.[62] But the juxtaposition of "Bede" 3.19 and 3.39 strongly suggests this connection.

Sodomy was more gravely punished when it involved monks, as "Bede's" text shows. In contrast to Theodore's *Penitential,* which contains no canons concerning homosexual acts between members of the clergy, Egbert's *Penitential,* like some Irish handbooks, mentions sins of clerical fornication several times. Egbert's text contains one reference to homosexual fornication involving a priest (part of a canon assessing

penance for fornication with a woman or a nun), assigning seven years
of penance if the sin is habitual (5.4, *CED* 3:421). The *Scriftboc* includes
this canon but does not include the reference to fornication with a man
(1c, *DAB* 176). The penitential assigns men who fornicate "in terga" a
penance of three years (Egbert 5.19, *CED* 3:422).

Egbert's *Penitential* does not use references of Sodom to identify
intercourse "in terga" but refers to sodomy in some form ("sodomita")
three times. The first is in a list of capital sins ("De capitalia crimina").
As in "Bede's" and Theodore's handbooks, the form given is "sodomitae" ("sodomite," which means "the inhabitants of Sodom" [1, *CED*
3:419]). (Another list of sins, not part of a penitential, uses a nomina-
tive form, "sodomy," "sodomiticum.")[63] Egbert's second reference to
sodomy ("sodomitae") occurs in the chapter "De minoribus peccatis":
"Again concerning sodomy, if it is habitual, for a bishop, fifteen years,
for a priest, twelve years, for a deacon, ten years, for a subdeacon, nine
years, for a cleric, seven years, for a layperson, five years" (2.2, *CED*
3:419).[64] An important English manuscript of the *Penitential* of Egbert
calls attention to sodomy by beginning a new chapter at this point, "De
sodomitis."[65] The third reference to "sodomites" deals with both laity
and clergy and occurs in a chapter of penances for the clergy: "Again
concerning the sodomite, sometimes ten years, that is for he who does
it often, or is in orders; sometimes seven, sometimes one for the
'molles,' sometimes 100 days for boys" (5.17, *CED* 3:422).[66] Once again
a penance of ten years is specified for the habitual sodomite. But lesser
penalties are also offered. Egbert's is the only penitential that both
makes reference to Sodom and requires a ten-year penance. When the
sinner is called a sodomite, Theodore's text offers lesser penances that
correspond to those found in "Bede's" penitential (i.e., four to seven
years). It is tempting to believe that the sodomite was punished less
severely for a reason—perhaps because he was seen as younger (i.e., a
boy) or weaker than other penitents. This evidence does suggest that
the "sodomite" was seen as *a type* of person in the period, although we
cannot step from that claim to the assertion that sodomite was a sexual
identity in the sense we think of it.

Sex Acts between Adult Males in Anglo-Saxon Penitentials

All four vernacular handbooks include penances for same-sex acts between men. The all-purpose canon concerning one who does "unnatural things" "against God's creation" (seen above) pertains to male as
well as female homosexual acts (Additamenta 1, *DAV* 69; *Old English
Handbook*, 25, lines 275–78). Translating Theodore 1.2.2, the *Scriftboc*

stipulates a penance of ten years for intercourse with a man or with an animal: "Whoever fornicates with an animal or a male person is to fast ten years" (9d, *DAB* 178). The *Old English Penitential* draws penances for male homosexual intercourse from the *Penitential* of Halitgar, which assigns somewhat longer penances of fifteen years (for a man age twenty or older) or a lifelong fast (for a married man of forty; 2.6, *DAV* 18–19). In the *Old English Penitential* this canon appears in a chapter entitled "Concerning those men who have illicit fornication, that is with animals, or soil themselves with young ones, or a man who has sex with another" (2.6, *DAV* 18). But the canon itself is some- what less comprehensive than the heading suggests.[67] The *Old English Handbook* repeats this canon, without the chapter heading (22, lines 164–70). The provisions differ significantly from standards defined by the *Penitential* of Theodore or by texts attributed to "Bede" and Egbert. Nowhere else in the English evidence are the ages of twenty and forty used as benchmarks for the severity of penances, and nowhere else is marriage mentioned as a factor in the penance of a man who has sex with another man. The demand of a lifelong penance is rare, although it is also used in the general canon prohibiting acts "against God's cre- ation" in the *Old English Penitential* and *Old English Handbook* (Addi- tamenta 1, *DAV* 69; *Old English Handbook*, 25, lines 275–78).

The *Canons of Theodore (CTH)* contains two general references to male homosexual intercourse. Neither makes reference to Sodom, but both contain vocabulary that poses special problems. According to the first reference, "If a 'bædling' fornicate with a 'bædling,' he is to fast for ten years. He who does this as a grown man ['werlice'] fasts for four years" (*CTH* 138–39, Mone 521). The first sentence translates the *Penitential* of Theodore 1.2.5 ("Si masculus cum masculo"). The second sentence translates Theodore 1.2.7 ("virile scelus semel faciens IIII. an- nos peniteat"), but fails to include "semel" (once) and so offers no jus- tification for the lighter penance. The *Canons of Theodore, Supplement (CTHS)* substitutes "unwærlice" (incautiously, foolishly, heedlessly) for "werlice," and so justifies the lighter penance (*CTHS* 68.6, *ALI* 2:228).

CTHS is a short but important text. It contains only twenty-two canons, all of them concerning sexual acts found in the *Penitential* of Theodore. Most of the canons in Theodore's *Penitential* pertaining to male homosexual acts (1.2.2–1.2.7) are included in *CTHS*. *CTHS* mer- its special attention because two of its canons (68.5–6) are the only evi- dence in the Anglo-Saxon penitentials for the use of the word "sod- omy" (*ALI* 2:228). Unfortunately, the text of *CTHS* is sometimes ambiguous because, like *CTH, CTHS* uses no chapter headings or other organizational plan. In Theodore's *Penitential* the target of a particular penance is almost always clear from the context of a given chapter. Theodore's chapter on "various failings of the servants of God," for example, gives penances for priests and then for monks, including a canon pertaining to boys in the latter sequence (1.8.1–14; 1–5 concern priests, 6–14 concern monks; 1.8.11 includes boys). Thus it is always clear to whom a general pronoun or "qui" refers. *CTH* includes a number of these canons (1.8.1–2, 5–7, 10–11) but does not indicate precisely to whom they apply, and in some cases important ambiguities arise. This is the case with the canons referring to sodomy.

As we have seen, the *Penitential* of Theodore 1.2.6 is a two-part canon that assigns the sodomite a penance of seven years and specifies that the "mollis" receives the same penance as the adulteress, also seven years (*CED* 3:178). The first clause is directly translated into Old English: "sodomisce .vii. gear. fæston" (*CTHS* 68.5). However, Theodore's reference to the "molles" is not; instead the translator writes "hi beoð hnesclice swa forlegene" (*CTHS* 68.6). Rather than account for the "molles" with a single Old English word, the translator uses an adjective and describes the molles (plural) as "hneslice," as in "they are as wanton [or soft, or weak] as the adulteress." The Old English "forlegene," used substantively, is ambiguous. "Forlegene" can mean simply "fornicator," but that category is inadequate to the meaning of the source, which clearly specifies an adulteress ("adultera"); the word used elsewhere for adulteress (and also for prostitute) is "forlegis."[68] The translator in *CTH* simplifies and clarifies the meaning but also omits the crucial point that the man's penance could be adjusted so that it matched a woman's.

Intramale intercourse between brothers was also prohibited. This sin is never associated with Sodom or the sins of sodomites. Theodore's *Penitential* assigns natural brothers who engage in sex a penance of fifteen years (1.2.19, *CED* 3:179); the regulation is repeated in the *Penitential* of Egbert (4.5, *CED* 3:420). *CTH* and *CTHS* are the only Anglo-Saxon penitentials to repeat this prohibition (*CTH* 147, Mone 521; *CTHS* 68.14, *ALI* 2:230). Both retain the penance of fifteen years, which equals the most severe penance for male homosexual intercourse, reserved in Theodore's *Penitential* and the Old English translation of the *Penitential* of Halitgar for those over the age of twenty (*Penitential* of Theodore 1.2.4, *CED* 3:178; *DAV* 2.6, 18–19).

Sex Acts between Boys and Men

Irish penitentials and those by Theodore, "Bede," and Egbert contain several canons concerning the sexual activities of boys. The Anglo-

Saxon vernacular penitentials devote more canons to sexual acts involving boys than they do to those in which only adults engaged. Concern with the sexuality of boys was not a particular feature of medieval Irish or English culture, however; the topic is familiar in studies of ancient Greece and spans the period from late Rome to the twelfth century and beyond.[69] References to boys' sex acts fall into two categories, sex acts between boys and sex acts between boys and men, with most canons in the former category.

The Latin vocabulary divides references to children into two groups: regulations concerning "infantes," children up to seven years of age who are mentioned only in the context of others' confessions, not their own, and "pueri," from seven to twenty, who confessed themselves.[70] Sex acts between boys were first described in Irish penitentials and usually received mild penances. The *Penitential* of Cummean contains a chapter "on the sinful playing of boys," which included kissing, masturbating, imitating acts of fornication, bestiality, interfemoral intercourse, fellatio, anal intercourse, and heterosexual intercourse.[71] Penances for kissing with or without "pollution," meaning ejaculation, ranged from a few "special fasts" (undefined) for boys to a harsh remedy for anyone twenty years of age or older. At that point, the sinner had to live on bread and water and was "excluded from the church" (Cummean 10.6–7, *IP* 126–27). Mutual masturbation between "boys of twenty years" required a penance of twenty or forty days, one hundred days if the sin were repeated, and one year if more frequently (Cummean 10.6–7, *IP* 128–29). Interfemoral intercourse between boys received a penance of one hundred days for the first offense or one year upon repetition (Cummean 10.8, *IP* 128–29). The next canon deals with sex between two boys, requiring the younger boy to perform penance: "If a small boy is abused by an older one, if he is ten years of age, he shall fast for a week; if he consents, for twenty days" ("Puer paruulus oppressus a maiore annum aetatis habens decimum, ebdomadam dierum ieiunet; si consentit, .xx. diebus"; Cummean 10.9, *IP* 128–29).

Theodore's *Penitential* provides just one canon for same-sex acts between boys: "If boys fornicate between themselves, he [Theodore] judged that they are to be beaten" (1.2.11, *CED* 3:178). Elsewhere in Theodore's *Penitential* and in Egbert's *Penitential,* references to boys' sexual activity occur in canons primarily devoted to men's sexual behavior. Theodore 1.2.7 is an example. A corresponding canon in Egbert's *Penitential* (5.17, *CED* 3:422) likewise includes boys. Theodore assessed boys a penance of two years for the first offense and four years upon repetition. Egbert's penance of one hundred days for boys is much milder. The sin for which the boy receives penance was the same as for the man, sodomy; the "boy" in question could be up to twenty years old. Egbert's *Penitential* requires boys who fornicate "in terga" to do penance for two years (5.19, *CED* 3:422).

The *Penitential* of "Bede" contains a series of penances for the sex acts of boys, including mutual masturbation (forty days of penance) and interfemoral intercourse (one hundred days or, for older boys, three forty-day fasts; "Bede" 3.31, *CED* 3:329). This text also includes two different penances for a boy who is forced into intercourse: "3.22 If a boy suffers being oppressed in such a way [raped], forty days, or psalms, [or] he is admonished to continence. . . . 3.32 If a small boy is forced [into intercourse] by an older boy, one week; if he consents [to it], twenty days" (*CED* 3:328, 329). The second canon derives from the canon in the *Penitential* of Cummean seen above.

All four of the Anglo-Saxon penitentials include canons concerning the sexual conduct of boys. The *Scriftboc* includes the following canons in a chapter on the "unlawful deeds of young men," a heading derived directly from a chapter on the "sinful playing of boys" from Cummean's penitential.[72] These two canons concern boys who have sexual intercourse. The first requires the boy forced into sex by an older boy to do penance for either seven or twenty days, the latter number if he consented to the act: "If a small boy has been forced by a larger one into intercourse, he (is to fast) seven [five] nights; if he consents to it, he is to fast twenty nights" (7a, *DAB* 177).[73] The second concerns boys who have sex together: "Boys who fornicate are to be beaten" (9e, *DAB* 178–79). The second canon derives from Theodore 1.2.11, the first from "Bede" 3.32.

The interrelationship between men's and boys' sex acts appears more complicated in the *Old English Penitential* (2.6, *DAV* 18–19), which contains a provision for boys who have sex that is repeated without change in the *Old English Handbook* (22, lines 164–70). The heading announces penances for men who have intercourse with animals, young men or boys, or other men. But the canon that follows, as we have seen, makes no reference to sexual intercourse between men and boys. At the end, however, it requires that young and ignorant ones are to be beaten if they engage in intercourse, as in Theodore 1.2.11. ("Geonglicum" should be translated "with young men, or boys," rather than "with children," which is a possible translation, since the intercourse is unlawful, and since the text elsewhere provides for unlawful sex with young women.)

CTH lays down similar provisions concerning interfemoral intercourse between boys: "183. If [an adult male] does it between (the limbs, i.e., interfemorally), [he is to fast] one year or the three forty-day periods. 184. If it is a boy, he is to fast twenty days or be beaten. 185. If he [the boy] does it with one in orders, he is to fast the three forty-day periods or one year" (Mone 525). It appears that the young boy received the same penance for interfemoral intercourse as an adult, although this is a case in which the lack of a chapter heading targeting the penance is significant. *CTH* 180 concerns monks and nuns; the next two canons concern men who ejaculate because they stimulate their thoughts, including when they sleep in church; canon 183 addresses "he" who has interfemoral intercourse; canon 184 names the boy; and canon 185 seems to continue to be concerned with a boy, since the adult involved is a monk (canon 180), who is a "man in orders," and whose penalty for interfemoral intercourse has already been given (canon 183).

Thus canon 185 seems to require that a boy who has sex with a man in orders must fast one year, or the three fasting periods, a requirement similar to that seen above in the canons concerning a small boy forced into intercourse by an older one (although their penances, of five or twenty days of fasting, were much lighter). It is the younger boy who had to do penance, not the older one who abused him or, in the canon from *CTH,* the man in orders. It would seem logical that such provisions would seek to protect boys from the sexual advances of older men, but that does not seem to be the intent of the canons. These penances were probably intended to purify the boy and remove the pollution of sexual intercourse from him. The demand that the boy do penance for an act he did not initiate, or even participate in willingly, also suggests that he is seen as a temptation to older men, and that even though he is young, he must be held accountable for his effect on them. In reference to these punishments, Payer commented that the penitentials "usually do not penance an act in which consent is lacking" and suggested that the canon "was meant to serve an educational function and was not simply punitive."[74] I would be less inclined to distinguish the punitive from the educational function of the canon. Violence was a fundamental part of classical and medieval pedagogical traditions; beatings were part of the students' routine. This violence was not a gratuitous form of abuse but rather served a pedagogical principle that stressed the role of physical pain in training the memory.[75] The young boy who was exploited by an older boy or a man was punished—more severely if he consented to the act—to help him remember that the experience was not to be repeated. We have seen above that boys who had sex with each other were beaten; sexual misbehavior was just one of many acts that involved them with a violent form of discipline.

However, from the very beginning of Western monasticism, physical contact between men and boys was strictly prohibited. Greenberg cites examples beginning with the early fourth-century rule of Pachomius.[76] Such rules inveighed against monks who took advantage of young boys or novices, forbidding the men from touching the boys or kissing them on the lips. Fierce prohibition of such contact is found in *Libri duo de synodalibus causis et disciplinis ecclesiasticis* by Regino of Prüm (published in 906). The cleric or monk who had intimate contact with a young man or boy was whipped in public; his head was shaved, he was spat on, imprisoned in chains, and lived on bread and water for part of the day for six months. For six months following this humiliation he was allowed to move about only with supervision. According to Michael Goodich, who sums up this ordeal, "This penance for wayward monks became a standard text in all later penitentials and was later inserted in Gratian's authoritative canon law collection of the twelfth century."[77]

Some idea of the reputations of monasteries as places of sexual temptation in the later medieval period can be gleaned from Boswell's version of an anecdote told by the twelfth-century chronicler Walter Mapp:

> When Bernard of Clairvaux was asked to restore life to the dead son of a Marquess of Burgundy he had the boy taken into a private room and lay down upon him. No cure transpired; the boy remained lifeless. The chronicler, who had been present, nonetheless found humor in the incident and remarked, "That was the unhappiest monk of all. For I've never heard of any monk who lay down upon a boy that did not straightaway rise up after him." The abbot blushed and they went out as many laughed.[78]

This anecdote is shadowed by the act described in "Bede's" *Penitential,* in which "a small boy is forced [into intercourse] by an older boy" and is made to perform a week's penance, or a penance of twenty days "if he consents [to it]" (3.32, *CED* 3:328). The custom joked about at Bernard's expense was not new to his time. The abbot's blush indicates that there is nothing "closeted" about the act.

Latin colloquies used to teach boys suggest that at certain times the propriety of intimate relations was openly discussed. In a passage in a Latin colloquy, Dominus (an older brother) asks Fraterculus (a boy) to accompany him to the lavatory. Fraterculus refuses but then receives permission from the master to do so in order to carry a lamp. This text also suggests that sex and gender were separated in monastic education so that boys could play roles when instructors required them to do so.

At one point the speaker calls to his "wife" to kiss him; his companion calls to a "young girl."[79] Colloquies, we know from the famous Latin and Old English example of the form, required boys to play roles of various kinds (taking the voices of those in certain occupations, for example).[80] We should see these works in the context of an educational tradition that allowed children—boys, at least—access to texts that were considered dangerous for adults.[81] Texts that permitted what we think of as role playing were used to help boys understand both sides of situations in which erotic violence could be a factor (e.g., the view of a rape victim as well as the perpetrator of the crime). Texts that required a boy to play a woman's part, or that described boys in compromising situations (the visit to the lavatory) belonged to a school tradition that taught boys important lessons of adolescence and control. Marjorie Woods has described the boys' situation as "a site of anxiety about control in two directions: those who control the boy and those whom he might be able to control."[82] If the dialogue can be thought of as a script for a performance, both female roles would have been taken by boys, just as boys would have taken women's roles in early liturgical performances, such as the Easter trope of the three women who approached Christ's tomb. In this tradition the *Regularis concordia,* which was written at Winchester near the end of the tenth century, assigned brothers to take these roles in imitation of the women.[83]

A queer theorist might want to argue at this point that the liturgical tradition supported or even introduced a certain "instability" of genders into the training of boys at monastic schools. But gender instability was a secondary issue; the primary tension being explored was that between child and adult. Boys "can try out the roles of both genders" in such exercises as those Woods describes because the focus was on power relations rather than sexual relations. "Rape scenes function in this tradition as the paradigmatic site for working out issues of power and powerlessness," Woods writes.[84] Exercises in which boys took girls' or women's parts, or the parts of boys in dangerous situations, were used to teach boys the right thing to do (ask for permission, for example). We must distinguish between such exercises or rituals— a young man performing a woman's role in sacred liturgy, for example—and the same young man, or a boy, being forced into sexual intercourse by an older monk. In the former act, taking a woman's part was a "manly" (i.e., appropriate and honorable) thing to do; in the latter it was not, and, as we have seen, the boy or young man was punished for being taken advantage of, whether he consented to the act or not. The penitential is not an exercise that teaches the powerless how to resist the powerful or how to behave correctly. It is, rather, a text that testifies to the complete success of an often-violent pedagogical tradition that allowed the powerless to speak only through subject positions created by the powerful. Boys did not create the texts that described their behavior. They learned how to argue both sides of a case through declamatory exercises that include examples of male prostitution.[85] But there was no argument in the case of the abused young boy. The Irish penitentials focus on the discipline of boys within monastic life. None of the Anglo-Saxon penitentials is a monastic document, but they retain canons concerning young boys, although reducing them in number. Even the *Old English Handbook,* the latest and shortest of these texts, includes a canon about boys, although canons concerning many other offenses are omitted. Boys and young men were thought to be capable of sexual intercourse—they were "sexually active"—and their sexual conduct formed part of a larger regulatory code. If we see the penitentials as a pedagogical as well as a disciplinary part of this code, they would, in their treatment of boys, seem to illustrate the principle that violence is a powerful teacher of proper behavior.

OTHER SEX ACTS

Nearly all the homosexual acts prohibited by the penitentials have been discussed in the canons analyzed up to this point. Two—interfemoral intercourse and oral sex or fellatio—have not. Theodore's *Penitential* assessed a penance of one year or the three forty-day fasting periods for interfemoral intercourse (1.2.8, *CED* 3:178). "Bede" required only a fast of the three forty-day periods (3.21, *CED* 3:328), while Egbert's *Penitential* required men who fornicated interfemorally to accept a penance of one year the first time and two years the second (5.18, *CED* 3:422). "Bede" assessed a penance for interfemoral intercourse involving boys of one hundred days or, for older boys, of three forty-day fasts (3.31, *CED* 3:329). As we have seen, both *CTH* and *CTHS* include interfemoral intercourse, assigning the same penance as Theodore did (*CTH* 140, Mone 521; *CTHS* 68.6, *ALI* 2:228).

Oral intercourse, or fellatio, carried a penance of seven years. According to the *Penitential* of Theodore, "Who releases semen into the mouth, seven years of penance; this is the worst evil" (1.2.15, *CED* 3:178). This could be a heterosexual or homosexual offense. It seems that in the *Scriftboc* the penance is addressed to men, since it follows the penance for bestiality (6e–6g, *DAB* 177). In *CTH* the canon follows one concerning fornication between boys (144–45, Mone 521). In *CTHS* the canon carries an added comment concerning its gravity:

"from some it was judged that they should do penance for it until the end of their lives" (68.10, *ALI* 2:228–30). The plural forms are important, since both partners seem to be assessed a penance. The severity of the lifelong penance is remarkable, especially since *CTHS* assesses lesser penalties for other sexual acts, including anal sex between men and incest. An offense that would seem to be related, drinking blood or semen, carries a penance of only three years (Theodore 1.7.3, *CED* 3:182), and the same penance is given to a woman for mixing semen in food as an aphrodisiac (Theodore 1.14.15, *CED* 3:188). Both penances are also found in the *Scriftboc* (9b, 19h, *DAB* 178, 184).

Sodom and Sexual Identities

The most intriguing evidence amid the data just surveyed is the terminology used to describe men who engaged in same-sex intercourse and the differences in the number of years of penance assessed for this behavior. The sodomite received a lesser penance than other men who engaged in homosexual acts. Two vernacular sources, *CTH* and *CTHS*, specify penances for the "bædling," a term without precise correspondence to the Latin terms "molles" or "sodomite." This lack of correspondence raises questions of sexual identity. Were there categories of identity for men who engaged in same-sex behavior? Were they seen as "types" of men and recognized as such by the church?

Theodore's *Penitential* uses three categories to describe men who have sex with other men: "masculus," "sidomitae," and "molles" (1.2.2, 1.2.5–6, *CED* 3:178). The Old English translator(s) used two terms, "bædling" and "wæpendman," to translate Latin "masculus," perhaps supplying the Anglo-Saxon equivalents of Latin "sodomite" and "molles." Theodore 1.2.2 identifies two parties, "whoever" ("qui") and a "man" ("masculo," "with a man"): "Qui sepe cum masculo aut cum pecude fornicat, X. annos ut peniteret judicavit." This could be rewritten as "[Si masculus] sepe cum masculo aut cum pecude fornicat, X. annos ut peniteret judicavit." The Anglo-Saxon author translates "qui" as "se ðe," and "masculo" as "bædlinge," but then, before translating "pecude," which means "animal," adds "oþþe mid oþrum wæpnedman" (with other males): "Se ðe mid bædlinge hæme. oððe mid oðrum wæpnedmen. oððe mid nytene. fæste X. winter." The translator distinguishes two kinds of men, naming first the "bædling" and then all other men. The penance is not for the "bædling" but for the man (whoever, "qui" or "se ðe") who has sex with him or "with other males," "mid oþrum wæpnedman." It appears that the translator differentiated between the "bædling" and other men, "real men" or manly men, "wæpnedmen." This would suggest that the "bædling" is the *kind* of man who was known for having sex with other men, perhaps a male prostitute, or a man who took the passive role and was notorious, or at least labeled, for doing so. The "bædling" was not just another male, a "wæpnedman." But why was he called a "bædling"?

The word "bædling" is used again in the translation of Theodore 1.2.5 ("si masculus cum masculo"). Both *CTH* 138 and *CTHS* 68.6 translate this phrase as "se bædling mid bædlinge." This canon seems to narrow the meaning of the first reference to the "bædling," no longer distinguishing between the "bædling" and the "wæpnedman" (the ordinary man) but now dealing only with "bædlings" who have sex with each other. Even though his penance is the same as that for a "real" man, a "masculus" who has sex with a "bædling"—that is, ten years— he is given a different label, suggesting that the "bædling" was seen as a special kind of man with reference to his sexual habits.

"Bædling" is a very rare word in Old English but it has enjoyed more celebrity than most esoteric vocabulary from the period and is attested in the *OED* as late as 1600. Apart from *CTH* and *CTHS,* the word occurs only in a gloss for the Latin "molles" and "effeminati." "Bædling" is defined in the century-old standard Anglo-Saxon dictionary as "homo delicatus," "a delicate fellow, tenderling, one who lies much in bed," with its roots in "bed." But no authority for this interpretation is offered.[86] The word is translated in the new *Dictionary of Old English,* with appropriate caution, as "homosexual?"[87] It has been suggested that "bædling" is a derivative of "bæddel," "hermaphrodite," but also meaning "effeminate fellow, womanish man," and that "bædling" is therefore related to the root of Modern English "bad." Citing Julius Zupitza, the *OED* says that Middle English "badde" (Modern English "bad") derives from "bæddel," a suggestion repeated in the *Middle English Dictionary.*[88] It would indeed be striking if the Modern English word for general, undefined evil, "not good," were to have come from contemptuous application of an Old English word meaning "hermaphrodite," and possibly, by extension, "effeminate person." This suggestion has been noted in the *Times Literary Supplement* as an example of how "the evil imputed to a sexual minority has been universalized." Making this observation, Wayne Dynes asks, "Could one ask for a clearer case of the linguistic oppression imposed by the majority on a sexual minority?"[89] Greenberg offers the suggestion too, without citing his source, presumably the *OED.*[90]

The word "bædling" is also noteworthy because the suffix "-ling" is diminutive, suggesting possibly a younger person or one marked by this term for subordinate status.[91] But the matter is hardly settled. The

OED (with less enthusiasm) also cites Gregor Sarrazin's proposal that "badde" is derived from Old English "ge-bædd, ge-badd," meaning "forced, oppressed," "with a sense-development parallel to that of L. 'captivus,' 'taken by force, enslaved,'" as in French "chetif," and ME "caitiff," 'worthless, wretch.' This etymology would link "bædling" to one of "oppressed status." Old English "bædan" means "to impel, to afflict, to oppress." If Sarrazin were right, the "bædling" was named after his status in society, that is, "oppressed one." This derivation would connote sexual submissiveness, suggesting that the "bædling" was the passive partner. A pun between "bædling" and "bædan" is possible in any case. The term "bædling" might have developed from "bæddel," "hermaphrodite," because this man could be either "man" or "woman," either the active partner (when having sex with another "bædling") or the passive partner (when having sex with a "masculus," "wæpnedman").

The linguistic value of this evidence is considerable, but it is important to remember that in the penitentials the word occurs only in two closely related translations of the *Penitential* of Theodore, both of them possibly contemporary with the earliest of the vernacular handbooks, the *Scriftboc.* The three vernacular handbooks whose development is closely related—the *Scriftboc,* the *Old English Penitential,* and the *Old English Handbook*—do not use "bædling" to refer either to adult males or to boys in relation to same-sex behavior. The term was obviously not in wide use in the period, and attaching great significance to it might well exaggerate its relation to the sexual terminology of the Anglo-Saxons. I suggest that the "bædling" was a man who was known to have sex with other men. He was not the *only* kind of man who had homosexual intercourse; other men, "wæpnedmen," as *CTHS* 68.6 makes clear, could also be sexual partners of "whomever" this canon was directed at. The "bædling" evidently could have sex with two kinds of men: ordinary men, who usually preferred women partners, or "bædlings," men like himself who usually had sex with other men or with each other. This seems a plausible interpretation of both Theodore 1.2.2 and *CTHS* 68.6, although Theodore does not use a special term for this man but simply refers to him as "masculo."

It is confusing that the Anglo-Saxon translator introduced a special term, "bædling," where Theodore used none, but did not do so in two cases when Theodore's text required it, "sodomite" and "molles." Theodore assigned sodomites a penance of seven years, and the "molles" the same penance as the adulteress, also seven years (1.2.6). Recent scholars are in general agreement on the meaning of "molles." Boswell argued that "molles" means "weak-willed" or "debauched," possibly "wanton" or "unrestrained."[92] According to Halperin, in Greek texts "molles" describes bisexual rather than exclusively homosexual males.[93] Payer identifies the "mollis" as the passive partner.[94]

The translator of *CTHS* seems not to have understood who or what the "mollis" was. Theodore's text states: "Sidomitae VII. annos peniteat; molles sicut adultera" (1.2.6); the translator, however, wrote, "Sodomisce .vii. gear. fæston. hi beoð hnesclice swa forlegene." "Sodomisce" looks like an adjective, not a noun, but should be translated as a substantive, "sodomitical ones." The translator did not know what to make of the "molles" and elided the difference between the sodomite and the "molles," so that sodomites, not the "molles," are described as being "as wanton as the adulteress." It appears that the translator thought that the "molles" and the "sodomite" were the same persons, that they were as "soft" or corrupt as adulteresses, and that they hence received the same penance as these women.

The distinction between the Latin terms is clear. Theodore's usage is mirrored in Egbert's *Penitential,* which includes the "molles" in a list of "capital sins" (or, more precisely, capital sinners): "molles, sodomita, maledici, perjuri" ("De capitalia crimina," 1, *CED* 3:419). The source for this list is Paul's first letter to the Corinthians (1 Corinthians 6:9–10), which lists the "molles" among those who shall not enter the kingdom of heaven: "neque fornicarii, neque idolis servientes, neque adulteri, neque molles, neque masculorum concubitores, neque fures, neque avari, neque ebriosi, neque maledici, neque rapaces regnum Dei possidebunt." Modern translators interpret these terms variously, and the distinctions among them—for example, between the "molles" and the "masculorum concubitores" (male prostitutes or concubines)—might not be absolute.[95] Significantly, "sodomite" is not one of the categories named in Paul's letter. The Pseudo-Theodore *Penitential,* a mid-ninth-century compilation based on Theodore, Egbert, and Bede, quotes part of Paul's list: "Neque molles, neque masculorum concubitores, regnum Dei possidebunt."[96] (A copy of this Latin text is found in the same manuscript as *CTHS,* the text containing the canons concerning the "bædling.")

The translator might have thought that the "molles" and the "sodomites" were one and the same, although they were not the same in Latin sources. The surprising thing is that the translator did not equate the "mollis" and the "bædling" or the sodomite and the "bædling." His terminology does not parallel Theodore's, suggesting that the Anglo-Saxon translator did not understand what his source was referring to, which, given other errors in the text, is a strong possibility. But this failure does not invalidate the fact that the translator *did* distinguish between the "masculus," who had sex with another man, and the "bæd-ling." Like Theodore, the translator assesses the sodomite a lighter penance than other men who engage in homosexual intercourse— seven years for the sodomite, compared to ten for the "bædling" and the "wæpnedman." Perhaps the sodomite received a seemingly lighter penance because he was a "womanly" man, an effeminate, rather than a "manly" man. But I say "seemingly lighter" because part of the pen-ance seems to be being degraded to the category of woman.

No absolutely certain answers to the identity of the "bædling" or the "molles" are forthcoming. But the language of the Latin penitentials and the Anglo-Saxon *CTH* and *CTHS* raises the intriguing possibility that there were social categories of men defined by their sexual behav-ior in Anglo-Saxon England. We can easily distinguish the manly man from the sodomite, whose penance was less. But we cannot readily dis-tinguish the manly man (the "wæpnedman") from the "bædling" (the effeminate man) because they received the same penance. It is difficult to imagine why, if these men had the same identity, their categories had different names. At the same time, if they had different identities, it is difficult to imagine why their penances for certain acts were the same.

A SOCIOLOGY OF SEX

No sociology of sex could be constructed from these details, but some conclusions about the sociology of sex in the Anglo-Saxon period can be drawn at this point, in three areas at least: the proportion of sexual sins relative to other sins in the penitentials; the proportion of homo-sexual to heterosexual acts; and the severity of penances for homo-sexual sins relative to those assigned for sinful heterosexual acts.

First, the sex acts punished in the laws—always heterosexual acts— take up a relatively small proportion of most codes. For example, of the ninety statutes of Æthelberht's laws, seven concern sex acts and another twelve concern marriage and social situations related to marital status (e.g., the protection of women, provisions for divorce, compensation for unmarried women), or about 21 percent of the code. Four of the twenty-eight laws of Wihtred, 14 percent, concern sexual unions; no particular sex acts are mentioned. Eight of the seventy-seven statutes of Alfred, nearly 10 percent, concern sexual crimes. The Treaty of Ed-ward and Guthrum stipulates twelve points, three of which concern sexual conduct. But some collections—I and II Edward; I–III and V Æthelstan—do not mention sexual offenses at all, and no law codes deal with same-sex acts.

There were no legal consequences for either intramale or intra-female sex, but presumably there were social consequences for the men and women who accepted the Church's harsh penalties for these acts, and those penalties would have created loss of face in their communities. Severe as the Church's penalties were, lack of legal sanctions undoubtedly eased conditions for men and women who had sex with their own kind. There must have been those who engaged in this behavior without confessing it, or perhaps without going to confession at all, even though they were expected to do so. Avoiding an encounter with the law was more difficult than avoiding confession, and the ubiquitous laments in homilies and other texts that Christians were failing to perform their required duties suggest that many Anglo-Saxons did not obey the Church's teachings simply because obedience was demanded or expected.

Regulations concerning sex form a much higher percentage of most penitentials. Using Latin penitentials thought to have been written in England, and the Anglo-Saxon penitentials, I have calculated the percentage of canons that concern sex acts and the ratio between heterosexual and homosexual acts (see table 3 for a summary). According to Payer, from 24 to 45 percent of various early Latin penitentials concern matters related to sex.[97] What constitutes a "sex-related" canon is not always obvious. An example is a provision concerning women who mix semen with their food "for an increase of love." The preparation of this aphrodisiac is not a sex act, but obviously one had to take place before the recipe could be prepared. The canon itself, however, does not involve a sex act.[98] My figures correspond closely to Payer's. In the Irish penitentials, from 25 to 36 percent of the canons are sex-related. Among the Anglo-Latin texts the range is slightly greater, from 25 percent (Theodore) to 56 percent ("Bede") and 51 percent (Egbert). The Anglo-Saxon texts pay noticeably less attention to sex acts, especially in the *Old English Penitential,* where they account for only 15 percent of the total; they account for 34 to 39 percent of the *Scriftboc,* the *Old English Handbook* and *CTH. CTHS* is almost entirely concerned with sexual acts (85 percent), but it is only a fragmentary penitential.[99]

Second, in the penitentials only a small number of the sex-related canons deal with homosexual sins. Greenberg claimed that from 4 to 8 percent of the canons of the penitentials are given to homosexual relations.[100] According to the calculations I have recorded in table 3, homosexual acts account for up to 10 percent of the canons in some handbooks, while only one contains no reference to same-sex behavior.

In the Irish penitentials, the data range from no such canons in Finnian's *Penitential* to 8 percent in the *Penitential* of Cummean and 10 percent in the *Old Irish Penitential* and the *Penitential* of Columbanus.[101] In the Anglo-Latin penitentials the percentage of homosexual canons is mostly lower: Theodore, 3 percent; "Bede," 10 percent, and Egbert, 6 percent.[102] These percentages drop sharply in the vernacular penitentials. Canons concerning homosexual acts occupy just 1 percent of the *Scriftboc* and 2 percent of the *Old English Penitential,* but 5 percent of *CTH,* 7 percent of the *Old English Handbook,* and 31 percent of *CTHS* (again, only a fragment of a penitential since it deals only with sexual sins). Approximately 14 percent of all the sexual canons in the *Old English Penitential* concern same-sex acts; the figure for *CTH* is 16 percent. Only 4 percent of all the sex acts in the *Scriftboc* concern same-sex acts, but same-sex acts account for 21 percent of the sex acts mentioned in the *Old English Handbook* and 57 percent of all those included in *CTHS.*

With the exception of *CTHS,* the Anglo-Saxon penitentials devote a smaller percentage of canons to sex acts than either Irish or Anglo-Latin handbooks. The three Anglo-Latin penitentials discussed here, attributed to Theodore, "Bede," and Egbert, make a combined total of six general references to male homosexual acts and six references to intramale sex using "Sodom" in some form (see table 1). This is an average of four references per handbook. Eight Irish penitentials (which I have not included in my survey) contain six canons referring to Sodom in some way and seventeen references to male homosexual intercourse (including canons pertaining to boys), an average of just under three references per handbook.[103] In comparison, the four vernacular Anglo-Saxon penitentials make eight references to male homosexual intercourse, but only two of them invoke Sodom (see table 2), an average of two canons per handbook. One explanation for the drop in the number of canons in the vernacular texts might be that the number of homosexual acts correlates with the proximity of a given handbook to same-sex communities, in particular to the monastery. That would explain why a higher percentage of all the sex acts mentioned in the Irish penitentials concerns homosexual acts (up to 39 percent in the *Old Irish Penitential,* although this too is a vernacular text).[104] On the one hand, it appears that male homosexual acts were of less concern to the translators of the Anglo-Latin texts than to the authors of those texts, or to the authors of Irish penitentials. However, the Irish handbooks are much more concerned with monastic milieux than the vernacular Anglo-Saxon texts, and given this shift in provenance, it is impressive that male homosexual acts continued to be of concern to church officials whose penitentials were composed largely with lay rather than monastic or clerical penitents in mind.

These figures suggest that homosexual acts are far less important than heterosexual acts in the penitentials, and in themselves they do not suggest that same-sex acts presented particular dangers to social order. Indeed, this data could be read as indicating either tolerance of homosexual acts or, since the Anglo-Saxon penitentials are later than the Latin texts, an increasing lack of concern with them. When the evidence is seen synchronically—an important perspective, since many manuscripts contain several handbooks and sometimes show that scribes attempted to conflate them—the contrast is even more striking.[105] Although the Anglo-Saxon penitentials written in the tenth and eleventh centuries capture, as a group, nearly all the regulations against homosexual acts in the earlier Latin sources, they are less concerned with sex acts in general and with homosexual acts in particular than the Latin texts are. At the same time, as we saw earlier, the laws become increasingly concerned with sexual conduct and Christian behavior more generally. But the evidence is deceptive. The latest of the vernacular penitentials, the *Old English Handbook,* contains the highest percentage of same-sex acts relative to other sins. It is clear that same-sex acts never ceased to concern the custodians of ecclesiastical discipline in the Anglo-Saxon period, even as handbooks were revised into more compact documents.

Third, comparisons show that homosexual acts were sometimes punished more heavily than heterosexual sex acts. The *Penitential* of Theodore, for example, assigns a penance of one year to a man who fornicates with a virgin and a penance of four years to a man who fornicates with another man's wife (1.2.1, *CED* 3:178). Men who fornicated with other men once received a penance of four years but penances of ten or fifteen years if they did it again and penances of seven years if they were "sodomites" or "molles" (1.2.2–7, *CED* 3:178). The only comparable penance for a heterosexual act is intercourse with one's sister, which received a penance of seven or twelve years. Sex between brothers, however, received a penance of fifteen years.[106] Another sanction for some of the men involved in these acts was their classification as women (i.e., as adulteresses). These men were also shamed by the proximity of male homosexual intercourse to bestiality (which is seen in all the vernacular penitentials). Their conduct was classified among the "unnatural things" done "against God's creation," a severe condemnation that of course would have included intrafemale intercourse too. Bailey argued that the penances in Theodore's *Penitential* manifest no "harsh discrimination" toward those "who own themselves guilty of homosexual practices." But it is clear that penances of ten to fifteen years (for repeated male homosexual intercourse and sex between brothers) are the most severe in the penitential, comparable only to penances for incest and greater than penances for acts that caused greater social disruption, including homicide, theft, and perjury.[107]

CONCLUSION

Amid all the detail about same-sex practices available in the Anglo-Saxon penitentials, three points are especially important. First, all the Latin and vernacular texts specify penances for male homosexual acts. Second, all these texts specify penances for those who repeatedly perform such acts, suggesting that for some penitents these acts were habitual and, in a word, preferred, no matter the consequences. The texts provide for sinners who committed these acts just once, assigning them lighter penances, but also provide for those who performed these acts many times. Third, two texts, *CTH* and *CTHS*, offer evidence that certain men who preferred to have sex with other men had a special name in Anglo-Saxon England. We can conclude that there were men and women in the Middle Ages who preferred to have sex with their own kind, and perhaps even exclusively with their own kind, and that some of these men were known for or identified with this preference (no comparable evidence for women exists).

The very rarity of such evidence tells us that what was true of Renaissance and other medieval cultures was true for this one. "[T]he terms in which we now speak of homosexuality cannot readily be translated into those of the sixteenth and seventeenth centuries," Alan Bray warned. "We need to carry our preconceptions lightly if we are to see in Renaissance England more than a distorted image of ourselves."[108] Halperin's words on this topic are also worth repeating.

> To the extent, in fact, that histories of "sexuality" succeed in concerning themselves with *sexuality,* to just that extent are they doomed to fail as *histories* (Foucault himself taught us that much), unless they also include as an essential part of their proper enterprise the task of demonstrating the historicity, conditions of emergence, modes of construction, and ideological contingencies of the very categories of analysis that undergird their own practice.[109]

Halperin's language, rich and suggestive, could be used to gloss the evidence of "sexuality" I have examined in this chapter. But that language is not much help in telling us about the "history" this evidence contains. Many more sources, and different kinds of sources, would be needed to give concrete detail to the "modes of construction" employed by cultural authorities in Anglo-Saxon England or to the "ideological contingencies" framing their work and complicating its reception. Certain new lines of investigation might contribute to our knowledge of the "historicity" of these texts. But the most productive investigations will, for some time to come, concentrate on describing and analyzing the primary evidence, not a particularly Foucauldian task (as I suggested in chapter 1), rather than applying poststructuralist or Foucauldian terminology to it.

The penitentials offer no clues about where the homosexual (or, for that matter, heterosexual) acts they prohibit would have taken place. But we can, I think, learn from Alan Bray's demonstration that in the Renaissance same-sex contact took place within acknowledged social institutions that disguised that contact and kept it from being recognized or identified as a particular form of social behavior, as a way of life. Those institutions existed in Anglo-Saxon England. They included single-sex education and extended households and another that Bray does not examine but that surely promoted male-male intimacy, military service.

Same-sex monasteries were primary locations for same-sex contact, as we see in "Bede's" reference to nuns who stimulate each other with a "device" and in the many canons prohibiting same-sex between boys or between men in Irish and other early penitentials. Other environments in Anglo-Saxon England might have been conducive to same-sex intimacy. One was the nonmonastic school to which nobility, at King Alfred's direction, sent their sons.[110]

Not all the boys schooled in these experiences became monks; many who were trained in monasteries were destined for military or administrative careers. Boys might well have been introduced to same-sex acts in school in this period, just as they are now, and to gender-crossing performances, which they are likely to have witnessed in the liturgy and in colloquies. Some of them might have chosen, when the occasion presented itself, to continue that behavior as adults, or continued that behavior without realizing that they might have chosen to do otherwise. Thus it is possible that the regulations against boys' homosexual acts in the vernacular penitentials are not necessarily mere vestiges of the monastic regulations. The Old English penitentials might well have been aiming at acts that boys learned about at school and continued afterwards.

Other social institutions that absorbed educated young men might also have prompted same-sex intimacy. Bray shows that the household in Renaissance England was an extended organization in which children and servants spent considerable time together. Similar conditions existed in Anglo-Saxon England, creating opportunities for men or women to engage in sex with their own sex. The penitentials point to these opportunities for intimacy between family members, including incest between mothers and sons and between brothers, and mothers who imitated acts of fornication with their sons.[111] Class lines were also crossed, at least in heterosexual acts, by men who had intercourse with servant girls or slaves. Obviously there was ample opportunity for liaisons that the church condemned. Intramale and intrafemale sexual acts were only some of those that were forbidden.

References to the "bædling" suggest a society of stratified and known social types, but such distinctions were no doubt observed most faithfully only in the upper reaches of Christian Anglo-Saxon society. Far more common must have been men and boys in rural, agrarian culture who, then as now, learned about the mechanics of sex from animals and, if the penitentials are to be believed, had sex with animals and with each other. Such traditions were passed on from older men to younger ones, from older boys to younger ones, as the references to same-sex intercourse in monastic documents suggest, moving almost automatically from one generation to the next. No records of such same-sex contacts exist for secular Anglo-Saxon culture. But such patterns are ubiquitous in sociological and anthropological studies, and it is at the least very likely that this sexual behavior was known to the Anglo-Saxons and that its existence underlies references to intramale sex and intergenerational male homosexual acts in the Old English penitentials.

I have argued that the evidence shows that some men and women in the Anglo-Saxon period preferred partners of their own sex and, if the penitentials' reference to repeated same-sex acts have any meaning, that some men and women persisted in this behavior despite the Church's and the culture's prohibitions against it. The existence of such people was known to the Church, which did everything in its power to change their behavior, demanding that they confess, inquiring into the details of their sexual experience when they did so, and handing them severe penances—even lifelong penances, in some cases—in an effort to reform and save them. There appear to have been no details of sexual experience that confessors did not inquire about. Did the nun use a "device" or not? Did the small boy forced into sex somehow consent to it? Did the man who had intercourse with another man do so once or several times? How old was his partner? Was the man married? Was he a "bædling"? Was his partner also a "bædling"?

To the extent that such discourse constitutes a community identity, isolating a pool or category of offenders who knew and talked to each other, we can speak of a sexual identity based on same-sex acts in the Anglo-Saxon period. Moreover, since all the vernacular evidence is derived from Latin texts that circulated widely in western Europe in the Middle Ages, especially through Carolingian and Frankish territories, as well as Italy, this hypothesis can be extended much more widely. In this evidence there is no sign of tolerance of same-sex acts, or even of compassion for those who confessed them, whether adults or children. But there is some sign that the sinners in question were identified as part of a group, since some individuals were known as "sodomites," or "molles," or, in England, as "bædlings," and those labels constitute some kind of group identity—that is, a category of male persons known by their sexual practices. Such a category is not the same as "homosexual," however, a term with far greater implications in discussions of identity. Furthermore, evidence in chapter 5 will show that the kind of identity created by the term "sodomite" was not exclusive to sexual behavior in the Middle Ages, so that whatever identity was created by that word was not necessarily specific to sexual practices.

The evidence suggests that some men and women chose to engage in forbidden sexual acts. But it cannot be assumed that those men, women, boys, and girls who engaged in homosexual acts did so in the knowledge that they were committing grave sins. Part of the influence of the penitentials was not merely to enforce sexual standards but to introduce them. This would have been true throughout the early Middle Ages, not only in the period of the first conversion to Christianity. Penitentials and homilies show that the Church continued to combat magic and superstition, worship of idols, and other practices throughout the Anglo-Saxon period. The Church faced a considerably more daunting task in trying to prohibit all sex acts outside of marriage. Those that could be classified as adultery also entailed the force of the secular government and were therefore easier to suppress, since sanctions against them were not new. Those that could not be classified in this way—and that included all homosexual acts discussed in this chapter—must have been more difficult to eradicate, not because the Anglo-Saxons were especially prone to same-sex acts but simply because such acts arose in their culture out of vagaries of human desire, curiosity, and loneliness, as well as choice. Those whose same-sex acts were discovered by parents, monastic supervisors, or other authorities might have been compelled to confess. But some of those whose acts remained private might never have realized that they were violating some of the Church's gravest prohibitions.

The Anglo-Saxons did not need an identified tradition of same-sex behavior, a core group identity, or any other modern-seeming means to lead them to the homosexual acts they wanted to engage in. Nor did their practice of such acts mean that they were "homosexuals," any more than the intramale and intrafemale sexual behavior of the men and women described by Bray constituted a sexual identity for them. Even though the Church punished same-sex acts severely and warned Christians in ominous terms about the consequences of that behavior, there is no reason to suppose that the bishops and priests succeeded. Indeed, the Latin penitentials show that they were even expected to confess these sins themselves (e.g., *Penitential* of Egbert 2.2, *CED* 3:219).

Penitentials offer the most specific and, I believe, the most important evidence of same-sex relations and attempts to regulate them in the Anglo-Saxon period. But these texts were just one form of discourse with which the Church pursued its aim of confining sex to marriage and, within marriage, structuring sexual relations within very limited parameters. Not all of this discourse is as straightforward as the handbooks of penance, but some of it takes equally direct aim at same-sex relations. Because the other genres are more discursive than the handbooks, they tell us more about how those who engaged in same-sex relations were taught to think of themselves. The most powerful tool for shaping an image of the sexually deviant was the destruction of Sodom and Gomorrah, a tale that figures in both prose and poetry that sought to persuade the Anglo-Saxons to restrict their sexual activities sharply or to pay a heavy price for indulging their desires.

APPENDIX I

Male and Female Homosexual Acts in the Penitentials of Theodore, "Bede," and Egbert

Theodore
(*CED* 3:176–204; the translation, with some modifications, is taken from McNeill and Gamer, *MHP* 182–215.)

1.2.2   Qui sepe cum masculo aut cum pecude fornicat, X. annos ut peniteret judicavit.

1.2.3   Item aliud. Qui cum pecoribus coierit, XV. annos peniteat.

does it often, or is in orders; sometimes seven, sometimes one for the "molles," sometimes 100 days for boys.

5.18   If men fornicate interfemorally, one year or, if repeated, two years.

5.19   If however they fornicate anally, three years; if it is a boy, two years.

APPENDIX 2

Male and Female Homosexual Acts in the Anglo-Saxon Penitentials

Scriftboc
(*DAB* 170–94)

6g   Swa hwylc man swa on muð sæd forlæteð, fæste VII winter.

7a   Lytel cniht gif he byð fram maran ofðrycced in hæmede, fæste V niht; gif
he him geðafige, fæste XX nihta.

9d   Se ðe mid neate hæme oððe wæpnede, fæste X winter.

9e   Cnihtas gyf hi heom betweonan hæmed fremman, swinge hi man.

19q   Wif gif heo mid oðre hæme, fæste III winter.

6g   Whoever releases seed into the mouth is to fast seven years.

7a   If a small boy has been forced by a larger one into intercourse, he (is to fast)
five days. If he consents to it, he is to fast twenty days.

9d   Whoever fornicates with an animal or a male person is to fast ten years.

9e   Boys who fornicate are to be beaten.

19q   If a woman has intercourse with another woman, she is to fast three years.

Old English Penitential
(*DAV* 18–19)

2.6   Be þam men þe ungedafenlice hæmð, þæt is wið nytenum, oððe hine mid
geonglingum besmiteð, oððe wæpnedman wið oðerne. Se man þe hine wið
nytenu besmiteð, oððe wæpnedman wið oðerne mid ungesceadelicum
þinge: gif he bið XX wintra eald man, þæt he understandan mæg þæt he þa
sceamlican þing 7 þa manfullan begæð, geswice 7 andette 7 fæste XV
(winter); 7 gif se man his gemæccan hæbbe 7 he beo XL wintra 7 swylce
þing begæð, geswice 7 fæste þa hwile þe his lif beo 7 ne gedyrstlæce þæt he
drihtnes lichaman underfo ær his endedæge. Geonge men 7 andgitlease
man sceal þearle swingan ðe swylce ðinge begað.

Concerning those who fornicate unlawfully, that is with animals, or one
who soils himself with young ones, or a male who has intercourse with another male.
The man who soils himself with an animal or the male who (fornicates)
with another, in an irrational way, if he is twenty years old, so that he can
understand that shameful and evil thing, let him desist and confess and
fast fifteen years; and if he has a spouse (wife), and he is forty years old and
does such a thing, desist and he is to fast for the rest of his life, and not be
allowed to receive God's body before the end of his life. If young men and
witless men do such a thing, they are to be beaten.

Additamenta 1
(DAV 69)

Gif hwa fullice on ungecyndelicum ðingum ongean godes gesceafte ðurh ænig ðinc hine sylfne besmite, bereowsige þæt æfre þa hwile ðe he libbe be ðam þe seo dæd sy.

If anyone foully through unnatural things soils himself [or herself] against God's creation in any way, he [or she] is to repent that forever while he [or she] lives, until he or she be dead.

Old English Handbook
(Fowler, "Handbook," 22)

Lines 164–70   Gyf hwa hyne wið nytenu besmyteð, oððe wæpnedman wið oðerne, gif he bið xx wintra, fæste xv winter; and gif se man his gemæccan habbe and he beo xl wintra and swilce þingc begæð, geswice and fæste þa hwile þe his lif beo, and ne geþristlæce þæt he Drihtenes lichaman underfo ær his endetiman. Geonge men and andgitlease man sceal þearle swingan þe swilce þingc begæð.

Lines 275–78   Gyf hwa fullice on ungecyndelicum þingum ongean Godes gesceafte þurh ænig þingc hine sylfne besmyte, bereowsige þæt æfre ða hwile þe he libbe, be þam þe seo dæd sy.

(Translations correspond closely to those for the *Old English Penitential* above.)

Canons of Theodore
(Mone 520–25)

138   Gyf bædling mid bædlinge hæme X winter fæste.
139   Se ðe þis werlice man deð, IV gear fæste.
140   Gyf hit cniht sy, æt ærestan II gear, gif he hit æft do, IV gear fæste.
141   Gyf he be leoðum deð, an gear oððe III and XL.
144   Cnihtas þa ðe hæmað heom betweonan, hit is demed, þæt hy man swinge.
145   Se ðe sæd on muð sendeð, þæt is wyrreste.
147   Gyf broðor mid breðer hæme þurh his lichoman gemegnysse, XV winter fæste buton flæsce.
183   Gyf he betuh ðeoh do, an gear oððe III feowertigo.
184   Gyf hit cnyht sy, XX daga fæste, oððe hine man swynge.
185   Gyf he hit mid gehadedum men do, III feowertigo oððe cal gear fæstc.

138   If a "bædling" fornicate with a "bædlinge," he is to fast ten years.
139   Who does this as an adult man (werlice) is to fast for four years.
140   If he is a boy and it is the first time, two years; if he does it again, four years.
141   If he does it between the limbs (i.e., interfemorally), one year or the three forty-day periods.
144   If boys fornicate, it has been judged that they are to be beaten.
145   Who sends seed into the mouth, that is the greatest evil.

147   If a brother fornicates with a brother through the mingling of their flesh, he is to fast for fifteen years without meat.

183   If he does it between (the limbs, i.e., interfemorally), one year of the three forty-day periods.

184   If it is a boy, he is to fast twenty days or be beaten.

185   If he does it with one in orders, he is to fast the three forty-day periods or one year.

Canons of Theodore, Supplement
(*ALI* 2:228–30)

68.5   Se ðe mid bædlinge hæme. oððe mid oðrum wæpnedmen. oððe mid nytene. fæste .x. winter. On oðre stowe hit cwyð. se ðe mid nytene hæme. fæste. .xv. winter. & *sodomisce .vii. gear. fæston.*†

68.6   Gif se bædling mid bædlinge hæme .x. winter bete. *hi beoð hnesclice swa forlegene.* Se ðe þis werlice ‡ deð æne. fæste .iiii. gear. gif hit gewuna byð. swa Basilius cwæð. gif hig beoð butan hade .xv. winter. an gear eallswa wif. gif hit cniht bið. æt þam ærestan cysse. ii. gear. gif he hit eft do. fæste .iiii. gear. gif he betwyh liþum deð .i. gear. oþþe .iii. feowertigo.

68.8   Gif wif hæmeð .iii. gear bete. gif heo sylf sig mid hire sylfre hæmed onhyrgende on þa ylcan wisan .i. gear hreowsige.

68.10 Se ðe sæd on muð sendeð. fæste .vii. gear. þæt is wyrreste. fram sumum hyt wæs demed þæt hi butu oð hyra lifes ende hit betton.

68.14 Gif broðor mid breðer hæme þurh his lichaman gemengnysse .xv. winter fæste butan flæsce.

68.5   Whoever fornicates with a "bædling" or with another male or with an animal is to fast for ten years. In another place it says that he who fornicates with an animal is to fast for fifteen years. (*and sodomites are to fast seven years*).

68.6   If a "bædling" fornicate with a "bædlinge," he is to fast ten years. (*they are as soft as the adulteress*). Who does this unaware (of what he is doing) is to fast for one year but four years if it is habitual, as Basil said. If he is not in orders, fifteen years, one year (more?) as with the woman. If it is a child and is the first time, two years; if he does it again, four years; if he does it interfemorally, one year or the three forty-day periods.

68.8   If a woman fornicate [with a woman], she is to fast for three years. If she fornicate with herself in imitation of that act, she is to do penance for one year.

68.10 Whoever sends seed into the mouth, that is the worst (evil). From some it was judged that they should do penance for it until the end of their lives.

68.14 If a brother fornicate with a brother through mingling of the flesh, he is to fast for fifteen years without meat.

   † It appears that at some point a scribe copied a translation of Theodore 1.2.6 into the margin in two lines; evidently this canon had been omitted and had to be added. However, a subsequent copyist took the first line as a continuation of Theodore 1.2.4 and the second line as a continuation of Theodore 1.2.5. I have italicized the lines to show that at an earlier stage this canon was translated correctly.

   ‡ Thorpe, *ALI* 2:228, notes that the Cambridge manuscript reads "unwærlice."

Table 1 *Penances for Same-Sex Intercourse in Penitentials of Theodore, "Bede," and Egbert*

Penitential		Sin	Penance	Use of "Sodom"
Theodore	1.2.2	man with man, often	10 years	no
	1.2.4	man with man, over 20	15 years	no
	1.2.5	man with man	10 years	no
	1.2.6	sodomite	7 years	yes
		molles	as adulteress	
	1.2.7	same	4 years	(yes; "item")
		habitual	15 years	
		not habitual	as a woman	
		boy, first time	2 years	
		boy, repeated	4 years	
	1.2.8	interfemoral sex	1 year, 3 40-day fasts	no
	1.2.11	boys with boys	beaten	no
	1.2.12	woman with woman	3 years	no
	1.2.15	fellatio	7 years	no
	1.2.19	brother with brother	15 years	no
"Bede"	3.19	sodomite	4 years	yes
	3.20	habitual sodomite	7 years	yes
		monk	7 years	
	3.21	interfemoral sex	3 40-day fasts	no
	3.22	boy (with older boy)	40 days, psalms	no
	3.23	woman with woman	3 years	no
	3.24	nun & nun with device	7 years	no
	3.31	boys, interfemoral sex	100 days, 3 40-day fasts	no
	3.32	boy with older boy	20 days with consent	no
Egbert	2.2	sodomy: bishop	14 years	yes
		priest	12 years	
		deacon	10 years	
		subdeacon	9 years	
		cleric	7 years	
		layman	5 years	
	4.5	brother with brother	15 years	no
	5.4	priest with man	7 years	no
	5.17	sodomite, repeated	10 years	yes
		man in orders	10 years	
		some men	7 years	
		molles	1 year	
		boy	100 days	
	5.18	interfemoral sex	1 or 2 years	no
	5.19	men/boys "in terga"	3/2 years	no

Table 2 *Penances for Same-Sex Intercourse in the Anglo-Saxon Penitentials*

Penitential	Sin	Penance	Use of "Sodom"
Scriftboc 6g	fellatio	7 years	no
7a	boy with older boy	5 or 20 days	no
9d	man with man	10 years	no
9e	boys with boys	beating	no
19q	woman with woman	3 or 10 years	no
Old English Penitential 2.6	man with men over 20	15 years	no
	man with married man over 40	lifelong	
Additamenta 1	unnatural acts	lifelong	no
Old English Handbook Lines 164–70	man with men over 20	15 years	no
	man with married man over 40	lifelong	
Lines 275–78	unnatural acts	lifelong	no
Canons of Theodore 138	bædling with bædling	10 years	no
139	adult male	4 years	no
140	boys once	2 years	no
	boys repeated	4 years	no
141	interfemoral	1 year or 40 days	no
144	boys with boys	beating	no
145	fellatio	[none specified]	no
147	brother with brother	15 years	no
183	interfemoral	1 year or 40 days	no
184	interfemoral, boy	20 days or beating	no
185	interfemoral with cleric	3 40-days or 1 year	no
Canons of Theodore, Supplement 68.5	whoever with bædling or with other male sodomite	10 years 7 years	(yes; "item")
68.6	bædling with bædling	10 years	yes
	bædling with bædling,	4 years	
	heedlessly	15 years	
	if habitual	1 year less	
	if not habitual	2 years	
	boy, first time	4 years	
	boy, repeated		
68.8	woman with woman	3 years	no
68.10	fellatio	7 years or lifelong	no
68.14	brother with brother	15 years	no

Table 3   *Heterosexual and Homosexual Acts in Irish, Anglo-Latin, and Anglo-Saxon Penitentials*

Penitential Texts	No. of Canons/ no. of Canons Dealing with Sex	Hetero-sexual Canons/ Homo-sexual Canons	Percent-age of Canons Dealing with Sex	Percent-age of All Canons Dealing with Homo-sexual Acts	Percent-age of Sex Canons Dealing with Homo-sexual Acts
Finnian	53/19	19/0	36	0	0
Columbanus	42/15	11/4	36	10	36
Cummean	173/58	45/13	34	8	29
Irish Penitential	113/39	28/11	35	10	39
Theodore 1	154/65	55/10	42	6	18
Theodore 2	155/12	12/0	8	0	0
Theodore 1 + 2	309/76	67/9	25	3	13
"Bede"	88/49	40/9	56	10	23
Egbert	111/57	50/7	51	6	14
Scriftboc	206/70	67/3	34	1	4
Old English Penitential	164/25	22/3	15	2	14
Old English Handbook	44/17	14/3	39	7	21
Canons of Theodore	133/51	44/7	38	5	16
Canons of Theodore, Supplement	26/22	14/8	85	31	57

The Shadow of Sodom

Same-Sex Relations in Pastoral Prose and Poetry

Handbooks of penance offer straightforward evidence that same-sex relations, especially those involving boys but also those between men, were vigorously opposed by the Church in the early Middle Ages. These regulatory documents, however, formed only a part of ecclesiastical discourse on the subject. Other Anglo-Saxon sources are less specific, but they too refer to homosexual acts, sometimes explicitly, sometimes in the context of general reference to sexual misconduct. In the "Sermo Lupi ad Anglos," for example, Wulfstan, archbishop of York (d. 1023), presumably included homosexual acts when denouncing "various fornications" ("mistlice forligru") and "foul adulterous fornicators" ("fule forlegene horingas").[1] Other texts ambiguously but tellingly refer to forms of sexual intercourse that are "against nature" ("ongean gecynde"). This as-yet vague but inclusive formulation encompassed same-sex acts and other forms of "deviant" sex, including heterosexual anal sex, bestiality, and anything that could be considered excessive, which meant that it went beyond what was necessary for sexual reproduction.

The chief narrative and iconographic vehicle for representing sexual excess in the Anglo-Saxon period was the destruction of Sodom and Gomorrah. Recounted in the book of Genesis, the history of these cities provided commentators with a rich store of images to use in denouncing immorality. Many Anglo-Saxon sources condemned the wicked practices of these cities, and some of them specified male homosexual intercourse among the cities' sexual excesses. Once Sodom had been associated with same-sex sex—and we have seen that this association was established in early Latin penitentials in Ireland and England—the name of the city could be used to encode and denounce male homosexual intercourse as well as other forms of sexual corruption. But same-sex sex is not Sodom's identifying sin or the nexus of the city's wickedness. In most Anglo-Saxon accounts, same-sex sex is, instead, the city's shadow.

The destruction of Sodom was regarded as the most vivid event in the history of sexual excess. But it was also the most amorphous. "There is no Sodom," writes Paul Hallam, "there are only Sodom texts. Stories of Sodom, commentaries, footnotes, elaborations and annotations upon Sodom."[2] In Anglo-Saxon England too there are commentaries, elaborations, and annotations upon Sodom, but few straightforward accounts of the evils of the city. My aim in this chapter is to examine references to Sodom in a variety of prose genres, including scriptural exegesis, vernacular homilies, and letters about the education of priests, and in poetry, in order to discover how prominent same-sex sex was in catalogues of the city's wicked deeds.

Some of the relevant Anglo-Saxon texts are "learned," by which I mean that they were written by the educated for the educated—for teachers, bishops, abbots, and others who led the ecclesiastical establishment. Among the Latin works I will discuss are two by Bede, the *Ecclesiastical History* (731) and Bede's commentary on the book of Genesis (725–31); works of Aldhelm (c. 639–709); and letters of Boniface (c. 675–754) and Alcuin (c. 731–804).[3] Relevant vernacular prose, also learned, was written later, between King Alfred's reign (871–99) and the early eleventh century. These texts include pastoral letters and homilies that guided priests in specific catechetical matters and addressed the routine concerns and daily conduct of Anglo-Saxon society. I begin by summarizing the history of Sodom as seen in a prose translation of Genesis in the *Old English Heptateuch,* a text accompanied with illustrations representing the history of Lot and Abraham and the destruction of Sodom.[4] Then, after examining various prose sources, I turn to the longest narrative devoted to the fall of Sodom and Gomorrah and the only poem among the Old English "Sodom texts," *Genesis A.*

SODOM IN SCRIPTURE

Scholars have long known that Sodom and Gomorrah were neither explicitly nor exclusively linked to homosexual sins in Scripture.[5] John Boswell went farther than most writers in his claim that, after the time of John Cassian, who wrote in the early fifth century, "many subsequent Christian authors *completely* ignored *any* sexual implications of Sodom's fate" (emphasis added).[6] This view plainly contradicts not only the Anglo-Saxon evidence but also the commentary of important writers such as Gregory the Great and Bede. M. R. Godden has agreed with those who maintain that "the sexual issue" (specifically, the issue of male homosexual intercourse in Sodom) may have been "a minor aspect of the story to the original writers and readers of Genesis."[7] Many Anglo-Saxon sources do not stress the episode's sexual implications. Instead they condemn the city for *luxuria,* the deadly or capital sin under which sexual sins were grouped. The sources also cite Sodom as an especially powerful example of the vengeance God takes on those who fail to keep their covenant with him. We will see that a variety of Anglo-Saxon texts contemporary with the handbooks of penance specify that sins of sexual excess prompted God's wrath. A few of them, including *Genesis A,* support this claim by specifically including male homosexual intercourse among the Sodomites' sins.

Mark D. Jordan has recently argued that "Latin exegesis had by the end of the patristic period fixed on a sexual interpretation of Sodomitic sin." Although other, non-sexual interpretations continued to be offered, after the time of Gregory they became "alternate readings" that were "pushed out of the way by sexual ones."[8] Gregory divided *luxuria* into two parts: a general sin that excited the soul to self-indulgence and a sin specifically linked to the genitals, to the loins of men and the "umbilical" or center of women. As a sin "housed in the genitals," *luxuria* led to effeminacy and animality, "softness" and bestiality,[9] characteristics that the Anglo-Saxon penitentials associate with the "sodomite" and with male homosexual intercourse. Jordan acknowledges that in penitentials from the seventh and eighth centuries "Sodom and its inhabitants were being mentioned as a way of designating a particular kind of sexual intercourse" but notes that these references can be cryptic. He stresses that "prescriptions against Sodomitic intercourse are not the same as the construction of the category of *sodomia,*" and this of course is correct.[10] Yet, as we have seen, Latin penitentials associated with the early Irish and English churches, including the *Penitential* of Theodore and those attributed to Egbert and to "Bede," refer to sodomy and sodomites, as do the Anglo-Saxon penitentials (although less frequently; see table 1 in chapter 4). The penitentials' descriptions of the sin and those guilty of it show that the city and the sin—however vaguely it was defined—were firmly connected.

In Genesis the destruction of Sodom is interwoven with the story of Abraham in a plot contrasting the just and unjust, the pious and the impious, the saved and the damned. These large themes frame Anglo-Saxon narratives based on the event and identify the sins of Sodom. According to Richard Kay, the history of Sodom is "an integral part of the origins of Israel as recounted in Genesis." The episode retains special significance as one of God's earliest contacts with man; it "set the patterns for the future history of the race in general and for His chosen people in particular."[11] In the history of Sodom, the careers of Abram (later Abraham) and Lot, his nephew and coheir, are closely paralleled. Their joint history began with the dispute concerning rights to pasturage. Lot settled in the plain of the Jordan river "in the direction of Zoar" (Genesis 13:10), while Abram stayed in Canaan, in the promised land. Lot "moved his tent as far as Sodom," a city where the people were "wicked, great sinners against the Lord" (Genesis 13:12–13).[12] Summing up rabbinic commentary on Sodom, Kay regarded its "outstanding feature" as "the insistence that the Sodomites sinned together as a community, by committing injustice against one another, against the rest of mankind, and against God."[13] Among the Sodomites, Lot was deeply involved with what Kay described as "the community of his choice." Once accustomed to city life, Lot intermarried with "mocking infidels." When informed that Sodom would be destroyed, he made "a hesitant and forced departure from one city only to seek out another," hindered by a wife who could not forget Sodom and was turned into a pillar as punishment (219). The scriptural narrative is less concerned with Abraham and Lot than with Abraham and Sodom, for Sodom, according to Kay, was "opposed to Abraham and everything that he represents" (220). His fertility is contrasted to the sterility of their sexual perversion, his rural habits to their urban ways, his obedient and ordered world to their disobedience and anarchy.

There is more to the story of Sodom than the city's destruction. After Lot arrived in Sodom, five kings of northern tribes, led by Chedorlaomer, made war on Sodom, Gomorrah, Admah, Zeboim, and Zoar (the five Cities of the Plain) and took Lot and many others captive. Abram heard of Lot's fate and, although leading a far inferior army, defeated Chedorlaomer. "Then he brought back all the goods, and also brought back his nephew Lot with his goods, and the women and the people" (Genesis 14:16). Returning to the city, the defeated king of Sodom met Abram, offered him rewards, and asked for the return of his men. Abram treated the king dismissively, implying that the king and his people were not righteous (Genesis 14:22–24), and refused the king's gifts.

After Abram rescued Lot, God renamed him Abraham, the new father of the Chosen People, and made a covenant with him (Genesis 15). In the form of three men ("ðry weras," 18.2), God visited Abraham and announced his plan to destroy Sodom. The *Old English Heptateuch* (figure 6, folio 29r) shows God, surrounded by winged angels, descending from heaven and appearing to Abraham, who prostrates himself before him. The illustration and the text differ at this point, since God seems to be alone and no "weras" apart from Abraham are to be seen. According to Kurt Weitzmann and Herbert L. Kessler, in some versions of the scene "the angels that greet Abraham are often wingless and the differentiation of one of them is particularly emphatic." They cite the illustrations from the *Old English Heptateuch* as examples.[14] God discloses the fate of Sodom to Abraham, who has been chosen "to keep the way of the Lord by doing righteousness and justice." In a culture of obedience, no secrets are possible. "Shall I hide from Abraham what I am about to do?" God asks (Genesis 18:17). "No, for I have chosen him, that he may charge his children and his household after him to keep the way of the Lord by doing righteousness and justice; so that the Lord may bring about for Abraham what he has promised him" (Genesis 18:19). It is God's suspicion that the Sodomites have secrets—he himself does not know exactly what their crimes are—that causes him to send his messengers to the city. But however great the sins of Sodom, they remain unspecified in Genesis. God complains of a single sin among the Sodomites, "peccatum" in the Vulgate ("peccatum eorum aggravatum est nimis," Genesis 18:20).[15] In the Old English translation, God complains to Abraham that "the noise of the Sodomites and of the dwellers of Gomorrah is very great, and their sin is very grievous. Now I wish to go there and to see if they fulfill with work the noise that comes to me, or if it is not so, (so) that I may know" ("Ðæra Sodomitiscra hream 7 ðære burhware of Gomorra ys gemenifyld, 7 heora synn ys swyðe gehefegod. Ic wylle nu faran to 7 geseon hwæðer hi gefyllað mid weorce þone hream ðe me to com, oððe hyt swa nys, ðæt ic wite," 129.20–130.21). It is their "hream," their noise or outcry, representing the Sodomites' open and shameless sinning, that draws first God's attention and then his ire.

Seeking to protect Lot, Abraham bargains with God so that the just would not be destroyed with the wicked. God agrees and then sends his companions to Sodom. Abraham returns to his dwelling. His three visitors, with God now clearly differentiated from his two companions, walk toward the city (figure 7, 31r). At this point and on folio 30v God's companions appear to be two men, although they are in fact wingless angels, not "weras." God is distinguished from them by his aureole. In the following illustration, however, the companions are no longer shown as "weras" but as winged angels. This change is signaled in the text, which says that in the evening two angels sent by God entered the city ("Comon ða on æfnunge twegen englas fram Gode asende," 131.1). Although their robes are the same as before, the angels now have wings like those on the angels who appear when God descends to earth. In the *Old English Heptateuch* the angels are wingless when they stand

Fig. 6. *The Old English Version of the Heptateuch,* folio 29r. God descends a ladder and appears to Abraham; Abraham, shown twice, welcomes him. London, British Library, Cotton Claudius B.iv. Photo reproduced by permission of The British Library.

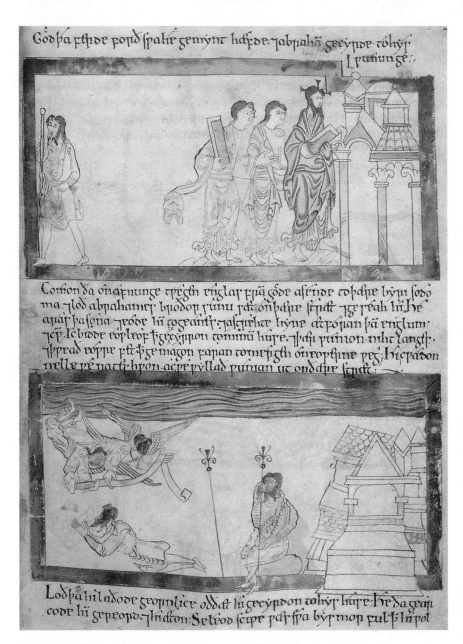

Fig. 7. *The Old English Version of the Heptateuch,* folio 31r (top). Abraham returns to his dwelling; God and two companions, beardless, wearing long, flowing robes, one carrying a tablet, look toward Sodom. London, British Library, Cotton Claudius B.iv.

Fig. 8. *The Old English Version of the Heptateuch,* folio 31r (bottom). God's companions enter Sodom. They are now flying angels, although their robes are identical to those in the previous illustration. Lot bows to them, as Abraham bowed to God (figure 6). London, British Library, Cotton Claudius B.iv. Photo reproduced by permission of The British Library.

before Abraham but winged when they approach Lot.[16] Their wings ensure that Lot will not mistake the visitors for beautiful men, which is how the Sodomites see them. The Sodomites subsequently gather at Lot's house to demand that he send his visitors out to them. Obviously they do not know the visitors are angels. In some later versions, however, the angels are described as beautiful men who are understandably attractive to the promiscuous Sodomites.[17] The narrative of Abraham's conduct is mirrored in Lot's and is juxtaposed to that of the Sodomites, and the parallel between Abraham and Lot is explicit in the illustration. Abraham bows when God appears to him, and this gesture is repeated by Lot, who bows to receive the angels when they enter Sodom (figure 8, 31r). The Sodomites demand that Lot turn over his guests to them, but Lot refuses, offering his daughters to the men instead.[18] The angels blind the Sodomites with a storm and the next morning lead Lot and his family to safety. Throughout their stay in Sodom, the visitors are represented as angels: it is as angels that they sit down to supper in Lot's house (folio 32v) and as angels that they firmly grasp Lot's wrist and his wife's when they lead them from the city (figure 9, 32r). *The Cotton Genesis* makes similar use of the angels' grasp; as Lot speaks to the Sodomites outside his house, a hand from inside the house reaches out to restrain and possibly to protect him.[19] This scene is not, unfortunately, portrayed in the *Heptateuch,* and indeed, as we will see in discussing the Old English translation (which was written by Ælfric), the episode itself is barely mentioned.

    Lot and his daughters continue on to Zoar, where the daughters, realizing that they would have no descendants, make Lot drunk and have intercourse with him. From these seeds they produced the nations of the Moabites and Ammonites.[20] While Lot is en route to Zoar (Segor), God sends rain showers mixed with darkness ("renscur mid swefle gemencged," 133.24) and engulfs Sodom and the other cities in fire and sulfur (figure 10, 32v). The narrative expends little energy on the event, noting that "God then cast down the city with rage, and completely destroyed the earth, and all the inhabitants were burned up, and everything that was growing was annihilated" ("God towearp ða swa mid graman ða burga, 7 ealne ðone eard endemes towende, 7 eall þa burhwara forbærnde ætgædere, 7 eall ðæt growende wæs, wearð adylegod," 133.25). The illustrator's restrained interpretation of this apocalypse matches the reticence of the text. In front of a collection of houses, the Sodomites (eleven men and five women) seem to be experiencing an earthquake, grasping columns and even the drawing's bottom frame for support. One man (extreme left) falls headlong,

Fig. 9. *The Old English Version of the Heptateuch,* folio 32r. The angels lead Lot, his wife, and their two daughters from the city, firmly clasping Lot and his wife. The scene is otherwise deserted. London, British Library, Cotton Claudius B.iv. Photo reproduced by permission of The British Library.

others seem to have fallen; two men (right-center and extreme right) seem to be blown into a horizontal position. Very little effort was made to differentiate the Sodomites from each another—the figures are more or less interchangeable—but neither do they form a close community. Some bodies seem intertwined, with a hand grasping a wrist (lower left) and another hand grasping a leg (lower right). But there are no embraces to suggest intimacy of any kind—affection or sexual relationships—among those who are about to die. Signs of luxury or indulgence are also absent. This is not an incoherent illustration, but neither is it powerfully suggestive of the devastation that other Anglo-Saxon sources describe so vividly. Rather, it illustrates incoherence and disorder that seem as much a preface to the judgment descending from the heavens as a consequence of it. Looking at this illustration, Anglo-Saxons would have seen men and women more or less like themselves, not exotic creatures bearing the marks of monstrous wickedness. That, as we will see, seems to be the point of the representation of the Sodomites in the *Heptateuch* and in many other Anglo-Saxon texts.

Fig. 10. *The Old English Version of the Heptateuch,* folio 32v. Those figures with closed eyes seem already to be dead; all wear expressions of repose rather than terror or shock. London, British Library, Cotton Claudius B.iv. Photo reproduced by permission of The British Library.

Sodom in Some Anglo-Latin texts

Anglo-Saxon understandings of Sodom and Gomorrah were strongly influenced by patristic commentary and by Bede's commentary on Genesis, which transmitted key points of the scholarly consensus up to his time.[21] According to Kay, "Like the rabbis before him, Bede—under the influence of Ezekiel—stressed the social injustice of the Sodomites as a community." Their injustice constituted impiety. "Piety consists in the proper use of God's gifts; impiety, in their malversation to *luxuria*." Thus luxury is not simply overindulgence of the flesh; it is also the sin of forgetting that one can use only a just portion of creation for oneself and that surplus is intended for others. Luxury must be seen as the root of the Sodomites' crimes.[22] Bede argued that the Sodomites were aware of their obligations to act justly under the Noachic laws. He regarded their defeat by the kings of the north and their rescue by Abram as a call to repentance. This lesson was lost on them but not on Lot, who lived among the sinful ones without being corrupted by them. Commenting on the sins of the Sodomites in Genesis 13:13, Bede carefully notes Lot's goodness:

> The sins to which the Sodomites were subject—except the unspeakable one recorded below—are sufficiently expounded by the prophet Ezekiel, who said, speaking to Jerusalem, "Behold this was the iniquity of Sodom thy sister, pride, fulness of bread, and abundance, and the idleness of her, and of her daughters: and they did not put forth their hand to the needy, and to the poor. And they were lifted up, and committed abominations before me." Lot himself was free from all of these faults, as is evident from the text of Genesis, for we are told there that he received the angels with hospitality and was seized by them from the impious infatuation of the Sodomites.

In connection with Lot's purity among the fallen people, Bede also cites the second letter of Peter, who writes that the Sodomites "from day to day vexed the just soul [Lot] with unjust works" (2 Peter 2:7–8).[23]

Bede's reference to the "unspeakable" sin ("excepto illo infando quod in sequentibus scriptura commemorat") is one of the earliest indications in the English tradition that the sin of the Sodomites is dangerous to mention (I discuss an earlier example by Aldhelm below). His reticence might have resulted partly from a sense of decorum and partly from a belief that his audience knew what the "unspeakable" sin was and did not need elaboration. But his commentary on Genesis 19:4 shows that Bede was not afraid of being more specific and that he understood the "unspeakable" or "infamous" sins of the Sodomites to include homosexual acts. When the Sodomites storm Lot's house, they demand that they be allowed "to know" his guests ("ut cognoscamus eos"). In his commentary Bede quoted Isaiah 3:9: "'They proclaim their sin like Sodom; they do not hide it.' Like the Sodomites, they proclaim and do not hide their sin, because with no thought of modesty, as a group, from youth to the most extreme old age, they practiced the shameful act of men on men, not only not hiding their sin in the presence of strangers and guests but forcing them to participate in this grievous and outrageous immorality."[24]

"Bede does not doubt that the Sodomites were homosexuals," Kay concludes, "but he thinks it far worse that they were so far from being ashamed of their vice that they both practiced it openly and forced others to join them" (231). Indeed, Bede specifically denounced the noise of the Sodomites, their "clamor," as a sign of the enormity of their wrongdoing ("Verum multiplicato clamore peccatorum, id est enormi illorum scelere").[25] Bede clearly understood the sexual sins of the Sodomites to be at least partially sins of male homosexual intercourse. He plainly indicated the homosexual character of the Sodomites' sin, described as "masculi in masculos turpitudinem," "the shameful act of men on men." I regard this statement as unambiguous evidence that Bede knew about and abhorred same-sex acts and associated them with the Sodomites. According to Kay, Bede found "no special significance to the sexual aspect of Sodom's crimes" and expressed no particular outrage at them. But because Bede obviously exercised extreme caution in referring to same-sex acts, it is difficult to agree entirely with Kay's assessment. There are, it is true, "no particular" signs of outrage. But there are very particular signs of Bede's fear of mentioning the act or acts in question. He may have subsumed male homosexual acts "under his previous general definition of the sin of Sodom [as impiety]," as Kay argues, since Bede described the fiery destruction of Sodom "as a prefiguration of the penalty that is to be inflicted at the Last Judgment on 'all the impious' ('omnes impii')."[26] Nonetheless, few subsequent sources are as clear in their linking of the city and these sins as this quotation from Bede. The vernacular tradition had to wait nearly three hundred years, the late tenth century, the time of Ælfric, for a voice as cautious and wary of Sodom and its sins as Bede's.

In the *Ecclesiastical History* (completed in 731), Bede attached no sexual significance to Sodom and its sins of luxury. Following the example of one of his sources, Gildas's *Ruin of Britain,* Bede adapted the story of the English to the motif of the Chosen People who violate their covenant with God and are destroyed as a result.[27] The British drove out their Irish and Pictish assailants; their victory was followed by "an abundance of corn in the island as had never before been known. With this affluence came an increase of luxury, followed by every kind of foul crime" ("tantis frugum copiis insula quantas nulla retro aetas meminit, affluere coepit, cum quibus et luxuria crescere et hanc continuo omnium lues scelerum comitair adcelerauit").[28] Restored to peace for a time, the British kept alive the memory of this calamity; when that memory faded, however, they again lapsed into evil ways. "To other unspeakable crimes, which Gildas their own historian describes in doleful words, was added this crime, that they never preached the faith to the Saxons or Angles who inhabited Britain with them." [29] Bede must be understood, however broadly, to have included sexual sins in the category of *luxuria*, although his reference to "unspeakable crimes" need not point to the sin of intramale intercourse only.

What was it that Gildas found unspeakable? Gildas did not mention specific sexual practices in references to Sodom and Gomorrah included in the inventory of archetypal disasters to which he compared the Saxon conquest of Roman Britain. He admired Britain's Roman heritage and used Sodom as an analogy for the British who failed to spread God's word and who fell to the Saxons. Gildas considered their moral lapses so great, N. J. Higham writes, that the British "were as the 'princes of Sodom' or the very Saxons themselves." [30] This comment puts the Saxons and the Sodomites on the same level but does so without describing the Saxons as Sodomites. The British king Constantine, among his other evil deeds, was guilty of "the stench of frequent and successive adulteries." "For, from the bitter vine of the men of Sodom, he had planted a slip of unbelieving folly in the soil of his heart—soil that bore no fruit to good seed." [31] Again echoing the book of Deuteronomy, which describes the poisonous grapes from the vines of Sodom (Deuteronomy 32:32), Gildas reported that the British king Maglocunus behaved "like a man drunk on wine pressed from the vine of the Sodomites" (chap. 33, p. 32). Gildas denounced adultery and whoring but made no reference to same-sex acts. He specified a range of sins— for example, he accused Aurelius Caninus, another British king, of "parricides, fornications, adulteries"—but he did not mention other sexual or homosexual sins associated with Sodom (chap. 20, p. 30).[32] When he referred to an "unspeakable sin" that was "not unknown to Constantine" ("Cuius tam nefandi piaculi non ignarus . . . Constantinus"), it was not a sexual offense but rather swearing false oaths on holy altars (chap. 28, p. 29).[33]

The work of another learned figure before Bede, Aldhelm, suggests an understanding of Sodom much closer to Bede's. In the versification of his prose treatise *De virginitate,* Aldhelm produced an extended allegorical account of the battle between vices and virtues. He made reference to Sodomites not in the section on fornication but in the opening discussion of gluttony, one of the branches of luxury. Aldhelm's primary concern was not the Sodomites but Lot and his behavior with his daughters. Lot "lived generously among wicked men," Aldhelm wrote. However, "when dark thunderbolts with sulphuric flashes set afire the fornicators and sodomites, softened by baseness, who were committing vile deeds of Sodom in a heinous fashion," Lot became drunk and knew "his grown daughters in debauchery." Had he not been drunk, he would never have committed "this deed, unspeakable in its perversity."[34] Aldhelm used a key term examined in chapter 4, "molles," to describe the acts of the Sodomites themselves: "scortatores et molles sorde cenidos [cinaedus] qui Sodomae facinus patrabant more nefando," literally "harlots and molles [effeminate men] who were performing the act of Sodom in an unspeakable way."[35] Aldhelm might be understood as referring to both male and female prostitution, but the reference would seem to include intramale intercourse. The sins Aldhelm cannot name include the Sodomites' sexual sin and also Lot's incest. Sodom has no specific association with same-sex offenses in Bede's *Ecclesiastical History* or in the work of Aldhelm and Gildas. But once we have read Bede's straightforward reference to the evil sin men commit with men, we unavoidably detect a shadow of same-sex sex when the sexual vices of the city are discussed.

A number of sources written up to a century after Bede's time, including texts written by key English figures on the Continent, Boniface, "the apostle of Germany," and Alcuin, a leading figure of Charlemagne's court, confirm that Sodom's sins were not only homosexual acts. Yet a shadow of same-sex sex accompanies many of their references to the city. In fact some scholars have seen far more than a shadow of homosexual sex in the correspondence of Boniface, the Anglo-Saxon archbishop of Mainz who was martyred in 754.[36] Derrick Sherwin Bailey and David F. Greenberg both find a reference to "homosexuality" in a letter written by Boniface and five other bishops that was sent to Æthelbald, king of the Mercians. The letter asserts that "[i]f the English people, as is reported here and as is charged against us in France and Italy and even by the heathens themselves, are scorning lawful marriage and living in wanton adultery like the people of Sodom, then we must expect that a degenerate and degraded people with unbridled desires will be produced."[37] True, this reference to Sodom alleges

sexual corruption, but not of a homosexual kind. Boswell noted that
Bailey truncated this quotation at the word "Sodom," thus concealing
the reference to marriage that removes any suggestion that homosexual
acts are invoked by the reference to Sodom.[38] Bailey did, however, admit that the letter permitted no firm conclusions.[39] Greenberg used a
somewhat different translation and cited the passage as evidence that
no early Germanic law codes mention homosexual behavior. He too
ended the quotation with the word "Sodom" and commented, "The
literary and historical sources suggest that, gender stereotypes aside,
this is because there was no prejudice against [homosexuality]."[40]
Hence Boniface protested against a custom that flourished because the
law codes did not restrain it. But the letter is primarily concerned with
fornication with consecrated women and the murder of children born
to them. Boswell was right to assert that in Boniface's letter "[h]omo-
sexuality is neither mentioned nor implied" (203). Boniface's comment
is indeed striking, not because it constructs an analogy between "filthy
unions" in England and the adulterous lust of Sodom but because it
hypothesizes "a degenerate and ignoble people, burning with lust" as
the *offspring* of such unions. Sodomitic intercourse is seldom associated
with fertility and procreation, even if only the procreation of the foul
from the foul. Boniface's letter clearly implies an understanding of
Sodom as a place of "adultery and lust." Lust would include intramale
or intrafemale sex, of course, but the letter makes no direct reference
to homosexual acts. Although same-sex sex is part of "lust," it can, in
this context, be seen only as part of lust's shadow.

Another English figure whose work on the Continent has been used
to attest to knowledge of same-sex relations is Alcuin, one of Charlemagne's teachers. Boswell argued that there is a "distinctly erotic element" in Alcuin's court circle, especially between Alcuin and his pupils.
Boswell quoted some fragments of Alcuin's poetry and a letter to a
bishop in which Alcuin wrote that if he were somehow transported
to the man's presence he would "cover, with tightly pressed lips, not
only your eyes, ears, and mouth but also your every finger and toe, not
once but many a time" (188, 190). Such effusions, as Peter Dronke
pointed out, belong to a venerable tradition of "Christian *amicitia*" and
need not have any direct relation to sexual passion. Boswell disputed
Dronke's point, arguing (quite reasonably) that "such phrases could later
be used in an erotic context regardless of their original setting" (190–
91 note 81). More telling is a letter Alcuin wrote to a student guilty of
what, according to Boswell, "appears to be a homosexual indiscretion."
Alcuin registered "no shock or outrage, simply annoyance" at this

behavior, Boswell reported, and added that "Alcuin simply threatens the youth with the prospect of losing his place in the clerics' affections" and points to the penalty of "eventual judgment" for his sins.[41]

The letter, however, reveals much more. In it Alcuin charged that his correspondent is "still addicted to the filthy practices of boys" and that he is unwilling to give up "what should never have been done." "[Where is] your fear of hell?" Alcuin asked. He warned the student to change his ways and says he will pray for his soul, "which will burn in the flames of Sodom."[42] The conjunction of Sodom and this accusation of "the filthy practices of boys"—acts described in the penitentials—shows not only that Alcuin deplored same-sex intercourse but that such behavior might be expected of boys (monastic boys in particular, it would seem), but not of older men. Allowing full measure for the passionate elements in Alcuin's correspondence, one does not have to read very many of his letters before realizing that the writer was as severe a moralist as Boniface, and also an ascetic. Boswell's suggestion (178 note 31) that Alcuin's "own inclinations" helped him modify regulations of the Carolingian church against same-sex acts is gratuitous. Alcuin's own inclinations are not a matter of record; whatever inferences we draw from his correspondence have to take into account the censure this letter makes plain. In a timely corrective to Boswell's reading of amatory letters such as this one, Stephen Jaeger has argued that erotic and passionate language had to be firmly isolated from same-sex sex in order to become available for such correspondence. He argued that erotic language between men was permitted in such correspondence to the exact degree that it was *not* sexual.[43] In chapter 2 I have taken a similar position in discussing the sexual content of Anglo-Saxon references to same-sex love.

Alcuin is agreed to have been the author of a catechetical work, the *Interrogationes Sigewulfi,* that associates Sodom with same-sex sexual practices "against nature" and explicitly condemns them. The work asks and answers questions about the meaning of the book of Genesis, synthesizing "precious pearls of wisdom" for the "weary traveler." In answer to the question, "Why were the world's sins destroyed by water in Noah's time, but the sins of the Sodomites by fire?" Alcuin, drawing on Bede, claimed that the sin of "natural" desire with women was punished by water, a lighter punishment than that used to avenge the sin of desire "against nature" with men ("Because that natural sin of desire [performed] with women is damned as if with the less harsh element; on the other hand, the sin of desire against nature [when performed] with men is punished by the fiercer element"; "Quia illud naturale li-

bidinis cum feminis peccatum quasi leviori elemento damnatur; hoc
vero contra naturam libidinis peccatum cum viris, acrioris elementi
vindicatur incendio").[44] The opposition of heterosexual to homosexual
intercourse is clear, for the sinner in each case is presumed to be male.
His "natural" sin is one of desire for women; his sin "against nature"
is one of desire for men. Alcuin thought of Sodom as a sinful place
where men unnaturally desired other men. Because Sodom's sins were
greater—that is, unnatural—they received greater punishment. Nature resumed its course when the earth was restored to life after the
flood, but the earth remained desolate after Sodom was destroyed by
fire. Water symbolizes baptism and repentance; fire, eternal damnation.
Thus one kind of sin was absorbed into a natural cycle of recovery, the
other was not.

The complete tradition of Sodom and Gomorrah in patristic commentary and exegesis cannot be inferred only from the writings just
sampled.[45] But little is found in the work of Aldhelm, Bede, Boniface,
and Alcuin that is not also found in commentaries on this popular subject by Gregory, Augustine, Ambrose, and others. By the end of the
eighth century, Sodom and Gomorrah had been explicitly (but not exclusively) associated with homosexual behavior by Bede, who made direct reference to intramale intercourse in his commentary on Genesis,
and by Alcuin and Aldhelm, although not by Boniface. The learned
Latin tradition does not name the sin—none of the authors I cite called
intramale sex "sodomy"—but clearly identifies male homosexual intercourse as the "unnatural" partner to the "natural" coupling of male and
female.

Like the Latin evidence, vernacular texts represent homosexual acts
as an excess to which the undisciplined, licentious, and indulgent were
prone. Some vernacular authors linked Sodom and Gomorrah to same-
sex intercourse, but most used a more general concept of excess to describe the character of those who dwelled in these cities. Sodomitical
excess takes obvious forms, such as gluttony and compulsive fornication. Other signs of Sodom's disregard for accepted social boundaries
include their noise or clamor and their suspicious preference for acting
at night. Christian moralists stressed that no sin (sexual or otherwise)
could escape God's sight and that Sodomites were neither silent nor
unseen. These writers were not constructing what we might think of
as a closet for same-sex acts and those who committed them. There
was no place for Sodomites to hide. Eventually Sodom disappeared
into darkness, but not a secret darkness. The oblivion that descended
on Sodomites in fire and sulfur was a punishment they called down on

themselves through their shameless outcry, their acts of blasphemy, indulgence, and sexual excess.

SODOM IN THE PROSE OF ALFRED'S REIGN

Vernacular prose texts that instructed priests and bishops in their duties, including preaching and hearing confession, bring us close to the
life of the Anglo-Saxon laity. Among these texts are several that date
from the reign of King Alfred (871–99) and pastoral letters and homilies from the tenth and eleventh centuries, which reinforced the harsh
view of intramale and intrafemale sexual relations found in the penitentials. Four translations undertaken during Alfred's reign are relevant.[46] The most important of them is the translation of Gregory's *Cura
pastoralis*. Others include the Old English translation of Gregory's *Dialogi*, a series of miracle stories told by Gregory to his deacon, Peter; the
translation of Orosius's *Historiarum adversum paganos libri septem*,
which contains the story of Sardanapallus; and Augustine's *Soliloquies*,
which contains a striking passage about physical intimacy between
men (both the translation of Orosius and the *Soliloquies* are discussed
in chapter 2; the *Soliloquies* makes no reference to Sodom and Gomorrah). Compared to references to Sodom in the handbooks of penance,
these texts show that the Anglo-Saxons associated many sins, sexual
and nonsexual, with the city.

The *Pastoral Care*, as it is usually known, was one of the most influential pastoral texts in the Middle Ages, early or late. The book describes sixty-five circumstances that the priest must consider when ad-
vising penitents. Sodom appears twice in Alfred's text, once to supply
an allegory about sexual continence in marriage and again to illustrate
the sins of those who are without shame. Both examples emphasize
excess and lack of restraint. Gregory juxtaposed the practices of Sodom
to marital continence and advised that "those who are bound in marriage are to be admonished in one way [and] in another those who are
free from those ties."[47] Gregory quoted familiar Pauline texts about
fornication that warn that it is better to fall "on the soft bed of marriage
rather than the hard earth of fornication" (397.22–23). He allegorized
Lot's escape from the flames of Sodom and Gomorrah to the city of
Zoar (Segor). In Zoar, Lot stood at the midpoint between the marsh of
Sodom and the mountain of continence, between sinful and procreative
sex. In this allegory Sodom represents excess, described as "the unlawful heat of our bodies" ("ðone unliefedan byrne ures lichoman"), and is
juxtaposed to mountain, which represents "the purity of continence"

("ða clænnesse ðære forhæfdnesse"), the righteous conduct of those who have intercourse only if they wish to beget children ("buton ðonne hi wilniað bearn to gestrienanne," 397.35–399.4). Gregory's chief concern was not homosexual unions, which would be included among the unlawful fornications of Sodom, but excessive sexual lust within marriage—and also, surprisingly, too little sex in marriage, the error of those "do not enjoy their own lawful partners as they should" ("hie gehealdað wið unryhthæmed and swaðeah his agenra ryhthiwena ne brycð swa swa he mid ryhte sceolde," 399.7–9). Marriage might be a "soft bed," but it is also an earthly burden that, if possible, one should escape, choosing instead a life of virginity. Gregory not only advised the clergy's instruction of the laity but also advised the clergy about their own sexual conduct, warning priests that they were not to associate with unmarried women ("æmtegan wifmen," 401.24). (Needless to say, they were not to associate with married women, either.) The Anglo-Saxon clergy were not, however, celibate, although certain reform-minded authors, Ælfric among them, advocated this practice.

Gregory quoted a passage from Paul's first letter to the Corinthians (1 Corinthians 6:9–10) that includes the list of sexual offenders who shall not enter heaven: "neque fornicarii, neque idolis servientes, neque adulteri, neque molles, neque masculorum concubitores, neque fures."[48] The Old English does not translate this language precisely: "Nawðer ne ða wohhæmendan, ne ða ðe diofulgieldum ðiowiað, ne ða unfæsðradan, ðe ne magon hira unryhthæmdes geswican, ne ða ðiofas" ("Neither fornicators, nor idolaters, nor the inconstant, who are unable to cease from fornication, nor thieves," 401.26–27). I noted in the last chapter that one term mentioned in this list, "molles," probably referred to a man who took the passive role in homosexual intercourse, and another, "masculorum concubitores," referred to male prostitutes. Other sinners mentioned include the "fornicarii" and "adulteri." Alfred's translation offers an opportunity to see how well these terms were understood in England near the end of the ninth century. Three categories, "adulteri," "molles," and "masculorum concubitores" are conflated into one, "ða unfæsðradan, ðe ne magon hira unryhthæmdes geswican," that is, "the inconstant, who are unable to cease from fornication." The "wohhæmendan," "fornicators," are those who have sex outside of marriage (clergy who did this were Gregory's immediate concern). All the others are "unfæsðradan," "the inconstant," whose sins, heterosexual or homosexual, are signs of uncontrollable lust. The link to Sodom is clear, since Gregory wrote elsewhere that inconstancy is one of the outgrowths of *luxuria*.[49] The distinguishing feature of the second category is excess: the "unfæsðradan" not only fornicated outside the proper context of marriage but also fornicated uncontrollably. (Like so much in the literature of Sodom, this accusation has a familiar ring. It is an early appearance of a stigma still current in homophobic discourse, which is that homosexuals are obsessed with sex and cannot restrain their lust—a stigma elevated to a lifestyle by those in what Gabriel Rotello has called the "fast lane" of gay male life, who argue that those who have the most sex are also the most gay.)[50]

Chapter 55 of the *Pastoral Care* cautions that "those who praise their unlawful deeds are to be admonished in one way [and] in another those who blame and yet do them" (427.9–10). Gregory quoted Isaiah's denunciation of those who "proclaimed their sins as the men of Sodom did, and did not conceal them" (427.28–29; Isaiah 3:9). Although this chapter makes no overt reference to sexual conduct or to homosexual acts, it associates the Sodomites both with lack of shame at their excess, a connection also made by Bede, and with the refusal to repent. The Sodomites continued in sin even though they knew what they did was wrong. Had they been ashamed of their sins and concealed them, they would have lived in fear; instead "they completely relinquished the bridle of fear when they cared not whether it was day or night when they sinned" ("hi forleton eallinga ðone bridels ðæs eges, ða hi ne scrifon hwæðer hit wære ðe dæg ðe niht, ðonne ðonne hi syngodon," 427.30–32). The Sodomites refused to keep their sexual misdeeds in the dark. But it is to darkness that those deeds will consign them, for those who know their sins and fail to relinquish them meet a terrible fate. "The more clearly they know [their sins], the greater their ruin, because they received the light of understanding, and yet would not relinquish the darkness of the wicked deed ("Swa hi hit ðonne swutolor witon, swa hi swiður forweorðað, forðæmðe hi onfengon ðæt leoht ðæs ondgietes, & ðeah noldon forlætan ða ðistro ðæs won weorces, ac ðæt andgiet ðæt him God sende to fultome hi agimeleasedon," 429.10–14).

Gregory did not elaborate the connection between those who knowingly persist in sin and the shameless Sodomites, but subsequent comments strengthen this association. The most pointed is Gregory's quotation of Psalm 54, "They shall go living into hell" (429.23–24). Those who do not know they are doing wrong will descend into hell after death, but "those who know, and yet do it, go living and conscious into hell" ("ac ða ðe hit witon, & swaðeah doð, ða gað libbende & witende on helle," 429.27–28). It would be difficult to imagine a better description of the punishment of the women and men swallowed into hell than God's rain of fire and brimstone on Sodom.

The *Pastoral Care* describes the Sodomites' shameless sinning as hell on earth. Some medieval accounts of the cities' destruction make that point by emphasizing stench, a prominent feature of the representation of Sodom in Gregory's *Dialogues*. Gregory elaborated a quotation from Matthew (7:14), "For the gate is narrow and the road is hard that leads to life, and there are few who find it," with a vision of the afterlife. A soldier sees a black and smoky river of stench and, opposite it, a sweet-smelling meadow where white-clad men behold shining mansions built of the good works done in the present life. These worlds are connected by a bridge. This topography—two opposed states and a transitional point between them—is similar to that Gregory provided for Sodom, Zoar, and the mountain of continence in the *Pastoral Care*. Evil ones who cross the bridge fall into the river; the just easily reach the meadow. When Peter asks for a scriptural text to prove that carnal sins are punished with stench, Gregory describes Sodom and Gomorrah, referring once again to the excessive desires of the Sodomites and the figurative relationship between their sins and their damnation.

> Soðlice eac we leornodon in genese þære bec, þæt drihten sende fyr 7 swefl samod ofer Sodoma folc, to þon þæt þæt fyr hi forbærnde, 7 se fula stenc þæs swefles hi acwealde. forþon þe hi burnon on þære unalyfdan lufe þæs gebrosniendan lichaman, hi forþon eac samod to lore wurdon in þam bryne 7 fulan stence, þæt hi ongæton on heora sylfra wite, þæt hi sealdon ær hi sylfe mid heora synlustum to þam ecan deaþe þære fulnesse.[51]

> Truly we learn in the book of Genesis that the Lord sent fire and sulfur together over the people of Sodom, in order that the fire might burn them and the foul stink of sulfur might kill them. Because they burned with the unlawful love of the corruptible body, they were brought to destruction in the fire and in the foul stink together, so that in their own punishment they might know that already in their sinful desires they gave themselves to the eternal death of that foulness.

As in the *Pastoral Care,* Gregory indicts all sexual sins and makes no specific reference to homosexual acts. The Sodomites apparently learned only at the last moment that the foulness of their lives anticipated the foulness of their death. The stench of "unlawful love" merely prefigures the stench of the eternal death these lovers bring on themselves. They pass from one stinking state into another, sinking into a punishment that literalizes their moral corruption.

The Old English translation of the *Historiarum adversum Paganos Libri Septem,* or *The Seven Books of History against the Pagans,* by Orosius lacks the rhetorical fervor of the *Dialogues* and the *Pastoral Care.*

This text neither analyzes nor allegorizes the destruction of Sodom, referring merely to the heavenly fire and its destructive power ("Hu þæt heofenisce fyr forbærnde þæt lond on þæm wæron þa twa byrig on getimbred, Sodome 7 Gomorre").[52] But this text provides an exceptionally clear understanding of Sodom's association with abundance or luxury. Excessive pleasure taken in the abundance of fruit—that is, luxury—arouses sexual lusts: "At that time the people were enjoying wealth excessively, until great fiery lust began to awake inside them and God's vengeance came to them because of this lust, so that he burned the whole land with sulfurous fire" ("Þa wæs þæt folc þæs micclan welan ungemetlice brucende, oð ðæt him on se miccla firenlust oninnan aweox. 7 him com of þæm firenluste Godes wraco, þæt he eal þæt land mid sweflenum fyre forbærnde," 22.29–23.11). Once a fruitful place, Sodom became dead and sterile; many kinds of fruit still grow there, "but when one takes it in hand, it turns to ashes" ("ac þonne hig man on hand nymð, þonne weorðað hig to acxan," 23.10–11). The physiology of the passage is fully in harmony with what we have seen in the *Pastoral Care*. The excess of the Sodomites is clear in their immoderate ("ungemetlice") enjoyment of wealth, which in turn awakens lust, which in turn provokes God's destruction. This, as Jordan has shown, is Gregory's understanding of *luxuria*, a sin which follows "the logic of mutation, infiltration, reactivation."[53]

SODOM IN ANONYMOUS HOMILIES

A group of anonymous homilies likely to have been written after Alfred's reign suggest further representations of Sodom. Two homilies in the anonymous Blickling collection, thought to have been produced before the last decade of the tenth century, use Sodom as an example of God's rage against sinful humanity. In a Palm Sunday homily, Christ sees that the people of Jerusalem will not repent ("þæt hie nænige bote ne hreowe don noldan") and sends them greater destruction than had ever been seen before, except by the Sodomites alone ("maran wræce þonne æfre ær ænigu oþru gelumpe, buton Sodomwarum anum").[54] A homily on the Assumption of Mary emphasizes another aspect of the Sodomites' punishment, the blindness that struck them immediately after they assaulted Lot's house. A powerful metaphor for ignorance and death, blindness is a punishment for wilful rejection of righteous behavior; it is a form of darkness visited upon those who, like the Sodomites, choose to live in it.[55] In the homily, a Jewish leader touches Mary's coffin and is converted. His people, already blinded like the Sodomites, cry out, but this noise is different from the clamor of

Sodom. The Jews fear that their blindness will followed by an inferno such as that visited upon the Sodomites, a terrible precedent that inspires them to humility and a confession of faith. "Woe to us," they cry, "for now it has happened to us as it was in Sodom" ("Wa us la, forþon be us is nu geworden swa swa on Sodoma byrig wæs"). Their belief restores their sight.[56] The sin of Sodom in this account is not luxury or some form of sexual misconduct but the refusal to believe.

Sodom and Sodomites appear in Old English homilies in several guises—as clamorous, unrepentant sinners, as examples of the fate awaiting the wicked, as those struck blind by their refusal to believe. Only once in the homiletic corpus are Sodom and Sodomites unambiguously linked to homosexual acts. *Vercelli Homily 7,* an anonymous homily from the tenth century, denounces luxury and warns that strife creates honor, that easy lives are fruitless, and that idleness is evil. After the manner of Gregory's *Dialogues,* the text quotes Matthew 7:14 to say that the narrow way leads to life and the wide way to death. Those in Sodom "perished because of their unlawful desires," as did those who lived in Noah's time. Their sin, named by Ezekiel (16:49), was luxury, which leads to unrighteous living.[57]

> Geþenceað eac þara þe in Sodome for hira unalyfedum gewilnungum forwurdon, 7 þara þe on Noes dagum wæron. Witodlice be ðam þe ðam yðan life lyfedon on Sodome hit wæs gecweden ðætte on hlafes fylnesse flowen. Þonne sio fylnes ðæs hlafes unriht wyrceð, hwæt is to cweðanne be ðam mænigfealdum smeamettum? Gemunað hu Esaw his dagas on ehtnesse lædde, 7 hu ða ðe ær in þam ryne Godes bearn wæron þurh ænlicra wifa sceawunga to fyrenlustum gehæfte on helle gehruron. Gemunaþ eac hu þa forwurdon þe mid wodheortnesse willan to wæpnedmannum hæmed sohton, 7 eallra Babilone 7 Egypta cyninga ealle hie swiðe ungesæliglice hira life geendedon 7 nu syndon on ecum witum. (135.38–49)

Remember also those who perished in Sodom because of their unlawful desires, and those who lived in Noah's time. Surely concerning those who lived the easy life in Sodom it was said that they flow in the fullness of bread. Then, (if) the fullness of the bread leads to unrighteousness, what is to be said concerning manifold delicacies? Remember how Esau spent his days in persecution, and how those who before were the children of God in that age were bound to fiery lusts through seeing their own wives (and) fell down to hell. Remember also how they perished who with mad desire sought fornication with men, and all the kings of Babylon and Egypt who ended their lives unhappily and now dwell in eternal torment.

The homily plainly contrasts two kinds of fornication, heterosexual (lust from the sight of men's own wives, "ænlicra wifa sceawunga") and homosexual, those who madly "sought fornication with men" ("to wæpnedmannum hæmed sohton"). A life of luxury, of excess—represented by the fullness of bread and manifold delicacies—is seen as the root of the Sodomites' (and others') sinfulness. The homily also underscores the irrationality of intramale sexual intercourse, characterizing it, beyond lust, as the desire of madness ("wodheortnesse willan"). "Just so are the same torments now prepared for those men who now live such lives as they lived," the homilist adds ("Eac swylce þa ilcan witu syndon gearuwe þam mannum þe nu swylcum lifum lifiað swylce hie lyfedon," 135.49–50). The force of the Sodomites' example carries into the present.

A pseudo-Wulfstan homily on the observance of Sunday, likely to have been written after the homilies in the Vercelli and Blickling collections, warns that certain sinful works are especially to be abstained from on Sunday. They include adultery, drunkenness, manslaughter, lying, plunder and theft, fornication and strife, hatred, and other evil deeds. Those who do not honor Sunday will be punished terribly by God, with hunger, the sword's edge, death, and captivity. The homily anticipates the speech God will deliver to those who do not honor Sunday: "I will sink your souls in misery in hell, just as I did previously to the two cities of Sodom and Gomorrah, which were consumed with heavenly fire before in this place, and all those who dwelled in them forever burn in the hell ground in hot fire, because they infamously enraged the merciful God" ("Ic besence eowre sawla on susle on helle, swa swa ic hwilon dyde þa twa burh Sodomam and Gomorram, þe mid heofonlicum fyre her wurdan forbærnde, and ealle þa þe him on eardodon, æfre byrnað on helle grunde on hatan fyre, forþan hi þone mildan god manfullice gremedon").[58]

These homilies illustrate the power of Sodom and Gomorrah to inspire the laity to righteous living through negative example, the cities' destruction supplying a spectacle of unthinkable horror. But the vices that occasioned it are, for the most part, only vaguely sketched. Most of the homilies do not associate Sodom and Gomorrah with specific sins. The Sunday sermon, for example, merely lists "adultery" and "fornication." The Blickling homily on the Assumption attacks doubt of Christian truth rather than sexual sin. There are many references to the "shameful deeds" of the Sodomites, but only the Vercelli homilist explained what at least one of those deeds was: men fornicating with other men.

In the homiletic discourse, the lesson of Sodom and Gomorrah was

a general warning that people would receive the punishment warranted by their evil deeds. If Sodom and Gomorrah had been *exclusively* associated with homosexual sins, we might conclude that the
homilists were not being straightforward about references to same-sex
acts. A few voices in their culture did name the sin of Sodom as same-
sex intercourse. But the cities were thought to have been guilty of many
other kinds of excess, not same-sex acts only. The homilists emphasized the justice and thoroughness of God's wrath rather than the
wicked deeds—homosexual, heterosexual, and nonsexual—that provoked it.

Sodom in the Works of Ælfric

One important Anglo-Saxon figure, Ælfric, shows a distinctive wari-
ness of explicit references to same-sex acts. His work, which includes
homilies, saints' lives, pastoral letters, and other texts, contains the most
important and certainly the most revealing references to Sodom in Old
English prose. They are found in Ælfric's version of the *Interrogationes
Sigewulfi* by Alcuin. Ælfric reduced Alcuin's 280 questions and answers
to 69 and added a preface and some other features to the work.[59] Explaining why God told Abraham that the sins of the Sodomites rose up
to heaven, Ælfric wrote, "The sin is with the voice when the guilt is
(committed) in deed. And the sin is (committed) with clamor, or noise,
when one sins freely, without shame, so that he shows his wrongdoing
to other men" ("Seo syn bið mid stemne þonne se gylt bið on dæde.
And seo syn bið mid hreame þon se man syngað freolice butan ælcere
sceame, swilce he his yfel oþrum mannum bodige," 46.449–48.452).
The noise or clamor of Sodom represents excess, a lack of shame. In
answer to the question, "Why did God punish these same Sodomites
with burning sulfur while the sinful in Noah's flood were punished by
water?" Ælfric offers a compressed translation of Alcuin's original: "In
Noah's flood God punished mankind's wickedness with water, with a
lighter fate, because they sinned with women [mid wifum], and the
Sodomites sinned abysmally against nature [ongean gecynd] and therefore were consumed with sulfurous fire, so that their foul lust was punished with foul sulfur" ("On noes dagum gewitnode god manna gal-
nysse mid wætere mid liðran gesceafte: forþan þe hi syngodan mid
wifum. 7 þa sodomitiscan syngodon bysmorlice ongean gecynd. 7
wurdon forþi mid swæflenum fyre forswælede. þæt heora fule galnys
wurde mid þam fulan swæfle gewitnod," 48.455–60). God forgave
mankind after the flood, saying that he would not damn his creatures
for all time but would punish them in the world instead "because they

are weak" ("forþam þe hi synd tyddre," 48.468). "But nothing like that is written concerning the Sodomites," Ælfric added, "who sinned shamefully against nature; therefore were they eternally damned" ("Nis na þus awriten be þam sodomitiscan þe ongean gecynd sceamlice syngodon. forþan þe hi synd ecelice fordemede," 48.469–72). Ælfric twice used the expression "against nature," "ongean gecynd," to describe the Sodomite's sin. His Latin source, as we saw above, juxtaposed two kinds of sinful behavior, "the sin of natural desire with women" ("naturale libidinis cum feminis peccatum") and "the sin of desire against nature with men" ("contra naturam libidinis peccatum cum viris"), thus making the contrast between what is "natural" and "unnatural" explicit.[60]

The distinction between "natural" and "unnatural" sins in Old English does not by itself indicate homosexual acts. Priests and other clergyman reading or hearing this text would have associated the phrase "against nature" with a variety of forbidden sexual acts, including same-sex relations and any other sex acts that frustrated procreation. In chapter 4 we noted a canon in the Old English Penitential and the Old English Handbook that states, "If anyone foully through unnatural things soils himself [or herself] against God's creation in any way, he [or she] is to repent that forever while he [or she] lives, until he [or she] be dead" (see chapter 4, appendix 2, for texts). The penitential's proscription would seem to encompass many evil acts. Ælfric's statement narrows and points the meaning. Noah's people sinned "mid wifum," "with women," while the Sodomites sinned "ongean gecynde," "against nature." Ælfric obscures the parallel structure. His asymmetrical construction fails to specify intramale sexual intercourse, but style and syntax together underscore that very possibility. In the murky realm of acts "against nature," we detect the phrase "mid werum," "with men," absent from Ælfric's sentence but clearly visible in its shadow.

Most of Ælfric's discussions of Sodom and Gomorrah make no reference to the Sodomites' sins. Another text addressed to the clergy, a letter written to the priest Sigeweard, after 1005, offers a condensed version of Christian history and describes the eight ages of the world. Sodom and Gomorrah belong to the second age of the world, spanning the Flood and Abraham's lifetime: "On ðissere ylde þa yfela leoda, fif burhscira ðæs fulestan mennisces Sodomitisces eardes, mid swæflene fyre, færlice wurdon ealle forbearnde, 7 heora burga samod, buton Loth ane, ðe God lædde ðanon mid his þrim hiwum for his rihtwisnesse" ("In this age the evil people of the five cities of the land of the most foul people of the Sodomites were suddenly entirely consumed with flames, together with their cities, all except Lot alone, whom God

led from thence with three women on account of his righteousness").⁶¹
The catastrophe is unmotivated because Ælfric made no reference to
the Sodomites' sexual sins. Lot's righteous behavior merely suggests
the impiety (unrighteous conduct by women and men) that caused the
Sodomites' destruction.

We can compare this text with Ælfric's mid-Lent homily known as
the "Prayer of Moses," included in his *Lives of Saints,* a book written
"about the passions and lives of the saints whom the monks honor
with offices" ("boc be þæra halgena ðrowungum and life gedihton þe
mynster-menn mid heora þenungum betwux him wurðiað"), completed before 998.⁶² The text describes God's vengeance on three often-
associated groups who held him in contempt: the angels, mankind in
the days of Noah, and the Sodomites; the special crimes of Sodom are
apparent. Men and women in the age of Noah acted very foolishly and
angered God greatly with fornication ("dysgodon to swyðe and mid
forligre gegremedon god ælmihtigne þearle," 296.185–86). God punished them with the Flood. The Sodomites, however, committed "foul
fornications" and were "the most vile people" ("þa fulan forligeras
þæs fracodostan mennisces sodomitiscra ðeoda," 296.191–92). God sent
"fire and foul brimstone, and burned them all up, and destroyed their
cities, and all that country with awful fire" ("God sende ða fyr on meri-
gen and fulne swefel him to and forbærnde hi ealle and heora burga
towende and ealne þone eard mid egeslicum fyre," 298.211–13). Where
those foul men lived, there is now foul water instead. The particular
lesson to be drawn from this example is not that Ælfric's audience
should refrain from foul fornication (although that too, of course), but
that there are two kinds of fornication, one typical of Noah's age, and
the other, "foul fornication," typical of the Sodomites. The latter is
worse than the former. But why? And how precisely did these sins
differ? Ælfric does not say. Once again he acknowledges a distinction
between two (or more) kinds of sexual misbehavior but fails to make
his meaning specific. The lesson that Ælfric himself draws from the
episode make a different point. He likens clergymen like himself,
"learned servants of God [who] greatly benefit the laity," to Abraham
because they too intercede with God for the faithful ("þæt micclum
fremiað þam læwedum mannum," 298.216–17). This collection of texts
was intended for the instruction of the laity (it is dedicated to two al-
dermen, Æthelweard and Æthelmær). The emphasis on clerical authority is underscored by Ælfric's comment that the collection contains
nothing new but is rather a translation of texts written in Latin and
previously unknown to laymen ("awriten on ledenbocum þeah þe þa
læwedan man þæt nyston," 4.47–48). The contrast between Abraham

and the clergy on one hand, the Sodomites and the laity on the other, is of course most unflattering to the audience.

Ælfric offered another compressed history of Sodom in a sermon on the Last Judgment, "Sermo de die iudicii," which stresses the unknowable nature and swiftness of the Second Coming. Ælfric noted that the story of Sodom is less well-known than that of the Flood. The remarkable banality of Sodom's affairs as he described them might explain why.

> And swa swa on Loðes dagum eft syððan gelamp,
> menn æton and druncon, bohtan and sealdan,
> byttlodan and plantodan, and beeodon heora tilunga;
> þa sende God færlice, sona swa Loð wæs
> of þære byrig alæd, ofer þam fif burhscirum
> fyr and swefel, swylce hit renscur wære,
> and mid ealle forbærnde þa fif burhscira.
> Eall swa bið on þam dæge þe ure Drihten bið æteowed,
> and he cymð to demenne on þam micclan dome
> eallum manncynne, ælcum be hys weorcum.[63]

> It happened in Lot's day that men ate and drank, bought and sold, built and planted, and went about their business. Then suddenly, as soon as Lot was led out of the city, God sent fire and sulfur over the five cities, as if it were a shower of rain, and the five cities burned up completely. Just so will it be on the day when our Lord will be revealed and he will come to judge all mankind in the great judgment, each according to his works.

This example differs from others because it does not imply the existence of two orders of evil deeds, with Sodom typifying the worse. Lot lived among the Sodomites, "sinful men, miserably condemned in shameful deeds" ("se eardode þa on þam yfelan leodscipe / Sodomitiscre burhware, þa wæron synfulle menn, / and bysmorlice forscyldgode on sceamlicum dædum," 593.67–69). But God sent two shining angels to the loyal Lot and led him out from that foul people ("of þam fulan mancynne," 593.74), so that Lot would not be destroyed with them. Only a few lines earlier Ælfric has mentioned that God will come on the Last Day with shining angels (592.48). Thus Sodom serves as a reminder of the final judgment, the terror of its destruction more important than the wickedness that provoked it. Ælfric made a similar reference to the cities in a Lenten homily about Jonah and the Ninevites, who averted God's anger because they fasted and were spared, unlike the Sodomites, who were burned with heavenly fire for their crimes ("for heora leahtrum, mid heofonlicum fyre forbærnde").[64]

Ælfric drew many morals from the story of Sodom, but he was reluctant to identify same-sex sex as one of the sins that made the city such an effective example. The high point of his restraint comes in his own translation of Genesis, parts of which were incorporated into the translation of this material found in the *Old English Heptateuch*. When describing the confrontation between Lot and the Sodomites, Ælfric departs abruptly from the text. It is in the night—their hour—when the Sodomites appear and demand that Lot hand over his visitors to them. "That people was very shameful, in that they would foully, against nature, fulfill their lust, not with women but so foully that it disgraces us to tell about it openly. And that was their uproar [outcry, "hream"], that they performed their filth openly" ("Se leodscipe wæs swa bysmorful, þæt hi woldon fullice ongean gecynd heora galnyssæ gefyllan, na mid wimmannum, ac swa fullice þæt us sceamað hyt openlice to secgenne, 7 þæt wæs heora hream, þæt hi openlice heora fylðe gefremedon" 132.3).[65] As Godden notes, "se leodscipe," "the nation," "is silently interpreted as the adult male inhabitants" of Sodom. He concludes that "[f]or Ælfric, male homosexuality was evidently the prevailing practice at Sodom and the reason for the city's destruction, and it was a sin so appalling that it could not be described."[66] What the Sodomites would not conceal, Ælfric himself chose to obscure, and what they proclaimed, he silenced, saying that he would not describe the acts that the Sodomites intended to commit. Unaware that Ælfric was the author, A. N. Doane remarked that the translator "feels so strongly that he replaces [Genesis] 19.4–11 with a little homily."[67] It is not much of a homily, of course, as opposed to an indignant concealment of what the author regards as an unmentionable offense. It is also a moment of significant irony, since his concealment flatly contradicts the translation policy Ælfric proclaimed at the start of the work. Ælfric's distinction between language and sense and his concern about the potential of misrepresenting the word of God in a translation is well known. Jonathan Wilcox has called his translation of Genesis "his most literal translation."[68] "We write no more than the plain [or "naked"] narrative," Ælfric writes ("We ne writaþ na mare buton þa nacedan gerecednisse," *Heptateuch* 77:42–43). In this case, Ælfric chose to write a good deal less.

Genesis 19:3–11 explains not only what the men wanted—intercourse with the visitors—but also Lot's offer of his daughters to them instead. But the translator's reluctance is directed not at Lot's proposal, whatever Ælfric thought of it, but at the Sodomites' demand for male

homosexual intercourse, which is "against nature" ("ongean gecynd").
It is ironic that Ælfric would not name this sin openly ("openlice"),
since his sentence makes the nature of the Sodomite's sin clear. Their
act, "foully against nature," "fullice ongean gecynd," is again juxtaposed to the sin "mid wimmanum." Members of the Anglo-Saxon audience, whether hearing or reading this text, would easily have substi-
tuted the missing term, "mid mannum" (or "mid werum"), just as they
would have done when reading Ælfric's translation of the *Interrogationes Sigewulfi*, in order to construct the sentence the author chose not
to write.

The texts examined up to this point had diverse audiences. Some of
these texts were clearly intended for a learned audience who would
read or hear the texts ("sine legendo, seu audiendo," as Ælfric put it in
the Latin preface to *Lives of Saints*, 1.2.4), and others for the unlearned
who would hear them only. Ælfric worried that translation was dangerous, since it might misrepresent sacred doctrine and cause "the
pearls of Christ [to] be had in disrespect" ("ne forte despectui habean-
tur margarite christi," 1.2.11–12). He did not hesitate to clarify certain
points about which he expected his audience to be in doubt. For example, he explained the meaning of circumcision and warned that it
was to be observed only figuratively (by controlling lust) rather than
physically.[69] Likewise, his comments on Sodom suggest that he concentrated on the spiritual or figurative meaning of the Sodomites' behavior, not wanting to risk creating a misunderstanding. Ælfric seemed
less concerned with giving scandal than with misinforming and misleading his audiences. At the same time, he clearly did not overestimate
the sophistication of his readers and hearers, and he might well have
considered discretion in his description of sexual matters all the more
important as a result.

SODOMITICAL SIN IN PRAYERS

Certain members of Ælfric's audience—educated and pious Anglo-
Saxons—would have found references to Sodom in another discursive
realm, private prayers used to prepare for confession to the priest or to
confess sins directly to God. Two prayers, recited by the priest and
penitent before confession, suggest how sexual sins figured into private
devotion. One of these texts forms part of the penitential known as the
Old English Handbook and is found in two eleventh-century manuscripts. The prayer refers to "all the sins that ever through cursed spirits
have defiled me, in deed or in thought, with men or with women or
with any creature, natural sins or unnatural sins ("ealle þa synna þe me

æfre þurh awirgede gastas on besmitene wurdon: oððe on dæde oððe
on geþohte, oððe wið wæpmen oððe wið wifmen oððe wið ænige ges-
ceaft gecyndelicra sinna oððe ungecyndelicra").[70] Instead of a sin "ongean gecynde," the sin is "of an unnatural kind," "ungecyndelicra."
Whether the speaker were male or female, this list would seem to include same-sex acts; sins "with men or with women or with any creature" are inclusive.

A similar prayer, part of a devotional exercise, is also found in two
manuscripts. In this version the speaker confesses to natural and unnatural sins and lists "sodomitical sins."

> Ic ondette ealra synna cynn þe me æfre þurh owiht awiergde gæstas
> on besmitan oððe ic self þurh ænige unnytnesse to wo gefremede on
> geðohtum oððe on wordum oððe on dædum on me selfum. on sun-
> dran oððe wið wæpned men. oððe wið wifmen oððe wið ænige ges-
> ceafte gecyndelicra synna oððe ungecyndelicra ðara þe deofla cyn be
> rað sawlum to besmitenesse. Ic eom ondetta sodomiscre synne þe hie
> on gegyltan þæt is geligre leasunga gitsunga getreowleasnesse. yfelre
> recceleasnesse. 7 ðristlæcnesse minra synna.[71]

> I confess all kinds of sins that cursed spirits defiled me with in any way
> or I myself through any folly did in error in thought or in word or in
> deed, by myself in private (alone) or with men or with women or with
> any creature, natural or unnatural, of those [through] which the devil's
> kin quickly [draws] the soul to defilement. I confess the sodomitical sins
> that they [i.e., the devil's kin] committed, that is fornication, lies, avarice,
> unbelief, carelessness, and boldness in my sins.

In this prayer sins that are implicitly sexual, those committed with men
or with women, natural or unnatural, are not associated with Sodom,
while only one of the "sodomitical" sins—fornication—is sexual. Numerous though the entries in this long catalogue of wrongdoing are,
nothing in the list is more explicitly sexual than this reference to
fornication. This prayer suggests that the sins of Sodom were not exclusively sexual and, given the curious and in some cases not very serious sins called "sodomitical" (lies, carelessness), that almost any sin
could be linked to Sodom. The sins in this list that would seem to be
connected to the city are fornication, unbelief, and especially boldness
in sinning, a reference to the Sodomites' lack of shame and their noise
or outcry ("hream" in Old English), all of them already seen as characteristic of the Sodomites in Bede's commentary on Genesis.

Seen in the light of the Latin prayer that is their source, these two confessional prayers tell us at least a little more. They derive ultimately from a Latin confessional prayer in the early-ninth-century Book of Cerne. The source also includes a list in its confession, "Confiteor tibi sodomitam, fornicationem falsum testimonium, adulterium, gulam," and so forth, which the Anglo-Saxon translation follows closely up to the sin of obstinacy, or "boldness in my sins" ("ðristlæcnesse minra synna"). The Latin continues with a confession of "all my sins" ("omnia peccata mea"), which include "natural or unnatural fornication, both with women and with men, adultery in the heart, and the shameful emission of semen" ("fornicationem naturalem et innaturalem, tam apud masculos quam apud feminas, cordisque mechationem et turpem effusionem semini").[72] The Old English omits the reference to natural and unnatural fornication, whether with men or with women, and re-places it with a more general list of sins, none of them sexual. It is curious that the translator would have kept the reference to Sodom but would have omitted the subsequent and more specific references to sexual sins. It seems clear that "sodomitical sins" were neither unthink-able nor unspeakable so long as they were broadly defined, and plainly *not* homosexual. No connection is made between the "sodomitical sins" and the specific acts of unnatural fornication that they would have encompassed.

The texts discussed thus far are but a sliver of the homiletic and devotional corpus of Old English. Those texts discussing same-sex be-havior are probably no more than 1 or 2 percent of the corpus. Most homilies have nothing specific to do with sexual behavior. Those that do, denounce fornication and adultery but rarely more specifically than Wulfstan denounced them in the text quoted at the start of this chap-ter. We have to evaluate references to Sodom and Gomorrah and to "unnatural" and "natural" acts in the context of this general cultural reticence on sexual matters. On the one hand, there are few references to Sodom and Gomorrah, and few of them point specifically to homo-sexual behavior. On the other hand, it is remarkable, given how little is written about same-sex acts even in the penitentials, the most privi-leged and powerful of these discursive forms, that homosexual inter-course is mentioned in more popular and public texts at all.

GENESIS A: A STORY OF SODOM IN VERSE

Against the broad outline of historical and allegorical understandings of Sodom, and homiletic allusions to figurative meanings of the Sod-omites' conduct, the poem known as *Genesis A* stands out. The poem is found in Oxford, Bodleian Library, Junius 11, an illustrated manuscript; unfortunately, no drawings accompany the account of Sodom in this text.[73] Ælfric refused to be explicit about same-sex sex but seems to make the homosexual nature of the Sodomites' sin clear anyway. The poem, on the other hand, is straightforward in representing Sodom as a place of many sexual evils, including male homosexual intercourse. Longer than any Old English poem except for *Beowulf,*[74] *Genesis A* dominates other Old Testament narratives in Junius 11 *(Exodus, Daniel,* and *Christ and Satan).* Likewise, the history of Sodom dominates the other episodes in the poem, accounting for some 700 of 2,936 lines. The best-known fact about *Genesis A* is not its unique account of Sodom but rather its relation to another, more distinctive poem known as *Genesis B,* which forms lines 235–851 of *Genesis A* in the manuscript.[75] Very little has been written about *Genesis A,* but the critical literature on *Genesis B,* which contains a famous speech in which Satan mourns the loss of heaven and decries the injustice that sent him and his cohorts to hell, is enormous *(Genesis B,* lines 356–441; comparisons with *Paradise Lost* are inevitable).[76] *Genesis B* is a kind of biblical poetry that seizes on an episode "as the formal means for presenting a specific doctrine of the Church which does not explicitly appear in the original text," an approach that Doane contrasts to that taken in *Genesis A,* which paraphrases Scripture and follows both its form and meaning.[77] According to Doane, the poet of *Genesis A* was "primarily interested in establishing the literal sense according to the broad medieval understanding of that term," incorporating unobtrusive and "traditional narrative and explanatory material as was thought necessary to complete and clarify the literal meaning of the text" (50). The poet's concentration on the literal level is usually taken as a sign that he lacked artistic ambition and insight into his subject. But his account of the destruction of Sodom, which includes a summary of the city's history, skillfully expresses disapproval of the Sodomites and their sins. The poem adheres to a military ethos expressed in familiar Anglo-Saxon tropes of battle poetry, a manly atmosphere in which kinship obligations and the communal bond are defended at all costs. Thus *Genesis A* provides a sober background of discipline and obedience against which to contrast the excesses of Sodom and the weaknesses of her people.

The poem recounts the defeat of Sodom and the other Cities of the Plain by the northern kings. In the confrontation between Abram and the king of Sodom, *Genesis A* undermines the manliness of Sodom in no subtle way. The king of Sodom has lost his men; he asks Abram to accept gold in place of the captives whom Abram has freed. But the king's honor is immediately compromised by Abram and by the poet, who continually associates Abram with warriors and victory and the king of Sodom with women and defeat.

    Þa spræc guðcyning,
Sodoma aldor,   secgum befylled,
to Abrahame   —him wæs ara þearf—
"Forgif me mennen   minra leoda,
þe þu ahreddest   herges cræftum
wera wælclommum.   Hafa þe wunden gold
þæt ær agen wæs   ussum folce,
feoh and frætwa.   Læt me freo lædan
eft on eðel   æðelinga bearn,
on weste wic   wif and cnihtas,
earme wydewan.   Eaforan syndon deade,
folcgesiðas,   nymðe fea ane,
þe me mid sceoldon   mearce healdan." (2123–35)

Then spoke the war king, the man of Sodom, deprived of warriors, to Abraham (to him [the king] was need of honor). "Grant me the men of my people whom you rescued with the strength of the army, fatal bondage of men. Keep the wound gold that was the possession of my people, the cattle and the treasures. Let me lead the offspring of nobles again to their homeland, free, to the empty place, to women and boys, poor widows. The sons are dead, the nobles of the country, except just a few who must hold the territory with me."

In his reply, Abram not only shuns the Sodomite's gold but repudiates Sodom as a kingdom of the weak, a place of women and boys. As he does so, he emphasizes his victory and the valor of his troops.

Ic þe gehate,   hæleða waldend,
for þam halgan,   þe heofona is
and þisse eorðan   agendfrea,
wordum minum,   nis woruldfeoh,
þe ic me agan wille,
sceat ne scilling   þæs ic on sceotendum,
þeoden mæra,   þines ahredde,
æðelinga helm,   þy læs þu eft cweðe
þæt ic wurde,   willgesteallum,
eadig on eorðan   ærgestreonum,
Sodoma rice.   Ac þu most heonon
huðe lædan,   þe ic þe æt hilde gesloh,
ealle buton dæle   þissa drihtwera,
Aneres and Mamres   and Escoles.

Nelle ic þa rincas   rihte benæman,
ac hie me fulleodon   æt æscþræce,
fuhton þe æfter frofre.   Gewit þu ferian nu
ham hyrsted gold   and healsmægeð,
leoda idesa.   Þu þe laðra ne þearft
hæleða hildþræce   hwile onsittan,
norðmanna wig.   Eacne fuglas
under beorhhleoþum   blodig sittað,
þeodherga wæl,   þicce gefylled. (2139–61)

I promise you, keeper of heroes, before the holy one who is lord of
heaven and of this earth, with my words, it is not worldly possessions
that I wish to have, goods or money, because I rescued your warriors,
glorious prince, protector of noble ones, lest you say afterwards that I
became blessed on the earth by you, pleasant companions, in ancient
treasures of the kingdom of Sodom. But you yourselves may from here
take the booty that I obtained for you by fighting, all except the part
(belonging to) these chieftains of Mamre, Aneres, and Escoles. I do not
wish to deprive the warriors rightly, for they kept their promise to me
at the spear points, fought as a comfort to you. Go now to carry home
decorated gold and the women who clasp one about the neck, the
women of the people. You have no cause, for a moment, to fear the
violence of battles of warriors, the warfare of the Northmen. Birds of
prey sit bloody on the slaughter of heathen armies, thickly filled with
the slain of the army of the nation.

Abram's speech drips with sarcasm, contempt, and ironic praise for
the defeated Sodomite king, whom he calls "keeper of heroes," "hæleða
waldend," "glorious prince," "þeoden mæra," and "protector of noble
ones," "æðelinga helm." He characterizes the Sodomites as "pleasant
companions," "willgesteallum" (2147), a compound whose elements
(will-ge-) the poet uses here and elsewhere, according to Doane, with
"sinister and ironic overtones. Probably the poet makes Abraham re-
ject the king of Sodom's offer in this way because of the traditional
distaste for this people, even though it involves getting ahead of the
story."[78] What Doane means is that the poet looks ahead to Genesis 19
and the destruction that punished the Sodomites' sexual immorality
and allows his contempt for that conduct to color his representation
of the king and his defeated people. Abraham's scorn is pronounced.
He calls on the king to lead home "the women who clasp one about
the neck." The women are in mourning, their desolation and dependence cruelly mocked in the gesture Abram describes. The warriors of

Sodom have been slain, and the king now has only women (and boys) to return to. Abram's attack is not directed at these victims, however, but at a king who must associate with them as his only companions. The king is implicitly ridiculed as effeminate, although his association with women comes not by his own choice but by obligation to his people, a duty that otherwise one would expect this poet, ordinarily so fond of noble conduct, to honor.

When the poet narrates God's destruction of Sodom, his approach is again unsparing. I begin with God's words to Abraham regarding rumors of the city's corruption.

> Ic on þisse byrig   bearhtm gehyre,
> synnigra cyrm   swiðe hludne,
> ealogalra gylp,   yfele spræce
> werod under weallum habban.   Forþon wærlogona sint
> folce firena hefige.   Ic wille fandigan nu,
> mago Ebrea,   hwæt þa men don,
> gif hie swa swiðe   synna fremmað
> þeawum and geþancum   swa hie on þweorh sprecað
> facen and inwit.   Þæt sceal wrecan
> swefyl and sweart lig,   sare and grimme,
> hat and hæste   hæðnum folce. (2408–18)

I hear a clamor from this city, an outcry of sin very loud, an ale-foolish boast, of evil speech, (that) troops have under the walls. For they are faithless ones, a people of oppressive sin. I wish to find out, son of the Hebrews, what the men do, if they commit sins so great in customs and thoughts, as they evilly speak deceit and malice. Sulfur and dark flames shall avenge that, painful and bitter, hot and violent for the heathen folk.

God's speech suggests a well-known triad of thought, word, and deed found in prayers (e.g., one on p. 214 above) and other texts related to confession and penance.[79] God has heard their words, it would seem ("they speak deceit," "þweorh sprecað / facen and inwit") and now goes to examine their acts ("customs," "þeawum") and thoughts ("geþancum"). God wants to see if their customs and thoughts match their speech. If the Sodomites will not confess their sins, the confessor will come to them, although the hour for absolution will by then have passed. The narrative is interrupted at this point because the manuscript is missing a leaf containing Abraham's successful attempt to bargain for the lives of the faithful who live in Sodom (Genesis 18:22–33).[80] The poem resumes with the assault of the Sodomites on Lot and his guests, a passage that offers blunt evidence of the Sodomites' sexual natures.

> Comon Sodomware
> geonge and ealde,   gode unleofe
> corðrum miclum   cuman acsian,
> þæt hie behæfdon   herges mægne
> Loth mid giestum.   Heton lædan ut
> of þam hean hofe   halige aras,
> weras to gewealde.   Wordum cwædon
> þæt mid þam hæleðum   hæman wolden
> unscomlice,   arna ne gymden.
> Ða aras hraðe   se ðe oft ræd ongeat,
> Loth on recede,   eode lungre ut,
> spræc þa ofer ealle   æðelinga gedriht
> sunu Arones,   snytra gemyndig:
> "Her syndon inne   unwemme twa
> dohtor mine.   Doð swa ic eow bidde
> —ne can þara idesa   owðer gieta
> þurh gebedscipe   beorna neawest—
> and geswicað þære synne.   Ic eow sylle þa
> ær ge sceonde   wið gesceapu fremmen,
> ungifre yfel   ylda bearnum.
> Onfoð þæm fæmnum,   lætað frið agon
> gistas mine   þa ic for gode wille
> gemundbyrdan,   gif ic mot for eow." (2453–75)

Then the men of Sodom came, young and old, unloved by God, with a great host, so that they surrounded Lot and his guests with a mighty army. They commanded him to lead the holy messengers out of the high house, the men in(to their) power, said with words that they wanted to have intercourse with the men shamelessly, not mindful of honor. Then Lot arose quickly, he who often perceived good advice, went out quickly, spoke over all the company of nobles, the son of Aaron, mindful of wisdom: "Inside are my two daughters, untouched. Do as I bid you (neither of the women yet knows the company of men through 'bedship'), and give up that sin. I will give them to you, before you commit disgrace against nature, very greedy evil for the sons of men. Take the women, allow my guests to have peace, whom I wish, before God, to protect, if I may, from you."

This passage straightforwardly acknowledges that one of the sins of Sodom was male homosexual intercourse. The Old English verb used in this passage is "hæman" (2460), the same word for "to fornicate" or "to have sexual intercourse with" that is found in the penitentials and other sources.[81] Doane and Paul Remley have shown that the poet had access to two translations of Genesis. The Vulgate text specifies that the Sodomites demanded "to know" Lot's guests: "ubi sunt viri qui introierunt ad te nocte; educ illos huc ut cognoscamus eos." In the Vetus Latina, an older translation, the Sodomites demand sexual intercourse: "educ illos ad nos ut coitum faciamus cum eis." [82] The poem follows the Vetus Latina in reporting that the Sodomites want to fornicate with Lot's guests, not to "know" them in a sense commensurate with traditional hospitality.

When Lot offers the Sodomites his daughters, he hopes to save the men from a sin that is "against [their] natures," "wið gesceapu" (2471). Old English "gesceap" (plural "gesceapu") means "nature" or "shape" but also "fate," and, elsewhere in *Genesis A,* "genitals," the "house" of the sin of *luxuria,* according to Gregory, as we saw above. Given other Anglo-Saxon sources that accuse the Sodomites of "unnatural" acts, and given this poet's flair for wordplay, the passage warrants close scrutiny.[83] Lot tells the Sodomites that intercourse between men is "against [their] natures," which might mean either that it is not their custom or that, although it is customary among them, it is against their natures anyway; the latter reading seems more likely. When Noah drank the wine from his vineyard and fell asleep naked, hc was unable to cover his genitals, his "shameful parts" ("he ne mihte . . . sceome þeccan," 1571–73),[84] in contrast to the genitals of Adam and Eve, which were covered when they were driven from Paradise ("swa gesceapu wæron / werum and wifum," 1574–75). Adam and Eve could cover their genitals, but they could not hide their fate, or their shame. Doane has suggested that "gesceapu" is a pun on the "fate" of Adam and Eve.[85] The pun in the passage concerning the Sodomites seems even more pointed. When Lot tells the Sodomites that homosexual intercourse is against their "natures," he could also be telling them that this act is "against their genitals," contrary to the natural use of their sex organs. But the act is not, ironically, "against thcir fatcs"; given the retribution in store for the Sodomites, homosexual intercourse does not impede their fate but rather hastens it.

The men of Sodom reply scornfully that Lot is a foreigner who is thus in no position to lecture them about the rules of their community. "Do you want, if you are able, / to be our supreme judge here [and] to teach the people?" they ask (2482–84). The Sodomites seize Lot, but the angels rescue him and blind them. Almost immediately the angels order Lot and his family to leave the city. Then the angels announce

God's plan to destroy Sodom. The poet's description of the city's destruction is vivid if brief.

> Bearwas wurdon
> to axan and to yslan,   eorðan wæstma,
> efne swa wide   swa ða witelac
> reðe geræhton   rum land wera.
> Strudende fyr   steapes and geapes,
> swogende for   swealh eall eador
> þæt on Sodoma byrig   secgas ahton
> and on Gomorra.   Eall þæt god spilde,
> frea mid þy folce. (2554–62)

Groves changed into cinders and ashes, the fruit of the earth, just as widely as the fierce punishment reached the broad land of men. Ravaging fire rushing forth swallowed all the possessions, the steep and broad together, that men had in the cities of Sodom and Gomorrah. God destroyed all that, the Lord, along with the people.

The poet describes the fate of Lot's wife and then celebrates the Sodomites' destruction as testimony of God's protection of those in his care.

> Hie þæs wlenco onwod   and wingedrync
> þæt hie firendæda   to frece wurdon,
> synna þriste.   Soð ofergeaton,
> drihtnes domas   and hwa him dugeða forgeaf,
> blæd on burgum.   Forþon him brego engla
> wylmhatne lig   to wræce sende.
> Waldend usser   gemunde wærfæst þa
> Abraham arlice   swa he oft dyde
> leofne mannan.   Loth generede,
> mæg þæs oðres,   þa seo mænegeo forwearð.
> Ne dorste þa   dædrof hæle
> for frean egesan   on þam fæstenne
> leng eardigean.   Ac him Loth gewat
> of byrig gangan   and his bearn somed
> wælstowe fyrr   wic sceawian
> oð þæt hie be hliðe   heare dune
> eorðscræf fundon.   Þær se eadega Loth
> wærfæst wunode,   waldende leof,
> dægrimes worn   and his dohtor twa. (2581–99)

They made way into that pride and drunkenness so that they were too greedy for evil deeds, bold of sin, and forgot the truth, the judgment of

God, and what he granted to the retainers [duguð], glory in the city. Therefore the prince of angels sent surging flames to them as a punishment. Our creator kept faithful Abraham, the dear man, honorably in mind, as he often did. Lot was saved, kin of the other one, when the great tribe perished. Nor dare the man strong in deeds for terror of the Lord long dwell in the stronghold, but Lot went from the city with his children together, farther from the place of slaughter, looked for a place until they came to a cave in a high hillside. There blessed Lot dwelled, true to his promise, the dear savior, a multitude of days with his two daughters.

Another leaf is missing at this point, corresponding to events in Genesis 19:31–32, which concerns the plan according to which Lot's daughters became pregnant by their father. A trace of disapproval is directed at them in the poet's description of them as "willgesweostor," possibly "loving sisters," a compound that recalls "willgebroðor," used to describe Cain and Abel, and "willgesteallum" (*Genesis A* 971), the scornful expression Abraham uses in referring to the Sodomites as "dear companions" (*Genesis A* 2147).[86] But incest is not discussed. Instead the poet stresses the reconstitution of kin around Lot. After the destruction of Sodom, Lot was reinstated in rural life, in a cave in the mountains. His "descendants returned to a way of life that was not too different from the one that they would have led had he elected to remain in Canaan."[87] In this sense the story of Abraham and Lot returns at its end to its beginnings (Genesis 13).

In distinguishing rural from city life in Genesis, Kay showed how virtue was associated with the former and corruption with the latter; he suggested that urban life is condemned in the episode, an observation that reinforces Boswell's hypothesis that cities were seen as places where homosexual activities were tolerated.[88] Anglo-Saxon society was overwhelmingly, if not exclusively, rural, with nothing like urban centers—apart from monastic establishments—to compare to the fabled cities of Scripture. This demographic fact might have underscored the remote and foreign qualities of Sodom and the other cities among Anglo-Saxons, and indeed among all early medieval people who learned about the wickedness and the fate of these places. But cities themselves were not seen as inherently evil. According to an analysis of Sodom as an urban setting by Hugh Magennis, the Anglo-Saxons followed Augustine in believing that Cain had built the first earthly city and that Abel's city was with God, a point echoed in Bede's commentary on Genesis.[89] The city and what Magennis calls "the good landscape" are common tropes in Old English poetry, both signs of God's favor. It is not the setting but those who inhabit it who cause the city's destruction; the fault of Sodom that Magennis stresses is drunkenness and consequent unruly behavior, sins of *luxuria* (92–93). Hence Sodom was remembered as a place of darkness and dark deeds that Sodomites refused to keep hidden. Anglo-Saxon authors repeatedly returned to the Sodomites' lack of shame, their open sinning, their insistence on doing in daylight what should not be done even in the dark, as the reason for the extraordinary means of their destruction. The Sodomites were sent living into hell because, by their refusal to heed God's word, restrain themselves, and repent, they had created a hellish kingdom on earth. How did the sometimes-shadowy behavior of such creatures resonate with Anglo-Saxon men and women who heard about it from their priests and poets?

The darkness surrounding Sodom before and after its destruction evokes the figure of the shadow I have used to suggest the presence of same-sex acts in Anglo-Saxon culture. Darkness keeps us from seeing clearly what the Sodomites did; at the same time, darkness carries a dire moral valence, representing the Sodomites' damnation. But when that world is seen from the Sodomites' perspective (as we reconstruct it), it is difficult to imagine same-sex relations as merely a shadow of the sexual world. The city seems to have been the one culture known to the Anglo-Saxons—and Christians before or after them—in which homosexual and heterosexual intercourse had equal standing. The belief that women lived in Sodom was never questioned; it was always assumed that heterosexual fornication was one of the city's ongoing excesses. What held Sodom apart was the acknowledged belief that the city also accepted another form—in fact, *the* other form—of fornication, usually disguised as that "against nature" but sometimes straightforwardly identified as male homosexual intercourse.

For Sodomites, same-sex love was not a shadow; for them, no such figure of secondary sexual relations was necessary. In most Anglo-Saxon descriptions of Sodom, however, including those that specify intramale intercourse as one of the city's sins, same-sex sex must be discerned in the darkness of acts "against nature," which are consigned to the shadows of "natural" acts (they too are sinful). All the accounts I have surveyed in this chapter represent homosexual acts and any other forms of excess in sexual conduct as sinful and "unnatural." They do not, of course, acknowledge the inevitability of "unnatural" acts in the presence of socially constructed and defined "natural acts," and that inevitability, that inescapableness, is part of what I mean by the "shadow" of same-sex love in Anglo-Saxon culture. Some accounts, Ælfric's in particular, seem conscious of the shadow in another sense, not as an inescapable fact but as a discursive strategy, a dark and unknowable place where shameful same-sex acts and "foul fornications" should be located. Ælfric does not differentiate between the living shadow and the dead blackness of damnation. He does not say that the Sodomites had both "natural" intercourse with women and "unnatural" intercourse with men but rather only that they had intercourse "with women" and intercourse "against nature." Although he refused to name or describe same-sex sex, Ælfric invoked it anyway by using a parallel structure that invites the hearer to interpret "against nature" as "with men" (for an example of a similar parallel structure see *Genesis A* 1573–75: "swa gesceapu wæron / werum and wifum . . . ussum fæder and meder"). Like other Anglo-Saxons, Ælfric knew what the Sodomites did, homosexually and heterosexually. Bishops, priests, and other teachers assumed that in their audiences sodomites of all sorts—blind disbelievers, clamorous sinners, compulsive fornicators of all kinds—shared this knowledge.

CONCLUSION

The texts surveyed in this chapter were, for the most part, written in the late tenth and the early eleventh centuries. Almost without exception they were intended for the clergy to use in instructing the laity. Even *Genesis A* strives to instruct, although as a heroic narrative it furnishes more entertainment in the process than other accounts of Sodom and Gomorrah. In every case, sodomy and Sodom are alternatives juxtaposed to chastity, usually defined within the permissible limits of sexual intercourse in marriage. Sexual intercourse defined as "unnatural" is intramale intercourse, we know, because it is juxtaposed to intercourse "mid wifum." The discourse of sodomy in Anglo-Saxon England is largely contained within these terms: first, sex in marriage, or no sex at all, as opposed to sex outside of marriage; second, sex between men and women as opposed to sex between men (or, theoretically, between women, but the narrative texts do not make this act explicit). What is natural conforms perfectly to what is lawful; whatever falls outside either definition is, by definition, excessive, "against nature," and therefore damned.

Given that literate Anglo-Saxons were explicitly informed about homosexual acts in Sodom, we must ask if there was a sense of shared identity linking some of them to the inhabitants of Sodom. Did Anglo-Saxons who engaged in same-sex relations have more reason to think of themselves as sodomites than those whose sins were equally grave if more conventional? Alan Bray argued that the representation of sodomites as monstrous, demonic, and bestial made it difficult for men in sixteenth-century England to recognize themselves as belonging to such a group. "[H]ow possible was it to avoid identifying with the 'sod-omite' who was the companion of witches and Papists, of werewolves and agents of the king of Spain? When the world inhabited by the conventional image of the sodomite was so distant from everyday life," Bray claimed, "it cannot have been hard."[90] The image of the sodomite in Anglo-Saxon texts is not so fully developed or so extreme. Images of Sodom from Anglo-Saxon texts associated the city and its people with hellish stench and unimaginable destruction. But the Sodomites are also imagined as a defeated nation of weaklings even before the city's annihilation. They burned with lust and hence went living into the fires of hell. These expressions of contempt hardly invoke the other-worldly described by Bray, the subhuman, the monstrous, and the bestial.

The mythical or symbolic context of sodomy—Gregory's river of stench, the unnatural world destroyed by fire and sulfur—is only one side of the picture, a set of representations that seems far from the social practices of same-sex relations in Anglo-Saxon England, so far indeed that one is tempted to compare the disparity between the representa-tions and the acts of ordinary people to that seen by Bray in later evi-dence. But less vivid representations of Sodom would have spoken to at least some Anglo-Saxons. The weakness of the Sodomite king and his people, for example, would have resonated with "bædlings" who were given penances that the handbooks compare to those given for women. Any notorious adulterers who refused to reform and repent would likewise have recognized themselves in accounts of the Sodom-ites as adamant sinners. Taken at its most general level, the example of Sodom could have applied to anybody who had sex or anybody who had ever worked on Sunday. Only the most pious were able to observe all the church's laws and never stray from Matthew's straight and nar-row path. They must have looked in considerable dismay at the mass of "Sodomites"—anybody living less piously, that is—around them.

Stories of Sodom in Anglo-Saxon England, with few exceptions, characterized the Sodomites unremarkably. But contemporary with the texts I have discussed is another that uses same-sex desire as a de-vice for ridicule and extreme abuse. This is the Latin poem *Moriuht,* named after its fictional Irish protagonist. *Moriuht,* a Norman work written before 1026 by Warner of Rouen, shows that poets of this pe-riod could be as vicious as their classical counterparts in using sex acts to defame the targets of their satire.[91] The poem mocks Moriuht's eth-nic origins and shows that Continental authors held émigré authors in low regard. A poet and would-be grammarian, Moriuht sets out from Ireland to find his lost wife. He is twice captured by Vikings and raped, "forced by the Vikings to perform the sexual service of a wife," although "not unwillingly does he play Ravola for everyone with his arse. Struck by a penis, he groans—alas for the unfortunate man!" ("Svbditur obprobriis et tunc pro coniuge Danis / Coniugis officium cogitur esse suum . . . Non tamen inuitis fit Rauola podice cunctis, / Percussus genio ingem[u]it, heu! misero," 75–80).[92] During a short stay in the Anglo-Saxon port of Corbridge, in Northumbria, Moriuht, "luke-warm for learning, but hot-blooded for sex" ("Minerue tepidus, sed Veneri calidus," 102), ravages a convent of willing nuns and is "recognized and available to all with his penis" ("Agnosci coepit cunctis ramoque pateri," 113), revealing his taste for homosexual as well as heterosexual intercourse. Christopher J. McDonough notes that Warner uses "the metaphor of monstrosity" to characterize Moriuht and employs sexual references to satirize the Irishman's second-rate learning. In the poem, moral sensibility and literary skill are closely connected; poetry was understood as a branch of ethics. Thus "[s]odomy and other sexual acts become tropes for contradictions and antitheses in the literary sphere," and Moriuht himself is a "comic subject of discourse on disorder" (3). Warner's poem is roughly contemporary with the homilies of Ælfric. It reminds us that medieval authors observed very different levels of decorum, and it suggests the kind of language and figures of speech used to characterize sodomites in the Renaissance satires and polemics studied by Bray. Nothing in the Anglo-Saxon stories of Sodom approaches the explicitness or the intense scorn that Warner deploys in his characterization of Moriuht.

Warner's poem also demonstrates a conjunction of national prejudice and sexual prejudice that later became a characteristic part of the discourse of Sodom. Moriuht is not exclusively homosexual in his taste; just as he is subjugated by the Vikings who rape him, he in turn exploits the nuns he seduces at Corbridge. It is not just his sexual passivity that is mocked and scorned but also his sexual excess, taken as symptomatic of his stupidity and lack of taste. His portrait suggests what at least one Norman author thought of Irish travelers to the Continent; England is implicated in the slander, since at least for a time Moriuht is welcomed in Northumbria by nuns (and men, too) fascinated by his bald head. In the next chapter, we will see some Normans and Anglo-Normans accusing other Normans of sexual excess and, centuries later, English historians accepting the canard that the Normans introduced sodomy into Anglo-Saxon England.

In the centuries that followed the Norman Conquest the discourse

of sodomy changed in two important ways. First, it became specialized rather than nonspecific, targeted at courts, attributed to notorious
princes and kings, attached to identifiable figures. Second, the discourse of sodomy came to be used in partisan polemics by reforming
factions eager to condemn traditional practices of the Church, especially the celibacy of the clergy. Ælfric opposed the practice of married
clergy, which was widespread in Anglo-Saxon England, but without
success. The Anglo-Saxon author who referred most often to Sodom,
he did not attach the discourse of sodomy to this issue. In the twelfth
century, sodomy acquired a new position in polemic as the vice of Norman princes and kings whose example, so certain church authorities
claimed, had allowed the sin to become widespread. Twelfth-century
officials, influenced by new reforms in Rome, advocated clerical celibacy but seemed unaware that Anglo-Saxon teachers like Ælfric had
shared their views. In the fourteenth century the discourse of sodomy
mirrored a division between a different kind of reform politics, outside
the Church rather than inside it, and at this point sodomy acquired
significance as the sin even holy men—men in holy orders—would
turn to if they were denied the right to marry.

Part

3

From
Angles to
Angels

6

Sex and the Anglo-Saxons from the Norman Conquest to the Renaissance

OUT OF THE SHADOWS

In the twelfth century, in learned circles at least, sodomy acquired a specific history as a sin particular to the Norman court. Even though English ecclesiastical legislation condemning sodomy was, by that time, at least four hundred years old, chroniclers and church officials claimed that the sin had been unknown in England before the Conquest. From a modern perspective, it would seem that those most likely to make such a charge would have been those who lost the most in the Conquest—that is, the Anglo-Saxons. But the Anglo-Saxons, in no position to criticize their conquerors, did not accuse the Normans of sodomy. Nor did the Normans make those accusations against the Anglo-Saxons. Rather, sodomy was a sin with which Norman clergymen reproached their own lay leaders. Most of the nationalistic flavor of the discourse of sodomy entered the discussion with the debates of nineteenth-century historians, many of them vigorous defenders of Anglo-Saxon virtues against Norman assaults on them.

As Clare A. Simmons has demonstrated, the nineteenth-century debates about the Normans and the Saxons are founded on the belief "that the Saxon age and the Norman Conquest are a material reality that can be evinced as proof either of the way England used to be, or more polemically, of the way England should be." We might substitute "the English church" for "England" in this quotation, with equal accuracy. Saxons and Normans were seen as exemplars much earlier, she notes, figuring prominently in sixteenth- and seventeenth-century debates.[1] In this chapter I want to look at three periods in which the clash between Saxon and Norman values was seen from English perspectives and used to valorize Anglo-Saxon practices. My particular focus at each point is the perceived relationship between the Anglo-Saxons and same-sex love.

The first period I describe is known as "Anglo-Norman England," roughly 1066–1200. During this period the legislation of the Anglo-Saxon church was revised by Norman administrators and clerics following recent reforms ordered in Rome. These reforms sought to standardize ecclesiastical law and to raise standards of clerical discipline. In this period the discourse of sodomy was deployed by Anglo-Norman churchmen against Norman rulers rather than against the laity and the clergy, who had been the chief targets of the antisodomy discourse of the Anglo-Saxon period. Resistance to ecclesiastical reforms predictably came from two fronts: secular authorities whose influence was being curbed, and clergy who had been ordered to separate from wives if married or to leave their concubines.

In the second period, the fourteenth century, early English history was idealized as a time when the Church taught people in their own language, and English began to regain status as an official vernacular language that had been lost to French. Lollard reformers used this precedent to demand the right to use English in teaching and preaching. Sodomy played a part in their arguments against the enforced celibacy of the clergy; same-sex intercourse was cited as a damnable recourse for priests who were not allowed to marry. A term notably missing in orthodox works, sodomy is mentioned in Lollard writings, some of which I discuss below. A few Lollard works challenge the prohibition against mentioning the word that was observed by Chaucer's Parson and some others.[2]

Scholars in the English reformation, the third period I discuss, also looked back to the Anglo-Saxons' use of the vernacular as they urged that the clergy be allowed to marry. Clerical celibacy had traditionally been encouraged in England, but never effectively. Marriage and concubinage had been allowed as alternatives to promiscuity. Early in the eleventh century, Ælfric advocated clerical celibacy in his pastoral letters. His arguments did not prevail, and reformers of even a century later did not cite them.[3] By the early sixteenth century the real views of the Anglo-Saxons were unknown. It was assumed that marriage was the proper state for the Anglo-Saxon clergy, one of several ancient practices to which the new Church of England ought to return. (This was not the only point on which officials in the English reformation preferred to misunderstand the traditions of the Anglo-Saxon church.)[4]

These three periods mark a shifting relationship between the Anglo-Saxons and same-sex sexual practices. As the homilies, penitentials, and other sources surveyed in the previous two chapters make clear, the Anglo-Saxon church directed the discourse of sodomy at both laity and clergy. Among the Normans this discourse acquired a literary dimension that it had not previously had in England. Sodomy was no longer described simply as a grave sin committed by evil men and women but as a set of social practices flaunted by the people's rulers and their courtly advisers—in other words, as a scandal. The scandal involved behavior and fashions that bespoke indulgence and moral laxness, however, rather than specific same-sex acts. There was nothing new in this. As we saw in chapter 5, those guilty of undisciplined and impious acts were thought of as "Sodomites" in the Anglo-Saxon period, especially if they lacked shame.

There were no major changes in official ecclesiastical thinking about same-sex acts at the time of the Norman Conquest, although the single most powerful polemic against same-sex behavior written in the Middle Ages, Peter Damian's *Book of Gomorrah*, had been written shortly before, between 1048 and 1054. Damian's work marked a newly aggressive phase in the war of words against sodomites, but his text had no influence on discussions of sodomy in England (or elsewhere) before or after the Conquest.[5] After the Gregorian reforms of the eleventh century, the definition of sodomy was broadened to include an array of nonprocreative heterosexual sex acts as well as same-sex acts, masturbation, and bestiality. There is thirteenth-century evidence that the new definition of sodomy was applied retroactively to the Anglo-Saxon penitentials, although we also find some thirteenth-century examples that show that sodomy retained its more limited meaning, clear in some early Latin and Anglo-Saxon sources, as male homosexual intercourse. In the fourteenth century, Lollards claimed scriptural precedent as they defied conventional wisdom and used the word "sodomy" to describe male homosexual intercourse. Restrictions on the word had disappeared by the sixteenth century, when sodomy acquired broad polemical force, especially as a charge to be used against the Roman church and its policy of clerical celibacy.

Each phase of this development incorporated an understanding of the Anglo-Saxon church as a touchstone. The distinct character of the Anglo-Saxons is, as we would expect, least obvious in Anglo-Norman writing closest to the Anglo-Saxon age and most obvious among Reformation polemicists far removed from that period. As definitions of sodomy broadened to include not just an array of sex acts but provocative fashions, the shadow of the word itself also grew. Same-sex acts still existed within it, but they shared their obscurity with acts unrelated to sexual intercourse. At the same time, sodomy always carried at least some implication of sexual relations "against nature," and same-sex relations were always included in that category.

The Norman Conquest had dire consequences for the English language and its records and for the traditions of the Anglo-Saxon church.
Following his victory at Hastings on 28 September 1066, William I (the
Conqueror) subdued England through forcible and often violent conquest, mounting a reign of terror to control the Anglo-Saxons. He set
about reforming the English church, replacing English with Norman
bishops, and transformed all the country's legal institutions.[6] William
was succeeded by his son, William Rufus, who ruled from 1087 to 1100
and who was particularly despised by ecclesiastical chroniclers as indifferent to religion and rapacious; his court was supposedly very dissolute.[7] William was killed in an apparent hunting accident in 1100 and
was succeeded by his brother, Henry I, a king more disciplined and
austere. Reforms instituted during Henry's long reign (1100–35) supposedly curbed the excesses of the court. Robert Curthose, duke of
Normandy, the elder brother of William Rufus and Henry, attempted
to wrest the throne from Henry and was defeated by him in a battle in
Normandy on 28 September 1106. Henry's victory over his brother,
won forty years to the day after the Norman conquest of England,
seemed to signal the English conquest of Normandy. Imprisoned for
twenty-eight years, Robert died in 1134.[8] Henry died in 1135. Because
the death of William Atheling had deprived the nation of an obvious
heir, Henry's reign was followed by a period of chaos concluded only
when Henry II was crowned in 1154. The reign of Henry I understandably came to be seen as a time of reform and renewed discipline
in the court.

One of the Conquest's beneficial effects was a new stimulus to write
history. According to Nancy F. Partner, "The Norman Conquest,
which brought to England men with no English traditions or loyalties
and thus threatened to erase English memories of saints and saintly
kings, had its quickening effect on the notable twelfth-century English
gift for memory-keeping, history-writing."[9] James Campbell has made
a bolder claim. "The greatest advances in the study and understanding
of Anglo-Saxon history made before the nineteenth century were those
of the twelfth," he wrote (a view, incidentally, that greatly underesti-
mates the importance of the sixteenth-century scholarly recovery of
Anglo-Saxon historical texts).[10] Campbell stressed that twelfth-century
history was not merely defensive of Anglo-Saxon traditions and critical of those (i.e., the Normans) who were transforming the English
church. Earlier, R. W. Southern had argued that much history after the
Norman Conquest was written out of "outrage, resentment and nos-
talgia" by those who had known Anglo-Saxon England and who deplored the transformation of church conditions under the Normans.[11]

While acknowledging the truth of Southern's view, Campbell argued that the histories of the twelfth century also had broader, positive motives and that they "extended beyond monasteries, beyond the church and beyond the wish to preserve the memory of a lost world." [12] Some of the most powerful Anglo-Norman voices belonged to ecclesiastics, including Anselm; his biographer, Eadmer; and Ordericus Vitalis. But not all were monks; Henry of Huntingdon was a secular historian and so was Geoffrey of Monmouth, although, given the mythical nature of the latter's work, not everyone would want to classify both of them as "historians." I begin with the Anglo-Norman voices.

SODOMY AND THE ANGLO-NORMANS

On 25 November 1120, William Atheling, son and heir apparent of Henry I, and his brother Richard, along with three hundred others, died when their ship, the *Blanche-Nef,* sank shortly after leaving Normandy for a return voyage to England. According to William of Malmesbury, William Atheling would have survived had he not, once free of the sinking ship, returned to try to rescue his sister Mathilda, an act of bravery for which he has received little credit. [13] Medieval commentators judged the disaster harshly, claiming that William and his companions were sodomites and effeminates whose immorality God punished with a violent and sudden end.

The chronicler who wrote at greatest length about William's death was Ordericus Vitalis, an Anglo-Norman who was born in England in 1075 and who lived in Normandy, where, between 1123 and 1141, he wrote the *Ecclesiastical History of England and Normandy.* [14] "[B]oth the love of his father and the hope of the people were confidently fixed on him," Ordericus wrote of William Atheling, "But indeed sinners in their guilty blindness cannot see or understand the things which the heavenly king rightly ordains for his creation, until the sinful man is captured like a fish on a hook or a bird in a net and entangled in sufferings beyond hope of escape." [15] Thomas Forester applauded Ordericus's "usual discretion" in making "only a very slight allusion to the prevalent opinion of the times, particularly among the clergy, that the shipwreck was a just judgment of Heaven on an unnatural vice which was very common among the young nobles who were lost in the Blanche-Nef." Forester added that Robert Curthose, Henry's brother, "was commonly accused of such practices . . . and is said to have introduced them into Normandy on his return from the east [where he fought in the Crusades]." [16] The sinking of the *Blanche-Nef* acquired emblematic significance, not merely as the end of a ship of fools but also as the destruction of a boatload of sodomites bringing their corrupt ways to England and meeting God's wrath en route. Norman rule was well established when William Atheling died, of course, and the supposed corruption of England by foreign sexual mores was by then already far advanced. But the chroniclers' response to William's death suggests their wish for a sign that God had punished the Normans for the vices they brought with them.

The chroniclers lead us to believe that a transformation in sexual mores had taken place long before William Atheling and his companions died. Ordericus did not describe the sexual behavior of the crew and passengers on the *Blanche-Nef;* he merely observed that they were drunk and rowdy and that they dismissed and mocked the priests who came to bless their departure.[17] Such general descriptions of loose living, characterized by a few disapproving moralists, have had far-reaching effect. Historians of earlier eras were inclined not only to accept the moralists' analyses but to weave them into narratives of the history of sex in England and Normandy. The claim that Robert brought "an unnatural vice" to Normandy from "the east" is a necessary forerunner to the claim that the Norman conquerors introduced sodomy and other homosexual practices into Anglo-Saxon England. As John Boswell has shown, the view that homosexual behavior was learned, and that it could be communicated by "cross-cultural contact," has been a staple in the medieval history of sex. In these narratives one point of origin served as well as another. Some argued that crusaders introduced homosexual behavior into Europe from the Middle East, while Giraldus Cambrensis, the twelfth-century Welsh historian, asserted that the English "picked it up from the Normans, who in their turn had gotten in from the French."[18] The juxtaposition of Robert's visit to the East and the Normans' relation to Anglo-Saxon England is revealing: sodomy and homosexual acts are unthinkable not only as part of the Anglo-Saxons' culture but as part of that of the Normans. Both nations had to acquire these vices from elsewhere.

Among the clergymen accusing the Normans of sodomy was Anselm, who was born at Aosta in Italy c. 1034. Anselm studied at Bec, in Normandy, with Lanfranc, who was appointed archbishop of Canterbury by William the Conqueror. Upon Lanfranc's death, William Rufus had to force Anselm to accept Lanfranc's position; Anselm became archbishop of York in the same year, 1093.[19] Anselm speaks to us through his biographer, Eadmer, who reports that, in a private meeting with William Rufus, Anselm warned that the king was talked about daily by "everyone in the whole kingdom" and that the people said "such things as by no means befitted the dignity of a king."[20] On a later occasion Anselm is said to have raised "the matter of sodomy" with William and asked for a church council to keep the whole country from becoming like Sodom itself. William declined, and Anselm had to wait until the Council of London of 1102, when Henry was king, for the opportunity he desired.[21] Eadmer's account has become part of the historical record. J. S. P. Tatlock, for example, writes that "St. Anselm and probably Henry of Huntingdon make it clear that the vice [of homosexual behavior] was regarded as something new in England."[22] According to Frank Barlow, Anselm thought that "the vice was rampant at the English and Norman courts."[23]

A close examination of the texts used to substantiate these charges against the Normans reveals very few specific references either to homosexual or to heterosexual acts. One event that bears close scrutiny is the Council of London of 1102, which passed statutes condemning sodomy and demanding clerical celibacy, although not connecting these two points. The council required that "those who commit the shameful sin of sodomy, and especially those who of their own free will take pleasure in doing so, were [to be] condemned by a weighty anathema, until by penitence and confession they should show themselves worthy of absolution." A clergyman found guilty of this sin was to be deposed; a layman "should be deprived of his legal status and dignity in the whole realm of England."[24]

The council treated "the shameful sin of sodomy" as a serious offense, reserving absolution for the sin to the bishop in some cases and assessing laity penances for sodomy according to their age, length of involvement in the sin, marital status, and willingness to do penance. Anselm recommended heavier penances for those who indulged in the sin after they knew it had been forbidden, but even he permitted priests discretion in assessing penances for them. This measured response to an almost certainly overstated problem (public acts of sodomy are unlikely to have taken place) was given eighteen years before the *Blanche-Nef* set sail. An unidentified prelate wrote to Anselm about sodomy in 1105, lamenting that even after the council sodomites remained unmolested.[25] Because a council held in 1108 made no mention of sodomy, Bailey asserted that the example of William Rufus had not taken hold and that the 1102 decree against sodomy was "immediately successful." Boswell rightly ridiculed Bailey's view as highly implausible. But his own account minimized the effect of the council's decrees and exaggerated their novelty.[26]

According to Boswell, the canon was an effort to "introduce ecclesiastical legislation in England designating homosexual behavior as sinful. (There had been no statutes against it previously.) The London

Council of 1102 took measures to see that the general public was informed of the impropriety of such acts and insisted that in the future
'sodomy' be confessed as a sin." Furthermore, Anselm wrote to an
archdeacon that "this sin has hitherto been so public that hardly anyone
is embarrassed by it, and many have therefore fallen into it because they
were unaware of its seriousness."[27] It was clear, Boswell concluded, that
"the average Englishman was not already aware" of sodomy as a sin
(215). Given the lack of specific public discourse (e.g., in homilies) defining sodomy, this is a plausible claim. But the Anglo-Saxon texts surveyed in chapters 4 and 5 show that the Anglo-Saxons clearly abominated same-sex intercourse, especially sex acts "against nature" and acts
between men. We cannot be too sure what the "average Englishman"
did or did not know. If he or she were a churchgoer—and most people
were compelled to attend church with some regularity—some knowledge of sodomy could be presumed. Anselm seems to have been unaware of the prohibitions of the penitentials against homosexual acts—
this is surprising—and did not expect Christians in England to know
about them either.

Boswell argued that Anselm and Henry worked together to suppress the decrees of the council. Henry supposedly tolerated the homosexual behavior of his son, William Atheling, since "[i]t was under his
reign and presumably with his approval that Anselm quashed the antigay legislation of the Council of London in 1102" (231 note 78). But
Anselm did not "quash" the legislation, which prohibited more than
"gay" sex in any case. Boswell's argument was conditioned by his decision to recruit Anselm himself to the ranks of the "gay." He suggested
that the archbishop suppressed the decrees of the council—which, we
must remember, Anselm himself wanted to take place—for "personal
reasons." Boswell claimed that the decree "was apparently never published," but this appears to be wishful thinking. A canon requiring the
new standards to be proclaimed every Sunday in all churches follows
the one prohibiting sodomy.[28] The council's chief focus was not sodomy but, as we have seen, the new Gregorian requirement that the
clergy be celibate—a point of reform that met with extreme resistance—and related matters, including the sale of the clergy's wives as
slaves. These issues are discussed in other sources and appear to have
been genuine, not manufactured, concerns.[29]

Anselm's objective was not just the celibacy of the clergy but also
the clergy's continence. Although the connection between celibacy and
sodomy is not made in the canon prohibiting sodomy, one cause of
opposition to the imposition of celibacy was the fear that the new rule
would lead to worse evils. Henry of Huntingdon, whose *Historia An-*

glorum appeared in 1129, wrote that the demand for clerical celibacy was controversial. "The prohibition seemed quite proper to some, but dangerous to others; for in their attempt at purity, many [priests] might fall into disgusting filth, to the great shame of the name of Christian."[30] "Disgusting filth" could cover a multitude of sins, not just sodomy, but sodomy was the sin that brought greater shame than most others to Christians guilty of it.

The council's attempt at reform was subverted rather than suppressed by Henry I, who used the demand for celibacy for the crown's financial gain. He heavily fined clergy who would not leave their wives but also accepted large sums from those who wished to continue living with women, a practice for which Anselm sharply rebuked him. A. L. Poole suggested that many of the lower-ranking clergy also disregarded the rule of celibacy, since it was shunned by their superiors.[31] Henry's interference shows that the conciliar edict was indeed promulgated. Anselm clearly wanted the council's provisions enforced and objected when Henry turned its decrees to his own uses. Indeed, Anselm's letter to the archdeacon provides for punishment of those who have "committed the sin of Sodom . . . not knowing that [legislation against it] had been promulgated."[32] It seems clear that Anselm sought to intensify restrictions against possible same-sex sexual practices, not that he sought to "quash" what Boswell calls "antigay legislation." Anselm was not aware of the teachings of the Anglo-Saxon church on same-sex intercourse between men or women, but his own position accords fully with the severity with which the Anglo-Saxons regarded the practice.

The *Ecclesiastical History* of Ordericus Vitalis is another key source for the Normans' understanding of sodomy. Ordericus did not disguise his contempt for the state of England and its peoples when the Normans conquered them. Describing the destruction wrought by the Danish kings of England (Æthelred, Harold, and Harthacnut), Ordericus wanted his readers to understand "why the Normans found the English a rustic and nearly illiterate people, although they had once been fully instructed in the best customs by the Roman pontiffs." He followed Bede's example (and that of Gildas) in blaming the defeated for their loss. A "lack of discipline affected clergy and laity alike, and inclined both sexes to every kind of lust," Ordericus wrote, but he made no mention of sodomy as one of those evils.[33] William introduced reforms and order into this moral and social chaos. His firm hand maintained order in both Normandy and England. Ordericus reported a hermit's dream in which a meadow (Normandy) was once protected by a fierce horse (William), who kept greedy animals from the meadow. One day the horse disappeared and was replaced by a "wanton cow" (Duke Robert), who allowed the animals to overrun and ruin the meadow. "Catamites and effeminates will govern" ("catamitæ et effeminati dominabuntur"), the hermit predicted (book 5, chap. 10, pp. 106–7). Ordericus confirmed that this prophecy came true when Robert returned from the Crusades. Robert "was sunk beyond redemption in indolence and voluptuousness" ("socordia nempe mollicieque damnabiliter detentus est"; book 10, chap. 17, pp. 300–301). During Robert's reign "sodomy walked abroad unpunished, flaunting its tender allurements and foully corrupting the effeminate, dragging them down to Hell" ("inter haec impune procedebat petulans illecebra molles flammisque cremandos turpiter fedabat uenus sodomestica").[34] The sodomites might have been fit for burning—a pointed reference to the fiery end of Sodom and Gomorrah that all sodomites should anticipate—but that was not a punishment either church or state dealt to them. Sodomites were not burned in England, and were not burned in Italy until the late thirteenth century.[35]

Ordericus did not point to specifically homosexual behavior. Describing the court of William Rufus, Ordericus claimed, "At that time effeminates set the fashion in many parts of the world: foul catamites, doomed to eternal fire, unrestrainedly pursued their revels and shamelessly gave themselves up to the filth of sodomy" ("Tunc effeminati passim in orbe dominabantur indisciplinate debachabantur sodomiticisque spurciciis foedi catamitæ flammis urendi turpiter abutebantur"). What were these practices? Ordericus listed them: hair parted to the forehead, "long and luxurious locks like women"; tight shirts and tunics; time wasted or spent eating, drinking, and dicing. "Our wanton youth is sunk in effeminacy," he wrote, "and courtiers, fawning, seek the favours of women with every kind of lewdness." Long hair, beards, shoes with pointed toes were exterior signs that exhibited inward thoughts and showed how little reverence these youths had for God (book 8, chap. 10, pp. 88–89). But the courtiers Ordericus denounced were continually studying "how to make themselves agreeable to women," not how to make themselves attractive to other men. Ordericus used "effeminacy" in the sense of excessive fondness of women and their ways. His charges have nothing obvious to do with same-sex behavior between men or intramale sexual intercourse.

Some references in the decades before the *Blanche-Nef* incident are more ambiguous. Hugh of Flavigny, a visitor to England on a papal mission in 1096, wrote about a royal clerk named Gerard who had been appointed bishop of Hereford. Hugh wrote that Gerard planned to make his acquaintances "communicants of the devil." His chamberlain brought him a pig, according to Hugh, which Gerard, at the devil's behest, "worshiped," presumably a euphemism for "copulated with"; the chamberlain was then ordered to serve the pig to Gerard's guests. Gerard's brother Peter, also a royal chaplain, "confessed to having been impregnated by a man, and died of the monstrous growth."[36] This is one of the few specific references to homosexual intercourse in the historical writing I have surveyed. Hugh's anecdotes do not concern William Rufus but rather the corrupt clergy in his court. Neither episode, obviously, can be taken as a reliable indication of the moral tone of William or those around him.

Nowhere do we find evidence to substantiate the widely accepted view that William Rufus was homosexual, any more than there is evidence that his uncle, Robert of Normandy, brought homosexual practices back with him from the Crusades. Most modern claims about William Rufus reflect the influence of Edward A. Freeman, the nineteenth-century's greatest Norman scholar and a fierce Anglo-Saxon partisan. In *The History of the Norman Conquest of England* (1870–79), Freeman regarded the Conquest as a severe but temporary setback in the development of the English nation. Freeman emphasized that after the Battle of Hastings William fought against local resistance but "never again met Englishmen in a pitched battle" and never fought against a rival king at the head of a national force. Thus it was that "from the memorable day of Saint Calixtus [14 October] that we may fairly date the overthrow, what we know to have been only the imperfect and temporary overthrow, of our ancient and free Teutonic England."[37] England belonged to one of three great national groups, the Teutonic, which was destined to rule the world, as the nations of the Greeks and Romans had once done.[38] England's greatness lay in its ability to rise above the Conquest. Freeman was reacting against the earlier views of Sir Francis Palgrave, who minimized the contrast between life in England before and after the Conquest. Palgrave's *History of Normandy* (1831) represented the Norman Conquest as a development that preserved vital English traditions and legal institutions.[39]

Hugh A. MacDougall has demonstrated the power of the myth of progress as an inspiration to nineteenth-century authors enamored of the "Teutonic" view of English culture.[40] Simmons has shown that many authors who viewed the Conquest as the overthrow of "Teutonic" institutions were, in the early nineteenth century, political radicals who supported egalitarian constitutional reforms. Palgrave, no reformer, argued that the very term "Anglo-Saxon" conveyed "a most false idea" that "disguises the continuity of affairs, and substitutes the appearance of a new formation in the place of a progressive evolution."[41] Another who minimized differences between the Normans and the Anglo-Saxons was Thomas Carlyle, who distinguished the Saxons from the "gluttonous race of Jutes and Angles"[42] and who memorably declared that "the Normans were Saxons who had learned to speak French."[43] Palgrave, Carlyle, and others who downplayed differences between the Saxons and the Normans represented the Conquest as a correction of excesses and decay and as a reinvigoration of a Saxon or "Teutonic" tradition. A sexual stereotype that lay beneath the surface of many of these studies emerges in the writings of Charles Kingsley, a lecturer at Oxford who argued that the late Anglo-Saxon period was decaying because "the Anglo-Saxon, (a female race) required impregnation by the great male race,—the Norse introduction of Northmen by Edward paving the way for the Conquest, etc."[44] Most commentators preferred to reverse the positions, however, and placed the Normans in the passive sexual role.

Freeman is the principal historian who associated the Normans with weakness and passivity. Running through Freeman's and other accounts is an affiliation of the Normans not just with sexual profligacy but with effeminacy and homosexuality. Freeman took a dim view of Anglo-Saxon civilization before the Conquest, especially the reign of Edward the Confessor. Although Edward's coronation in 1043 restored the ancient native dynasty to the English throne after many years of Danish rule, he had strong connections to the Normans. One of the sons of Æthelred and Emma, Edward lived in exile in Normandy and was invited back to England in 1041 by King Harthacnut, whose sudden death that same year cleared the way for Edward's coronation. Because his court included some Norman knights and priests, Edward was seen as something other than a truly Anglo-Saxon king. He was more renowned for asceticism and piety—he is the only canonized English king—than for military skills. He also failed to provide an heir, thus failing "a central duty of a king—preservation of the bloodline."[45]

In *The Norman Conquest,* Freeman portrayed Edward as an example of Teutonic virtue corrupted by Norman influence. Freeman indicted Edward's sexual conduct, claiming that he enjoyed the company of Tostig, the brother of Harold (who succeeded Edward for a short reign of nine months, and who was defeated by William at Hastings), as his "favorite." Freeman condemned Edward's actions as "un-English" and suggested that Edward placed his "favorite" before the nation's interest

(2:28–29, 382–84). Simmons has proposed that Freeman's readers would have connected Edward's behavior to that of Edward II and James I, both reputed homosexuals, thus implicitly accusing Edward of homosexual sins.[46] But Freeman exaggerated. Sir Frank Stenton took pains to deny that Edward's court was dominated by Normans, pointedly noting that "the idea that he surrounded himself with Norman favourites will not survive an examination of the witnesses to his charters."[47]

More than any other nineteenth-century historian, Freeman gave credence to the comments of the chroniclers about the Normans' supposed association with "sodomy," effeminacy, and other "homosexual" vices. Freeman claimed that Rufus was "deepest of all in guilt." "Into the details of the private life of Rufus," Freeman declared somewhat indecorously, "it is not well to grope too narrowly. In him England might see on her own soil the habits of the ancient Greek and the modern Turk." His courtiers "altogether forsook the law of God and the customs of their fathers," Freeman wrote. "Vices before unknown, the vices of the East, the special sin, as the Englishmen then deemed, of the Norman, were rife among them."[48] Freeman's long appendix "The Character of William Rufus" surveyed the chroniclers' works, but nothing more than long hair, pointed shoes, and repeated accusations of "softness" or "effeminacy" are to be found there (2:490–504). Indeed, much of the writers' wrath is directed not at sex acts but at specific fashions—in particular concerning hair and shoes—that were seen as threatening to the moral order. Other sources speak to the same concern; Tatlock fills two pages with them. For example, the Council of Rouen forbade long hair in 1095. The Council of Westminster (1102) that Anselm promoted ordered that mens' hair should be cut to show both eyes and ears. Bishop Wulfstan of Worcester used to cut men's hair, "chiding their effeminacy and hinting at worse," in other words, perhaps suggesting that same-sex relations could be found in their shadow.[49] Ordericus reported that in 1105 Bishop Serlo of Séez preached against "effeminate men with curls, debased fornicators and catamites" who were "bearded like goats or Saracens."[50] In 1130 William of Malmesbury reported a tale about a knight who dreamed that he strangled in his long hair. William also denounced men who dressed effeminately and "wanted to be women," "assailers of others' chastity, prodigal of their own," describing this style as typical of the court of William Rufus and observing that it would not have been tolerated by Henry.[51]

Why this fuss about long hair and fancy clothes? The reason for these diatribes, Tatlock argued, was only partly a practical concern that long hair and elegant attire, "growing elegance and diminishing masculinity," were unsuitable to hunting. "The indignation of churchmen was due not only to regret for the good old days of dirty clothes and bristly faces," Tatlock continued, "but . . . to association of the new manners with homosexuality."[52] Barlow wisely pointed out that the "moralists," as he called the fuming chroniclers, were at a sartorial disadvantage. "Their own locks were mutilated by the tonsure—an unpopular disfiguration"; thus "hairiness in men of noble rank" was seen as degenerate.[53] Indeed, a haircut was essential for women who sought to disguise themselves as novices in male monasteries, as we saw in the saints' lives in chapter 2, and has long been known to have played a symbolic role in culture.[54]

Prominent historians of sexuality in the last century and this one accepted Freeman's view of Norman morals. At the end of the nineteenth century, Havelock Ellis claimed that "homosexual practices flourished among the Normans, as among other warlike peoples." Ellis actually claimed very little for the Normans that could not have been claimed for the Anglo-Saxons. At one point in *Sexual Inversion* he cited the Normans as a warlike people (along with the Dorians, Scythians, Tartars, and Celts). "During war and the separation from women that war involves, the homosexual instinct tends to develop," according to Ellis. Elsewhere he commented that "[a]mong the Normans, everywhere, homosexuality was markedly prevalent," and he attributed the "spread" of sodomy in France in the eleventh century and later in England to the Normans. Ellis's evidence for these wide-ranging claims consists of a few references to Anselm, Ordericus, and other chroniclers (most of them discussed above).[55] Another nineteenth-century scholar who argued for "a marked increase in homosexuality" in the twelfth century, attributable to the Norman Conquest, was G. Rattray Taylor.[56]

Twentieth-century historians have also repeated Freeman's assessment, or merely reiterated and confirmed what the chroniclers had said.[57] Bailey, for example, asserted that William Rufus was without doubt an "invert" or homosexual because he was unmarried and (illogically enough) because some historians have denounced his personal morals.[58] Tatlock took it as a fact that homosexuality was widespread at the courts of Robert of Normandy and William Rufus.[59] Christopher Brooke noted that William never married and had no children, and that "his private life is said to have shocked even his younger brother" (Henry, that is). Brooke added that William has been charged with "homosexual vice"; although specific evidence is lacking, "conditions of

his age and his life make it perfectly possible."[60] Poole likewise concluded from the chroniclers' accounts and from the "effeminate character" of William's court that the king "indulged in unnatural vice"
and that "[f]rom the moral standpoint he was probably the worst king
that has occupied the throne of England."[61] Jack Lindsay argued that
in a "semimilitary caste like that of the Norman nobles, sodomy was
no doubt common practice,"[62] although he did not explain why sodomy was not a common practice in the equally military castes of the
Anglo-Saxons.

Chief among historians who took a fuller view of the matter is
Barlow. He noted that the charges against William Rufus were not
specific but rather that they concerned debauchery in general. Although he concluded that William was either bisexual or homosexual,
since "the chroniclers were in no doubt" and would not have made up
this accusation, Barlow was at pains to show that the charges against
the king did not concern specific sexual acts. Barlow noted that William's court, thought to have been the nexus of this wickedness, was
also said to have been "thronged" with harlots. Nor was William accused of having a "favorite," although he also did not marry and had
no bastard children.[63] Barlow also sketched a short history revealing
how Norman morals had been corrupted in England. He claimed that
the Normans were, at first, rough and crude and that they "mocked
the English nobles whom they thought of as girls." Eventually, however, newfound wealth softened the conquerors. They "aped some English fashions, and by William II's reign moralists were denouncing
their effeminacy."[64]

Historians of sexuality have also taken broad exception to the standard view of the Normans and sex. Alan Bray dismissed Ellis's work
as "propaganda."[65] Bailey contradicted the view that the Normans had
introduced homosexual practices into England, discounting Taylor's
views while pointing out that Ellis's claims about the Normans and homosexuality rested on "nothing more than a large and unwarranted inference from the lives and conduct" of William Rufus and Robert.
William was clearly an "invert," Bailey agreed, but he stressed that there
was "no reason to assume, against all the historical evidence, that the
vices of the court or of a coterie of nobles and their sycophants were imitated in the country at large."[66] Boswell accurately traced the vagueness
and circularity of the tradition regarding sodomy and the Normans.
He noted that "where chroniclers comment specifically on William's
sexual excesses they do not mention homosexuality" but claim instead
that he was given to adultery, fornication, and effeminacy.[67]

The best reason to question the standard account of the Normans

and homosexual acts is that close association of the Normans with sodomy depends on the disassociation of the Anglo-Saxons with this sin.
It is apparent that the chroniclers used such terms as "sodomite" and
"catamite," "molles," and so forth, almost indiscriminately in their
eagerness to denounce fashionable excesses. References to "roving eyes"
and "mincing steps" are as frequent in the chroniclers' writing as references to Sodom. Sex between men is not mentioned by Ordericus,
and Anselm's view that the sin of Sodom ("scelus Sodomae") was newly
introduced to England is itself not specific to intramale sex. A central
fact, overlooked by many commentators on the subject—and not just
the nineteenth-century writers—is that the chroniclers did not have a
clear idea of what "sodomy" or the "sin of Sodom" was. Boswell suggested that Ordericus was "obsessed with homosexuality and imputed
it to most prominent Normans."[68] To say that Ordericus was "obsessed
with homosexuality" is to assume that he knew what "homosexuality"
and "homosexual" meant. It would be more accurate to say that Ordericus was obsessed with extravagance, indulgence, and anything that
suggested moral weakness and laxity.

Those "obsessed with homosexuality" should rather include subsequent commentators, perhaps beginning with Freeman and certainly
including those who wrote after him, who, like Freeman, unhesitat-
ingly interpreted the chroniclers' comments on dress and manners as
indications of sexual behavior. Accusations of same-sex misbehavior
are difficult to separate from more general charges of sexual indulgence that are themselves standard fare in the chroniclers' comments.
Charges of effeminacy, mincing steps, roving eyes, and elaborate dress
do not pertain to same-sex behavior. At the most they might be said
to anticipate the traditional view of the "fairy," i.e., a man marked
by "[a] limp wrist or an exaggerated swivel-hipped, mincing walk,"
or other stereotypical gestures indicating that he was effeminate and
womanlike.[69] The chroniclers did not make this connection themselves, but it is plain in the work of later historians who, working with
a simplistic, historically undifferentiated concept of "homosexuality,"
read their own understanding of "sodomy" and "homosexuality" into
the chroniclers' accounts and used those terms to categorize all the behavior to which the medieval authors objected.

The claim that sodomy had been "introduced" into England after
the Norman Conquest presumes that the Anglo-Saxon age had been a
kind of paradise in which only "natural" sexual relations were known.
The Anglo-Saxons supposedly lacked knowledge of "deviant" sexual
practices and therefore were vulnerable to corruption by outsiders who
did not. But as we have seen, Anglo-Saxon sources condemn same-sex

practices already in the early eighth century. Accounts of the Normans' sexual behavior would lead one to think that such evidence had simply disappeared. Such a view is, of course, preposterous. It is indicative of how little was known about the vernacular evidence of Anglo-Saxon ecclesiastical practice in the twelfth century and how little value modern historians of sexuality have attached to the Anglo-Saxon evidence more generally.

Many manuscripts of important Anglo-Saxon and Anglo-Latin texts, including the homilies of Ælfric and the Anglo-Saxon penitentials, were copied after the Conquest. Given this fact, the Normans' ignorance of Anglo-Saxon customs is difficult to understand.[70] All the manuscripts containing the vernacular Anglo-Saxon penitentials were written around or after the middle of the eleventh century, at Exeter, Canterbury, and especially Worcester.[71] Worcester has been called a "clearing house" for the works of Ordericus, Eadmer, and William of Malmesbury. All three historians argued that the Conquest was justified because the church in England, its monastic foundations especially, had fallen into states of decay.[72] It is significant that from the eleventh to the thirteenth century Worcester was also a preserve for Old English texts and knowledge of the Old English language. It is probable that some texts were copied—and, we can suppose, used, although less and less regularly—after the Conquest. The Normans replaced the ecclesiastical structures of the Anglo-Saxon church, but the establishment of new standards embodied in the Normans' language and administrative traditions required both time and effort. Even as the penitentials were being recopied, the administrative and intellectual systems in which they participated were weakening. Yet it is difficult to believe that the Anglo-Saxon church's opposition to same-sex relations, even more evident in Latin penitentials than in the vernacular documents, should have been illegible in any sense to the Normans. Ordericus Vitalis and other Anglo-Norman chroniclers wrote admiringly of such Anglo-Saxon figures as Bede and Alfred[73] but seem to have been either unaware of or cautiously suspicious of even the Latin texts used to govern the Anglo-Saxon church.

ANGLO-SAXON ENGLAND IN THE LATER MIDDLE AGES

While Ordericus and others indebted to Bede reconciled Anglo-Saxon and Norman histories, one author sought to elaborate—and to invent—English history before the Anglo-Saxons. This was Geoffrey of Monmouth, whose *History of the Kings of Britain,* completed c. 1136, traces the kings of England from the legendary Brutus, great-grandson of Aeneas of Troy, to Cadwallader, who abandoned Britain to the Saxons. Geoffrey's work, based on the writings of Gildas and on Arthurian folklore, generated an image of Anglo-Saxon England that prevailed in later medieval historiography and did much to obscure Anglo-Saxon history with claims for the origin of the English nation in Troy. Geoffrey's version of English history was not overturned until 1605, when Richard Verstegan published arguments that England's national origins did not lie in Brutus and Troy but rather with Saxons, Danes, and Normans, all of whom shared a racial origin.[74] What prompted the contempt of more serious and scholarly historians such as William of Newburgh for Geoffrey's writing was Geoffrey's approval of British kings and his elevation of Celtic heritage to the level of England's Saxon heritage. Partner has shown that Norman and Anglo-Norman writers often followed Bede in disapproving of the British as a weak and dissolute, even heretical, people—"treacherous apostates," in Partner's words—who betrayed Britain to Saxon invaders. As we have seen, Ordericus used this paradigm to suggest why the Anglo-Saxons, who triumphed over the British, had in turn fallen to the Danes.

Geoffrey took an ironic view of the chronicles and histories of his time. Valerie I. J. Flint has argued that the *Historia* was a sustained parody of monastic accounts that advocated the subordination of the clergy to the crown, clerical celibacy, and the subordination of women.[75] Seen in the light of these three issues in particular, Geoffrey's *Historia* appears as an unlikely cousin to ecclesiastical reform literature that acquired significant mass by the late fourteenth century and that, in its sixteenth-century form, helped to create the Church of England.

Gildas, and Bede after him, suggested that luxury—the category of sin to which sodomy belonged—was instrumental in the downfall of the Chosen People. Geoffrey's *Historia* claimed that two British kings were guilty of deviant sexual relations, and in one case he accused the king of sodomy. The first was Mempricius, who lived in the time of Homer, according to Geoffrey, and who "abandoned his own wife . . . and abandoned himself totally to unclean living, preferring unnatural intercourse to natural love" (literally, "abandoned himself to the pleasures of the sodomites," "sese sodomitane uoluptati dedit"). The second king was Malgo, "one of the comeliest men in the whole of Britain." He drove out tyrants but was "yet hateful in the sight of God, for his sodomitic vice" ("sodomitana peste").[76] Gildas, one of Geoffrey's sources, made reference to Sodom as a site of luxury and sin, but he did not specify sexual intercourse.[77] Given Flint's arguments for Geoffrey's sharp sense of parody, it seems reasonable to read these references, which greatly amplify the implications of Gildas's account, as exaggerated echoes of twelfth-century discourse of sodomy. Geoffrey satirizes both the sodomites and their historians. This conclusion seems especially warranted in reference to Mempricius, who, Tatlock suggested, was modeled on William Rufus. Both Mempricius and William Rufus died in hunting accidents, although the parallels are not exact. For example, according to Geoffrey Mempricius abandoned his wife, but William Rufus never had one.[78]

To the disgust of many of his readers, Geoffrey paid little attention to the history of Anglo-Saxon England. But subsequent revisers and translators of his work showed great interest in the subject and conflated their concerns with Geoffrey's. The Norman poet Wace translated Geoffrey's text into octosyllabic couplets in French in 1155, and this work, the *Roman de Brut,* was translated into English by Laȝamon, a parish priest in Areley Kings, Worcestershire, West Midlands. His *Historia Brutonum,* usually known as *Brut,* was probably composed in the first half of the thirteenth century (both surviving manuscripts are mid-thirteenth-century) and was certainly written after the death of Henry II in 1189.[79] The work begins with a short narrative that represents in neatly symbolic fashion the linguistic forces of English life in the twelfth century and creates a context for Geoffrey's work entirely out of keeping with the sense of history in the original.[80]

When Laȝamon set out to tell the story of England's nobles after the flood, he took three books with him:

> Laȝamon gon liðen wide ȝond þas leode
> & bi-won þa æðela boc þa he to bisne nom.
> He nom þa Englisca boc þa makede Seint Bede.
> An-oþer he nom on Latin þe makede Seint Albin.
> & þe feire Austin þe fulluht broute hider in.
> Boc he nom þe þridde leide þer amidden.
> þa makede a Frenchis clerc
> Wace wes ihoten þe wel couþe writen. (1.3.14–20)[81]

> Laȝamon began to travel widely through the land and acquired the noble books that he took as examples (i.e., accepted as authoritative); he took the book in English that Bede made, and another in Latin made by St. Alban and the fair Augustine, who brought baptism here, and he took the third book and set it between them that was made by the French clerk Wace, who knew how to write very well.

When Laȝamon translated Wace's book, he would have us believe, he positioned it between two others, one in Latin, written by Augustine, who brought Christianity to England, and the other an English book by Bede, "English" either by provenance (and in Latin) or in its use of the vernacular. The triad is symbolic. French is the dominant language, resting in the central position; Bede's text is merely a prop for it. Was this book of Bede a copy of the Anglo-Saxon translation of his *Ecclesiastical History,* produced in Alfred's reign? An eleventh-century copy made at Worcester, which is just ten miles from Areley Kings, still exists.[82] The use of English for Bede's text would not be merely symbolic, however subordinate it is in the arrangement of books, for Laʒamon is translating Geoffrey's book—already translated from Latin to French—from French to English.

When Laʒamon came to Wace's (and Geoffrey's) version of the two sodomitical kings, he sharpened the account in his sources. Geoffrey was less interested in Mempricius, the king perhaps modeled after William Rufus, than in Malgo. Mempricius ("Membriz" in the Middle English text) "abandoned his queen and took his retainers to bed, having forsaken women" ("for-heowede al his quene. / His hired-men he nom to bedde, 7 wifmen he al bilafde," 1.66.1289–90). Neither Geoffrey nor Wace explained that Mempricius had intercourse with his retainers. Laʒamon elaborated the somewhat similar sins of Malgo, which seem to have influenced the behavior of his retainers toward women.

> He luuede þane sunne þe lað [is] ure Drihtene.
> þa wifmen heo for-soken to mare sunne heo token.
> wapmon luuede wapmon wifmen heom laðe weoren.
> swa þat monie þusende wenden of þissen lond.
> wifmen swiðe feire ferden to oðere þeoden.
> for mucchel scome heo[m] þuhte. þat wepmen heom ne rohte.
> (2.756.14392–97)

> He loved the sin that is hateful to our Lord. He forsook women and embraced a great sin. Men loved men; women were hateful to them. Thus many thousand women, very fair ones, left this land and went to other nations because they thought it a great shame that men did not care for them.

Laʒamon did not call either king a sodomite. But his translation makes the sexual sin of both kings clear: they had sex with other men rather than with women.

In the works of Anselm and the Anglo-Norman chroniclers sodomy was a weapon used to attack the corruption of contemporary kings and princes. Like Anselm and the chroniclers, Geoffrey did not hesitate to use the word "sodomy" or some variant of it. But Geoffrey's participation in this discourse cannot simply be taken as another instance of an Anglo-Norman historian attacking the legendary vices of William's court. Rather, in the framework Flint has provided, we might expect to find Geoffrey deriding the chroniclers' "obsession" (to borrow Boswell's description of Anselm's interest in the matter) with William's conduct. Since he otherwise presented the British in a highly favorable light, it is difficult to believe that he would portray two kings as sodomites without an ulterior motive grounded in parody. No one, so far as I know, has ever imputed irony, or much in the way of wit, to Laȝamon, however, and his elaboration of Malgo's sin seems intended to amplify the injustice and wrong worked by the king's wickedness. Laȝamon did not use the word "sodomy," it is true, but he unambiguously accused the kings of having sexual intercourse with other men, and in keeping with the tenor of his time, he marked this sin as one especially hateful to God. Geoffrey deliberately pushed Anglo-Saxon memories to one side as he pursued a history of Britain before the Anglo-Saxon invasion. Although using Geoffrey's text, Laȝamon pushed history in the opposite direction, turning the history into English and returning the history of England before the Anglo-Saxons to the anti-British bias found in Gildas and Bede. In the case of the two sodomitical kings, Laȝamon also imported contemporary dogma into his text.

Although Anglo-Norman sodomitical discourse demonstrates an apparently complete lack of familiarity with Old English and Anglo-Latin writing about same-sex sex, the Anglo-Saxon language and memories of the English past did not disappear so completely as the authors of Anglo-Norman or Middle English chronicles suggest. There are several signs that the language and even some aspects of the culture of the Anglo-Saxons continued to be known, even revered, long after the Conquest. Many of these signs are superficial, registered only in the names of certain figures, especially Bede and Alfred, who are celebrated as translators of Latin works into English and as teachers who used the people's own language. Alfred was admired by Ordericus Vitalis as "the first king to hold sway over the whole of England" and a giant among those who came before or after him.[83] The *Proverbs of Alfred,* written before the end of the twelfth century and known to and apparently used by Laȝamon, belong to an entirely imaginary literature composed of Alfred's wise sayings (none of which have anything to do with his genuine writings).[84]

But some recognition of the Anglo-Saxons' learning is more substantial, and more significant examples are to be found in texts from

Worcester in the late twelfth and early thirteenth centuries. Worcester, not far from Laʒamon's home, was a site not merely for the preservation of Anglo-Saxon manuscripts but for scholarly study of the texts and the language they contained. At Worcester, English scholars after the Conquest asserted Anglo-Saxon traditions of learning and church discipline, even as they reconciled those traditions to the reformed standards being put into effect elsewhere in England. Worcester's ecclesiastical life was dominated by St. Wulfstan (not to be confused with the famous archbishop of London, York, and Worcester), who died in 1095 and was canonized in 1203. The last of Edward the Confessor's bishops and the last Anglo-Saxon bishop in England, Wulfstan remained in Worcester long after other sees in England had been given to Norman bishops. He actively promoted ecclesiastical reform in his diocese at a time when the Normans were busily transforming ecclesiastical practices elsewhere.[85]

Wulfstan's is a distinctively anti-Norman voice in the historical record of the twelfth century. Shortly before his death, he directed a monk named Hemming to organize a cartulary condemning "the violence of the Normans in our own time, who by force, guile and rapine have unjustly deprived this holy church of its lands, villages and possessions, until hardly anything is safe from their depredations."[86] Wulfstan had an unusual investment both in Anglo-Saxon standards of church discipline and in Anglo-Saxon texts. According to Christine Franzen, "a high proportion of the surviving late eleventh-century Worcester manuscripts were written in English," some of them for use in pastoral work with the laity.[87] Nor was Wulfstan the last Englishman to believe that Anglo-Saxon traditions were important. During the reign of Henry I many Anglo-Saxon laws were collected in translations intended for practical use, not merely as records of ancient customs but as "a modernized statement of the old law."[88] During the reign of Henry II, who died in 1189, Alfred's laws were translated from Anglo-Saxon into Latin.[89]

The spirit of Wulfstan's work was carried on by a scholar known to us as the Tremulous Hand of Worcester, who was probably a near contemporary of Laʒamon. According to Wendy E. J. Collier, "It seems to be more than a coincidence that two men of such similar commitment and interests should be working within a few miles and within a few years of each other, and in an area where the memory of the last Anglo-Saxon bishop was still venerated."[90] The Tremulous Hand wrote glosses and notes on a large number of Anglo-Saxon manuscripts. Worcester Cathedral Manuscript F. 174, the so-called Worcester Fragments, was written in the first half of the thirteenth century entirely in his hand. It contains an impressive range of Anglo-Saxon texts, including a version of the poem known as *The Soul's Address,* familiar to Anglo-Saxonists from copies in the *Vercelli Book* and the *Exeter Book,*[91] and an early Middle English version of Ælfric's *Grammar and Glossary.* In addition to these updated versions of Old English texts is a passage of rhythmical prose known as *Sanctus Beda.* This text laments that English is no longer the language used to instruct the people and mourns deaths of famous men who taught their people in English, including Bede, Ælfric, Æthelwold, and others.[92]

Bede's reputation as a translator of English works had particular durability and is attested in a range of Middle English sources, including, as we have seen, Laȝamon's *Brut,* from about 1200. No authentic work by Bede survives in Old English except the *Ecclesiastical History,* which was translated in the late ninth century, not during Bede's lifetime (Bede died in 735). The claim that Bede wrote in Old English is made in an eighth-century text known as "Cuthbert's Letter on the Death of Bede," which reports that there were two works that Bede wanted to finish at his death. One was the Gospel of St. John, which he "was turning into our mother tongue to the profit of the Church" ("in nostram linguam ad utilitatem ecclesiae Dei conuertit"). The other was a selection from Isidore, *De natura rerum.*[93]

The cathedral library at Worcester owned a number of Anglo-Saxon manuscripts, including a copy of the Old English version of Bede's *Ecclesiastical History* glossed by the Tremulous Hand. Among others was a famous copy of Alfred's translation of the *Cura pastoralis,* in which there are fifty or more glosses per page.[94] He also glossed a manuscript of Alfred's translation of Boethius's *Consolation of Philosophy,* the Old English translation of Gregory's *Dialogues,* and two manuscripts of the Anglo-Saxon penitentials.[95] As we saw in chapter 5, Alfred's translation of the *Cura pastoralis* and Gregory's *Dialogi* were among the texts that developed graphic images of Sodom and allegories about the city's sinfulness.

Amid all this material, it is the Tremulous Hand's work with the penitentials that reveals both his own interest in clerical discipline and his knowledge of definitions of sodomy established since the Anglo-Saxon period. The Tremulous Hand began but did not persist in an effort to render the penitentials and other texts into a new language; instead he simply entered the Latin translations of individual words.[96] Collier traces the extent of the Tremulous Hand's interest in penance and confession, showing that it ranged from general matters, such as commutations of penance and lists of the chief sins, to notes on penances for particular sins.[97] He marked various issues within the scope of penitential discipline, but he took particular interest in sexual sins inside and outside of marriage and unusual interest in unorthodox sexual acts. His most important notations accompany canons from the *Old English Penitential* that concerns "those men who have illicit fornication, that is with animals or soil themselves with young ones, or a man who has sex with another" ("Be þam men þe ungedafenlice hæmð, þæt is wið nytenum, oððe hine mid geonglingum besmiteð, oððe wæpnedman wið oðerne"; see chapter 4, appendix 2, *Old English Penitential* 2.6). Near the chapter heading the Tremulous Hand wrote "sodomit," meaning "sodomite." He placed a "Nota" mark opposite the canon that followed, which refers to bestiality (not to intercourse with boys, as the heading does), and another "Nota" mark opposite the canon that specified a penance of beating for young men who commit this sin.[98] Opposite another canon forbidding bestiality later in this text the Tremulous Hand also wrote "sodomit."[99] Next to what I have referred to as a general, all-purpose canon forbidding unnatural acts ("ungecyndelicum ðingum") he entered another "Nota" mark (see chapter 4, appendix 2, *Old English Penitential,* Additamenta 1). The Tremulous Hand entered fourteen annotations into one manuscript of the *Old English Penitential;* seven of them concern sex acts and two of them classify a sin as "sodomy."[100] Collier notes that the Tremulous Hand displayed an interest in Sodom itself, marking the name of "Lot," who dwelled among the sinful people of Sodom ("eardode þa on ðam yfelan leodscype sodomiscre burhware"), three times in one homily.[101]

In the early period, including the period of the Anglo-Saxon penitentials, which survive in manuscripts from the late tenth through the mid–eleventh century, homosexual acts are described with details that later penitentials omit, using description, as Payer has observed, because the church as yet lacked "accepted common nouns to cover different classes of sexual behavior."[102] Later penitentials reflect the full range of meanings attached to "sodomy" as a category including acts such as incest and bestiality. The Tremulous Hand, we can see, did not hesitate to use the word "sodomite," a term he would have known from old Latin penitentials available to him at Worcester.[103] But his use of the term does not correspond to uses found in earlier Latin or Anglo-Saxon penitentials. Rather, as we see above, the Tremulous Hand used "sodomite" both times to mark canons that deal with bestiality (the first example also includes male homosexual intercourse). He had derived this definition from contemporary penitentials, not the older texts.

The Tremulous Hand was the last scholar to comment on the

Anglo-Saxon penitentials until the English reformation. Highly selective and largely misguided rereadings of the Worcester manuscripts, including the Anglo-Saxon penitentials, were undertaken by various Renaissance scholars, including John Joscelyn, secretary to Archbishop Matthew Parker.[104] After the twelfth century, penitential literature in England was written in Latin, and nothing like the Old English handbooks of penance, with their straightforward accounts of same-sex offenses, ever reappeared. The discourse of sodomy, transformed by the Normans, developed within the parameters of standardized canonical collections, and "sodomy" itself, as the Tremulous Hand's work shows, was no longer understood as exclusively same-sex behavior, as it was in earlier penitentials. Subsequent references to "sodomy" in legal collections are both rare and confusing. For example, sodomy is mentioned in a thirteenth-century legal treatise known as *Fleta* in a chapter on arson. "Apostate Christians, sorcerers and the like should be drawn and burnt. Those who have connexion with Jews and Jewesses or are guilty of bestiality or sodomy shall be buried alive in the ground, provided that they be taken in the act and convicted by lawful and open testimony" ("Christiani autem apostate, sortilegii et huiusmodi detractari debent et conburi. Contrahentes vero cum Iudeis vel Iudeabus, pecorantes et sodomite in terra viui confodiantur, dum tamen manu opera capti, per testimonium legale vel publice conuicti").[105] This treatise claims to be based on the legal code known as *Bracton,* written in the mid–thirteenth century, which has been called "the crown and flower of English medieval jurisprudence."[106] But *Bracton* makes no reference to sodomy, and the source of the reference in *Fleta* remains obscure; the punishment of being buried alive, according to Bailey, dates from the early Germanic period and is a legal archaism.[107] About the same time, another compilation, known as *Britton,* appeared; it condemns sodomites to burning. *Britton* was written in French rather than Latin, and it is found in more manuscripts than *Fleta,* which has been described as "a failure."[108] The provisions of *Britton* regarding sodomy were probably not enacted. Sexual morality was the Church's domain, not the state's. Sodomy was made a felony in 1533, and the passing of that statute itself "affords an almost sufficient proof that the temporal courts had not punished it and that no one had been put to death for it for a very long time past."[109]

CHAUCER'S ANGLO-SAXON TALE

As we saw briefly in Laȝamon's *Brut,* appreciation for learned writing in the English vernacular seems never to have died out after the

Norman Conquest, even though such writing became very scarce. Bede and Alfred maintained steady reputations as learned men who wrote in English. In the fourteenth century, as Douglas Moffat has shown, English chronicles showed acute resentment at the loss of status that the Norman victory meant for the Anglo-Saxons. The context of this resentment in the early fourteenth century is, needless to say, very different from that surrounding Wulfstan's view of the Normans. Early-fourteenth-century English chroniclers identified the lowborn as those of Anglo-Saxon descent and contrasted them to the highborn, those of "French" descent, "who held positions of relative power and prestige."[110] The Normans were also seen as a foreign race that put the Anglo-Saxons under a burden of tyranny against which the English struggled for centuries. This is the so-called Norman yoke, a formulation with which reformers in the seventeenth century and after attributed the loss of the freedoms thought to have been characteristic of the Anglo-Saxon period.

The theory of the "Norman yoke" was used to articulate class differences as well as racial differences. It required an idealization of Anglo-Saxon institutions as representative of a superior social organization. The fourteenth-century chroniclers' perceptions of "lowborn" Anglo-Saxons can be seen as an early instance of the "Norman yoke" theory, but Moffat pointed out that the chroniclers did not idealize the Anglo-Saxons or their institutions or see pre-Conquest England as a perfect society.[111] The Conquest's linguistic consequences mirrored the fall of the English from power. Their language had become a mark of their inferior social status. But it was also a link to an ancient heritage. In the course of the fourteenth century, English regained its ascendancy over French as the powerful adopted the speech of those they dominated. As Moffat says, "[F]inding one's own language coming increasingly out of the mouths of those who are socially and economically one's superior, where before that was not the case, would not, I submit, be an unambiguous source of pride and satisfaction."[112]

References to Anglo-Saxon heritage reappear in a variety of Middle English contexts.[113] Two quite different voices at the end of the fourteenth century suggest that the Anglo-Saxons were remembered as valorous in the faith and as a people who read Scripture and taught in their own language. The demand of Lollard preachers to be able to teach and read the Scripture in English was a key feature of what Anne Hudson has called the "premature reformation" in England at the end of the fourteenth century.[114] Moffat and others have analyzed the shifting status of England's major languages in the fourteenth century.

Particularly contested, as Nicholas Watson has shown, was the use of English in theological study.[115] Lollard preachers knew of Bede's reputation as a translator. They mistakenly thought he had turned the Bible into English, citing this work as a precedent for their own wish for a vernacular Bible. One important record of their views is the "General Prologue" to the Wycliffite Bible, which survives in just 11 of the 250 manuscripts containing the Wycliffite Bible.[116] The "General Prologue" points to a long and neglected tradition of English as a sacred language.

> [F]or if worldli clerkis loken wel here croniclis and bokis, thei shulden fynde, that Bede translatide the bible, and expounide myche in Saxon, that was English, either comoun langage of this lond, in his tyme; and not oneli Bede, but also king Alured, that foundide Oxenford, translatide in hise laste daies the bigynning of the Sauter into Saxon, and wolde more, if he hadde lyued lengere. Also Frenshe men, Beemers [Bohemians], and Britons han the bible, and othere bokis of deuocioun and of exposicioun, translatid in here modir langage; whi shulden not English men haue the same in here modir langage, I can not wite, no but for falsnesse and necgligence of clerkis, either for oure puple is not worthi to haue so greet grace and ȝifte of God, in peyne of here olde synnes.[117]

Another tract on translating Scripture noted that "[a]lso venerabile Bede lede be þe spirit of God translatid þe Bible or a grete part of þe Bible into Englishe." The author must have been reading some text attributed to Bede—it cannot have been the Gospel of John, however, which does not survive—because he went on to say that the texts were written in "so oolde Englische þat vnneþe can any Englishe man rede hem, ffor þis Bede regnede an hooly doctor after þe Incarnation seuene hundred yeer and xxxij."[118] The treatise repeats the belief that "Alrede þe kynge ordined opone scolis of diurse artes in Oxenforde and he turnede þe best lawes into his modor tunge and þe sawter also."[119] Alfred is believed to have translated the prose psalms of the *Paris Psalter,*[120] but the claim that he founded Oxford University, part of his general reputation as a great and wise man, is of course spurious.[121] The reference to "oolde Englische" in this treatise is striking. Anglo-Saxon was first called "Old English" around 1200 by the author of *Seinte Marherete,* an early Middle English text that marks the end of the Old English tradition.[122] At that point, "Old English" could still be read. But the "oolde Englische" of the Wycliffite prologue is so remote that "scarcely anyone is able to read it." The author probably could not decipher Bede's *History* in Old English, but he was aware that English had been used as a sacred language long before his own time. His argument about its validity as a language for preaching and teaching is based on precedent and is sound.

Lollard enthusiasm for translation in English strongly opposed tradition. Lollards were radical on other fronts, including their deployment of the discourse of sodomy. The following excerpt from a Lollard text represents sodomy as a consequence of clerical celibacy and conveys a decidedly untraditional attitude toward the prohibition against speaking of the sin observed by Chaucer and many of his contemporaries:[123]

> Þe þridde conclusiun sorwful to here is þat þe lawe of continence annexyd to presthod, þat in preiudys of wimmen was first ordeynid, inducith sodomie in al holy chirche; but we excusin us be þe Bible for þe suspecte decre þat seyth we schulde not nemen it. Resun and experience prouit þis conclusiun. For delicious metis and drinkis of men of holi chirche welen han nedful purgaciun or werse. Experience for þe priue asay of syche men is, þat þe[i] like non wymmen; and whan þu prouist sich a man mark him wel for he is on of þo. Þe correlary of þis conclusiun is þat þe priuat religions, begynneris of þis synne, were most worthi to ben anullid. But God for his myth of priue synne sende opyn ueniaunce. [124]

The third conclusion sorrowful to hear is that the law of continence that is joined to priesthood, which was first established in prejudice of women, induces sodomy throughout the church. We excuse ourselves by means of the Bible from the suspect decree that says we should not name it [this sin]. Reason and experience prove this conclusion. Because of delicate meat and drink the men of holy church will have needful purgation or worse. The private test of such men is that they do not like women; when you detect such a man, mark him well, for he is one of them. The corollary of this conclusion is that the private orders, the originators of this sin, were most worthy to be abolished. But God, because of his sight of private sin, sends open vengeance (for them).

This commentary brings together several strains of argument: the antifeminist basis of clerical celibacy; the resulting sin of sodomy among those forced to live without women; the supposed scriptural basis for the demand that "sodomy" not be named (correctly said to be false); and the belief that the test of a sodomite is that he "like[s] non wymmen." These sentiments, we will see, were even more fully developed by John Bale, an early Reformation historian, and applied to the same conclusion—the belief that sodomites had to be found out and removed, and that regulations governing the clergy had to be revised to prevent the creation of more such damned creatures. Sixteenth-century authors learned from Lollard texts. Among Bale's contemporaries, both Matthew Parker and John Foxe owned copies of the Lollard tract on translating the Bible into English.[125]

The Lollards insisted on reading and teaching in the vernacular. Their efforts curiously parallel those of Geoffrey Chaucer, never to be mistaken for a radical, who was keen to establish English as a language with status comparable to Latin, French, and Italian. Chaucer is also increasingly recognized as an author who knew something about the Lollards, satirized the clerical corruption the Lollards deplored, and expressed "unabashed admiration" for ideals similar to theirs.[126] Significantly, some of these ideals figure in Chaucer's only Anglo-Saxon tale, *The Man of Law's Tale,* which begins with a joke about Chaucer's extensive English compositions. The Man of Law reports that he does not know a tale that Chaucer has not already told "in swich Englissh as he kan / Of olde tyme" (46–50).[127] The Man of Law himself claims to know quite a bit about England's history, since we are told in the *General Prologue* that "[i]n termes hadde he caas and domes alle / That from the tyme of kyng William were falle" (323–24)—that is to say, that he knew all the cases in the Court of Common Pleas from the time of the Norman Conquest.[128] Chaucer seldom turned to earlier English history to demonstrate the tradition he sought to bolster. When he did so in *The Man of Law's Tale,* he derived his knowledge from a French source, the *Chronicle* of Nicholas Trivet, written in the early fourteenth century.[129] Although Trivet did not clarify the nature of his sources, they included Anglo-Saxon and Anglo-Latin texts. According to Margaret Schlauch, "Trivet vaguely refers to 'chronicles of the Saxons,' otherwise unspecified," but she notes that "[n]o such story is contained in any Anglo-Saxon source known to us."[130] Trivet seems to have known Bede's *Ecclesiastical History* and derived the name of one of his major characters, Alla, from the Northumbrian king Bede calls Ælle. Trivet also compiled a commentary on Boethius's *Consolation of Philosophy* that strongly suggests direct use of the Old English translation of that work attributed to King Alfred.[131]

Chaucer begins *The Man of Law's Tale* in the East, with the marriage of the Roman emperor's daughter, Custance, to the sultan of Syria. His mother murders him for betraying their faith and becoming Christian and sets Custance adrift in a rudderless ship which, three years later, is driven aground off the coast of Northumbria, where she is found by a constable. The setting and the name of the king, Alla, are historically accurate. The account of persecution of Christians who fled to Wales conforms roughly to accounts of early British history found in Gildas and elsewhere.[132] Thereafter the tale becomes a conversion narrative about the earliest phases of English—or, more precisely, British—history. Other versions, including Chaucer's source, establish Northumbria as Saxon territory. Gower wrote that the constable's king, Ælle, was a "Saxon and a worthi knyht."[133] Trivet reported that the constable's name was Elda and noted that Custance, when questioned by Elda, answered him in his own language ("E ele lui respoundi en Sessoneys, qe fu la langage Elda").[134] Chaucer conjures a dark vision of Northumbria as a land lacking both religion and law,[135] and says only that Custance spoke "[a] maner Latyn corrupt" (519) that was intelligible to the constable.[136] This small detail points to a phrase used in the "General Prologue" to the Wycliffite Bible, where the speech of Italians is identified as "Latyn corrupt, as trewe men seyn, that han ben in Italie."[137]

Northumbria at this time was pagan, nearly all Christians, the Man of Law reports, having been driven into exile in Wales (541–46). The constable and his wife, Hermengyld, take Custance into their castle. Custance pleases everybody, so that "alle hir loven that looken in hir face" (532). Hermengyld is especially fond of this visitor, and "loved hire right as hir lyf" (535). Shortly thereafter, as a result of this bond of friendship, Hermengyld becomes a Christian (537–38). A blind man, one of the few Christians not in exile, encounters Hermengyld, Custance, and the constable, and asks that Custance give him his sight. She does, upon which Hermengyld's husband learns of her conversion and becomes a Christian too. A knight has fallen in love with Custance but is rejected when he tries to woo her. In revenge he plots against her. During the constable's absence the knight steals into Hermengyld's bedroom, where the two women, exhausted by their prayers, share a bed (596–602). The knight kills Hermengyld and puts the knife under Custance's pillow; he later accuses her of the crime, swearing on "[a] Britoun book, written with Evaungiles" (666), but is struck dead for his blasphemy. Alla is converted as a result of this miracle and Custance's intercession (680–86), and, much to the distress of his mother, Custance and the king are married. When Custance and Alla go to bed, the narrator marks the event with delicate reservations about its implications for Custance's sanctity.

> They goon to bedde, as it was skile and right;
> For thogh that wyves be ful hooly thynges,
> They moste take in pacience at nyght
> Swiche manere necessaries as been plesynges

To folk that han ywedded hem with rynges,
And leye a lite hir hoolynesse aside,
As for the tyme—it may no bet betide. (708–14)

They went to bed, as was suitable and right. For though wives are very holy, at night they must accept patiently those necessary things that please those who have wedded them with rings, and set their holiness aside for a bit—there is no other way.

Custance and Alla are separated through a fiendish plot created by his mother around the birth of Custance's son. As a result Custance is once again put out to sea, apparently at Alla's command but in fact at the behest of his mother, who is, when Alla learns of her treachery, killed (894–95). In the end Custance and Alla are reunited in Rome, where she is led by her ship and where he has gone on a pilgrimage of repentance for killing his mother. They return to England, where he dies; Custance then returns to her father in Rome.

The tale is a marriage of history and myth, Ælle having been a real Anglo-Saxon king mentioned in other sources, and Custance a distressed heroine of folktale, a "calumniated wife" like others set adrift in a ship by an evil mother-in-law.[138] Chaucer did not underscore the connection between the tale's Anglo-Saxon perspective and the Man of Law's joke about composition in English, although the "Britoun book," perhaps a book in the British tongue, might be an important clue to vernacular culture. For Trivet the book is a more significant prop than it is for Chaucer; Trivet notes that it is also the text the two women have used in their prayers together.[139] Chaucer also put less emphasis than other versions, including his source, on the physical intimacy between the two women, who share a bed the night Hermengyld is murdered. They sleep "en meme le lyt," according to Trivet, and John Gower said the same. Chaucer, less explicit, indicates that there are two women sleeping when the knight "[a]l softely is to the bed ygo"—that is, to one bed (599).[140] Chaucer uses this sleeping arrangement—a common one in the medieval world and, until recently, in the modern world as well[141]—to comic effect in *The Reeve's Tale,* when two students are forced to share a bed in a miller's house. In the course of taking revenge for a wrong he has done them, they play something like musical beds. Their game ends when one of them inadvertently ends up in the miller's bed and boasts about having had sex not once but three times with the miller's daughter during the night.[142]

Chaucer made nothing of the same-sex love that shadows the close relationship between Hermengyld and Custance—nothing sexual of it, in any case. Nor should we. But we should not forget that it *is* same-sex love. In some ways this community of two women recalls the single-sex environment of the Christian communities seen in the tales of Eugenia and Euphrosyne, the saints whose Old English lives describe their cross-dressing. Chaucer does not cross-dress characters, but he does cross-name them. In Trivet's account Hermengyld is a man, a prince of Spain converted to Christianity by his wife and martyred by his Arian father in 585, a story known to the Anglo-Saxons in a translation of the *Dialogues* of Gregory the Great undertaken at the end of the ninth century.[143] Chaucer's Hermengyld is a woman converted by her friend, Custance. The history of Hermengyld's name would have mattered, if only to those who knew Chaucer's source. For us, the name faintly masculinizes her and deepens the same-sex shadow of the love she and Custance share. The sexual implications of this love are also underscored, for the female-female pairing seems less innocent when one of the women is associated with masculine traits. Each woman in *The Man of Law's Tale* is positioned opposite the man who partners the other woman. When the constable is away, Custance replaces him in Hermengyld's bed, and after Hermengyld's death (and indeed because of it and the ensuing trial) Alla converts and marries Custance, in a sense replacing Hermengyld in Custance's bed. Although these juxtapositions intensify the sexual resonance of the women's relationship, the intimacy between Custance and Hermengyld plainly does not extend from the physical to the sexual. Given the stress the tale places on Custance's chastity, it would be ludicrous to queer their friendship into a sexual relationship. The narrator says that after Alla begot his son he left Custance with the constable and a bishop and went back to fight the Scots (715–21). She has a very brief career as a wife but a conspicuously successful career as maid and mother. When she and her child are sent from England, she speaks words of comfort that have been compared to Middle English lyrics expressing the Virgin's pity for Christ.[144]

The juxtaposition of Hermengyld's cut throat and the jealous knight's knife might touch off some Freudian or Lacanian speculations. But they could not overpower the tender basis of the friendship, formed before Christianity becomes its foundation, between two women. *The Man of Law's Tale* is not a story of same-sex love except in one limited and striking sense: Custance and Hermengyld are partners in love and in prayer. Chaucer's apostle from Rome and her first convert are women whose love for each other provokes a crime of passion by a man who has fallen into the wrong kind of love with one of them. In the next chapter I take up some implications of Alla's presence in this

tale and in Bede's *Ecclesiastical History,* and explore connections between Bede's text and Bale's. For the moment, however, I want to turn
the Man of Law's clock back to the night when Custance and Hermengyld, "wery, forwaked in hire orisouns" (exhausted from loss of sleep
because they have prayed so much, 596) fall into bed. The evil knight,
knife and murderous plan in hand, has not yet left his quarters. I pause
here because Chaucer does not. In this moment of love and friendship,
a prelude to tragedy, a better ending is still possible as the women,
surrounded by the same-sex shadow of their love, sleep.

Alla, Angli, and *Angels*
in America

Rome, not Northumbria, is the center of *The Man of Law's Tale,* and celibacy, not marital bliss, is the Man of Law's preferred mode for Christ's holy ministers. Chaucer's text looks neither to the vernacular tradition of married clergy that the Wycliffites sought nor to the celibate clerical world demanded by Roman canon law and espoused earlier by the Anglo-Saxon church of Ælfric and by Norman reformers. Instead, the Man of Law's heroine is a product of Chaucerian compromise. She practices what might be thought of as serial chastity. Custance marries Alla, but after she becomes pregnant she lives without his company for all but the last year of his life. Clerical ideals dominate *The Man of Law's Tale,* much of its domestic sentiment notoriously devalued not only by the narrator's self-dramatizing interruptions but by Chaucer's debt to the work of a great reforming cleric, Pope Innocent III, whose "De miseriis humane conditionis" (On the misery of the human condition) is quoted in the prologue to the tale and elsewhere in the text.[1]

Chaucer makes much of the dependence of the English church on Rome. His reform-minded contemporaries, the Lollards, regarded Rome as a dangerous influence; in the Reformation the city became a symbol used to attack Catholicism. But for the Anglo-Saxons and for orthodox Christians of Chaucer's time, Rome was the center of the Church on earth. Correspondence with the pope and travel to and from Rome were means by which the church of the frontier established its authenticity. In this chapter I examine one small part of this traffic, an episode from Bede's *Ecclesiastical History of the English People,* which describes the sale of angelic English boys in Rome, a story subsequently retold by Wace, Laȝamon, and others, including John Bale, a Reformation historian. I compare the juxtaposition of angels and Angli, meaning "English," in these texts to angelic powers in Tony Kushner's

Angels in America, a play in which the Anglo-Saxons, embodied in the stereotype of the WASP, play a small but significant role. For a moment, however, I return to Chaucer's Alla and a scene in which he too meets a boy in Rome.

ALLA AND ÆLLE

Alla registers a dim presence in *The Man of Law's Tale.* He is heard about after Custance converts Hermengyld and her husband but otherwise, except for letters to his mother, not heard from until a young boy (who proves to be his son) is set before him at a feast. This act is part of Custance's plan. She too has arrived in Rome but has refused to identify herself to the senator who rescued her from the ship on which she was set adrift from Northumbria. Now, in her husband's presence, she speaks through her son. "[A]t his moodres heeste / Biforn Alla, durynge the metes space, / The child stood, lookynge in the kynges face" (1013–15).[2] The child does not look like him, however, but "as lyk unto Custance / As possible is a creature to be" (1030–31). Because Alla has kept the faith (he is on a pilgrimage of repentance for killing his wicked mother), he realizes that Christ might have sent Custance to Rome just as he sent her to Northumbria. Shortly thereafter Alla and Custance are reconciled. Only then does she reveal herself to her father, the emperor, explaining for the first time who she is (1105–13).

The story of Custance reminds many readers of a saint's life and recalls some of the dynamics of stories about cross-dressed women saints recounted in chapter 2.[3] Like Euphrosyne, Custance is betrothed, in Custance's case to a sultan who becomes a Christian in order to marry her. His mother, outraged, kills him and sends Custance out to sea, a scenario repeated when Custance is expelled from Northumbria. Unlike Euphrosyne, Custance marries and has a child. But in many ways her life as a missionary is similar to the lives of the evangelizing saints commemorated in Anglo-Saxon texts. The moment at which Custance reveals herself to her father recalls the revelation made by both Euphrosyne and Eugenia to theirs. And, like Eugenia, Custance preaches the word of God from within a same-sex community. It is, of course, a tiny one, just Custance and Hermengyld, but their same-sex love, symbolized by the bed they share, is genuine and more warmly demonstrated than such love is in the Anglo-Saxon texts.

Having been reunited in Rome, Custance and Alla return to Northumbria for a year of wedded bliss. After Alla's death, Custance goes back to Rome and takes up a life of virtue and good works, never again parting from her father (1156–57). Chaucer rejoined his roving heroine to patriarchal structures identical to those governing the lives of Eugenia and Euphrosyne. The difference is that Chaucer's holy woman is not just a daughter but also a wife and mother—a married evangelist. To a surprising degree *The Man of Law's Tale* conforms to what might have been a Lollard vision of evangelism in the true church. Custance's language, for example, recognized as "a maner Latyn corrupt" in Northumbria, is what the Lollards thought Italians spoke—that is, a vernacular, albeit not English. The tale discreetly hints of controversies building in the Church in Chaucer's time by effecting a radical redescription of the origins of the Church in the Anglo-Saxon period. According to the Man of Law, Northumbria was converted by a woman who arrives from Rome by way of Syria, directed only by God's will and the winds. But as Bede's *Ecclesiastical History* makes clear, the territory was converted by Irish missionaries and by holy men who came at the pope's behest from Rome—Augustine sent by Gregory the Great in 596, Theodore and Hadrian sent by Pope Vitalian over half a century later. Equally bold is the Man of Law's revised account of Alla, Chaucer's version of the Northumbrian king Ælle, the only English character in the text who is known to have been a historical person. Chaucer's Alla is converted to Christianity by Custance and with her has a son, Maurice, who was crowned emperor by the pope (1122). Bede's Ælle was not Christian but rather served as a symbol of pagan kingship awaiting redemption. Ælle's son, Edwin, converted to Christianity because he wished to marry Æthelburh, the daughter of the Christian king Æthelberht.[4] Thereafter Edwin "held under his sway the whole realm of Britain, not only English kingdoms but those ruled over by the Britons as well."[5]

Ælle's role in Bede is much smaller on the historical level but much greater on the symbolic level. He appears in Bede's text but once, in a description of some boys who, like Maurice, ended up in Rome through circumstances not of their own choosing. They too looked into the face of an important man, Pope Gregory. Or I should say, rather, that he looked into their faces, and what he saw there, depending on whose account we accept, was either the image of a chosen people waiting to be converted (the preferred explanation)—or love.[6]

> It is said that one day, soon after some merchants had arrived in Rome, a quantity of merchandise was exposed for sale in the market place. Crowds came to buy and Gregory too amongst them. As well as other merchandise he saw some boys put up for sale, with fair complexions, handsome faces, and lovely hair. On seeing them he asked, so it is said,

from what region or land they had been brought. He was told that they came from the island of Britain, whose inhabitants were like that in appearance. He asked again whether those islanders were Christians or still entangled in the errors of heathenism. He was told that they were heathen. Then with a deep-drawn sigh he said, "Alas that the author of darkness should have men so bright of face in his grip, and that minds devoid of inward grace should bear so graceful an outward form." Again he asked for the name of the race. He was told that they were called *Angli.* "Good," he said, "they have the face of angels, and such men should be fellow-heirs of the angels in heaven." "What is the name," he asked, "of the kingdom from which they have been brought?" He was told that the men of the kingdom were called *Deiri. "Deiri,"* he replied, *"De ira!* good! snatched from the wrath of Christ and called to his mercy. And what is the name of the king of the land?" He was told that it was Ælle; and playing on the name, he said, "Alleluia! the praise of God the Creator must be sung in those parts." [7]

The story of the Anglian boys in Rome is found at the start of book 2 of the *Ecclesiastical History,* where Bede encloses a summary of Gregory's life within a larger narrative of the origins of the English nation. Like Gildas, Bede portrayed the early British as a Chosen People who violated their covenant with God and were destroyed as a result.[8] Bede effected a complete break between the histories of the lapsed early Christian communities of the British—the community that Custance encounters when she lands in Northumbria and reads a "Britoun book"—and the heathen tribes, the Anglo-Saxons, whom Gregory's missionaries would convert. Bede located his own origins in the Anglo-Saxons, the new rather than the old chosen people.

The boys whom Gregory saw in the marketplace were descendants of Anglo-Saxons who, 150 years after coming to Britain, were still pagan. Gregory and Bede call the boys "Angli," a term that generally means "English."[9] But Bede had a more particular understanding of the term, as his description of the settlements of Germanic tribes makes clear. Bede located the Jutes where the people of Kent live, and the Saxons where the West, East, and South Saxons live. He continued: "Besides this, from the country of the Angles, that is, the land between the kingdoms of the Jutes and the Saxons, which is called *Angulus,* came the East Angles, the Middle Angles, the Mercians, and all the Northumbrian race (that is those people who dwell north of the river Humber) as well as the other Anglian tribes. *Angulus* is said to have remained deserted from that day to this." [10] Bede seems to have meant "Anglian" in the more specific sense of "Northumbrian." He himself was born in the territory of Monkwearmouth-Jarrow, in Northumbria, and so was "Angli" in three senses—Northumbrian, Anglian, and English.[11] "Angli" also means "angels," of course, but Bede carefully understates this meaning, which in the anecdote is better left to Gregory. That the boys' beauty should make Gregory think of angels is significant, for it suggests a purely symbolic meaning for "angli" otherwise rare in Bede's *Ecclesiastical History*.

Bede affirms a natural affinity between Gregory and the Anglo-Saxons. It might seem curious that Gregory should find the boys attractive, since his admiration suggests that he prefers their unfamiliar appearance (light-complected and light-haired) to that of his own people. The discrepancy strongly suggests that the anecdote originates with an English author whose views Gregory is made to express. The episode is a pretext for witty verbal play that valorizes the boys' race, their nation, and their king. Young, innocent, and beautiful, the boys themselves represent a benign and neglected heathendom. When Gregory recognizes all the signs of a chosen people awaiting God's blessing, Bede is permitted to foresee the new Christian age of the English people that arrived in England with Gregory's missionaries.

For all its piety, the encounter between Gregory and the boys reflects earthly and political concerns. Bede shows us Gregory's interest in establishing the Church in England and in complementing the churches that Rome had already fostered so successfully elsewhere in western Europe. Bede's chief aim was to bolster the success of that Church especially in the land of his birth; he dedicated the work to the Northumbrian king Ceolwulf.[12] The reference to angels promotes this aim, symbolically affiliating the Anglo-Saxon church with Rome. When Gregory announced that the people of Anglia, represented by angelic youth, were ready to be changed into "fellow-heirs of the angels in heaven," a new age—the history of Bede's own beginnings—came into being. But these unhappy boys were not its heralds, any more than they were angels. Other messengers—missionaries brought to England by Augustine at Gregory's command, long after the boys had been forgotten—were charged with bringing the faith to the Anglo-Saxons. That the boys could be compared to angels was not testimony to their proximity to the divine, a role Bede reserved for real angels, but to the angel-like state of their descendants, who would be newly baptized, newly converted, and newly saved.

The boys, Bede notes, were "put up for sale." Gregory saw them amid stacks of other merchandise. What were they doing there? Peter Hunter Blair warned that readers should not "jump to the romantic conclusion that the boys whose purchase was envisaged by Gregory were English slaves on sale in a market-place." The boys might also have been held in service, he suggested, as four English boys were held in the service of Jews at Narbonne, or prisoners of war, mercenaries, or "merely young men in some way bound to the soil on Merovingian estates."[13] A letter survives from Gregory to the priest Candidus (written in September 595), asking him to buy "English boys who are seventeen or eighteen years old, that they may be given to God and educated in the monasteries" ("pueros Anglos qui sunt ab annis decem et septem vel decem et octo, ut in Monasteriis dati Deo proficiant comparet").[14] The boys Gregory sees in the marketplace are not destined for education and clerical status, however. Those who have looked closely at the episode, including Bertram Colgrave, R. A. B. Mynors, and David Pelteret, identify the boys as slaves—although Bede does not—and relate the episode to the well-documented practice of slavery by the Anglo-Saxons.[15] "The custom of buying or ransoming slaves to turn them into missionaries was known," according to Colgrave, and both Aidan and Willibrord observed it.[16]

In the later Anglo-Saxon period opposition to slavery seemed to intensify. In 1014 Wulfstan denounced those who sold their children into foreign servitude.[17] But foreign trade in slaves persisted until the Norman Conquest, after which opposition to slavery continued. The Council of London of 1102 criticized the custom, even as servile tenure was becoming a more prevalent form of bondage.[18] In almost all cases in Anglo-Saxon sources the slaves in question are penal slaves forced into slavery because they could not pay debts or because they were being punished for some offense. The boys' status depended on their age; if they were seventeen or eighteen, they could have been sold as slave labor. But it is also possible that the boys Gregory saw in Rome were captives who were too young to be penal slaves and who merely represented a benign and neglected heathendom. Bede's narrative exalted their innocence, youth, and beauty, even though its real subject was their race, their nation, and Ælle, their king. What was their value in the market place? Ruth Mazo Karras points out that sexual exploitation was among the many unfortunate facts of life for women slaves. It is possible that boys were also sexually exploited and that their commercial value was directly related to their beauty and fairness, underscored by Gregory's focus on their faces (they are "bright of face," they have "the face of angels").[19] The boys would have been exploited by men, obviously, a kind of same-sex sex that, as we saw in chapter 4, was of particular concern to the Anglo-Saxons.

Any sexual resonance in the anecdote is, of course, suppressed by Bede and, in turn, by all those who retold the episode after him. In the

version found in Laȝamon's *Brut,* the "angli" are men, not boys, whose
response anticipates Gregory's discovery and spoils the drama of his
curiosity and his good heart. "We are heathen men," they say, "and have
been brought here, and we were sold in England, and we seek baptism
from you if you would only free us" ("We beoð heðene men and hider
beoð iladde, / and we weoren ut isalde of Anglene lond; / and fulluht
we to þe ȝeorneð ȝef þe us wult ifreoiȝen," 14707–9). Gregory's reply
is obliging. "[O]f all the peoples who live on earth, you English are
assuredly most like angels; of all men alive your race is the fairest"
("Iwis ȝe beoð Ænglisce englen ilicchest / of alle þan folke þa wunieð
uppen uolde; / eouwer cun is feȝerest of alle quike monnen," 14713–
15).[20] Neither Laȝamon's nor other versions subsequent to Bede's include all of the episode's verbal play. Instead these versions overtly state
points implied in Bede's account, showing, first, that the Angli desired
baptism and requested it of Gregory, and, second, that they were captives who yearned to be free. But an ironic reading is also possible.
Laȝamon's version, which makes nothing of Gregory's insight, might
suggest that the Anglo-Saxons use the pope to effect a cynical exchange
of baptism for freedom; conversion is their idea, not his.

The first modern reader to comment on the sexual subtext of Bede's
story was John Boswell, who documented the Church's concern that
abandoned children would be sold into slavery and used for sexual
purposes. Some writers protested this practice, but not for the reasons
we might expect. Their concern was that fathers who abandoned their
children might later accidentally buy them as slaves and commit incest
by having intercourse with them. Boswell noted that the public sale of
slaves continued in Rome long after the empire was Christianized and
illustrated the practice with the episode as Bede recounted it.[21] In the
1540s, some seven hundred years after Bede's death, Boswell's point
was vividly anticipated by a remarkable figure named John Bale, the
first reader to see a same-sex shadow in the story that has charmed so
many.

Bede and Bale

Bale (1495–1563) was a Carmelite priest who left the Church of Rome
in the 1530s. The author of several large-scale surveys of English authors and the first biographer of Chaucer, Bale was also a collector of
early manuscripts, including those in Anglo-Saxon.[22] According to
John N. King, Bale was "the most influential English Protestant author
of his time."[23] He was also a prodigious instrument in the propaganda
efforts of Thomas Cromwell.[24] Bale recounted the episode of Gregory

and the slave boys in a revisionist narrative of English ecclesiastical history called *The Actes of Englysh Votaryes.*

> And as thys Gregorye behelde them fayre skynned and bewtyfullye faced, with heare upon their heades most comelye, anon he axed, of what regyon they were. And answere was made hym, that they were of an yle called Englande. Wele maye they be called *Angli* (sayth he) for they have verye Angelych vysages. Se how curyose these fathers were, in the wele eyenge of their wares. Here was no cyrcumstaunce unloked to, perteynynge to the sale. Yet have [has] thys Byshopp bene of all writers reckened the best sens hys tyme.[25]

Bale mockingly urged his readers to "[m]arke thys ghostlye mysterye, for the prelates had than no wyves." He plainly implied that Gregory had sexual designs on the boys. "[T]hese fathers" were "curyose" in the "wele eyenge" of the boys as "wares," he wrote, using an expression with strong sexual overtones. In sixteenth-century English, "ware" could mean "piece of goods" (an expression "jocularly applied to women," according to the *OED*) and "the privy parts of either sex."[26] Because priests were unmarried, Bale observes, with much sarcasm, "other spirytuall remedyes were sought out for them by their good prouvders and proctours, we maye (yf we wyll) call them apple squyres." "Apple-squires," according to the *OED,* means "pimp" or "panderer," thus further underscoring Bale's sexual innuendo. Stressing that this sale was not unique, Bale produces another witness, Machutus, who saw a similar event in Rome in AD 500 and bought the boys to protect them (23a). We are meant to conclude that Gregory, deprived of a wife by the Church's demand for clerical celibacy, sought out "other spirytuall remedyes" by purchasing boys for sex.

Bale's rewriting of the story of Gregory and the Anglian boys takes place in the context of an elaborate revision of England's Anglo-Saxon Christian history proposed in *The Actes of Englysh Votaryes* and *The Image of Bothe Churches.* In *The Actes of Englysh Votaryes* Bale boldly revised English history in order to describe the nation's struggles against the corrupt influences of the Church of Rome. The chief instrument of Roman domination, Bale argued, was clerical celibacy, which permitted the clergy to degrade marriage and advocate virginity, all the while using its own religious houses for immoral purposes. Bale vigorously defended the right of the clergy to wed and believed that the Roman clergy who claimed to be celibate had in fact indulged in every form of sexual corruption. In *The Image of Bothe Churches,* Bale set forth a thesis about the Church in England that, as it was later developed by his better-known contemporary, John Foxe, became a foundational strategy for Reformation anti-Roman polemic.[27] Bale argued that the Church had been divided during the reign of Constantine and that the See of Saint Peter stemmed from the corrupt division, while an isolated community of the faithful, who retained belief in the true Church, reestablished the true Church in England. Bale argued that the false Church of Rome had taken on the image of the true Church of antiquity and that from the time of St. Augustine's mission to the English (597) to the rejection of papal authority by Henry VIII (1533) the Church in England had been corrupt. Bale was among the historians who looked back to the Anglo-Saxon period, skipping over an internal period in which they perceived England as dominated by the Church of Rome to a point that they erroneously saw as a free, "native," English church unencumbered by Roman influence. This was an exercise in self-justification. Having recently thrown off Roman rule itself, the new "English" or "Anglican" church was searching for its origins in the Anglo-Saxon period, which was perceived as another time when England's Christians governed themselves justly and righteously.

For Bede, the mission of Augustine marked the permanent conversion of Britain. Bale reversed the significance of this event. He claimed that the English church had survived pure and uncorrupted until the coming of Roman missionaries. With them they brought pernicious doctrines such as clerical celibacy, and as a result they transformed the once-pure land and its church into a new Sodom. Seeking to open his readers' eyes to the false miracles used by "obstynate hypocrytes" still living under the pope's rules, Bale wrote *The Actes of Englysh Votaryes* in order to accuse Catholics of portraying "whoremongers, bawdes, brybers, idolaters, hypocrytes, traytors, and most fylthye Gomorreanes as Godlye men and women" (2a). His diatribes are laced with references to Sodom and Gomorrah. Although his definitions of the sins of these unholy places remain vague, they encompass theological error as well as sexual excess, including, at certain points, male homosexual intercourse.

Marriage, Bale wrote in *The Actes,* was the "first order of religion," created in order to protect against "beastlye abusyons of the fleshe that shuld after happen" if men and women disobeyed God's command to increase and multiply (7b). The Church sought to dissuade holy men and women from marriage, broke up existing marriages, venerated only unmarried saints, and demonized women as "spretes" ("sprites," 3a); these were the acts of "the Sodomytycall swarme or brode of Antichrist" (4a). According to Bale's extraordinary revision of the history of Anglo-Saxon holy men and women, clergymen fornicated with cloistered nuns and produced a race of bastards who were then venerated as saints, Cuthbert, Dunstan, Oswald, Anselm, and Becket among them (2b). Some did worse, since they refrained from women but "spared not to worke execrable fylthyness among themselves, and one to pollute the other," an obvious reference to male homosexual acts (12b). Devout in his praise of Mary, Bale was eager to insist that she was not abused by the clergy and that she was not a professed nun, "as the dottynge papystes have dreamed, to couer their sodometrye with a most precyouse coloure, but an honest mannys wyfe" (13a). Bale attacked "spirituall Sodomytes and knaves" who wrote the lives of these sinful saints (18a): "Come out of Sodome ye whoremongers and hypocrytes, popysh byshoppes and prestes" (18b). Bale used "sodometrie"— an obsolete word for sodomy, first used in 1530, according to the *OED*—to attack clergy who took the required vows of celibacy but who were unable to remain celibate: either men who had sex with each other because they could not have sex with women, or men who did have sex with cloistered nuns who were virtually the male clergy's sexual slaves. Shortly before he recounts the story about Gregory, Bale tells of a large group of women who joined a pilgrimage only to find that they had been taken from England to be forced to prostitute themselves to the clergy on the Continent (21a).

In leading up to his account of the boys, Bale followed Geoffrey of Monmouth, who embroidered Gildas's account into a claim that sodomy was pervasive among the early Britons, practiced by two of their kings (Malgo and Mempricius) and the cause of their overthrow by the Saxons. Gildas's version contains no hint of sexual slander, as we saw in chapter 5. Bale wrote that Malgo, who was possibly fashioned on William Rufus, was "the most comelye persone of all hys regyon," someone to whom God had given great victories against the "Saxons, Normeies, and Danes." But he was a sodomite. He imitated the ways of his predecessor Mempricius, who was "geuen to most abhomynable sodometrye, which he had lerned in hys youthe of the consecrate chastyte of the holie clergye" (21b–22a).[28] Thus the British were weak and were easily conquered by the Saxons. Bale believed that Roman Christianity entered England with the Saxons, who renamed the land England. "Then came therein a newe fashyoned christyanyte yet ones agayne from Rome with many more heythnysh yokes than afore." Bale then immediately introduced Gregory and told the story about the boys (22a–b, a section entitled "The Saxons entre with newe Christyanyte").

Elsewhere Bale underscored the charges of sodomy among Catholic clergy made in *The Image of Both Churches*. In his *Apology against a Rank Papist* (1550), Bale asked, "Whan the kynges grace of England by the autorite of Gods wurd, discharged the monkish sectes of his realme, from their vowed obedience to the byshop of Rome, did he not also discharge them in conscience of the vowe of Sodometry, whyche altogether made them Antichristes creatures?" Catholic clergy had set marriage and virginity "at variance" and replaced them with "two unhappy gestes, called whoredom and buggery."[29] In *The Pageant of Popes,* published in 1574 (after Bale's death), Bale recounted visitations to monasteries ordered by Henry VIII, which found "such swarmes of whoremongers, ruffians, filthie parsouns, giltye of sinne against nature, Ganimedes, and yet votaries and unmaryed all, so that thou wouldest thincke that there were a newer Gomorrah amonge them." At Battle Abbey, according to Bale, there were nearly twenty "gilty of sinne against nature" (their crimes included bigamy and adultery); at Canterbury there were eleven.[30] *The Pageant of Popes* shows that Bale saw another side to Gregory, casting him as the creator of a policy opposing clerical celibacy (no one could ever accuse Bale of consistency). Gregory was informed that priests "accompanied not only with virgins and wyves, but also even with their owne kindred, with mankind, yea and that whiche is horrible to be sayde, with brute beastes." ("Accompanied" is an obsolete euphemism for "cohabit with," according to the *OED.* Note that Bale regards bestiality as worse than same-sex acts.) Appalled at this conduct, Gregory revoked the canon requiring that priests not marry.[31] Gregory was given credit for being "the best man of all these Romaine Patriarkes, for learning and good life," and Bale praised his humility and his learning.[32]

Like many polemicists, Bale was an idealist. His attack on the Roman clergy can be explained by his high regard for marriage and his ardent defense of women's position. When he was a Carmelite priest, in the 1520s, Bale carried out extensive research into Carmelite archives and took special interest in the Church's view of women, in part at least because of his interest in Mary, the patron of the Carmelite order.[33] His recruitment to the Church of England came in the 1530s, when he lived in London and could see the drastic impact of Henry's marriage and decrees on all monastic orders, including his own. It was also at this time—in 1536—that Bale married, and undoubtedly this change in his life fueled his polemics about the Roman Church's demand for clerical celibacy.[34] Bale identified the ideal of marriage for the clergy as an Anglo-Saxon custom that had been brought to an end with the Norman Conquest. "I omit to declare for lengthe of the matter," he wrote in *Apology against a Rank Papist* (xiii), "what mischefe and confusion, vowes [vows] brought to this realme by the Danes and Normannes, whan the lyves of the vowers in their monasteries were more beastlye than eyther amonge paganes or Turkes." Bale, who was unaware that the Danes were not Christian, believed that the monks and clergymen, once forced to give up wives, turned to "bestlye" lives worse than those lived by pagans or Turks. In other words, he thought they had become sodomites.

Sodomy also figured in Bale's plays, his best-known works. In *A Comedy concernynge Thre Lawes, of Nature, Moses, & Christ, Corrupted by the Sodomytes, Pharysees, and Papystes* (1538), written before the historical studies just sampled, Bale created a character named Sodomismus, an allegorical figure unique in sixteenth-century English drama.[35] Sodomismus is one of six vice characters in the play. Attired "lyke a monke of all sectes," according to Bale,[36] Sodomismus repeatedly associates himself with both monks and the pope.

> I dwelt amonge the Sodomytes,
> The Benjamytes and Madyantes
> And now the popish hypocrytes
>   Embrace me every where.
> I am now become all spyrytuall [i.e., taken over by spiritual leaders],[37]
> For the clergye at Rome and over all
> For want of wyves, to me doth fall,
>   To God they have no feare. (2:571–78).

Pederastic unions are listed among the forms of sodomy he promotes.

> In Rome to me they fall,
> Both byshopp and cardynall,
> Monke, fryre, prest and all,
>   More ranke they are than antes.
> Example in Pope Julye,
> Whych sought to have in hys furye
> Two laddes, and to use them beastlye,
>   From the Cardinall of Nantes. (2:643–50).

Had he known about Gregory's letter to Candidus, Bale would have had an even more pertinent example of how a Roman pope allegedly abused innocent boys.

In *King Johan,* which casts the king as an opponent of clerical corruption, the king speaks for Bale's position. Johan (King John) regrets that the clergy

> Shuld thus bynd yowre selfe to the grett captyvyte
> Of blody Babulon the grownd and mother of whordom—
> The Romych Churche I meane, more vyle than ever was
>   Sodom.[38]

For Bale, "sodomites" were not only the unjust and impious but also those who turned from the lawful union of marriage and had illicit intercourse either with the opposite sex or with their own. In *A Comedy concernynge Thre Lawes,* Sodomismus claims to have inspired all manner of sexual sinners, ranging from the fallen angels who fornicated with the daughters of men (Genesis 6:1–4) to Onan (Genesis 38:9; see *A Comedy,* 580–610). The offense that seems most closely connected to sodomy in Bale's mind is idolatry, represented in the play as Idolatria, an old woman. Idolatria is the companion of Sodomismus, who speaks to her in terms of endearment, calling her "myne owne swetehart of golde" (481). Sodomismus is sexually profligate, not exclusively or even primarily interested in same-sex intercourse. His accusations against monks and popes, however, conform precisely to those Bale himself made in his nondramatic works.

The inference that Bale had accused Gregory of sodomy was drawn by Bale's Catholic opponent, who recognized the unacknowledged source of Bale's story in Bede's *Ecclesiastical History.* In 1565, in the first translation of Bede's *Ecclesiastical History* in modern English, Thomas Stapleton listed "a number of diuersities between the pretended religion of Protestants, and the primitive faith of the english Church" (he counted forty-five points of difference in all). Stapleton contrasted the authority of Bede, who wrote without prejudice, with that of Bale, Foxe, and other "pretended refourmers." Stapleton discussed the episode involving Gregory and the Anglian boys in his preface. Bede, who was close to this event, had told a story contrasting outer beauty with inner lack of belief. Bale had deliberately misread the event in order to charge Gregory "with a most outrageous vice and not to be named." Stapleton obviously understood Bale to have accused Gregory of sodomy. Bede was a bee who made honey (beautiful meaning) out of this episode, said Stapleton, but Bale was a "venimous spider being filthy and uncleane himself," an "olde ribauld," and "another Nero" who found "poisonned sence and meaning" therein.[39]

To be fair, Bale's interpretation, admittedly harsh, is somewhat better than Stapleton allowed. Bale forces us to reconsider Bede's treatment of the anecdote and calls our attention to its dark side, its shadow. The episode about Gregory and the boys is animated by the contrast between light and dark, outside and inside. Gregory calls Satan "the author of darkness" who holds "men so bright of face in his grip." He finds the Anglians "devoid of inward grace" while admiring their "graceful . . . outward form[s]." Gregory's language clearly recognizes that physical and moral beauty exist in close proximity to the evil and the ugly. Bede did not look beyond Gregory's words for these malignant forces. Instead he saw the brightness of the episode, which marked the "Angli" as a people elevated by their likeness, at least in Gregory's mind, to angels. Bale saw around Gregory's words and, like Gregory himself, recognized how near evil was to the good. But Bale reversed the field of Gregory's vision, casting Gregory into the darkness where Gregory himself saw Satan. What lived in that darkness was same-sex desire, the unholy appetite of Gregory and other reluctant celibates for the sexual favors of young Englishmen. Such shadows, dark places of evil and corruption, are not the only kind of shadows where same-sex relations can be seen. They are not the kinds of shadows I think of when I think of the presence of same-sex love in a heterosexual world. All the same, Bale's vision of the shadow, however distasteful it might seem, is, in context, accurate. The sexual abuse of young boys was a danger to which life in the monastery exposed them, as the penitentials show. Slavery was another danger, not unrelated, that lurked in the episode Bede describes. It is difficult to deny that the shadows seen by Bale are places where "the author of darkness," as Gregory called him, held sway.

Bale's recasting of Anglo-Saxon history had a prominent sexual aspect, if not a primary sexual character. He saw the Anglo-Saxons as a people who naturally observed God's lawful commandment to be fruitful and multiply. Their Roman oppressors, on the other hand, were those who denied clergy the right to marry and, as a result, spread sexual corruption wherever they were to be found. Gregory's "wele eyenge" of the slave boys' "wares" vividly emblematizes this exploitation and situates it in the heart of Rome. For Bale, Anglo-Saxon identity was continuous with British identity that predated the arrival of the Anglo-Saxons. English identity emerged out of this combined British-Anglo-Saxon identity in a struggle against the enslaving bonds of Roman and then Norman domination. Racial differences are but vaguely registered by Bale, and his chronology, not unexpectedly, is confused. Malgo won victories over "Saxons, Normeies, and Danes," for example, even though it was the Saxons who subverted the realm (22a). Bale's historical discourse, punctuated with numerous references to Sodom and allegations of homosexual acts among the clergy, is entirely free of allegory (his plays, obviously, are not). Bale did not need a figurative discourse about angels or origins to celebrate what was, for him, the distinguishing feature of his sources. His sense of who was Saxon, Norman, or Dane was imprecise, but Bale unquestionably understood that Gildas, Bede, Geoffrey of Monmouth, Chaucer, and others, were not mythical figures but were instead his predecessors, righteous as he was himself.[40] He was sure that the history he chronicled was as English as

he was. His association of corrupt sexual practices with foreign powers—Roman and Catholic especially—is therefore easily explained,
however disagreeable we find it. His polemical use of sodomy strongly
resembles that of the Anglo-Norman historians and chroniclers on
whose work he drew. But whereas they directed their diatribes against
their own princes and rulers, Bale directed his at the princes of the
Catholic Church. Among their agents he numbered the Norman conquerors of England, the despoilers of the True Church of the British.

ANGELS AND ANGLI

Another polemicist and dramatist with a vague sense of the Anglo-
Saxon past and strong views on its significance is Tony Kushner. His
celebrated two-part drama, *Angels in America: A Gay Fantasia on National Themes,* approaches the Anglo-Saxons through the stereotype of
the WASP. Kushner correlates same-sex relations with racial stereotypes and national heritage and makes revealing use of Anglo-Saxon
culture that is seldom noticed by the play's admirers. Kushner's AIDS-
infected hero is the play's only WASP, the thirty-second Prior Walter
in a line traced to the Norman Conquest so that it can represent the
Anglo-Saxon hegemony of the West. But *Angels* reverses a dynamic
that operates in all the other texts I have examined throughout this
study. Anglo-Saxon penitentials, histories, poems, and commentaries
ultimately side with the angels. And so, for that matter, do Chaucer
and Bale, Custance being Chaucer's angel, the English boys being
Bede's and Bale's. Angels are pure, either above sex or, if involved with
sexual relations, chastely married; they are on the side of order. Sodomites, however they have been defined, are not. They and same-sex relations are stigmatized and repressed because they subvert order, lack
shame, and threaten to lead others into sin.

In order to express Kushner's millennial vision, *Angels in America*
rewrites the social history of England (and America) in order to enable
a new era in which same-sex relations thrive while heterosexual relations wither. Kushner does not take the side of the angels but rather
represents them as weak, lost, and prejudiced. Amid their confusion,
paradoxically, their saving grace is that they retain their sexual prowess.
The Angel of America, as she will be known, enters the play as a messenger to a white, Anglo-Saxon, Protestant but exits taking advice
because the WASP is also a PWA, a "person with AIDS," prophet of a
new homosocial order and herald of a revolution so sweeping that it
offers redemption even for angels.

Rich in references to migratory voyages and the Chosen People, *An-*

gels in America advances a broad argument about history and progress. The play is a multicultural juxtaposition of WASP, Jewish, black, and Mormon traditions, among others. David Savran has argued that the "spiritual geography" of Mormonism is central to the play's "conceptualization of America as the site of a blessed past and a millennial future." Savran demonstrates that Mormonism was among the evangelical, communitarian sects formed in reaction to the individualism fostered by Jacksonian democracy and the ideology of Manifest Destiny.[41] A key element in the racial basis of Manifest Destiny, which claimed for the chosen people "a preeminent social worth, a distinctively lofty mission, and consequently unique rights in the application of moral principles,"[42] is Anglo-Saxonism. The premise of Anglo-Saxonism (familiar in earlier forms in the works of Gildas, Bede, Chaucer, and Bale, as we have seen, and many others, of course) is that the English are a Chosen People and a superior race.[43] Numerous nineteenth-century accounts used the racial purity of the Anglo-Saxons to justify westward expansion and empire building. Anglo-Saxon culture was thought to have been inherently democratic and the Anglo-Saxons egalitarian, self-governing, and free. The descendants of a people who so perfectly embodied the principles of American democracy had, it appeared, natural rights over lesser peoples and their lands. Anglo-Saxonism enters *Angels in America* through the lineage of Prior Walter. He is a token of the WASP culture—the only white Anglo-Saxon Protestant in the play, according to Kushner[44]—against which the oppressed peoples of the play, Jews and blacks in particular, strive.

The Anglo-Saxon subtext of *Angels* emerges in both parts of the drama, *Millennium Approaches* and *Perestroika,* through the association of Prior Walter with the angel. Kushner locates Prior's origins in the mid–eleventh century, but the Anglo-Saxon characteristics that Prior represents are prior to the Normans, whose conquest of England constitutes a particularly troubled originary moment for the chief Anglo-Saxon of the play. An early scene in each of the three acts of *Millennium Approaches* reveals something about Prior's Anglo-Saxon identity (act 1, scene 4; act 2, scene 3; and act 3, scene 1). In the first of the scenes about his lineage, Prior jokes with Louis, his Jewish lover, after a funeral service for Louis's grandmother. Prior comments on the difficulties that their relatives present for gay men: "Bloodlines," he says. "Jewish curses are the worst. I personally would dissolve if anyone ever looked me in the eye and said 'Feh.' Fortunately WASPs don't say 'Feh'" (1:20).[45] A few moments later he reveals his first AIDS lesions to Louis, who is horrified both by the lesions and by Prior's mordant jocularity about them. This scene establishes Prior's AIDS status and his WASP identity and introduces the largest of the cultural themes of *Angels in America:* the resistance that biological descent and inherited tradition, embodied here in the body of the WASP, pose to political change. Bloodlines are curses because they carry the past into the present, creating resistance to the possibilities of change that the present raises. WASP blood resists change because WASPs, as they are presented in this play, exist in a culture of stasis, while other races and creeds, denied that stability and permanence and driven by persecution and need from place to place, have developed migratory and transitional cultures open to, and indeed dependent on, change.

Having inherited a distinguished past, Prior faces an uncharacteristically grim future (for a WASP) because he carries a fatal new element in his bloodline, AIDS. The virus paradoxically reverses the deadening flow of WASP tradition and prepares for a new social order whose values the WASP himself will eventually espouse. The virus he bears is both literal (HIV) and figurative; it is eventually identified as "the virus of time," the "disease" of change and progress. The angel who appears to Prior at the end of *Millennium Approaches,* and who punctuates the play with intimations of her arrival, claims to herald a new age. When Prior receives his first intimation of the angelic, a feather drops into his room and an angelic voice ("an incredibly beautiful voice," the text specifies) commands, "Look up! . . . Prepare the way!" (1:34–35). But the side of the angels is not what we expect it to be. The angel is not pointing to a new age but instead calling for a return to a previous one. The tradition and stasis that constitute Prior's Anglo-Saxon heritage draw her. She believes that Prior will be a worthy prophet precisely because he is a worthy WASP.

Kushner happened on Prior's name when looking "for one of those WASP names that nobody gets called any more." Discussing Walter Benjamin with a friend so interested in the philosopher that she sometimes "thought she was Walter Benjamin reincarnated," Kushner referred to the real Benjamin as the "prior" Walter.[46] The significance of Prior's name unfolds in a subsequent dialogue between Louis and Emily, a nurse, after Prior has been hospitalized. "Weird name. Prior Walter," says Emily. "Like, 'The Walter before this one.'" Louis replies: "Lots of Walters before this one. Prior is an old old family name in an old old family. The Walters go back to the Mayflower and beyond. Back to the Norman Conquest. He says there's a Prior Walter stitched into the Bayeux tapestry" (1:51). The oldest medieval record mentioned in *Angels in America,* the tapestry would seem designed to surround Prior's origins with an aura of great antiquity.

The appearance of Prior Walter's name on the tapestry validates

Louis's claim that the Walter name is indeed an "old old" one. But the Bayeux tapestry is a record of the political and military events surrounding the Norman Conquest of Anglo-Saxon England in 1066. The tapestry testifies to the subjugation of the Anglo-Saxons and marks the point at which the government and official vernacular language of England were no longer English. Generations of Anglo-Saxonizing historians and writers regarded the arrival of the Normans as the pollution of the pure stock of the race.[47] Thus Kushner's announced aim of portraying Walter as a WASP is more than a little complicated by this decision to trace Walter's ancestry to a tapestry long accepted as a lucid statement of Norman claims to the English throne.[48] Notoriously ironic throughout *Angels in America*, Kushner might have chosen the tapestry to register precisely this compromised aspect of Prior's lineage.[49] But one's view of that lineage would seem to depend on the uses to which it is put in *Angels in America*, where it seems intended to represent the Anglo-Saxons as a monolithic, triumphant culture that has reached a symbolic end point in Prior's blood.

Emily (played by the actress who plays the angel) is somewhat baffled by Louis's high regard for Prior's ancient name and for the tapestry itself. Louis believes that the queen, "La Reine Mathilde," embroidered the tapestry while William was away fighting the English. In the long tradition of French historians and politicians who used the tapestry to arouse public sentiment to support nationalistic causes, including the Napoleonic wars against the English,[50] Louis pictures Mathilda waiting at home, "stitch[ing] for years," waiting for William to return. "And if he had returned mutilated, ugly, full of infection and horror, she would still have loved him," Louis says (1:52). He is thinking penitently of Prior, who is also "full of infection and horror," whom Louis will soon abandon for Joe, the married Mormon lawyer with whom Louis has an affair. Louis's view of when and where the tapestry was made is popular, but wrong. The tapestry was made in England, under the patronage of William's half-brother Odo, bishop of Bayeux and vice-regent of England, within a generation of 1066, not during the Conquest itself, and then taken to the Bayeux Cathedral.[51]

Kushner's mistaken ideas of when, where, and by whom the Bayeux tapestry was made have significant implications for his definition of "WASP." Kushner invokes the Conquest as if its chief force were to certify the antiquity and authenticity of Prior's Anglo-Saxon credentials and heritage, a point of origin for *English* identity, although, as I have shown, it traditionally represented the very betrayal of the racial purity that "Anglo-Saxon" came to represent. Louis's assertion that the name of a "Prior Walter" is stitched into the tapestry is also without foundation. Only four minor characters are named in the tapestry, none of them Anglo-Saxons ("Turold," "Ælfgyva," "Wadard," and "Vital"). The rest are important figures (Harold, William, and others), most of them Norman and well-known from contemporary sources.[52] If Prior Walter were an Anglo-Saxon, it is highly unlikely that he would be commemorated in the tapestry, although it is possible he could have been an English retainer of Harold (who was defeated by William).

But "Prior Walter" is a singularly inappropriate name for an Anglo-Saxon. It strongly suggests an ecclesiastical, monastic context, as if "Prior Walter" were "Walter, prior of" some abbey, instead of the secular and heroic ethos usually called to mind by "Anglo-Saxon." Apart from the tapestry, there is no evidence either for or against an argument about Prior's origins. Although it is possible that his ancestors were Anglo-Saxon, it is more likely that they were Normans who, after the Conquest, settled in England and established the line from which the Walters descended. Few Anglo-Saxons would expect to find their ancestors mentioned in the tapestry, while Normans would want to boast of this testimony to a family's distinguished history. The original Prior Walter might have been a Norman who took part in the conquest of the English. His family would have been prosperous. As we saw in the last chapter, the Anglo-Saxons were less well-to-do than their conquerors and resented the superiority of French into the fourteenth century. If so, as the last in a line of thirty-one men of the same name (or, by an alternative count, if bastard sons are included, thirty-three [1:86]), Prior Walter claims Norman rather than Anglo-Saxon ancestry, or, more likely, a heritage in which Norman and Anglo-Saxon blood is mixed—in other words, Anglo-Norman. His long genealogy, to which Louis proudly points, is hybrid at its origins. Kushner's stereotype of the WASP is itself a further hybrid, obviously, since it is a post-Reformation construct in which P ("Protestant") is a new element. WASP, we can see, is not only a recent vehicle for the representation of "Anglo-Saxon" culture, but an exceedingly shallow one.[53]

We learn more about Prior's ancestry at the start of the third act, when two prior Priors appear to him in a dream (1:85–89). The first to appear, the "fifth of the name," is the thirteenth-century squire who is known as "Prior 1." He tells of the plague that wiped out whole villages, the "spotty monster" that killed him (1:86). (This is another sign of Kushner's shaky historical sense; the first outbreak of the Black Death in England was a century later, in 1348.)[54] They are joined by "Prior 2," described as "an elegant 17th-century Londoner" (1:86), who preceded the current Prior by some seventeen others and also died of

the plague, "Black Jack." Priors 1 and 2 are not merely ancient ancestors, however. They are also the forerunners of the angel whose arrival
spectacularly concludes the play. To "distant, glorious music," they
recite the language later used by the angel; her messengers, they are
"sent to declare her fabulous incipience." "They [the angels] chose us,"
Prior 2 declares, "because of the mortal affinities. In a family as long-
descended as the Walters there are bound to be a few carried off by
plague" (1:87). Neither Prior 1 nor Prior 2 understands why Prior is
unmarried and has no wife, although the second Prior understands
that the plague infecting Prior is "the lamentable consequence of ven-
ery" (1:87). Only later, when they see him dancing with Louis, does
Prior 1 understand: "Hah. Now I see why he's got no children. He's a
sodomite" (1:114). Prior Walter is, therefore, the end of his line. After
him the WASP hegemony of the Walters, apparently unbroken from
the mid–eleventh century to the present, will cease to exist.

The vague and portentous sense of these genealogical relations is
clarified in the next scene (1:89–96), in which Louis engages in a long,
confused, and painfully naïve monologue about race and identity politics in America, much to the disgust of his friend Belize, a black nurse
and ex–drag queen.[55] Louis describes a difference between American
and European peoples that encapsulates the tension between Anglo-
Saxons and other races. "Ultimately what defines us [in America] isn't
race, but politics," he says. "Not like any European country where
there's an insurmountable fact of a kind of racial, or ethnic, monopoly,
or monolith, like all Dutchmen, I mean Dutch people, are, well, Dutch,
and the Jews of Europe were never Europeans, just a small problem"
(1:90). Significantly, Kushner chooses England as site for a scene
in which, according to Louis, the "racial destiny," not the "political
destiny," matters (1:91). A Jew in a gay bar in London, Louis found
himself looked down upon by a Jamaican man who still spoke with a
"lilt," even though his family had been in England for more than a
century. At first this man, who complained that he was still treated as
an outsider, struck Louis as a fellow traveler: "I said yeah, me too, these
people are anti-Semites." But then the man criticized British Jews for
keeping blacks out of the clothing business, and Louis realized how
pervasive racial stereotypes could be (1:91). In America, Louis believes,
there is no racial monopoly; in America the "monolith is missing," so
"reaching out for a spiritual past in a country where no indigenous
spirits exist" is futile (1:92). The native peoples have been killed off:
"there are no angels in America, no spiritual past, no racial past, there's
only the political and the decoys and the ploys to maneuver around the
inescapable battle of politics, the shifting downwards and outwards of

political power to the people" (1:92). Wiped clean of its indigenous spirits, the nation as Louis sees it would seem to be a blank slate not unlike England before the Anglo-Saxons, ready for migratory peoples (including Jews and Mormons) who bring their past with them as they seek to build a new future. Belize holds Louis's liberal interpretation of American government and culture in utter contempt. Kushner ensures that the naiveté of the Jew's liberalism will be exposed and contained by Belize's furious reply that in America race is more important than anything else.

Louis's speech reveals the meaning of Anglo-Saxon that is encapsulated in Prior's WASP identity. Even though Prior's mixed Norman and Anglo-Saxon genealogy contradicts Louis's point about the monolith of racial purity that the WASP supposedly represents, Prior is singled out as the recipient of the angel's visit because he is made to represent the cultural monolith of WASP America, fixed and unchanging, embodying what Louis calls "an insurmountable fact of a kind of racial, or ethnic, monopoly, or monolith" (1:90). WASP heritage stands conveniently juxtaposed both to Louis's vision and to Louis's own heritage of many small groups, "so many small problems" (1:90). Although Kushner might have wished to represent the Anglo-Saxons only as a hybrid people, and hence introduced evidence that points to the eleventh-century intermingling of Norman blood, it seems evident to me that the racial dynamics of the play require that the Anglo-Saxons represent the "monolith" about which Louis speaks. Only then can other races and groups be set up in opposition to them.

Indeed, even in motion, the Anglo-Saxons of *Angels in America* are oppressors. One of the most harrowing moments in *Millennium Approaches* is Prior's account of his ancestor, a ship's captain, who sent whale oil to Europe and brought back immigrants, "Irish mostly, packed in tight, so many dollars per head." The last ship he captained sank off Nova Scotia in a storm; the crew loaded seventy women and children onto an open boat but found that it was overcrowded and began throwing passengers overboard: "They walked up and down the longboat, eyes to the waterline, and when the boat rode low in the water they'd grab the nearest passenger and throw them into the sea" (1:41). The boat arrived in Halifax carrying nine people. Crewmen are the captain's agents; the captain is at the bottom of the sea, but his "implacable, unsmiling men, irresistibly strong, seize . . . maybe the person next to you, maybe you" (1:41–42). The agents of the Anglo-Saxons arbitrarily decide the fates of the Irish in their care. The episode is a stark political allegory, a nationally rendered reminder of the rights of one group to survive at the expense of another, a deft miniature that reveals the power of the conquerors over the conquered, the inter-relation of commerce and the immigration patterns of impoverished nations, and, most of all, "unique rights in the application of moral principles," a signature belief of Manifest Destiny.[56]

The point of the association of stasis with Anglo-Saxon heritage— the grand design of *Angels in America*—emerges fully in *Perestroika,* when the Angel of America articulates her ambitions for the WASP and discloses the assumed affiliations between the Anglo-Saxons and the angels. The angel attempts to persuade Prior to take up her prophecy. "I I I I / Am the Bird of America," she proclaims, saying that she has come to expose the fallacy of change and progress (2:44), "the Virus of TIME" that God released in man (2:49), enabling humans to explore and migrate. Angels do not migrate; instead, they stand firm (2:49). God himself found time irresistible and began to prefer human time to life in heaven. The angel says:

> Paradise itself Shivers and Splits
> Each day when You awake, as though WE are only
>   the Dream of YOU.
> PROGRESS! MOVEMENT!
> Shaking HIM. (2:50)

A few moments later she shouts, "*YOU HAVE DRIVEN HIM AWAY!* YOU MUST STOP MOVING!" (2:52). God became so bored with the angels that he abandoned them on the day of the 1906 San Francisco earthquake. And who could blame him? In the one scene that Kushner gives performers the permission to cut, if only in part (act 5, scene 5; see 2:9), the angels are shown sitting around heaven listening to a mal-functioning 1940s radio over which they hear the broadcast of the melt-down of the Chernobyl reactor. Their real concern, however, is the radio's malfunctioning vacuum tube (2:130). They are a picture of feckless paralysis, obviously unable to respond to the changes forced on them by human or heavenly time. "More nightmare than utopia, ma-rooned in history," Savran writes, "Heaven commemorates disaster, de-spair, and stasis."[57] The purpose of the angel's visitation is to recruit Prior as the angels' prophet on earth. Angels, we see, are not messen-gers from the divine or heralds of change, although that is how we conventionally think of them, and how Kushner and the play's pub-licity represent them. Angels are instead associated with stasis and with the power of ancient spirits to resist change. Opposed to the flow of power "downward and outward," as Louis puts it, of "power to the people," the angels want God to return to his place so that they can return to theirs.

The angel's visit is not intended to save Prior from his disease but to use his disease against him, to try to persuade this "long descended" man (like the angel in this) to stop the phenomenon of human progress, to get him to turn back the clock. The angel says to him that she has written "The End" in his blood. This could mean that the AIDS virus is supposed to ensure his desire to stop time—stop the progress of the disease—and prompt him to proclaim her message (2:53), although what is written in his blood could also be his homosexuality, which writes "The End" in a different sense, since it means that he is the last of his line. Later in the scene in which the angel commands Prior to stand still, symbolically appealing to his Anglo-Saxon love of stability and tradition, Belize dismisses the vision as Prior recounts it: "This is just you, Prior, afraid of the future, afraid of time. Longing to go backwards so bad you made this angel up, a cosmic reactionary" (2:55). Prior and Belize were once lovers; Belize knows him well. Like Prior, three other figures—the angel, Sister Ella Chapter (a friend of Joe's mother in Salt Lake City), and the nurse (all played by the actress who plays the angel)—are fearful of movement. Emily does not want Louis to leave the hospital room (1:52). Before Joe's mother moves to New York to help Joe cope with his schizophrenic wife, Harper, Ella reminds her that Salt Lake City is "the home of the saints" and "the godliest place on earth," and then cautions, "Every step a Believer takes away from here is a step fraught with peril" (1:83). But Ella's is not a view that the play endorses. Joe's mother leaves anyway. All the chosen people do.

Like her, Prior rejects the advice to stay put. He ignores the angel's command precisely because "The End" is written in his blood. He interprets these words as the angel's wish that he die: "You want me dead" (2:53). No longer the Prior who joked fatalistically about his lesions outside the funeral home in act 1 of *Millennium Approaches,* he refuses to die. Because he has contracted "the virus of time," the WASP, who has the most to lose, turns from the past to the future. All the "good" characters in the play are already on the move, already evolving, even Joe's drug-maddened wife, just as all the valorized nations and races in the play have migrated. The prominence of migration and the movement away from racial purity are basic elements of Kushner's thesis about change, which is based on an idea of the Anglo-Saxons, the WASPS, as static, permanent, and fixed. Politics change racial makeup and break down pure races and their racism. Kushner explains:

Prior is the only character in the play with a Yankee WASP background; he can trace his lineage back for centuries, something most Americans can't reliably do. African-American family trees have to start after ancestors were brought over as slaves. Jews emigrated from a world nearly completely destroyed by European genocide. And most immigrant populations have been from poor and oppressed communities among which accurate genealogy was a luxury or an impossibility. . . . a certain sense of rootlessness is part of the American character.[58]

Anglo-Saxon history prior to the Normans shows that "a certain sense of rootlessness" is also part of the Anglo-Saxon character. American rootlessness was inherited from the nation's Anglo-Saxon founders; the Anglo-Saxons in America were hardly a people who wanted to stay put. It is because of their restlessness and their desire to move westward that Louis, as Kushner's surrogate, can assert that there are no angels in America.[59]

Kushner's association of WASPs with stasis is his most interesting— but least accurate—reinterpretation of the historical record. Kushner seems to think that Anglo-Saxons—WASPs at least—are not a migratory people. At this point his play helps us see a truth in Bede's *Ecclesiastical History* that Bede himself did not acknowledge. Bede reported that after the migration of the Angles to Britain, the land of "Angulus" remained empty "from that day to this." Are there no angels in America? There are no angels in Angulus, either, because the entire population moved to Britain. Thus the Angles took *their* ancient spirits with them, just as did blacks, Jews, and other migrant peoples. Already in the eighth century the immigrants to Britain were known as Anglo-Saxons.[60]

Louis's tendentious view of history is easily discredited, and not only by Belize. The intermarrying of Anglo-Saxon and Norman families ended the pure monolith of "the English" that Prior Walter supposedly represents. What is true of Prior Walter and all WASPS was true for people in England even before the Conquest. "Apartheid is hard enough to maintain," Susan Reynolds writes, "even when physical differences are obvious, political control is firm, and records of births, deaths, and marriages are kept. After a generation or two of post-Roman Britain not everyone, perhaps comparatively few people, can have been of pure native or invading descent. Who can have known who was descended from whom?" Reynolds draws the inescapable conclusion that "those whom we call Anglo-Saxons were not consistently distinguishable from everyone else."[61] After the Conquest, of course, the Anglo-Saxons became less "Anglo-Saxon" than they had been earlier, but at no time were bloodlines in Anglo-Saxon England pure; like most bloodlines, they were even then more the consequence of politics than they were of race.

This severing of biological descent and culture is a denial of the power of race to unify a people. That is the good news of *Angels in America* for homosexuals, the new Chosen People of this epic (what epic does not have one?). Like Mormons, Jews, and other racial groups, gay people too are oppressed, without a homeland, and on the move. But unlike those groups, gays are, first of all, a *political* people, not bound by nation or race. They have no common descent; there is no link between their sexual identity, which the play sees as their central affiliation, and either their biological or their cultural ancestry. So seen, gays serve as a perfect prophetic vehicle for Kushner's newly multicultural America. Prior succeeds in subverting the angels' design and persuading them to become his messenger; he has refused to become theirs. Their message is that the clock should be turned back to old values and stasis, staying put. His message is that change is good. Won over to humanity's view of time and place, the angels sue God, resorting to time-bound human processes (litigation) to redress grievances. The joke apparently is that the angels' heavenly wishes are inferior to the desires of humanity. The new angels of America know better than the Angel of America because Prior, their WASP spokesman, resoundingly refutes the angel's call for stasis. God, however, will probably win; his lawyer is Roy Cohn, the demon in *Angels*. Discredited at this point, God is a disloyal lover who has abandoned his angels for (the men of?) San Francisco. The angels, in turn, are also discredited, for they have accepted Prior's suggestion that those who abandon their lovers should not be forgiven, just as Prior will not forgive or take back Louis (2:133, 136).

So Prior moves ahead, not in spite of AIDS but rather *because* of AIDS. The "virus of time" has jolted him out of torpor and self-pity and eventually transforms him into the play's strongest character, a position from which he waves an affectionate goodbye to the audience. This is an AIDS play with a difference—with a happy ending.[62] Because he is a WASP the angel singled him out, but because he is a PWA he rejects her. In *Angels in America,* AIDS retains its deadly force (Cohn and others die of it) without killing the play's central character. Obviously weakened, but strong nonetheless, Prior survives. Having been visited by an angel, Prior all but becomes one. "You are fabulous creatures, each and every one," he says to the audience. "And I bless you:

More Life. The Great Work begins" (2:148). He recapitulates the last lines of *Millennium Approaches,* in which the Angel declares, "Greetings, Prophet. The Great Work begins. The Messenger has arrived" (1:119). Another messenger has arrived at the end of *Perestroika,* and his name is Prior Walter. Prior's farewell to the audience, however moving, is a remarkable banality to which I will return.

Savran argues that the play, like *The Book of Mormon,* "demonstrates that there are angels in America, that America is in essence a utopian and theological construction, a nation with a divine mission."[63] It is possible to suggest that Bede and Kushner share a political purpose, which is to create the idea of a unified people. Bede does this with the term—the concept—"Angli," which comes to mean "the English," a people elevated by their likeness to angels. Like Chaucer and Bale, Kushner is also out to unify a people, but more ambitiously and inclusively, and not a people to be compared to angels, but a people to replace them. The threat that unifies the English in Bede's work is the heathen past. The same might be said for Chaucer's ancient British Christians, at least as the Man of Law imagines them. Bale too imagined the British as overwhelmed by Roman Catholicism as brought by the Anglo-Saxons; he saw the British of his own time triumphing over the same evil force. The threat that unifies Kushner's new angels is not AIDS, which only menaces a small percentage of them, but the old regimes of race that divide and weaken people and prevent change, the very forces of conservative national and religious identity that Bede, Chaucer, and Bale advocated so powerfully. Those forces are routed at the end of *Angels in America,* and the boards are clear for a new age. The promised land of *Angels in America* is a multicultural, tolerant world in which biological descent counts for little (there are no successful marriages in the play) and cultural inheritance imparts defining characteristics to people without imposing barriers among them.

MILLENNIUM APPROACHES

I began thinking about this study in 1993, when I saw *Angels in America* for the first time. I was troubled by the conflation of Anglo-Saxon and Norman identities and unclear about how Kushner meant to align his vaguely sketched history of Prior's family with the play's sexual politics. It seemed obvious that he had merely used the WASP as a rhetorical trope and that he had not thought about the Anglo-Saxonism contained in that acronym or how Anglo-Saxonism might be related to his historical thesis about Mormons or, for that matter, angels in America.

Kushner ignored the hybrid nature of WASP identity. Likewise, he missed the prominence of same-sex friendships in the nineteenth-century Mormon tradition. D. Michael Quinn has noted that Mormons, although sometimes seen as clannish and isolated, participated fully in what Quinn describes as the "extensive homocultural orientation among Americans generally" a century ago.[64] Same-sex relations, sexual and otherwise, figure prominently in the history of early Mormon leaders, male and female alike. Kushner's representation of the Mormons would lead one to believe otherwise, however, since his Mormons seem hardly aware that homosexuality exists.

In not knowing much about the Anglo-Saxons, Kushner shares a great deal with the authors I have examined in part 3 of this book. The Anglo-Norman chroniclers knew next to nothing about the Anglo-Saxons that they did not get from Bede's *Ecclesiastical History*. A few later writers, including thirteenth-century scholars, struggled to recover the Anglo-Saxons' language, but their efforts mostly reveal how quickly knowledge of the Anglo-Saxons' culture, even their ecclesiastical culture, had faded. Chaucer and his contemporaries knew even less, relying again on French chronicles to conjure images of the Anglo-Saxon past. For all his testy and repetitive declarations, Bale was closer than any of his predecessors to real knowledge of the Anglo-Saxons. Despite his errors and confusion, his knowledge of a continuous historical tradition and its sources shames both earlier and especially later efforts. The "scholarly recovery" of Anglo-Saxon language and texts advanced rapidly after Bale's time but did not, for many years, produce a representation of Anglo-Saxon culture any more accurate than his.

Kushner, unfortunately, did no better than the other authors I have named. I take *Angels in America* as a reasonable, if regrettable, reflection on popular understanding of Anglo-Saxon culture. Kushner seems to be more respectful of Mormon traditions than of Anglo-Saxon traditions. The play contains a diorama portraying the Mormons' westward journey but nothing about the migration of the Anglo-Saxons (2:62–72). Mormon culture seems alien to him and hence multiculturally significant; its history needs to be recaptured and represented. WASP culture, evidently, is familiar and does not need to be elaborated. But at least in the extended historical sense that Kushner evokes through his use of the Bayeux tapestry, WASP culture too is alien to him. Its multicultural significance is ignored, homogenized into stereotypical patterns and ideas. Absent the oversimplified WASP, would *Angels in America* have had a culture to demonize and denounce?

Angels in America is unique among the works I have discussed in not taking the side of the angels. More important, it is also unique in its perspective on same-sex love. As I showed in part 1, it is possible to glimpse satisfying moments of same-sex love—if not same-sex sex— in opera and dance, and even in a few Anglo-Saxon narrative texts. Gays and lesbians hoping to find representations of love as they know it can find it in these works, sometimes at a small cost (i.e., closing our eyes at the opera), often at no cost. But when we go to *Angels in America,* we have no need to deprive our senses in any way. This is a work that, like many others, not only aims to show gays and lesbians what the author assumes we want to see but even blesses its audience for show- ing up. There are many differences between the power of such a work and that of *Dido and Aeneas,* as danced by Mark Morris, and the power of *Der Rosenkavalier,* with its use of the convention of the trouser role. The central difference, it seems to me, conforms to the difference between liberation and legitimation as approaches to gay and lesbian rights. Kushner and Morris liberate a same-sex perspective; they empha- size the sexual—the homosexual—in a transgressive manner. That is one way to see homosexual sensibility in the modern world, demanding its due. But finding same-sex love in works that are not about homo- sexual desire—for example, in operas using trouser roles—also legiti- mates same-sex love by pointing out that it can exist, plainly if unobtru- sively, as the shadow of heteronormative desire.

The second time I saw *Angels in America* was New Year's Eve, 1995. My partner and I had bought tickets at a premium because the theater advertised a "party" to follow the performance, which concluded shortly before midnight. The "party" turned out to be glasses of cheap fizzy wine hurriedly passed out by staff members eager to clear the house. The cast reappeared to mock the management's fleecing of the audience and to lead us in "Auld Lang Syne," gracefully lifting the occasion above the circumstances provided for it. Shortly before mid- night, in a light snowfall, we walked down a street filled with people who were rushing into bars and restaurants. It was a relief to board the train. The cars were also full—some couples, some groups, some singles, some straight, some gay—but oddly quiet, a capsule of greater Chicago heading to parties or to bed. Between one stop and another the new year arrived. The car's little communities acknowledged the moment without ceremony. Gay, straight, alone, together, we rode happily along. For me the calm—the indifference—made a welcome change from the excitement and intensity of the play and the hustle of the street. No angels crashed through the roof, no heterosexuals were chastised, no homosexuals turned into saints (or demons), no call to a great work of liberation sounded. This is all right, I thought to my-self. This is how the millennium, Kushner's and any other, will come, and go.

That is also how I think same-sex love goes along in the world, how it works best for some of us at least—love that belongs in the picture, always there, an ever-present shadow. Political and social work will always be needed to win equal treatment for gays, lesbians, bisexuals, and others who make up sexual minority groups. But there are many ways in which that work can be undertaken. I know that many activists cannot see themselves resting until the difference between heterosexual and homosexual is obliterated and such institutions as marriage and the family are transformed and open partnerships and public sex be-come the new norms. These people see no reason why the institutions of heterosexual desire should be their institutions. Neither do I. Nor do I see why the institutions of homosexual desire should be mandated for all. My vision of same-sex love might seem tepid and diffuse, devoid of passion and revolutionary fervor, not queer enough. Perhaps it is. But I strongly believe that same-sex love cannot be reduced to genital sex, and I will always believe that life is more interesting, pleasurable, and meaningful if its erotic potential can be realized across a spectrum that includes but is not restricted to the sexual. A world that slowly gets used to that idea would seem a better home to me than any queer planet I have yet to see described.

Afterword
Me and My Shadows

Many studies of same-sex relations in the premodern and early modern periods focus on records produced by courts and schools—affectionate, even passionate letters of the kind used so effectively by John Boswell. Same-sex relations—sexual and otherwise—were probably as common in military establishments as in monasteries and were also a fact of life in the countryside. Because we lack documents from rural areas and the lower levels of military environments, we can never be sure. My analysis of same-sex relations in Anglo-Saxon England has been based on the texts that survive from this culture, a fraction of the books available in the Anglo-Saxon period. But even then regulatory and narrative texts would have recorded only a fraction of the experiences, same-sex and otherwise, known to the culture. In the course of my work I found myself wondering about the lost experience of the Anglo-Saxons. I found myself extrapolating from modern to medieval worlds of sexual behavior and from Anglo-Saxon texts to the larger, unknowable, and hence shadowy worlds around them. It is not the contemporary sexual culture of queer theory and media-generated homosexual stereotypes that I find comparable to medieval cultures, but rather the world of American life of the 1960s and before, the world in which I was raised. By way of concluding this study I want to speculate on similarities between some social conditions in my past and social conditions at levels of Anglo-Saxon society that the texts do not discuss, levels lost to us but perhaps recoverable if we consider some possible similarities between our culture and theirs.

Important studies of gay and lesbian life have demonstrated how recently some pervasive terms of modern sexual discourse have been invented. George Chauncey's *Gay New York: Gender, Urban Culture, and the Making of the Gay Male World, 1890–1940,* for example, reminds us that the "closet" is a relatively new idea and demonstrates how different the gay world of New York (and other cities, presumably) was even thirty years ago from what it is today.[1] Another book that stresses the difference between perceptions of sexual behavior before and after the 1970s is John D'Emilio's *Sexual Politics, Sexual Communities,* which positions the 1948 release of the Kinsey studies of sexuality as a dividing point.[2] D'Emilio stressed the role of military service in World War II, and the war itself, in transforming sexual codes for gays and lesbians. This phenomenon has since been amply demonstrated by Allan Bérubé in *Coming Out under Fire: Gay Men and Women in World War Two.*[3] Recently D. Michael Quinn's *Same-Sex Dynamics among Nineteenth-Century Americans: A Mormon Example* has shown how important same-sex friendships were to what he calls the "homocultural orientation" of America a century ago and how drastically those friendships were subsequently altered by homophobic responses.[4]

These books and others demonstrate that same-sex relations used to be understood more inclusively—less exclusively about sexual intercourse—than, in some quarters, they are now. It has been my aim to demonstrate that same-sex relations in Anglo-Saxon England are most apparent, and most fully integral to the culture, when they are understood to be inclusive of gestures of affection, expressions of devotion, and other evidence that, along with sexual intercourse, constitutes the discourse of same-sex love. I have tried to show that same-sex relations, and indeed same-sex sex, encompass more than sexual intercourse, and to argue that kisses, embraces, and other contact, verbal or physical, between members of the same sex attest to the vitality, necessity, and even the ubiquity of homosexual love and affection (very different in every sense from "homosexuality"). Such forms of same-sex contact in urban centers, courts, and schools of the Middle Ages are familiar. But what about same-sex relations outside these confines? Some of the evidence I have presented extends beyond elite circles. So does my own history as a boy growing up on a farm in Iowa in the 1950s and 1960s and as a young man stationed with the U.S. Army in Korea in the early 1970s.

When I graduated from college in 1969 I was faced with the certainty of being drafted into the U.S. Army, going to basic training and infantry school, and being shipped to Vietnam. I came from a farming community in a county with a tiny draft pool; the Selective Service Board instituted the lottery system too late to apply to me. The kinds of deferments handed out to my college friends were beyond reach. In the hope of avoiding the infantry and combat I enlisted; as a college graduate, luckily, I qualified for language school. The army offered me two alternatives for foreign-language instruction: Korean or Vietnamese. I spent forty-seven weeks studying Korean at a facility outside Washington, D.C., and was sent to Korea in April 1971. I left Korea, and the army, at the end of January 1972. January 1997 found me immersed in thinking about and writing this book, which was taking me into new areas of the medieval culture I had studied and written about for years and, simultaneously, leading me back to forgotten parts of my past. The time for a return to Korea seemed right. Twenty-five years to the day of my departure from Korea, I left Chicago to return to Seoul.

With me I took three books that stirred memories of my past. They were Will Fellows's *Farm Boys: Lives of Gay Men from the Rural Midwest,* a collection of first-person narratives by men who grew up on farms between the 1930s and the 1970s; *Korean Works and Days: Notes from the Diary of a Country Priest,* written by Richard Rutt, an Anglican bishop who lived in rural Korea in the 1950s and 1960s; and Bérubé's *Coming Out under Fire.*[5] Thinking about these books helped me understand the sexual codes of my past and those of the Anglo-Saxon age; explaining why and how seems to be a good way to conclude the process of writing about them.

Farm Boy

I read the narratives of gay life in *Farm Boys* amazed at the extent of sexual experience midwestern farm boys claim to have had, far beyond the kinds of childhood experimentation I expected to read about. Some of the contributors to the collection still live on farms, but most of them, like me, escaped rural life as soon as they could and, like me, have never thought about returning. Many of them had more fun than I did. Their stories show that even in isolated rural areas boys found many ways to learn about and experiment with sex. One condition that contributed to their freedom, especially in the prewar era, paradoxically, was ignorance—not theirs, but their families'. In many cases the boy's family did not know that intramale sex was possible. There are few examples in nature, and of course the formal or informal knowledge about sex made available to these parents when they were growing up was far more limited than that available to their children. What fathers and mothers did not know about they did not think to prohibit, and neither, usually, did the boys' teachers or preachers. Many farm boys reported that they experimented with themselves and with other boys whenever the opportunity presented itself—on camping trips, swimming, walking, even working in secluded places. A few boys were abused by men; some of them went on to abuse others (i.e., to force them into sex). Brothers had sex with brothers, boys had sex with each other and with animals.

In almost all cases the boys did not know names for what they were doing, much less did they have some idea of such actions as bearing on a "homosexual" orientation. The awakening to knowledge about sex, as opposed to sexual knowledge, often took place late. An exceptional story makes the point clear. One of the most aggressively sexual narratives is Steve Preston's. Raised without a mother by a violent father, he and his brothers, when small boys, were sexually abused by an uncle when he baby-sat with them. One day Preston and a cousin put a name to their sexual behavior: "About the time my mother died, Neil and I looked up homosexuality in the encyclopedia. It said something about males who engage in sexual contact with one another more than six times. So we were sitting there counting on our fingers and decided we were" (262). Reading this, I remembered how important it was to me when our parents, after much hesitation over the price, bought *The World Book Encyclopedia*. But I never looked up "homosexual" in it and I wonder how Steve Preston and his cousin knew the word. They were not only aware of their sexual preference but aware that it would be described in a standard reference work, information also available to their teachers and parents. The boys' confidence and their sense of a homosexual identity are unusual among those recounted in Fellows's book.

Preston was born in south-central Wisconsin; when he looked up "homosexual," he was nine years old. It was 1971. I was born in northeastern Iowa; when I was nine it was 1956. In rural areas then, and perhaps in some rural areas even now, the universal expectation that everyone would marry directed all public thoughts of sex along heterosexual lines. Before AIDS and a handful of movies and television programs about gay men and lesbians, and before campaigns such as those mounted by Anita Bryant and the religious right, fewer people were aware of what homosexuality was. The sexual histories of farm boys of my era could, with some changes, be sexual histories of boys in Anglo-Saxon England. They too were sometimes introduced to same-sex acts by men or older boys and experimented with other boys and with animals. Most of those who were not monks eventually left same-sex practices behind and married. Some of them, as *Farm Boys* makes clear, married *without* leaving these practices behind; the Anglo-Saxon penitentials make the same point.[6]

My life was very different, without experimentation, without sexual abuse. I had no idea that men had sex with each other even after I realized that I wanted to have sex with men myself. I assumed that I was the only person who had such ideas (this phenomenon is widely reported in *Farm Boys*), and because I had many other ideas that seemed to be mine alone, I supposed that my sexual desires were also unique. A television program about sex, and my father's response to it, made me realize my error. What can this program have been? Was it one of those "scare" broadcasts from the 1950s, part of the postwar reconstitution of the nuclear family and the attendant campaign to stigmatize homosexuals as sex offenders, sexual psychopaths, and deviates?[7] I always watched television lying on the floor and had to be reminded constantly not to get too close to it for fear of "ruining my eyes." (Apparently it occurred to no one that I might need glasses, which I most certainly did.) My father was sitting on the couch behind me. When someone described "homosexuals" as men who had sex with each other, my father asked, "What do they do?" I had no idea, but of course once the question had been asked, I began to wonder how it could be answered.

SPECIALIST FRANTZEN

Another book that made me aware of similarities between part of my personal experience and the conditions of sexual relations in the premodern period was *Coming Out under Fire*. This book shows how it was possible for women and especially for men to carry on same-sex relations without objection, even though sometimes they were observed, on ships, on military bases, and in other confined spaces where men were physically close, often fearful and alone, and deprived of contact with women. The buddy system encouraged men to pair up, Bérubé wrote, "and gave a respectability to devoted male couples, whether or not they included gay men, that was unusual in civilian life." Such intimacy was usually far removed from what we might think of as a "gay" relationship. "My Buddy" was a love song, heterosexual of course, from the 1920s. It became popular again during the war, when it expressed sentiments that described the buddy system. Later the song "became a signature piece for many gay men's choruses," according to Bérubé (38). The song was adopted by (mostly) heterosexual men to celebrate their closeness to other (mostly) heterosexual men, a same-sex union shadowed by conventions of romantic love that presumably did not embarrass the soldiers. When the song was taken up by gay men, heterosexual romance remained a shadow; the song itself, after the war, acquired a quality of military maleness with its own homoerotic appeal. Their response to this song is similar to my wish to see same-sex intimacy in operas using trouser roles; they sang

"My Buddy" hoping to hear what they wanted to hear. To the fulfillment of such wishes there are inevitable restrictions. Bérubé: "But during the war the combat soldiers' acceptance of one another's pairing
and physical intimacy was more a recognition of their need for closeness in life-threatening situations than any conscious tolerance of homosexuality" (188). Today, happily, conscious tolerance of homosexuality
prompts recognition of a need for closeness in situations less dire (although they can still be life-threatening).

Again a comparison with sexual behavior in the premodern period
seems possible. The Anglo-Saxons were a warrior culture; men lived
on intimate terms with each other, without women. When women
were permitted into some camps during the Crusades, church officials
were scandalized that a presumed safe same-sex environment had been
corrupted. Eleanor of Aquitaine was blamed for the failure of the
Second Crusade because she insisted on going into battle. William of
Newburgh wrote that "[h]er example was followed by many other
noble wives . . . with the result that the Christian camp which ought to
be chaste swarmed with a multitude of women."[8] Church officials had
long known that the same-sex environment of the monastery was not
free of sexual misbehavior; it was naïve to assume that those who
fought would behave better than those who prayed.

Bérubé points out how the medical profession collaborated with the
military to devise elaborate systems for detecting homosexuals during
physical exams and interviews before World War II, and how such
procedures codified certain stereotypical identities for lesbians and gay
men in the 1950s. Before these codes and procedures were in place, gay
people arguably had more freedom. They found each other in military
service in numbers that had not been possible to imagine previous to
that powerfully centralizing and democratic experience. But this opportunity for community building quickly turned dangerous when
doctors and military authorities began interrogating suspected homosexuals and forcing them to testify against themselves and their friends.
This culture of suspicion, shame, and punishment was well developed
when I entered the army in July 1969, landing in Fort Polk, Louisiana,
just a few days after Apollo 11 landed on the moon.

The army was an aggressively heterosexual place. I had no awareness of a homosexual culture on any of the bases I was stationed at,
even at Fort Meyer, Virginia, close to Washington, D.C., and hence
likely to benefit from the freedom of the urban environment. Homosexual culture was successfully hidden from me at all the places I was
stationed and confronted me first in Korea, in the person of a married
GI. It was June 30, 1971, according to the journal I kept during my

ten months in the country. One night three of us were having a drink after work. Suddenly a man named Mike leaned across Sam, who also worked our shift, and said, "Frantzen, I've decided that you are a homosexual, and I'll agree to have an affair with you if I can take the dominant role."[9] I was too embarrassed to reply, but privately my response was ambiguous. Ashamed and angry, I was also aware that I was at some level pleased. I liked this man (although, correctly as it turned out, I thought he was a little unpredictable). In my journal, in a disappointingly lame account of the evening, I described Mike's proposition as a "catastrophe." I recalled that I had discussed being gay with two friends (both seminarians) in San Francisco. But those conversations were "wisdom apparently lost, to judge from the way I've handled things here," I wrote. "It's just that I was totally taken by surprise." Taken by surprise, and outed, by a married man who had proposed this liaison in front of a third person, someone whose knowledge of the arrangement made it impossible even to consider. Later, to Sam, I felt obliged to express indignation at Mike's offer and to assume a stance of presumed heterosexuality. I did not want this proposition to brand me as a homosexual, whether my acquaintances assumed I was one or not.

I supposed that Mike had been driven to make this proposition not because of who I was but because of who he thought I was—somebody who would agree to his terms. He later had what we called a "nervous breakdown" and received a medical discharge after a period of hospitalization. I was hospitalized during some of that period and wrote benignly, indeed patronizingly, about him. "Johnson leaves for America today," I wrote (August 13, 1971). "His problem has gotten too big for him. I spent hours talking to him, and feel that I was instrumental in getting him here [into the hospital]—he's just down the hall—and enjoy talking to him now. He's much more relaxed." But two days later I no longer thought so. "His outlook isn't very good," I wrote disapprovingly, a testy Florence Nightingale after all, "and he won't do much better elsewhere without some changes." Obviously Mike's proposition did not rupture our friendship; indeed it seems to have strengthened it.

The experience answers perfectly to a phenomenon Bérubé described in basic training during World War II. "Not all trainees who approached other men for sex were gay," he wrote. "Heterosexual recruits who had had the most sexual experience with women or who felt strong sex drives could initiate sex without being afraid that they were queer, especially if their partner was gay and played the 'passive' sexual role" (41). Absent from my journal notes on this experience are any responses that a self-aware gay man might have had. Mike wanted his wife, and I was presumably the only man he knew who he thought would agree to have sex with him. He made me aware that he had been watching and thinking about me; I was flattered. Being in the closet did not mean that I was invisible (of course, Mike might have been in the closet himself). When I think about this period now, I wonder if what Henning Bech outlines as a standard explanation for same-sex relations in prison can be applied to men in the military. Deprived of women's company, they "seize on surrogate satisfactions" and have sex with other men. "In this way the needs for emotional ties are satisfied as well as the needs for the demonstration of masculine dominance and potency, or for security."[10] Bech suggests that such relations indicate instead that men are attracted to other men *as men* and not as substitutes for women (25).

Moon Ch'e-Hun

The third book that figures into this meditation, Rutt's *Korean Works and Days: Notes from the Diary of a Country Priest,* helped me set this proposition into the context of my life not just as a GI but as a GI in Korea. Rutt's book is a reminiscence of old Korea, the rural country whose folk customs could have changed but little between 1950 and a century, perhaps centuries, before. I had not remembered anything about homosexuality in this book, which I had taken with me because I thought it would help me remember not only the vanished country-side that I had admired on my travels but also the sense of adventure and mystery that surrounded my stay there. Then I came upon Rutt's description of a conversation he once had with a churchwarden under his jurisdiction.

> Not long ago I was sitting in the tiring room [i.e., dressing room] of one of my smaller churches, chatting with the churchwarden while the supper was being prepared. There was a lull in the conversation, and then he chuckled and said: "You know, I never realized paederasty was a sin till I read the Epistle to the Romans." After hearing the rest of his chatter I was left wondering to myself just what memories lay behind his chuckle.
>
> He said that when he was a boy, only forty years ago, there were often "pretty boys" in a village. They were especially the favourites of young widowers and sometimes of older and richer men. The boy would receive nice clothes and would be fairly conspicuous. But his po-

sition would involve no ostracism and would not impair his chances of marriage.

But among the itinerant players—the dancers and acrobats and puppet-show people—paederasty, male prostitution, and regular homosexual marriages, sometimes with transvestitism, were common and well known (just as formal tribadistic unions were common among the palace women in the capital).

Rutt appended a note to this last sentence: "According to the late Song Sokha, in his *Korean Folklore Studies,* these bands of players were formed in the late Yi dynasty [i.e., sixteenth century] in direct imitation of highly organized groups of low-class female prostitute-entertainers such as can still occasionally be met with" (112–13). The churchwarden had knowledge, and perhaps experience, of same-sex relations between men and "pretty boys." The boys engaged in these affairs without damaging their chances to marry later. The situation sounds very much like pederasty among the ancient Greeks.

Christianity's disapproving interpretation of this custom, St. Paul's condemnation of it, and the presence of the bishop, did not stop the churchwarden from recalling the custom with evident pleasure. Had he been a "pretty boy"? Had he been the lover of one? He had learned from the Church that pederasty was a "sin." But he had a special Christian education; he was a churchwarden, although not otherwise, presumably, in orders. How many men like him were Christians but had *not* read St. Paul or other texts that were construed as prohibiting same-sex intercourse? The topic, we may be sure, did not often come up in homiletic discourse; the sexual sins denounced there (vaguely, as impurity) were almost certainly heterosexual, not homosexual. The topic did not come up in my education, either. We have seen that it did come up, in a limited context, in the education of men and boys in Anglo-Saxon England, in penitentials that punished small boys forced into intercourse by older ones (see chapter 4, tables 1 and 2). In this regard, at least, Anglo-Saxon culture was straightforward about a topic that many who have studied it have chosen to ignore. But the evidence does not suggest that the Anglo-Saxons' prohibition was effective. Steve Preston was a small boy who was abused and who went on to pressure others into sex; some of the small boys similarly exploited in Anglo-Saxon England no doubt became older boys or men who took advantage of young ones.

I had no knowledge of these lost traditions and heard nothing about them during my stay in Korea, where I lived in two worlds. One was

Fig. 11. The 226th United States Army Security Agency Operations Company, Kang-hwa Do, Korea, 1971.

the army base, a small unit of about one hundred GIs located on the island of Kang-hwa, situated about forty miles from Seoul over a road that was, at the time, little more than a dirt track thronged with small, noisy buses, trucks, and military traffic. The company, officially known as the 226th United States Army Security Agency Operations Company, occupied a small base, known to the Koreans as "226." It was a grim mix of Quonset huts and cinder-block buildings pitched on a hillside below a top-secret facility that monitored radio and radar activity in North Korea and China (figure 11). The base was a tedious and fearful place, so close to North Korea that "alerts" anticipating enemy attacks were frequent (we could hear North Korean propaganda broadcast over loudspeakers across the Han River estuary at night). There I was Specialist 4th Class Frantzen.

Kang-hwa was another world, and for my life on the island I adopted a Korean name, Moon Ch'e-Hun, "Frantzen" being too difficult to work into the Korean alphabet. Kang-hwa was covered with mountains and valleys terraced with rice paddies; it had a beautiful coastline. I loved to look to the west and watch as the islands stretching into the Yellow Sea vanished in purple light at sunset. The island of Kang-hwa was once a fortress, the refuge of the Koryo court during the thirteenth century and the site of a battle between Koreans and some French and American invaders in the late nineteenth century. When I returned in 1997 I discovered that much of the island's beauty and all of its rural charm had disappeared. "Overrated as a tourist attraction," a guidebook warned, adding, unpromisingly, "[i]f your time is limited, you can skip all this without feeling a deep sense of loss." [11] The army base closed long ago, the island is covered with good roads, Kang-hwa is full of sport-utility vehicles driven by Seoulites up for the weekend. Kang-hwa is no longer a place of mystery or romance, but life there is obviously better for everybody. So my visit evoked a deep sense of loss, but I had already begun to experience it before I left Chicago.

As a GI on the island I organized a Korean universe to parallel army life. Shortly after I arrived there, I met some teachers and began tutoring school children in English. I found a hospital clinic run by Maryknoll nuns who knew a great deal about Korea and taught me much. I met a Peace Corps volunteer and shared two rooms with him in a splendid old house, built, we were told, by the Japanese during the occupation of Korea (1910–45). I do not recall that my roommate and I ever discussed sex; in 1997 this wonderful house and its Western-style sitting room, complete with a Japanese poster advertising *White Christmas,* was nowhere to be found. I also became acquainted with some men stationed at a Republic of Korea (ROK) marine base known as 3637, not far from the base where I was stationed.

I frequently spent time with Korean military and police personnel, easier for me than for many GIs because I spoke some Korean. I used to find the demonstrative curiosity and affection of these men exciting. In summer, sitting in a tearoom or riding on a ferry between Kang-hwa and the small islands to the west, I would talk to the police or marines who regularly patrolled streets and the coastline (figure 12). Most Korean men have little body hair. Some of the men I knew were fascinated by the hair on my arms and legs and, without asking, used to touch me. Nobody—least of all good-looking men in uniform— had ever stroked my arms or legs. They expressed delight and surprise while, in some embarrassment, I tried to explain that many Westerners were the same as me, even as I derived pleasure from this contact that differentiated me from most men, Western or Eastern.

From time to time I visited the ROK marine base and sometimes

Fig. 12. Allen Frantzen and two unidentified policemen aboard a police patrol boat between Kang-hwa Do and Song-mo Do, Korea, 1971.

even stayed overnight, relishing the dangerous thrill of being where I was not supposed to be and enjoying the rough and ready atmosphere of a camp far more Spartan than the base where I lived and worked. My quarters at 226 were primitive, but at least they had running water; 3637 did not. During these visits I felt very much like a civilian who was not expected to tolerate the rigors of a ROK marine's life (and indeed I could not have tolerated them for long). To the extent that comforts were possible at 3637, I enjoyed them. My friends and I would hike into the hills and sit there, overlooking the island, the sea, and the distant shores of the North. They always wanted to sing, although I never really knew what they were singing about. When it was my turn, I would sing "She'll Be Comin' 'round the Mountain" (I do not know why) or "Yesterday," a song with special meaning to anybody far from home.

One of these men was a navy captain named Dr. Lee, a dark and handsome man with a devastating smile whom I met shortly after arriving on Kang-hwa. When I realized that I was captivated by him, I reflected on prior experiences with men—emotional, not sexual—and dutifully, if ambiguously, wrote in my journal that "fascinations are mostly dangerous." I would not have written "crushes" for the world, but that was what I meant. I wrote about Lee every time I saw him, but I never once wrote his full name. I have hundreds of pictures from my time in Korea but not a single picture of him and only a few post-cards and letters (in one, sent after I had left Korea, he offered to send my "promised girl" or, absent her, my mother, a traditional Korean woman's costume). He was the most important person I met that year. I saw him every chance I got and wrote about him frequently. When he was transferred off the island to the other side of the country, I took long bus trips to see him, and he did the same for me. I must have been in love with him, reading our bond of friendship through a lens of homosexual attraction that I was sure he did not share. Like many Korean men he was affectionate and polite, deferential to me as a visitor, and pleased to act as a cultural intermediary and protector whenever he could. I was happy to depend on him. Wary as I was of telling myself anything I did not want to know, in my journal I described my time with him on the island as "romantic" and "excited." After he left Kang-hwa, I used to stand on the mountain where our listening post was located, look at the marine base where he had lived, and—there is no other word for it—pine for his company.

So to a few observations on how these experiences and cultural situations connect to the study of same-sex relations in Anglo-Saxon England. First is the power of texts produced by a heterosexual culture to name the elements and actors within same-sex cultures. Texts identify sexual practices and hence the people who engage in them, as we see in the boys who looked up "homosexual" in the encyclopedia and the churchwarden who read St. Paul. When people recognize their own actions in texts, texts acquire the power to confer identity, welcome or not.

Second is the lack of texts produced by those who inhabit same-sex cultures. It was only in retrospect, and in most cases in isolation from farm culture, that farm boys spoke about rural same-sex culture. I never wrote about my homosexual desires as a high school or college student, any more than I acted on them. Until I read *Farm Boys,* I had seen nothing that remotely resembled accounts of my experiences and thoughts about sex as a boy or teenager; the literature seems largely dominated by the coming out stories of well-known men in urban cultures.[12] One could not guess at my experience from official documents or begin to reconstruct it from most available narratives of gay men's lives. I kept my own records, hundreds of pages of a journal that I started when I was sixteen. I am glad that I still have these notebooks, although they studiously mask my thoughts about sex. There are no heart-broken paeans to would-be boyfriends, no intimate details about same-sex relations, no speculations on sexual feelings. Even in my late teens and early twenties I did not talk about sex freely. I was intimidated by the sexual sophistication of some of my friends in college and by the military culture that persistently encouraged the very feelings it forbade me to have.

Third, the gap between sexual experience and textual power. Not all writing about same-sex relations, obviously, makes the world a safer place for gays, lesbians, and bisexuals. For every book or essay that reflects on same-sex experiences positively there is one (or more?) that has the opposite effect. But too much of this writing, whether it affirms gay behavior or not, tells people that they are *either* straight *or* gay. Such work crudely reduces the range of human sexual experience to categories that cannot accommodate the same-sex relations I have recalled here. My experiences, especially in the army, especially in Korea, taught me, in retrospect, about the possibilities for same-sex relations between men and women who are not constrained by the demands of politics (queer, lesbian, gay, straight, repressive—it does not matter) to classify themselves and make their sexual behavior a calling card of political identity.

It was still possible, when I was a young man, to have same-sex experiences without being "gay," and to be "gay" without having sexual experiences. It still is. It was possible for boys to have affairs with men and later to marry and become fathers. It still is. It was possible for two men in the army to have sex together and go back to their wives. It still is. It was possible for two men who were in love to have sex only with each other or with other men, or for men who were not in love to have sex only with other men. Those options too are still possible. They were also possible in the Anglo-Saxon age, at least for men. The domestic worlds of women and the worlds of women's religious communities also created many opportunities for same-sex love, affection, and sex (I think of Hermengyld and Custance in their bed). I conclude that my own experiences as a boy and a young man, quite recent experiences from the perspective of history, were similar to experiences that the records suggest boys and men had in early medieval Europe. When it comes to sex, those cultures are not so remote as they seem.

My trip to Korea stirred many old memories. Before I went, I sorted through photograph albums and boxes of pictures and memorabilia that had lain unexamined for twenty-five years. I read journal entries unread for all that time. At certain moments during my visit—for

example, when, on a bright but very cold morning, I left my gloves on
the bus that took me from Seoul to Kang-hwa—I suddenly remembered Korean words and phrases that I had not spoken since I had left
the country. My experience in Korea, like my Korean, had been as
good as lost because I had no occasion to remember it. The experiences
of the Anglo-Saxons—some of them, I contend, not so different from
a farm boy's or a modern soldier's, when it comes to sex—are likewise
as good as lost unless we make occasions to recall them. I do not know
if it was permissible for two men who enjoyed each other's company—
let's say they were thegns of Alfred—to embrace or otherwise show
affection as they ended a night of eating, drinking, and singing. *Beowulf* and *The Wanderer* suggest that at certain times men kissed and
embraced and went their separate ways. I hope that some of those who
kissed and embraced did not part and that not all their nights were as
conventional as my nights with Dr. Lee.

Two Nights

One night before he left Kang-hwa, Lee took me to dinner with some
of his officer friends at a little restaurant well off the main street of the
city of Kang-hwa, where we left the Jeep. They ordered dinner, joking
with the mama-san and the girl who brought the food. We drank beer,
sitting around a low table and talking about army life and ROK marine life, their work, my work, where I should go in Korea and what I
should see, and when I could visit their families. When it was time to
go, they paid the bill. Amid an extended exchange of bows and thanks
we struggled into boots and shoes left under a wooden bench outside
the room where we had eaten. Lee started for the alley, boxy cap tipped
back on his head, shirttail hanging out, fatigue pants loosely stuffed
into his unlaced boots (a look I would not see in the United States for
years). His cohort followed, joking and laughing. As we walked down
the dirt path to the jeep, Lee turned and took my hand. Once or twice
I glanced at him, hoping to see what he was thinking. He was not,
probably, thinking about anything. But I was. Beside myself with pleasure and excitement, dizzy with beer, overwhelmed with a sense of
intimacy, I thought, "Can this be happening? This must be love. This
is what I have always wanted."

I had held hands with a few women, but not many, before Lee took
my hand that night. This innocent gesture of affection from a man was
unique in my experience. To me it represented closeness, friendship,
intimacy, even sex. I was twenty-four years old. Such a gesture is still
forbidden to gay men and women most of the time, in most places. If

we hold hands walking down the street or sitting in a restaurant, we make a political statement (unconventional, too gay!). If we do so in a gay neighborhood, we make a different political statement (conventional, too straight!). When I returned to Korea in 1997, I saw young and old women and children holding hands, but no boys and certainly no men. I doubt that today matters are much different in the countryside.

I remember another night one summer on the farm when I was in high school. For some reason I was home alone, a rare event; I seldom felt unwatched. The moon was full and my room was bright with its light. I got up, took off my pajamas and walked down the stairs and outside, where I stood on the porch in the warm silence. Then I ran to an old swing that hung from a huge elm tree by the garage. I jumped on the seat, surprised at how smooth the old wood felt under me, and began to swing as fast and as high as I could, leaning back, legs spread, sailing naked through the night and the warm air, hearing only the creaking of the rope and the wind rushing past me. Eventually I saw headlights in the distance, surely from my parents' car. I continued to swing until there was only one more hill for the car to climb and descend before its lights would rush up the road and into the shadows where I sailed back and forth. I jumped off the swing and raced across the lawn into the house. As the gravel crunched and my father's Impala pulled into the driveway, I fell into bed. There I lay, heart pounding, scandalized, sweaty, thrilled. I never wrote about that experience. Neither boy nor man shared it. No catechism — or any other book I knew — described such an adventure, or forbade it. I was sure that I had broken a rule (I was sure that I did not want to be caught), but I did not know which one. It was a moment of awakening to the nearness of forbidden pleasure, to danger, darkness, and mystery, and to the possibility of being at home in my body, which was, just then, in every sense and for once, my own.

Notes

NOTES TO THE INTRODUCTION

1. John Boswell, *Christianity, Social Tolerance, and Homosexuality: Gay People in Western Europe from the Beginning of the Christian Era to the Fourteenth Century* (Chicago: University of Chicago Press, 1980).

2. Without proposing a model of Anglo-Saxon sexuality, I echo Robert Padgug's view that "sexuality is relational" and that it consists of "active social relations." See Padgug, "Sexual Matters: Rethinking Sexuality in History," in *Hidden from History: Reclaiming the Gay and Lesbian Past,* ed. Martin Duberman, Martha Vicinus, and George Chauncey, Jr. (New York: Penguin, 1989), 58.

3. Richard Smith, "Queer Indeed," *Gay Times* 183 (December 1993): 72, quoted in Alan Stewart, *Close Readers: Humanism and Sodomy in Early Modern England* (Princeton: Princeton University Press, 1997), xxii.

4. Boswell, *Christianity, Social Tolerance,* 269–302.

5. Larry Scanlon, "Unspeakable Pleasure: Alain de Lille, Sexual Regulation, and the Priesthood of Genius," *Romanic Review* 86 (1995): 217. In addition to Boswell's *Christianity, Social Tolerance, and Homosexuality,* Scanlon cites Boswell's *Same-Sex Unions in Premodern Europe* (New York: Villard Books, 1994).

6. See Stewart, "Epistemologies of the Early Modern Closet," in *Close Readers,* 161–87, for a discussion of the architecture of the closet in the Renaissance.

7. Eve Kosofsky Sedgwick, *Epistemology of the Closet* (Berkeley and Los Angeles: University of California Press, 1990), 71.

8. The "impossibly contradictory" nature of the closet is explained by David M. Halperin, *Saint Foucault: Towards a Gay Hagiography* (New York: Oxford, 1995), 34–35.

9. Robert Spindler, *Das altenglische Bussbuch (sog. Confessionale Pseudo-Egberti)* (Leipzig: B. Tauchnitz, 1934), 171. For a discussion of this motif, see M. R. Godden, "An Old English Penitential Motif," *Anglo-Saxon England* 2 (1973): 22–39; my translation.

10. Terry Castle, *The Apparitional Lesbian: Female Homosexuality and Modern Culture* (New York: Columbia University Press, 1993), 14, taking issue with Judith Butler's essay "Imitation and Gender Insubordination," in *Inside/Out: Lesbian Theories, Gay Theories,* ed. Diana Fuss (New York: Routledge, 1991), 15.

11. For a concise and lively survey of queer critical practices, see Alexander Doty, *Making Things Perfectly Queer* (Minneapolis: University of Minnesota Press, 1993), xi–xix.

12. See Teresa de Lauretis, "Queer Theory: Lesbian and Gay Sexualities: An Introduction," *Differences* 3 (1991): iii. De Lauretis describes gay sexuality as "both interactive and yet resistant, both participatory and yet distinct, claiming at once equality and difference."

13. On "messiness," see Doty, *Making Things Perfectly Queer*, xiii–xiv; Lauren Berlant and Michael Warner, "What Does Queer Theory Teach Us about X?" *PMLA* 110 (1995): 343–49; and Michael Warner, *Fear of a Queer Planet* (Minneapolis: University of Minnesota Press, 1993).

14. Sedgwick, *Epistemology of the Closet*, 3. Sedgwick's debt to Foucault is examined by Halperin, *Saint Foucault*, 37–38.

15. Judith Butler, *Bodies that Matter: On the Discursive Limits of "Sex"* (New York: Routledge, 1993), especially 223–42. Gender performativity is the subject of Butler, *Gender Trouble: Feminism and the Subversion of Identity* (New York: Routledge, 1991), a book that does not otherwise treat queer theory.

16. Michel Foucault, *The History of Sexuality*, vol. 1, trans. Robert Hurley (New York: Vintage, 1980).

17. For the original assessment, see David M. Halperin, *One Hundred Years of Homosexuality: And Other Essays on Greek Love* (New York: Routledge, 1990), 64 (originally published in a 1986 review). For the recanting, see Halperin, *Saint Foucault*, 5.

18. Karma Lochrie, "Desiring Foucault," *Journal of Medieval and Early Modern Studies* 27 (1997): 9.

19. Michel Foucault, *The Use of Pleasure*, trans. Robert Hurley (New York: Vintage, 1986).

20. Foucault, *History of Sexuality*, 1:162 (confession), 164 (penance).

21. Lochrie, "Desiring Foucault," 8.

22. Halperin, *Saint Foucault*, 30–31.

23. Halperin's *Saint Foucault* is the most thorough treatment of Foucault's contribution; see also comments by Louise Fradenburg and Carla Freccero, "Caxton, Foucault, and the Pleasures of History," in *Premodern Sexualities*, ed. Fradenburg and Freccero (New York: Routledge, 1996), xvi–xvii.

24. Foucault, *History of Sexuality*, 1:35.

25. Foucault, *History of Sexuality*, 1:101.

26. Foucault, *History of Sexuality*, 1:100–101. For elaboration and an application of this concept, see my essay, "The Disclosure of Sodomy in the Middle English *Cleanness*," *PMLA* 111 (1996): 451–64.

27. J. J. Francis Firth, ed., *Robert of Flamborough: Liber poenitentialis* (Toronto: Pontifical Institute of Mediaeval Studies, 1971), 196.

28. Geoffrey Chaucer, *The Parson's Tale*, in *The Riverside Chaucer*, ed. Larry D. Benson, 3rd ed. (Boston: Houghton Mifflin, 1987), 288–327.

29. James Creech, *Closet Writing/Gay Reading: The Case of Melville's "Pierre"* (Chicago: University of Chicago Press, 1993), 94.

30. Sedgwick, *Epistemology of the Closet*, 56.

31. F. W. H. Wasserschleben, ed., *Die Bussordnungen der abendländischen Kirche* (1851; reprint, Graz: Akademische Druck–U. Verlagsanstalt, 1958), 253. See further Pierre J. Payer, *Sex and the Penitentials: The Development of a Sexual Code, 550–1150* (Toronto: University of Toronto Press, 1984), 77–79.

32. Mark D. Jordan, *The Invention of Sodomy in Christian Theology* (Chicago: University of Chicago Press, 1997), 42.

33. George Chauncey, *Gay New York: Gender, Urban Culture, and the Making of the Gay Male World, 1890–1940* (New York: Basic Books, 1994), 6.

34. Sedgwick, *Epistemology of the Closet,* 56.

35. Castle, *Apparitional Lesbian,* 2.

36. Doty, *Making Things Perfectly Queer,* xi.

37. Alan Bray, *Homosexuality in Renaissance England* (1982; reprinted with a new afterword, New York: Columbia University Press, 1995), 24–25, 26.

38. *Webster's New World Dictionary of the American Language* (Cleveland: World Publishing, 1956), 1337.

39. Lee Edelman, *Homographesis: Essays in Gay Literary and Cultural Theory* (New York: Routledge, 1994).

40. Bray, *Homosexuality in Renaissance England,* 56.

41. Lochrie, "Desiring Foucault"; and Karma Lochrie, "Don't Ask, Don't Tell: Murderous Plots and Medieval Secrets," in *Premodern Sexualities,* ed. Fradenburg and Freccero, 137–52. For arguments about the consistency of Foucault's thoughts on sexuality and his creativity, "pervasive political and ethical dispositions" that "persist through his late thought," see Carolyn Dinshaw, "Getting Medieval: *Pulp Fiction,* Gawain, Foucault," in *The Book and the Body,* ed. Dolores Warwick Frese and Katherine O'Brien O'Keeffe (Notre Dame: University of Notre Dame Press, 1997), 137.

42. Fradenburg and Freccero, *Premodern Sexualities,* viii.

43. Jonathan Goldberg, ed., *Queering the Renaissance* (Durham: Duke University Press, 1994), 9.

44. Bruce W. Holsinger, "Sodomy and Resurrection: The Homoerotic Subject of the *Divine Comedy,*" in *Premodern Sexualities,* ed. Fradenburg and Freccero, 244.

45. Holsinger, "Sodomy and Resurrection," 245–46, quoting Caroline Walker Bynum, *Fragmentation and Redemption: Essays on Gender and the Human Body in Medieval Religion* (New York: Zone Books, 1992), "Genitality and Sexuality," 85–88.

46. Holsinger, "Sodomy and Resurrection," 246.

47. Carolyn Dinshaw, "Chaucer's Queer Touches/A Queer Touches Chaucer," *Exemplaria* 7 (1995): 82. I comment on this argument in "Between the Lines: Queer Theory, the History of Homosexuality, and the Anglo-Saxon Penitentials," *Journal of Medieval and Early Renaissance Studies* 26 (1996): 245–96.

48. Seemingly aware of the weakness of her case, Dinshaw points out that Zephyr and the sun are also male and that these references provide "generous evidence for a reading of 'his' [in the first line] as 'his'" (81–82). But the maleness of these later figures has nothing to do with the fact that, in Chaucer's configuration, April is male and March female.

49. Butler, *Bodies that Matter,* 228.

50. Berlant and Warner, "What Does Queer Theory Teach Us?" 343.

51. Carla Freccero, "Queer Philology with Marguerite de Navarre: Nationalism and the Castigation of Desire," in *Queering the Renaissance,* ed. Goldberg, 120.

52. Holsinger, "Sodomy and Resurrection," 245.

53. Warner, *Fear of a Queer Planet,* xxvi.

54. Urvashi Vaid, *Virtual Equality: The Mainstreaming of Gay and Lesbian Liberation* (New York: Doubleday, 1995), 37.

55. Callen is quoted by Gabriel Rotello, *Sexual Ecology: AIDS and the Destiny of Gay Men* (New York: Dutton, 1997), 204.

56. Rotello argues against "a male-oriented notion of sexual entitlement" that

presents men as "victims of our hormones." See *Sexual Ecology,* 203–4. For a more ambiguous view of the return of the culture of the 1970s, see Douglas Sadownick, *Sex between Men: An Intimate History of the Sex Lives of Gay Men Postwar to Present* (New York: HarperCollins, 1996). Sadownick acknowledges that he no longer thinks "that sex is the *sine qua non* of homosexual life," arguing instead that "homosexual libido (one's vital energies) is the motivating energy that informs . . . gay life" (12).

57. Vaid, *Virtual Equality,* 38. For an adamant position on the importance of sexualizing discourse (i.e., making everything about sex) and the supposed homophobia of "de-gaying gayness," see Leo Bersani, *Homos* (Cambridge: Harvard University Press, 1995), 4–6.

58. The usual point of origin for this expression is Adrienne Rich, "Compulsory Heterosexuality and Lesbian Existence," *Signs* 5 (1980): 631–60, reprinted in *The Lesbian and Gay Studies Reader,* ed. Henry Abelove, Michèle Aina Barale, and David M. Halperin (New York: Routledge, 1993), 227–54. But according to D. Michael Quinn, the phrase was first used by Jean Lipman-Blumen, "Changing Sex Roles in American Culture: Future Directions for Research," *Archives of Sexual Behavior* 4 (1975): 439–40. See Quinn, *Same-Sex Dynamics among Nineteenth-Century Americans: A Mormon Example* (Urbana: University of Illinois Press, 1996), 16 note 7. For an endorsement of Rich's claims with some additional reflections, see Deborah Cameron, "Ten Years On: 'Compulsory Heterosexuality' and Lesbian Existence," in *Women's Studies: Essential Readings,* ed. Stevi Jackson (New York: New York University Press, 1993), 246–48, cited in Quinn, *Same-Sex Dynamics,* 18 note 7.

59. I used Foucault in this way in "Disclosure of Sodomy."

60. Bruce Bawer, *A Place at the Table* (New York: Simon and Schuster, 1993), 56, quoted in Vaid, *Virtual Equality,* 38.

61. See, for example, Justin Hayford's review of Sullivan's *Virtually Normal* (New York: Knopf, 1995), in *Chicago Reader,* 8 September 1995, 10, 12, 14 (a review circulated nationally). For related essays by Sullivan, Bawer, and others, see Bruce Bawer, ed., *Beyond Queer: Challenging Gay Left Orthodoxy* (New York: Free Press, 1996). Sullivan, Michelangelo Signorile, Larry Kramer, and Gabriel Rotello have been labeled "turdz," meaning neoconservatives, by the New York group known as Sex Panic, led by Phillip Brian Harper, Lisa Duggen, and Michael Warner, among others. See Caleb Crain, "Pleasure Principles," *Linguafranca* 7 (October 1997): 26–37.

62. For a summary of the impact of the Kinsey studies, see John D'Emilio, *Sexual Politics, Sexual Communities: The Making of a Homosexual Minority in the United States, 1940–1970* (Chicago: University of Chicago Press, 1983), 33–37, 42–43, 93–95.

63. Barry Adam, *The Making of a Gay and Lesbian Movement* (Boston: Twayne, 1987), 67.

NOTES TO CHAPTER ONE

1. Edith Wharton, *The Age of Innocence* (New York: Scribner's Sons, 1968), 3; further references are to this edition. Nilsson, one of the great opera stars of the late nineteenth century, sang the role of Marguerite in *Faust* in the production that opened the Metropolitan Opera, the new "Opera House" Wharton mentions, in 1883. On her career, see John Dizikes, *Opera in America: A Cultural History* (New Haven: Yale University Press, 1993), 175, 215–16, 219.

2. Today, the soprano taking the role of Marguerite sings "Il m'aime," not "M'ama." It has been some time since operas were sung only in languages their audi-

ences were presumed to understand. A century ago, many operas were translated into the national language of the house staging the production. In New York, that meant not English but Italian or German, with German favored exclusively from 1884 to 1891, partly as a concession to the lower fees of German artists and partly to the large number of German immigrants in the audience. Outside New York and the Met, however, "there was plenty of opera in English." See Andrew Porter, "Translation," in *The Metropolitan Opera Encyclopedia,* ed. David Hamilton (New York: Simon and Schuster, 1987), 370–71; see also Martin Mayer, "The Metropolitan Opera," in the same volume, 226–29.

3. *Faust,* an opera in five acts, with music by Charles Gounod and text by Jules Barbier and Michel Carré, premiered in Paris in March 1859. My references are to pages in the text of the performance recorded by Carlo Rizzi, conductor, with Orchestra of the Welsh National Opera, Teldec Classics International 4509-90872-2.

4. Joseph Victor Amadée Capoul was well-known for his performances as Faust. See *The New Kobbé's Complete Opera Book,* edited and revised by the Earl of Harewood (New York: G. P. Putnam's Sons, 1976), 782.

5. Hans-Christian Schmidt, "Faust/Margarete," essay included in the text of *Faust* cited above, 26.

6. *Faust* was so popular that by 1894 New Yorkers sometimes called the Metropolitan Opera House the "Faustspielehaus." See Dizikes, *Opera in America,* 288.

7. *Faust* played thirty-seven times in Paris in 1858, its first season. Gounod added a ballet and set spoken dialogue to music for a revival in 1869. By 1887, the work had been performed 500 times in Paris; eight years later another 500 performances had been given, and by 1902 *Faust* had been performed 1,250 times in the city. See "Faust," the introductory essay by H. E. Krehbiel, in *Faust: A Lyric Drama in Five Acts,* libretto by J. Barbier and M. Carré, music by Charles Gounod (New York: Schirmer, 1902), xi. Charles O'Connell reports the even greater, and no doubt exaggerated, figure of 1,000 performances between 1869 and 1878; see *The Victor Book of the Opera* (Camden, N.J.: RCA Manufacturing Co., 1936), 133.

8. Schmidt, "Faust/Margarete," 24.

9. I echo Caroline Walker Bynum's comments on representations of the Christ child in religious art, *Fragmentation and Redemption: Essays on Gender and the Human Body in Medieval Religion* (New York: Zone Books, 1992), 79.

10. Ralph P. Locke, "What Are These Women Doing in Opera?" in Corinne E. Blackmer and Patricia Juliana Smith, eds., *En Travesti: Women, Gender Subversion, Opera* (New York: Columbia University Press, 1995), 76.

11. Dizikes, *Opera in America,* 218. For his sources see 577 note 4.

12. Arthur Laurents is a screenwriter interviewed in *The Celluloid Closet,* a 1996 film directed by Jeffrey Friedman and Rob Epstein and distributed by Sony Classics Pictures, based on Vito Russo, *The Celluloid Closet: Homosexuality in the Movies,* rev. ed. (New York: Harper and Row, 1987).

13. See Corinne E. Blackmer and Patricia Juliana Smith, introduction to *En Travesti,* ed. Blackmer and Smith, 7–8. For an analysis of the relation of boys in women's costumes in Renaissance drama, see Bruce R. Smith, *Homosexual Desire in Shakespeare's England: A Cultural Poetics* (Chicago: University of Chicago Press, 1991), 120–57; and Stephen Orgel, "Nobody's Perfect, or Why Did the English Stage Take Boys for Women?" *South Atlantic Quarterly* 88 (1989): 7–29. Orgel argues that the threat of same-sex relations posed by cross-dressed boys was taken less seriously than dangers

that the stage posed to the control of women in the culture. See 26–28 for a summary, and, for qualifications to Orgel's connection between cross-dressing and same-sex desire, see Jonathan Goldberg, *Sodometries: Renaissance Texts, Modern Sexualities* (Stanford: Stanford University Press, 1992), 110–12. On transvestite traditions in medieval drama, see Vern L. Bullough, "Transvestism in the Middle Ages," in *Sexual Practices and the Medieval Church,* ed. Bullough and James A. Brundage (Buffalo: Prometheus Books, 1982), 52–54 (originally published as "Transvestism in the Middle Ages: A Sociological Analysis," *American Journal of Sociology* 79 [1974]: 1381–94), quote from 45.

14. This information is taken from Julian Budden, "Breeches Part," in *The New Grove Dictionary of Opera,* ed. Stanley Sadie (London: Macmillan Press, 1992), 1:592–93. A number of singers in the mid–nineteenth century specialized in masculine roles, including Marietta Alboni, a singer who influenced Walt Whitman's "Out of the Cradle Endlessly Rocking." See Dizikes, *Opera in America,* 186–87; and Robert D. Faner, *Walt Whitman and Opera* (Philadelphia: University of Pennsylvania Press, 1951).

15. Cori Ellison, "Call Me Mister," liner notes to *Call Me Mister,* a recording of trouser-role arias by Jennifer Larmore, with the Welsh National Orchestra, conducted by Carlo Rizzi, Teldec Classics International 0630-10211-2, p. 2.

16. Some prominent examples of trouser roles include Orfeo in Gluck's *Orfeo ed Euridice* (1762), Cherubino in Mozart's *Le Nozze di Figaro* (1786), and Prince Orlofsky in Johann Strauss's *Die Fledermaus* (1874). In Tchaikovsky's *Maid of Orleans* (1881), on the other hand, the title role of Joan is sung by a mezzo in trousers who plays a woman. In addition to *Der Rosenkavalier* (1911) and *Ariadne auf Naxos* (1912), Strauss used trouser roles in *Arabella* (1933), where the heroine's sister has been dressed as a boy since birth. For a full list of trouser roles, see Budden, "Breeches Part," 592–93.

17. Blackmer and Smith, *En Travesti,* 11–13.

18. Ellison, "Call Me Mister," 2.

19. Paul Rudnick, interviewed in the film *The Celluloid Closet.*

20. I generally try to distinguish gay men and lesbians but sometimes group them together as "gay people," and include bisexuals. I reserve the words "gay" and "sexuality" (as well as "homosexuality" and "heterosexuality") for attitudes and choices of men and women after World War II.

21. See Russo's "Necrology," which lists gay characters from thirty-nine films and their violent deaths, *Celluloid Closet,* 347–49.

22. Steven F. Kruger, *AIDS Narratives: Gender and Sexuality, Fiction and Science* (New York: Garland, 1996), 81–104.

23. See O'Connell, *Victor Book of the Opera,* 441.

24. My references are to pages in the text of the performance of *Der Rosenkavalier* conducted by Herbert von Karajan with the Philharmonia Orchestra and Chorus, EMI 749354 2, translation by Walter Legg.

25. Lotte Lehmann, *Five Operas and Richard Strauss,* trans. Ernst Pawel (New York: Macmillan, 1964), 45.

26. Lehmann, *Five Operas,* 123.

27. Lehmann, *Five Operas,* 124.

28. Harewood, *New Kobbé's Complete Opera Book,* 1010.

29. Gary Schmidgall, *Literature as Opera* (New York: Oxford University Press, 1977), 278.

30. "Die ganze Steigerung von heir ab durchaus parodistisch." I quote the markings from Richard Strauss, *Der Rosenkavalier: Comedy for Music in Three Acts by Hugo*

von Hofmannsthal, English trans. by Alfred Kalisch (London: Fürstner Limited, 1911), 6–8. See the musical illustrations by William Mann, "Introductory Note," accompanying the recording conducted by Karajan, *Der Rosenkavalier,* 13.

31. See David M. Halperin, *One Hundred Years of Homosexuality: And Other Essays on Greek Love* (New York: Routledge, 1990), 29–38.

32. On love between a "feminine lesbian" and a "masculine one" in the context of a discussion of lesbian identity, see Teresa de Lauretis, "Sexual Indifference and Lesbian Representation," *Theater Journal* 40 (1988): 155–77, reprinted in *The Lesbian and Gay Studies Reader,* ed. Henry Abelove, Michèle Aina Barala, and David M. Halperin (New York: Routledge, 1993), 141–58.

33. Blackmer and Smith, *En Travesti,* 14. Another example is the trouser role of the Composer in Strauss's *Ariadne auf Naxos,* also with text by von Hofmannsthal, written immediately after *Der Rosenkavalier,* and first heard in 1912 in a one-act version designed to follow a performance of Molière's *Le Bourgeois Gentilhomme. Ariadne* premiered in a new, two-act version (without the play) in 1916. The opera was first performed in the United States in Philadelphia in 1928, with Nelson Eddy in the cast (Harewood, *New Kobbé's Complete Opera Book,* 1018–19).

34. Terry Castle, "In Praise of Brigitte Fassbänder: Reflections on Diva-Worship," in *En Travesti,* ed. Blackmer and Smith, 43–44. See also Castle, *The Apparitional Lesbian: Female Homosexuality and Modern Culture* (New York: Columbia University Press, 1993), 230.

35. It is a pleasure to thank John Ruffing for this and other intriguing suggestions.

36. I quote the English translation by Walter Legg that accompanies the 1957 recording conducted by Herbert von Karajan, *Der Rosenkavalier.*

37. Lehmann, *Five Operas,* 129.

38. Owen Jander, "Breeches Part," in *The New Grove Dictionary of Music and Musicians,* ed. Stanley Sadie (London: Macmillan, 1980), 3:249.

39. Lehmann, *Five Operas,* 144; the dialogue is included in the story adaptation by Anthony Burgess, *The Cavalier of the Rose* (New York: Little, Brown, and Co., 1982), 92–95.

40. Smith, *Homosexual Desire in Shakespeare's England,* 153.

41. For a discussion of cross-dressing, see Marjorie Garber, *Vested Interests: Cross-dressing and Cultural Anxiety* (New York: Routledge, 1991). For criticism of Garber's methodology and assumptions, see the review by Anne Hollander, "Dragtime: The Professor, the Transvestite, and the Meaning of Clothes," *New Republic,* 31 August 1992, 34–41.

42. See Catherine Clément, *Opera, or the Undoing of Women* (Minneapolis: University of Minnesota Press, 1988), 18–23, and Arthur Gross and Roger Parker, *Reading Opera* (Princeton: Princeton University Press, 1988), 1–11, for arguments about the importance of operatic text. Susan McClary has made a case for feminist readings of musical language; see *Feminine Endings: Music, Gender, and Sexuality* (Minnesota: University of Minnesota Press, 1991).

43. Performances at the Grand Ole Opry in Nashville are broadcast live; those in the audience hear the same commercials as those listening in their homes. This is not true at the Metropolitan Opera, where the audience attending the performance is not constrained by the broadcast program.

44. Wayne Koestenbaum, *The Queen's Throat: Opera, Homosexuality, and the Mystery of Desire* (New York: Poseidon Press, 1993), 42, 67. He comments that *Opera News*

included pictures of blind fans and asks if opera fans are "blind to the possibly queer ramifications of their taste? Or is queerness just another form of sightlessness?" (77).

45. Curtis Price, "*Dido and Aeneas* in Context," in *Purcell: "Dido and Aeneas," An Opera,* ed. Curtis Price (New York: W. W. Norton, 1986), 15–19; and, in the same edition, A. Margaret Laurie, "Allegory, Sources, and Early Performance History," 53–59.

46. Robert Worth Frank, Jr., *Chaucer and "The Legend of Good Women"* (Cambridge: Harvard University Press, 1972), 57.

47. The libretto of *Dido and Aeneas* is quoted from Price, *Purcell,* 63–76. References to act and line number are given in the text.

48. Morris's commentary is quoted from the program copy for the performances of *Dido and Aeneas* given in Chicago in April 1996.

49. Joan Acocella, *Mark Morris* (New York: Farrar, Strauss, Giroux, 1993), 98.

50. Price, "*Dido and Aeneas* in Context," 6–8. The opera has been seen as an allegory about the Glorious Revolution of 1688 and the Dutch king William and his marriage to Mary II.

51. Judith A. Periano, "I Am an Opera: Identifying with Purcell's *Dido and Aeneas,*" in *En Travesti,* ed. Blackmer and Smith, 124–25.

52. John von Rhein, review of *Dido and Aeneas,* Chicago *Tribune,* 18 April 1996, section B, p. 2.

53. Acocella, *Mark Morris,* 101.

54. Periano argues that the Sorceress "might have been a drag role." She also notes that "Curtis Price and Irena Cholij have argued that in the professional performances of *Dido and Aeneas,* the Sorceress was, indeed, sung by a bass." See "I Am an Opera," 125.

55. Curtis Price, "Dido and Aeneas," in *Grove Dictionary of Opera,* 1:1169. This view is contested in Periano, "I Am an Opera." Periano argues that there is really no authoritative text of the opera or its initial conditions of performance and believes that the girls' school performance could have been a substantial one, even though critics "deny the possibility of an entirely female and an entirely amateur cast" (105). "Given the fashionable and educated audience, the private forum, and the probable talent and amateurish enthusiasm of the young students, it is perfectly reasonable that Purcell took the opportunity to experiment and write a tragic opera 'at a time when operas were hardly ever tragic and when England had no real opera'" (106), quoting Price, introduction to *Purcell,* vii.

56. Morris follows the Hoffmann tale in naming characters; hence the young girl is named Marie, not Clara, in his dance.

57. I base my summary on *The Nutcracker* as produced by the American Ballet Theater and filmed in 1977, starring Mikhail Barishnikov and Gelsey Kirkland (MGM/UA Home Video).

58. Acocella, *Mark Morris,* 103; see also 112 on the absence of such partnering in Morris's work and much modern dance.

59. Andrew Sullivan, *Virtually Normal: An Argument about Homosexuality* (New York: Knopf, 1995), 154–55.

60. Locke, "What Are These Women Doing in Opera?" 74. Locke refers to Koestenbaum's *Queen's Throat,* a book that seems to take conventions of female hysteria as a point of departure for gay men's identification with the suffering heroines of opera. I think it is also true that gay men identify with these characters because, like them, some gay men are also scorned and mistreated by heterosexual men they desire,

admire, even love. For an analysis of Koestenbaum's work in the context of queer theory, see Kevin Kopelson, "Metropolitan Opera/Suburban Identity," in *The Work of Opera: Genre, Nationhood, and Sexual Difference,* ed. Richard Dellamora and Daniel Fischlin (New York: Columbia University Press, 1997), 297–313.

61. Sullivan, *Virtually Normal,* 9.

62. Urvashi Vaid, *Virtual Equality: The Mainstreaming of Gay and Lesbian Liberation* (New York: Doubleday, 1995), 1–34.

63. Smith, *Homosexual Desire in Shakespeare's England,* 17–18.

NOTES TO CHAPTER TWO

1. Bruce R. Smith, *Homosexual Desire in Shakespeare's England: A Cultural Poetics* (Chicago: University of Chicago Press, 1991), 17–18.

2. See Thomas Stehling, trans., *Medieval Latin Poems of Male Love and Friendship* (New York: Garland, 1984), for samples from the late classical period to the fourteenth century.

3. Clare A. Lees, "Engendering Religious Desire: Sex, Knowledge, and Christian Identity in Anglo-Saxon England," *Journal of Medieval and Early Modern Studies* 27 (1997): 19.

4. Lees, "Engendering Religious Desire," 19.

5. For arguments for and against the role of Aphrodite as a model for transvestite saints, see Hippolyte Delehaye, *The Legends of the Saints,* trans. Donald Attwater (London: Geoffrey Chapman, 1962), 119–69, especially 150–56, where Delehaye discusses several transvestite saints and vigorously disputes the relation of Aphrodite or Venus to any of them. The best discussion of medieval cross-dressing is Vern L. Bullough, *Sexual Variance in Society and History* (New York: John Wiley, 1976), 364–69.

6. See Vern L. Bullough, "Transvestism in the Middle Ages," in *Sexual Practices and the Medieval Church,* ed. Bullough and James A. Brundage (Buffalo: Prometheus Books, 1982), 45.

7. To gauge the relative frequencies of these terms, consult Antonette diPaolo Healey and Richard L. Venezky, eds., *A Microfiche Concordance to Old English* (Toronto: Pontifical Institute of Mediaeval Studies, 1980). Other words might be taken as ambiguous gender markers; "dryhtlic," for example, which means "lordly" as well as "noble," describes Hildeburh, the woman survivor (and victim) of the Finnsburg episode. See Fr. Klaeber, ed., *"Beowulf" and the Fight at Finnsburg,* 3d ed. with supplements (Lexington, Mass.: D. C. Heath and Co., 1953), line 1157.

8. Citations from Joseph Bosworth and T. Northcote Toller, eds., *An Anglo-Saxon Dictionary* (Oxford: Oxford University Press, 1898).

9. Ælfric, "De transitu Mariae Aegyptiace," in *Ælfric's Lives of Saints,* ed. Walter W. Skeat, EETS, OS, 76, 82, 94, 114 (London: Oxford University Press, 1966), 2:14. References to line number are given in the text; translations here and elsewhere are mine unless otherwise noted. *EETS, OS* refers to Early English Text Society, original series. Other series referred to below are ES (extra series) and SS (special series).

10. For a good overview of Ælfric's life, see Jonathan Wilcox, ed., *Ælfric's Prefaces,* Durham Medieval Texts 9 (Durham: Durham Medieval Texts, 1994), 1–15. On the authorship of the text, see Hugh Magennis, "Contrasting Features in the Non-Ælfrician Lives in the Old English *Lives of Saints,*" *Anglia* 104 (1996): 332–36.

11. Skeat, *Ælfric's Lives of Saints,* 1:4, lines 41–45. "National" saints are those honored by "angel-cynn mid freols-dagum," by the English nation with festivals, while

monastic saints are honored by "mynster-menn mid heora enungum betwux him," by monks in their offices among themselves.

12. Wilcox, *Ælfric's Prefaces,* 50. See 45–51 for a discussion of this preface, the variety of texts included in this collection, and the custom of reading aloud.

13. "Natale Sancte Agathe Uirginis," in *Ælfric's Lives of Saints,* ed. Skeat, 1:194–209. On authorship, see Paul E. Szarmach, *"Ælfric's Women Saints: Eugenia,"* in *New Readings on Women in Old English Literature,* ed. Helen Damico and Alexandra Hennessey Olsen (Bloomington: Indiana University Press, 1990), 156 note 3. See Gopa Roy, "Female Saints in Male Disguises: The Old English *Lives* of St Eugenia and St Euphrosyne: A Bibliographical Guide," *Medieval Sermon Studies Newsletter* 31 (1993): 47–53.

14. See Bullough, *Sexual Variance in Society and History,* 367–68.

15. Hans Hecht, ed., *Bischof Wærferths von Worcester Übersetzung der Dialoge Gregors des Grossen* (1900–1907; reprint, Darmstadt: Wissenschaftliche Buchgesellschaft, 1965), book 4, chap. 14, p. 279, lines 7–12. There is a brief commentary on Galla in Malcolm Godden, "Wærferth and King Alfred: The Fate of the Old English *Dialogues,"* in *Alfred the Wise,* ed. Jane Roberts and Janet L. Nelson with Malcolm Godden (Cambridge: D. S. Brewer, 1997), 49–50.

16. See Danielle Jacquart and Claude Thomasset, *Sexuality and Medicine in the Middle Ages* (Princeton: Princeton University Press, 1988), 73, for medical views that held that "men are hotter than women and for this reason are hairier." See also 13 and 59–62 regarding the association of heat with sperm.

17. "Eodem die natale Sancte Eugenie Uirginis," in *Ælfric's Lives of Saints,* ed. Skeat, 1:24–50; references to line number are given in the text. Ælfric compresses the historical material in his source and removes names and even whole episodes. His treatment of his source is examined by Gopa Roy, "A Virgin Acts Manfully: Ælfric's *Life of St. Eugenia* and the Latin Versions," *Leeds Studies in English* 23 (1992): 1–27. See also Magennis, "Contrasting Features," 322–23. By making the text less historically specific, Ælfric clearly increased its power to speak to his own time.

18. The word that I have translated as "wanton," "myltestre," is an Old English gloss for "prostitute," "meretricem," but it seems harsh to call Melantia a prostitute, and Skeat's "wanton woman" seems better for the context (35, line 21).

19. Szarmach comments that the scribes of the text were unsure which pronouns to use at this point. See "Ælfric's Women Saints," 150.

20. See *Aldhelm: The Poetic Works,* trans. Michael Lapidge and James L. Rosier (Cambridge: D. S. Brewer, 1985). The *Carmen de virginitate* is translated by Rosier, 97–167; see 145, line 1920.

21. Jane Tibbetts Schulenburg, "Women's Monastic Communities, 500–1100: Patterns of Expansion and Decline," *Signs* 14 (1988–89): 261–92. For a skeptical view of the early Anglo-Saxon period as a "golden age" of female monasticism and for additional bibliography, see Clare A. Lees and Gillian R. Overing, "Birthing Bishops and Fathering Poets: Bede, Hild, and the Relations of Cultural Production," *Exemplaria* 6 (1994): 35–65.

22. The life is incorrectly titled by Skeat "Euphrasia or Euphrosyne"; the text refers only to Euphrosyne ("Natale Sancte Eufrasiæ Virginis," in *Ælfric's Lives of Saints,* 2: 334–55; references to line number are given in the text). See Magennis, "Contrasting Features," 342–47, for observations on Ælfric's handling of his source.

23. Robert Spindler, *Das altenglische Bussbuch (sog. Confessionale Pseudo-Egberti)*

(Leipzig: B. Tauchnitz, 1934): "If a man sleeping in church releases his seed, he is to rise and sing the psalter" ("Gyf man on cyrican slæpende his sæd ageote, arise and singe psaltere," 8d, p. 178). "Whoever fornicates in church, let the bishop judge that and then punish as it seems right to him" ("Swa hwylc man swa on cyrcan hæme, deme þæt biscop and ðonne witnige swa him riht ðince," 9c, p. 178).

24. "Natale Sancte Eufrasiæ Virginis," 2:355, line 14.

25. The Latin text is quoted and translated by Szarmach, "Ælfric's Women Saints," from the *Vitae Patrum,* in *Patrologiae cursus completus, Series Latina,* 221 vols., ed. J. P. Migne (Paris: J. P. Migne, 1844–55), 73:153, col. 614.

26. I quote the New Revised Standard Version from *The Complete Parallel Bible* (New York: Oxford University Press, 1993), 3068.

27. Roy, "Virgin Acts Manfully," 9.

28. Roy, "Virgin Acts Manfully," 12.

29. Szarmach, "Ælfric's Women Saints," 153.

30. Benjamin Thorpe, ed., *The Sermones Catholici of Homilies of Ælfric,* 2 vols. (London, 1844), 1:188, quoted in part in Janet M. Bately, "Old English Prose," in *The Cambridge Companion to Old English Literature,* ed. Malcolm Godden and Michael Lapidge (Cambridge: Cambridge University Press, 1991), 79. For another translation and commentary, see Roy, "Virgin Acts Manfully," 6.

31. Quoted and translated in Roy, "Virgin Acts Manfully," 3.

32. Male homosexual intercourse was severely punished in the penitentials. Handbooks of penance repeatedly condemn such relations, and the Benedictine Rule repeatedly inveighs against even kissing between brothers. See Pierre J. Payer, *Sex and the Penitentials: The Development of a Sexual Code, 550–1150* (Toronto: University of Toronto Press, 1984), 135–39. The Anglo-Saxon regulations against same-sex intercourse are analyzed in chapter 4.

33. Simon Gaunt, "Straight Minds/'Queer' Wishes in Old French Hagiography," in *Premodern Sexualities,* ed. Louise Fradenburg and Carla Freccero (New York: Routledge, 1996), 164–65. The "risk" of same-sex attraction, he believes, is enhanced rather than curbed because the cross-dressing "forces us (and the monks . . .)" to question what is meant by "man" and "woman" as categories (166). As I have demonstrated, Old English discourse on manly women shows no confusion about these categories whatsoever. Gaunt responds to my analysis of this episode in "When Women Aren't Enough," *Speculum* 68 (1993): 445–71, reprinted in *Studying Medieval Women: Sex, Gender, Feminism,* ed. Nancy F. Partner (Cambridge, Mass.: Medieval Academy of America, 1993), 140–66. This episode in the life of Euphrosyne is also briefly noted by John Boswell, "Revolutions, Universals, and Sexual Categories," in *Hidden from History: Reclaiming the Gay and Lesbian Past,* ed. Martin Duberman, Martha Vicinus, and George Chauncey, Jr. (New York: Penguin, 1989), 28.

34. Seeking to historicize his analysis, Gaunt notes that the Old French text exists in four manuscripts (163) and suggests that "[t]he manuscript tradition indicates that this text is more central to medieval literary culture than modern scholarship has allowed." He asks, "Could this in part be a result of its casual treatment of transvestism and homosexuality?" (165). Presumably if such narratives were "central" or "more central" to medieval French culture, the culture could be said to have been accepting of same-sex behavior and to have regarded such behavior as casually as the texts supposedly do. But if texts in which Satan takes human form and cross-dresses to tempt men sexually are common in medieval French literature, Gaunt should have said so. He

notes that only two narratives about cross-dressed women saints have survived in Old French, so the odds are not good (162). The appeal of the text could also be attributed to its swift suppression of same-sex desire, and it is possible that medieval readers were less interested in the text's sexual content than in its other features.

35. Szarmach, "Ælfric's Women Saints," 155.

36. Lees, "Engendering Religious Desire," 31–35.

37. Michael Lapidge, "The Saintly Life in Anglo-Saxon England," in *Cambridge Companion,* ed. Godden and Lapidge, 261.

38. Bernadette J. Brooten, *Love between Women: Early Christian Responses to Female Homoeroticism* (Chicago: University of Chicago Press, 1996), 324–25, an analysis that emphasizes the asymmetry of the gender hierarchy.

39. On Clement and his influence, see Brooten, *Love between Women,* 320–36; for comments about women who "behave like men," see 325.

40. Bullough, *Sexual Variance in Society and History,* 362. Penitentials mentioning male transvestism include the *Penitential* of Silos, *St. Hubert's Penitential,* and the *Merseberg B Penitential.* The *St. Hubert's* and *Merseberg B* penitentials are found in *Paenitentialia minora Franciae et Italiae saeculi VIII–IX,* ed. Raymond Kottje with Ludger Körntgen and Ulrike Spengler-Reffgen (Turnhout, Belgium: Brepols, 1994); see canon 42, p. 60, and canon 29, p. 176, respectively.

41. Brooten, *Love between Women,* 104.

42. See the introduction to Paulus Orosius, *The Seven Books of History against the Pagans,* trans. Roy J. Deferrari, Fathers of the Church 50 (Washington, D.C.: Catholic University of America Press, 1964), xv–xx.

43. Orosius, *Seven Books of History,* 38, par. 19.

44. Janet M. Bately, ed., *The Old English Orosius,* EETS, ES, 6 (London: Oxford University Press, 1980), book 1, chap. 3, p. 32, lines 14–23.

45. See Alan Bray, *Homosexuality in Renaissance England* (1982; reprint, New York: Columbia University Press, 1995), 86–87, 130–31 note 77; and, for recent remarks, Jonathan Goldberg, *Sodometries: Renaissance Texts, Modern Sexualities* (Stanford: Stanford University Press, 1992), 110–11.

46. Bately notes that this is a rare word and that its meaning is ambiguous, either "very powerful" or "deserving of condemnation." See Bately, *Old English Orosius,* 222–23 note 32/16–17.

47. References to "softness" or "weakness" appear in the Anglo-Saxon penitentials. The *Canons of Theodore* describes men who have sex with men as "hnesclice swa forlegene" ("wanton or soft as the adulteress"; in *Ancient Laws and Institutes of England,* ed. Benjamin Thorpe [London: Commissioners on the Public Records, 1840], 2:228, canons 68.5–6). For the text, see below, chapter 4, appendix 2. Old English "hnescnysse" means "weakness." See Josef Raith, ed., *Die altenglische Version des Halitgar'schen Bussbuches (sog. Poenitentiale Pseudo-Ecgberti),* 2d ed., Bibliothek der Angelsächsischen Prosa 13 (1933; reprint, Darmstadt: Wissenschaftliche Buchgesellschaft, 1964), canon 57, pp. 66–67. A confessional prayer in another Anglo-Saxon penitential contrasts "anything soft or hard" ("æghwæt hnesces oððe heardes"). See Roger Fowler, "A Late Old English Handbook for the Use of a Confessor," *Anglia* 83 (1965): 18, lines 54–55. "Hneslice" would seem to correspond to Old Norse "blauðr," meaning "*soft, weak,*" answering Latin *mollis.* See Carol J. Clover, "Regardless of Sex: Men, Women, and Power in Early Northern Europe," in *Studying Medieval Women,* ed. Partner, 62.

48. Bately, *Old English Orosius,* 33:20–25.

49. See Clover, "Regardless of Sex," 70–75.

50. The hall is a complex symbol in Anglo-Saxon literature; for an extended analysis, see James W. Earl, *Thinking about "Beowulf"* (Stanford: Stanford University Press, 1994), 53–61, 67–71, 114–29.

51. Quotations are from Klaeber, *Beowulf;* references to line number are given in the text.

52. See Klaeber, *Beowulf,* 372, for "nobly" as the definition of "manlice," and for "generously" see E. Talbot Donaldson, trans., *Beowulf: A New Prose Translation* (New York: W. W. Norton, 1966), 19. Donaldson's translation is reprinted in the *Norton Anthology of English Literature,* vol. 1, ed. M. H. Abrams, 6th ed. (New York: W. W. Norton, 1993), 47. "Manlice" is translated as "manfully, generously" by Howell D. Chickering, Jr., *Beowulf: A Dual-Language Edition* (New York: Doubleday, 1977), 109, line 1045.

53. "Vir," the root of "virtue," is the Latin for "man," hence "virtuous," meaning "manly."

54. The other thing Hrothgar expects, or would like to, is that he and Beowulf will meet again; he has, after all, asked him to come back soon. For a different translation of the last lines, see Thomas Wright, "Hrothgar's Tears," *Modern Philology* 65 (1967): 39–44. Chickering (*Beowulf,* 348) comments unfavorably on Wright's version. For a survey of critical views and an analysis of this scene in Lacanian terms, see Mary Dockray-Miller, "*Beowulf*'s Tears of Fatherhood," *Exemplaria* 10 (1998): 1–28.

55. Chickering, *Beowulf,* 348. Chickering's reading of this episode, 347–48, is a model of good sense. He mentions Hrethel, Beowulf's foster father, and Beowulf's lack of a son.

56. John M. Hill, *The Cultural World in "Beowulf"* (Toronto: University of Toronto Press, 1994), 131.

57. David M. Halperin, *One Hundred Years of Homosexuality: And Other Essays on Greek Love* (New York: Routledge, 1990), 75–87.

58. Christopher Marlowe, *Edward II,* scene 4, line 394, in *The Complete Works of Christopher Marlowe,* vol. 3, ed. Richard Rowland (Oxford: Clarendon, 1994), 23.

59. Halperin, *One Hundred Years,* 86–87. See also Smith, *Homosexual Desire in Shakespeare's England,* 31–77, "Combatants and Comrades," a chapter concerned with Renaissance responses to male-male pairs in classical texts.

60. Halperin, *One Hundred Years,* 86–87.

61. Gillian R. Overing has suggested that Beowulf is both neurotic and hysteric (in the sense that, as a hero, he unsettles certain categories of meaning); see *Language, Sign, and Gender in "Beowulf"* (Carbondale: University of Southern Illinois Press, 1990), 84–85. These remarks, extended in a revealing way, prompted one reviewer to remark that "a book which describes Beowulf as both gay and a hysteric is unprofitable." See Alexander Hennessey Olsen's review, *Speculum* 67 (1992): 1026. Overing does not suggest that Beowulf is "gay," but she does analyze "the strength of expressed masculine desire in the poem" and observes that "marriage is valued as an extension" of the larger emotional context created by "the bonds of loyalty and friendship forged between men" (74). See also her discussion of "love of the same as a means of developing solidarity against the other," a bond she describes as "exclusively masculine" (72). This too is an apt context for analyzing *Beowulf.*

62. All editors seem to agree on the construction "wiflufan," but the "woman" ("wif") herself is missing from the manuscript, where only "ufan" now survives on

folio 175v, line 4 (Julius Zupitza, ed., *Beowulf: Reproduced in Facsimile from the Unique Manuscript, British Museum MS. Cotton Vitellius A.xv,* 2d ed., EETS, OS, 245 [1882; reprint, London: Oxford University Press, 1959], 95, line 4). See also Kevin S. Kiernan, *The Thorkelin Transcripts of "Beowulf,"* Anglistica 25 (Copenhagen: Rosenkilde and Bagger, 1986), 1–34; letters lost on folio 175v are noted on p. 77.

63. *The Wife's Lament* is found in *The Exeter Book,* ed. George Philip Krapp and Elliott van Kirk Dobbie, Anglo-Saxon Poetic Records 3 (1936; reprint, New York: Columbia University Press, 1966), 210–11. See Patricia A. Belanoff, "Women's Songs, Women's Language: *Wulf and Eadwacer* and *The Wife's Lament*," in *New Readings on Women in Old English Literature,* ed. Damico and Olsen, 193–203, especially 199 on the role of longing in *The Wife's Lament.*

64. Marilyn Desmond, "The Voice of Exile: Feminist Literary History and the Anonymous Anglo-Saxon Poem," *Critical Inquiry* 16 (1990): 587. *Wulf and Eadwacer* is found in *Exeter Book,* ed. Krapp and Dobbie, 179–80.

65. For an analysis of the speaker's role in this poem, see Desmond, "Voice of Exile"; Desmond discusses the question of the speaker's sex, 574–75 note 5. One translation that omits the hints of sexual contact in the lines I quote is S. A. J. Bradley, trans. and ed., *Anglo-Saxon Poetry* (London: J. M. Dent and Sons, 1982), 385: "My friends, loved while they lived, are in earth; they keep their rest while I in the dawning pace alone under the oak-tree around this earthen dug-out."

66. *The Wanderer* and *The Seafarer* are found in *Exeter Book,* ed. Krapp and Dobbie, 134–37 and 143–47, respectively. For an analysis of exile as a theme in these works, see Stanley B. Greenfield, "The Formulaic Expression of the Theme of 'Exile' in Anglo-Saxon Poetry," *Speculum* 30 (1955): 200–206, reprinted in *Essential Articles for the Study of Old English Poetry,* ed. J. B. Bessinger, Jr., and Stanley J. Kahrl (Hamdon, Conn.: Archon, 1968), 352–62.

67. *Maxims II,* ed. Elliott van Kirk Dobbie, in *The Anglo-Saxon Minor Poems,* Anglo-Saxon Poetic Records 6 (1941; reprint, New York: Columbia University Press, 1966), 55–57.

68. *Precepts* is found in *Exeter Book,* ed. Krapp and Dobbie, 140–43. In ten sections, it urges restraint in word and deed, a definition of wisdom or wise conduct generic in Old English.

69. Chickering, *Beowulf,* 348.

70. Chickering, *Beowulf,* 347.

71. *Wanderer,* in *Exeter Book,* ed. Krapp and Dobbie, 134–37.

72. T. P. Dunning and A. J. Bliss, eds., *The Wanderer* (London: Methuen, 1969), 112. They note that "he" in line 43 might well refer to the lord, not the retainer (113).

73. For a reading of the dream as *vana illusio,* bringing with it "an image of and the desire for a beloved who is no longer accessible," see Andrew Galloway, "Dream Theory in *The Dream of the Rood* and *The Wanderer,*" *Review of English Studies* 45 (1994): 482.

74. J. S. P. Tatlock, *The Legendary History of Britain: Geoffrey of Monmouth's "Historia regum Britanniae" and Its Early Vernacular Versions* (Berkeley and Los Angeles: University of California Press, 1950), 356–57.

75. L. J. Downer, ed., *Leges Henrici Primi* (Oxford: Clarendon, 1972), law 78, sec. 2c, p. 245.

76. For a general introduction to this text in the context of Alfred's other translations, see Allen J. Frantzen, *King Alfred* (Boston: G. K. Hall, 1986), 67–88. For a con-

troversial revision of Alfred's biography, see Alfred P. Smyth, *King Alfred the Great* (Oxford: Oxford University Press, 1995), 577–83; Smyth would seem to agree with my assessment that Alfred did not successfully come to terms with the complexity of the text he and his helpers set out to translate.

77. The Old English is quoted from Thomas A. Carnicelli, ed., *King Alfred's Version of St. Augustine's "Soliloquies"* (Cambridge: Harvard University Press, 1969), 75–76. References to page and line number are given in the text.

78. Ruth Waterhouse, "Tone in Alfred's Version of St. Augustine's *Soliloquies,"* in *Studies in Earlier Old English Prose,* ed. Paul E. Szarmach (Albany: State University of New York Press, 1986), 69. The "-ne" ending on "oðerne" is singular, not plural, and it is masculine; the plural or feminine ending would be "-e."

79. Henry Lee Hargrove, ed., *King Alfred's Old English Version of St. Augustine's "Soliloquies,"* Yale Studies in English 22 (New York: Henry Holt and Co., 1904), 26. Lees also treats Wisdom as neuter, "Engendering Religious Desire," 27.

80. This translation of Augustine's original is taken from Augustine, *The Solilo-quies,* trans. John H. S. Burleigh, in *Augustine: Earlier Writings,* Library of Christian Classics 6 (Philadelphia: Westminster Press, 1953), p. 37, chap. 13, par. 22.

81. Augustine, *Soliloquies,* pp. 35–36, chap. 12, par. 20.

82. Bodily pain would have been familiar to Alfred, a celebrated warrior whose *Life,* by Asser, one of Alfred's bishop, reports that the king was often ill. Asser's *Life* is translated by Simon Keynes and Michael Lapidge, *Alfred the Great* (Harmondsworth, Middlesex: Penguin, 1983), 67–110; see 88–91 for references to Alfred's illness. Smyth regards Asser's account of Alfred's health as greatly exaggerated and characterizes it as "hagiographical borrowing and invention." Smyth argues that the *Life* itself is a forg-ery. See Smyth, *King Alfred the Great,* 204.

83. Augustine, *Soliloquies,* p. 37, chap. 13, par. 23.

84. Ælfric uses the figure in "Preface to Genesis," in *The Old English Version of the Heptateuch: Ælfric's Treatise on the Old and New Testaments and His Preface to Genesis,* ed. S. J. Crawford, EETS, OS, 160 (1922; reprint, London: Oxford University Press, 1969), 77, lines 41–43.

85. Carolyn Dinshaw, "A Kiss Is Just a Kiss: Heterosexuality and Its Consolations in *Sir Gawain and the Green Knight,"* Diacritics 24 (1994): 210–11.

86. Thomas Symons, ed., *Regularis concordia* (London: Thomas Nelson and Sons, 1953), foreword, par. 11: "Domi uero degentes, non solum fratres sed etiam abbates, adolescentes uel puerulos non brachiis amplexando uel labris leuiter deosculando" ("In the monastery moreover let neither monks nor abbots embrace or kiss, as it were, youths or children"). Michael D. C. Drout has pointed out that the phrase would be more accurately translated "nor embrace with arms or lightly kiss with lips," language that underscores the sexual temptation created by this encounter. See Drout, "Imitat-ing Fathers: Tradition, Inheritance, and the Reproduction of Culture in Anglo-Saxon England," dissertation, Loyola University Chicago, 1997, 132–33.

87. According to the *Old English Handbook,* a layman who was required to lay aside his weapons was also forbidden from entering a church. "[N]e he innan cirican ne cume, ac þeah halige stowa georne sece and his giltas cyðe and him þingrædene bidde, and ænigne man ne cysse" ("he is not to come into church but should eagerly seek holy places and make his sins known, and ask intercession for himself, and he should kiss no one"; Fowler, "Late Old English Handbook," 28, lines 347–49.

88. Spindler, *Das altenglische Bussbuch,* "If a priest kisses a woman in his desire, he

is to repent that twenty days" ("Sacerd gif he mid his luste wifmon cysse, hreowsige þæ XX. daga," 8e, p. 178); "A baptized person is not allowed to eat with a catecumen nor give him the kiss; how much more so is he not allowed to do this with a heathen" ("Ne mot gefullad mid þæne gecristnodon etan ne hine cyssan, swa mycele ma swa he ne mot mid þæne hæðenan," 13b, p. 180). For Irish penitentials that punish boys who kiss, see the *Penitential* of Cummean, in *The Irish Penitentials,* ed. Ludwig Bieler, Scriptores Latini Hiberniae 5 (Dublin: Institute for Advanced Studies, 1963), "Ponamus nunc de ludis puerilibus priorum statuta patrum nostrorum," canons 2–3, pp. 126–27.

89. *Exeter Book,* ed. Krapp and Dobbie, contains several ceremonial riddles. See riddle 14, the solution being a horn (187 for text, 329 for solution); the solution to riddle 63 is cup or bowl (229–30 for text, 367 for solution); see also riddle 30a, ship (195–96 for text, 339 for solution).

90. "Each took the other in his arms; they kissed and embraced" ("Æghwæðer oðerne earme beþehte, / cyston hie ond clypton"). Compare *The Wanderer,* line 42, "clyppe ond cysse." See Kenneth R. Brooks, ed., *Andreas and the Fates of the Apostles* (Oxford: Clarendon, 1961), 33, lines 1015–16.

91. Richard North, "Getting to Know the General in the *Battle of Maldon,*" *Medium Ævum* 60 (1991): 1–15.

92. *The Battle of Maldon,* in *Anglo-Saxon Minor Poems,* ed. Dobbie, 7–16.

93. Antonette diPaolo Healey et al., *Dictionary of Old English* (Toronto: Pontifical Institute of Mediaeval Studies, 1996), fasc. E.

94. Clover, "Regardless of Sex," 77.

95. The glosses are quoted from Healey, *Dictionary of Old English,* fasc. E, definitions 3.b.iii.

NOTES TO CHAPTER THREE

1. This literature is surveyed in Allen J. Frantzen, *The Literature of Penance in Anglo-Saxon England* (New Brunswick: Rutgers University Press, 1983).

2. Glenn Burger, "Kissing the Pardoner," *PMLA* 107 (1992): 1143–56; Carolyn Dinshaw, "Chaucer's Queer Touches/A Queer Touches Chaucer," *Exemplaria* 7 (1995): 75–92; Dinshaw, "A Kiss Is Just a Kiss: Heterosexuality and Its Consolations in *Sir Gawain and the Green Knight,*" *Diacritics* 24 (1994): 205–26; Steven F. Kruger, "Claiming the Pardoner: Toward a Gay Reading of Chaucer's *Pardoner's Tale,*" *Exemplaria* 6 (1994): 115–39; Kathy Lavezzo, "Sobs and Sighs between Women: The Homoerotics of Compassion in *The Book of Margery Kempe,*" in *Premodern Sexualities,* ed. Louise Fradenburg and Carla Freccero (New York: Routledge, 1996), 175–98.

3. Ruth Mazo Karras and David Lorenzo Boyd, "'Ut cum muliere': A Male Transvestite Prostitute in Fourteenth-Century London," in *Premodern Sexualities,* ed. Fradenburg and Freccero, 101–16.

4. Alan Bray, *Homosexuality in Renaissance England* (1982; reprint, New York: Columbia University Press, 1995).

5. Havelock Ellis, *Sexual Inversion,* vol. 1, part 4 of *Studies in the Psychology of Sex,* 2 vols. (1905; reprint, New York: Random House, 1936).

6. Jonathan Goldberg, *Sodometries: Renaissance Texts, Modern Sexualities* (Stanford: Stanford University Press, 1992); Goldberg, ed., *Queering the Renaissance* (Durham: Duke University Press, 1994); Gregory W. Bredbeck, *Sodomy and Interpretation: Marlowe to Milton* (Ithaca: Cornell University Press, 1991); Alan Stewart, *Close Readers: Human-*

ism and Sodomy in Early Modern England (Princeton: Princeton University Press, 1997). In *Queering the Renaissance*, see Alan Bray, "Homosexuality and Signs of Male Friendship in Elizabethan England," 40–61.

7. Bruce R. Smith, *Homosexual Desire in Shakespeare's England: A Cultural Poetics* (Chicago: University of Chicago Press, 1991).

8. For an incisive introduction to the development of gay and lesbian history, see Martin Duberman, Martha Vicinus, and George Chauncey, Jr., eds., *Hidden from History: Reclaiming the Gay and Lesbian Past* (New York: Penguin, 1989), 1–13. See also, among others, John C. Fout, ed., *Forbidden History: The State, Society, and the Regulation of Sexuality in Modern Europe* (Chicago: University of Chicago Press, 1992); Randolph Trumbach, "Gender and the Homosexual Role in Modern Western Culture: The 18th and 19th Centuries Compared," in *Homosexuality, Which Homosexuality? International Conference on Gay and Lesbian Studies*, ed. Dennis Altman, Carole Vance, Martha Vicinus, and Jeffrey Weeks (London: GMP Publishers, 1989), 149–69; and Trumbach, "The Birth of the Queen: Sodomy and the Emergence of Gender Equality in Modern Culture, 1660–1750," in *Hidden from History*, ed. Duberman et al., 129–40.

9. Paul Hallam, *The Book of Sodom* (London: Verso, 1993); Derek Jarman, *At Your Own Risk: A Saint's Testament*, ed. Michael Christie (Woodstock, N.Y.: Overlook Press, 1993). See also Jarman, *Kicking the Pricks* (Woodstock, N.Y.: Overlook Press, 1997).

10. *Preface of Gildas on Penance*, canon 1, in *The Irish Penitentials*, ed. Ludwig Bieler, Scriptores Latini Hiberniae 5 (Dublin: Institute for Advanced Studies, 1963), 60–61.

11. *Penitential* of Cummean, chap. 2, canon 9, and chap. 10, canon 15, in *Irish Penitentials*, ed. Bieler, 114–15, 128–29.

12. *Penitential* of Theodore, book 1, chap. 2, canons 5–7, in *Councils and Ecclesiastical Documents Relating to Great Britain and Ireland*, 3 vols., ed. Arthur West Haddan and William Stubbs (1871; reprint, Oxford: Clarendon, 1964), 3:178; trans. John T. McNeill and Helena M. Gamer, *Medieval Handbooks of Penance: A Translation of the Principal "Libri poenitentiales"* (1938; reprint, New York: Columbia University Press, 1990), 185.

13. For an authoritative analysis of this process, see Pierre J. Payer, *Sex and the Penitentials: The Development of a Sexual Code, 550–1150* (Toronto: University of Toronto Press, 1984), 72–114.

14. Payer, *Sex and the Penitentials*, 81–83, 98–104. Selections from Burchard's *Corrector et medicus* are translated in *Medieval Handbooks of Penance*, 321–45.

15. Payer, *Sex and the Penitentials*, 82; Michael Goodich, *The Unmentionable Vice: Homosexuality in the Later Medieval Period* (Santa Barbara: ABC-Clio, 1979), 64.

16. Mark D. Jordan, *The Invention of Sodomy in Christian Theology* (Chicago: University of Chicago Press, 1997), 45–66.

17. Peter Damian, *Book of Gomorrah: An Eleventh-Century Treatise against Clerical Homosexual Practices*, trans. Pierre J. Payer (Waterloo, Ontario: Wilfrid Laurier University Press, 1982), chap. 11, p. 52.

18. Adrian Morey, ed., *Bartholomew of Exeter: Bishop and Canonist* (Cambridge: Cambridge University Press, 1937), 170, reports that Ivo used Burchard's text in some 1,600 of 1,784 sections. See also Payer, *Sex and the Penitentials*, 76, 85, 111–13; and Vern L. Bullough, *Sexual Variance in Society and History* (New York: John Wiley, 1976),

381–82. I discuss some of this evidence in "The Disclosure of Sodomy in the Middle English *Cleanness,*" *PMLA* 111 (1996): 451–64.

19. Bullough, *Sexual Variance in Society and History,* 382.

20. See Danielle Jacquart and Claude Thomasset, *Sexuality and Medicine in the Middle Ages* (Princeton: Princeton University Press, 1988), 116–22, 155–59.

21. Jacques Despars, quoted in Jacquart and Thomasset, *Sexuality and Medicine,* 159.

22. For these dates, see Morey, *Bartholomew of Exeter,* 174; and J. J. Francis Firth, ed., *Robert of Flamborough: Liber poenitentialis* (Toronto: Pontifical Institute of Mediaeval Studies, 1971), 8–9.

23. Firth, *Robert of Flamborough,* 229–31.

24. F. Broomfield, ed., *Thomae de Chobham summa confessorum,* Analecta Mediaevalia Namurcensia 25 (Louvain: Éditions Nauwelaerts, 1968), lxii (for the date), 398–400.

25. James A. Brundage, *Law, Sex, and Christian Society in Medieval Europe* (Chicago: University of Chicago Press, 1987), 399. See also Jordan, *Invention of Sodomy,* 108–9.

26. Geoffrey Chaucer, *The Parson's Tale,* in *The Riverside Chaucer,* ed. Larry D. Benson, 3d ed. (Boston: Houghton Mifflin, 1987), p. 320, fragment 10, lines 909–10.

27. W. Nelson Francis, *The Book of Vices and Virtues,* EETS, OS, 217 (London: Oxford University Press, 1942), p. 46, lines 4–5, 10, 18.

28. Gillis Kristensson, *John Mirk's Instructions for Parish Priests,* Lund Studies in English 49 (Lund: C. W. K. Gleerup, 1974), 80, lines 223, 230–31. Some of the references given in this paragraph are noted in a brief survey of Middle English evidence concerning sodomy by Vern L. Bullough, "The Sin against Nature and Homosexuality," in *Sexual Practices and the Medieval Church,* ed. Bullough and James A. Brundage (Buffalo: Prometheus Books, 1982), 66–71; and in Bullough, *Sexual Variance in Society and History,* 385–88.

29. Frantzen, *Literature of Penance,* 7–8, 14.

30. Pierre J. Payer, "Sex and Confession in the Thirteenth Century," in *Sex in the Middle Ages,* ed. Joyce E. Salisbury (New York: Garland, 1991), 127.

31. Jordan, *Invention of Sodomy,* a work discussed in detail below.

32. Firth, *Robert of Flamborough,* 196; this passage is translated by Goodich, *Unmentionable Vice,* 57, and is discussed by Brundage, *Law, Sex, and Christian Society,* 399.

33. Bray, *Homosexuality in Renaissance England,* 7. An early version of *Studies in the Psychology of Sex* was coauthored by Ellis and John Addington Symonds (*Sexual Inversion* [London: Wilson and Macmillan, 1897; reprint, New York: Arno Press/New York Times, 1975]). Symonds's heirs withdrew permission to use his name on subsequent editions. See D. Michael Quinn, *Same-Sex Dynamics among Nineteenth-Century Americans: A Mormon Example* (Urbana: University of Illinois Press, 1996), 181 note 24, 340 note 8.

34. Ellis, *Sexual Inversion,* 39–40. Ellis gives no evidence for his citation from the penitentials, but he might have been referring to the *Preface of Gildas on Penance,* cited above, which combines "natural fornication and sodomy."

35. Bray, *Homosexuality in Renaissance England,* 7, 8.

36. Ellis, *Sexual Inversion,* 59.

37. For his analysis of "sexual inversion in women," see Ellis, *Sexual Inversion,* 195–263.

38. John Boswell, *Christianity, Social Tolerance, and Homosexuality: Gay People in Western Europe from the Beginning of the Christian Era to the Fourteenth Century* (Chicago: University of Chicago Press, 1980); Boswell, "Revolutions, Universals, and Sexual Categories," in *Hidden from History,* ed. Duberman et al., 17–36; Bray, *Homosexuality in Renaissance England,* 7. Smith, *Homosexual Desire in Shakespeare's England,* 9–12, cites both of these works by Boswell.

39. Boswell, *Christianity, Social Tolerance,* 4 note 3.

40. *The Problem of Homosexuality* was produced for the Church of England Moral Welfare Council in 1954. See Derrick Sherwin Bailey, *Homosexuality and the Western Christian Tradition* (1955; reprint, Hamden, Conn.: Archon, 1975), vii.

41. John T. Noonan, Jr., *Contraception: A History of Its Treatment by the Catholic Theologians and Canonists* (Cambridge: Harvard University Press, 1965), 532.

42. *Penitential* of Bede, 3.39, in *Councils and Ecclesiastical Documents,* ed. Haddan and Stubbs, 329: "Si in tergo, IIII annos peniteat, quia sodomiticum scelus est."

43. Bullough, *Sexual Variance in Society and History,* 347–77, 378–413. For a more general overview, see also Vern L. Bullough, *Homosexuality: A History* (New York: New American Library, 1979), 17–62.

44. Payer, *Sex and the Penitentials,* 82.

45. With few exceptions the reception of Boswell's book by the scholarly press was largely negative. Many reviewers generously acknowledged the importance of the study, but many also expressed serious doubts about Boswell's methodology and his interpretation of evidence. See reviews by James A. Brundage, *Catholic Historical Review* 68 (1982): 62–64; Vern L. Bullough, *Inquiry* 3 (1980): 28–29; and E. Christensen, *English Historical Review* 96 (1981): 852–54. For an admiring review with important criticism, see Jeremy Adams, *Speculum* 56 (1981): 350–55, who comments that Boswell at one point uses "a definition of *gay* so broad as to be useless for social history" (352). For a critique of Boswell's handling of evidence pertaining to lesbian relations, see Bernadette J. Brooten, *Love between Women: Early Christian Responses to Female Homoeroticism* (Chicago: University of Chicago Press, 1996), 10–13; and Payer, *Sex and the Penitentials,* 138. I do not deal in detail with the more limited claims of Boswell's essay "Revolutions, Universals, and Sexual Categories," 17–36. Boswell argues that essentialist, constructionist, and even normative views of sexual identity can be found in classical and medieval cultures. This essay, which cites evidence from Greek, Arabic, Anglo-Saxon, Middle English, and Old French sources, loosely correlates modern and medieval categories in order to support Boswell's assertion. The Anglo-Saxon text briefly cited is the life of Euphrosyne, discussed in chapter 2.

46. Brooten, *Love between Women,* 260–62.

47. Boswell subsequently defended this usage in "Revolutions, Universals, and Sexual Categories." His evidence for this claim is highly selective, and his position on Greek texts is opposed by David M. Halperin, "Sex before Sexuality: Pederasty, Politics, and Power in Classical Athens," in *Hidden from History,* ed. Duberman et al., 37–53.

48. Rosamond McKitterick, *The Frankish Church and the Carolingian Reforms, 789–895* (London: Royal Historical Society, 1975), 1. McKitterick devotes an entire chapter (1–19) to the significance of this document.

49. Boswell's argument is littered with irrelevancies and verges on sophistry. First he claimed that the Frankish edict is not important because it did not recommend

specific penalties, even though harsh penances are recommended. Then he sought to undermine the edict by claiming that it lacks what he considered proper scriptural authority and that it cited instead a canon from what he calls "the little-known Council of Ancyra." He questioned the authority of this widely quoted canon, saying that "it was known in the West only through an inaccurate translation" (178). The accuracy of the translation is irrelevant, as is the claim that the Council of Ancyra was "little-known." Bullough notes that Derrick Sherwin Bailey doubted whether the statutes from Ancyra were originally "directed against homosexual activity" but adds, "this was the way they were interpreted by various councils in the West." See Bullough, *Sexual Variance in Society and History,* 353. Obviously the Franks thought that their source was both accurate and reliable. The lack of specific penances for bestiality or intramale intercourse is not, of course, a sign that the Frankish canon is half-hearted or a sign of tolerance. The edict plainly says, in language Boswell quotes, that the penances for these acts are to be "dura et districta" ("hard and difficult"). See 178 note 31.

50. Regino not only used but specifically recommended penitentials by Theodore of Canterbury and Bede. His chief source for these early canons was a document called the *Penitential of Pseudo-Bede,* composed of parts of separate handbooks attributed to Bede (d. 735) and Egbert (d. 766). Neither of these texts is likely to be genuine, that attributed to Bede certainly not. But this is an example of how early English authorities, through texts attributed to them, shaped the history of same-sex relations in ecclesiastical administration. On Regino's debt to the Bede-Egbert texts, see Payer, *Sex and the Penitentials,* 78.

51. Payer, *Sex and the Penitentials,* 92–93. Boswell incorrectly described Regino's collection as an "early penitential work" (*Christianity, Social Tolerance,* 182). When Regino published *De synodalibus causis et disciplinis ecclesiasticis* in 906, penitentials had been circulating on the Continent and elsewhere for over two hundred years.

52. "While his discussion is interesting," Boswell writes, "it gives a misleading impression of the importance of the English penitentials" (182 note 43). For a critique of Boswell's arguments see Payer, *Sex and the Penitentials,* 135–39; and Jeffrey Richards, *Sex, Dissidence, and Damnation: Minority Groups in the Middle Ages* (London: Routledge, 1991), 132–33, 148–49. See also David F. Greenberg, *The Construction of Homosexuality* (Chicago: University of Chicago Press, 1988), 16–17 on Boswell's methodology, and 263–64 on Boswell's use of the penitentials. Boswell made better use of these sources in *The Kindness of Strangers: The Abandonment of Children in Western Europe from Late Antiquity to the Renaissance* (New York: Random House, 1988), 219–23, but retained some unpersuasive reservations about them (219 note 141).

53. Theodore's *Penitential* attacked as "heretical" certain customs—for example, the system used to calculate the date of Easter—in use in the Irish church; see "De his qui per heresim decipiuntur" (Concerning those who are deceived by heresy), book 1, chap. 5, 3:180–82.

54. "Quos paenitentiales vocant, quorum sunt certi errores, incerti auctores" (quoted and discussed, with similar statements, in Frantzen, *Literature of Penance,* 97–99).

55. Frantzen, *Literature of Penance,* 100–101.

56. Boswell noted that one penitential punishes homosexual acts less severely than it punished a priest for hunting (180). As Greenberg demonstrated, a careful reading of the text Boswell cited would have disproved this claim. Greenberg generously calls Boswell's statement "somewhat misleading" (*Construction of Homosexuality,* 264 note 118).

57. See the discussion of the work of the author known as Tremulous Hand of Worcester, chapter 6.

58. Damian, *Book of Gomorrah,* 10.

59. See Brundage, *Law, Sex, and Christian Society,* 597–99, a useful table that arranges the penitentials in chronological sequence. Some information regarding the early "Frankish" penitentials should be read in the light of recent research, but the table itself continues to serve as a reliable and valuable guide to the sources.

60. Allan Bérubé, *Coming Out under Fire: Gay Men and Women in World War Two* (New York: Penguin, 1991).

61. Jordan, *Invention of Sodomy,* 30 note 1, in reference to Boswell's (and Bailey's) work on Old Testament references to Sodom. Jordan otherwise cites Boswell only once, to contradict Boswell's claim that Aquinas's categorization of homosexual acts is a "concession to popular sentiment" (147). See Boswell, *Christianity, Social Tolerance,* 328.

62. Payer, *Sex and the Penitentials,* 116.

63. Bray, *Homosexuality in Renaissance England,* 24–25.

NOTES TO CHAPTER FOUR

1. John W. Baldwin, *The Language of Sex: Five Voices from Northern France around 1200* (Chicago: University of Chicago Press, 1994), xxviii.

2. David F. Greenberg, *The Construction of Homosexuality* (Chicago: University of Chicago Press, 1988), 3–4.

3. Howard Becker, *Outsiders: Studies in the Sociology of Deviance* (New York: Free Press, 1963), 162, quoted in Greenberg, *Construction of Homosexuality,* 2.

4. Æthelberht 1 (Attenborough 4–5). The early laws are cited from the translation by F. L. Attenborough, *The Laws of the Earliest English Kings* (1922; reprint, New York: AMS Press, 1974). There is a good discussion of the interaction of Anglo-Saxon law and penance in Thomas Pollock Oakley, *English Penitential Discipline and Anglo-Saxon Law in Their Joint Influence* (1923; reprint, New York: AMS Press, 1969).

5. "Pecunia ecclesiis furata sive rapta reddatur quadruplum; sæcularibus dupliciter" (*Penitential* of Theodore, in *Councils and Ecclesiastical Documents Relating to Great Britain and Ireland,* ed. Arthur West Haddan and William Stubbs (Oxford: Clarendon, 1871), book 1, chap. 3, canon 2, 3:179. This edition is hereafter cited as *CED* and sections of Theodore's text by book, chapter, and canon, e.g., 1.3.2.

6. The source for the later law collections is the edition and translation by A. J. Robertson, *The Laws of the Kings of England from Edmund to Henry I* (1925; reprint, New York: AMS Press, 1974). The laws cited are V Æthelred 4, 5, 6, 9 (Robertson 80–83); VI Æthelred 2, 5, 41 (Robertson 90–93, 102–103); VIII Æthelred 30 (Robertson 126–27).

7. The text I call the *Scriftboc* is edited by Robert Spindler, *Das altenglische Bussbuch (sog. Confessionale Pseudo-Egberti)* (Leipzig: B. Tauchnitz, 1934), hereafter abbreviated *DAB.* I refer to this text throughout as the *Scriftboc* to avoid confusion with another vernacular text called the *Poenitentiale Pseudo-Ecgberti.* The manuscript is Oxford, Bodleian Library, Laud Misc. 482, a Worcester collection from the middle of the eleventh century. For the date, see N. R. Ker, *Catalogue of Manuscripts Containing Anglo-Saxon* (Oxford: Clarendon, 1957), no. 343. The contents of this manuscript can be discerned in Spindler's apparatus and in his comparative table of the manuscript contents, *DAB* 6–8. Missing are chapter 13 on marriage, "De coniunctione et aliorum

causis," and part of chapter 14 on adultery, "De lavacro mariti vel aliorum causis" (*DAB* 181–82); chapter 15 on the rights of children, "De etate pueri vel puelle quomodo sibi dominentur" (*DAB* 183); part of chapter 17 on sexual acts in marriage, "De homicidiis vel incestis mulieribus" (*DAB* 185).

8. *Scriftboc,* chap. 16, "Item de generationibus quomodo iungunter," 19b and notes to line 269, in *DAB* 184; see Spindler's comments, 50. The source is the *Penitential* of Egbert, chap. 7, canon 1 (*CED* 3:423): "Mulier abstineat se a viro tres menses, quando concepta est antequam pariat, et post partum XL dies."

9. I am preparing an electronic database of the Anglo-Saxon penitentials.

10. Dorothy Whitelock, ed., *English Historical Documents, c. 500–1042,* 2d ed. (London: Eyre Methuen, 1979), 358.

11. Mary P. Richards, "The Manuscript Contexts of the Old English Laws: Tradition and Innovation," in *Studies in Earlier Old English Prose,* ed. Paul E. Szarmach (Albany: State University of New York Press, 1986), 171–92.

12. See Vern L. Bullough, "Formulation of Ideals: Christian Theory and Christian Practice," in *Sexual Practices and the Medieval Church,* ed. Bullough and James A. Brundage (Buffalo: Prometheus Books, 1982), 20–21; and Bullough, *Sexual Variance in Society and History* (New York: John Wiley, 1976), 348–53.

13. James A. Brundage, "Adultery and Fornication: A Study in Legal Theology," in *Sexual Practices,* ed. Bullough and Brundage, 129–34.

14. James A. Brundage, *Law, Sex, and Christian Society in Medieval Europe* (Chicago: University of Chicago Press, 1987), 132.

15. On women in the laws, see Mary P. Richards and B. Jane Stanfield, "Concepts of Anglo-Saxon Women in the Laws," in *New Readings on Women in Old English Literature,* ed. Helen Damico and Alexandra Hennessey Olsen (Bloomington: Indiana University Press, 1990), 92–93. Other important studies are Christine Fell, *Women in Anglo-Saxon England and the Impact of 1066* (Indiana: University of Indiana Press, 1984), 56–64; and Sheila C. Dietrich, "An Introduction to Women in Anglo-Saxon Society," in *The Women of England from Anglo-Saxon Times to the Present,* ed. Barbara Kanner (Hamden, Conn.: Archon Books, 1979), 32–56.

16. Brundage, *Law, Sex, and Christian Society,* 146; Brundage cites Suzanne Wemple, *Women in Frankish Society: Marriage and the Cloister, 500 to 900* (Philadelphia: University of Pennsylvania Press, 1981), 70–71.

17. Æthelberht 10, 11, 14, 16 (Attenborough 4–7).

18. Æthelberht 31 (Attenborough 8–9). See Attenborough's note to Æthelberht 31 on p. 177. Wergeld is the sum of money to be paid to a man's family upon his death.

19. Æthelberht 85 (Attenborough 14–15).

20. Alfred 10 (Attenborough 71).

21. II Cnut 50 (for a man who commits adultery; Robertson 200–201); see Whitelock, *English Historical Documents,* 358–59, 928–29.

22. II Cnut 54 (adultery with his slave), 53 (the woman who commits adultery; Robertson 200–203).

23. Fell, *Women in Anglo-Saxon England,* 64, describes two charters that record estates forfeited, one by a woman and one by a man, because the holder committed adultery. For further discussion of the charters' evidence of women's status, see Marc A. Meyer, "Land Charters and the Legal Position of Anglo-Saxon Women," in *Women of England,* ed. Kanner, 57–82.

24. I Cnut 6a, 7.2 (Robertson 162–63), 24 (Robertson 172–73); II Cnut 50, 53, 54 (Robertson 200–203). Prostitution is mentioned in VI Æthelred 7 (Robertson 92–93) and II Cnut 4 (Robertson 176–77).

25. Alfred 8, 18 (Attenborough 68–69, 72–73); I Edmund 4 (Robertson 6–7).

26. On sex during Lent, see II Cnut 47 (Robertson 200–201); on confession, see I Cnut 18b.1 (Robertson 168–69); I Cnut 23 (Robertson 172–73); on saying prayers, see I Cnut 22 (Robertson 170–72). Cnut's proclamation of 1027 addressed to Ælfric, archbishop of York, is a Latin text reporting on the king's journey to Rome. The fourth paragraph refers to the power of the keys and uses other distinctively ecclesiastical language (Robertson 146–47).

27. For connections between the laws and a penitential known as the *Old English Handbook*, see Roger Fowler, "A Late Old English Handbook for the Use of a Confessor," *Anglia* 83 (1965): 10–11.

28. Wihtred 3, 4 (Attenborough 24–25).

29. For abduction, see Æthelberht 82 (Attenborough 14–15). See James A. Brundage, "Rape and Seduction in Medieval Canon Law," in *Sexual Practices,* ed. Bullough and Brundage, 141–48. The topic is discussed extensively in Brundage, *Law, Sex, and Christian Society.* See also Pierre J. Payer, *Sex and the Penitentials: The Development of a Sexual Code, 550–1150* (Toronto: University of Toronto Press, 1984), 38, 117.

30. Alfred 11 (Attenborough 70–71).

31. For rape of a girl, see Alfred 29 (Attenborough 76–77) and for the rape of a commoner's slave and of a slave by a slave, see Alfred 25 (Attenborough 74–75).

32. See Cnut's proclamation of 1020 (15) and II Cnut 51 (Robertson 144–45, 200–203).

33. The prostitute, "horcwen," is mentioned in Edward and Guthrum 11 (Attenborough 108–9). See also VI Æthelred 7 (= II Cnut 4a; Robertson 92–93, 176–77). For discussion see Fell, *Women in Anglo-Saxon England,* 64–66.

34. Derrick Sherwin Bailey, *Homosexuality and the Western Christian Tradition* (1955; reprint, Hamden, Conn.: Archon, 1975), 147. Bailey reviews two thirteenth-century law codes that deal with sodomy, 145–46. I discuss these collections in chapter 6.

35. See Allen J. Frantzen, *The Literature of Penance in Anglo-Saxon England* (New Brunswick: Rutgers University Press, 1983), 1–18, for an introduction to this genre and related texts in the Old English period. A new introduction to the book accompanies the translation by Michel Lejeune, *La Littérature de la pénitence dans L'Angleterre Anglo-Saxonne* (Fribourg: Éditions Universitaires, 1991), ix–xxx. Oakley's *English Penitential Discipline and Anglo-Saxon Law in Their Joint Influence* is still useful. A guide to penitentials, with translations, is John T. McNeill and Helena M. Gamer, *Medieval Handbooks of Penance* (1938; reprint, New York: Columbia University Press, 1965), hereafter *MHP.* Information on dates and manuscript traditions should be supplemented by Cyrille Vogel, *Les "Libri paenitentiales,"* Typologie des Sources du Moyen Age Occidental, vol. 27 (Turnhout, Belgium: Brepols, 1978), corrected and revised in part by Allen J. Frantzen, Mise à jour du fascicule no. 27 (Turnhout, Belgium: Brepols, 1985). See also *Paenitentialia minora Franciae et Italiae saeculi VIII–IX,* ed. Raymond Kottje with Ludger Körntgen and Ulrike Spengler-Reffgen (Turnhout, Belgium: Brepols, 1994).

36. Payer, *Sex and the Penitentials,* 12.

37. I cite the editions of all these texts as they are found in *CED*. These penitentials are also available in an older edition by F. W. H. Wasserschleben, ed., *Die Bussordnungen der abendländischen Kirche* (1851; reprint, Graz: Akademische Druck–U. Verlagsanstalt, 1958). But this edition is not readily available; references therefore are to the edition by Haddan and Stubbs *(CED)*. For manuscripts of the texts attributed to "Bede" and Egbert, see works cited in note 38. For manuscripts of the various forms of Theodore's handbook, see Paul Willem Finsterwalder, ed., *Die Canones Theodori Cantuariensis und ihre Überlieferungsformen* (Weimar: Hermann Böhlaus, 1929).

38. On the manuscript connections among these texts, see my discussion in "The Penitentials Attributed to Bede," *Speculum* 58 (1983): 573–97, especially 584–85 and notes. There I accept the authorship of Egbert as genuine. For reservations see Raymond Kottje, "Erfassung und Untersuchung der frühmittelalterlichen kontinentalen Bussbücher," *Studi Medievale* 26 (1985): 948. For a more recent analysis, see R. Haggenmüller, *Die Überlieferung der Beda und Egbert zugeschriebenen Bussbücher,* Europäische Hochschulschriften, series 3, vol. 461 (Frankfurt am Main: Peter Lang, 1991). There is a good summary of the problem in *CED* 3:413–16 and in *MHP* 217–38 (which includes partial translations).

39. Halitgar's penitential is edited by H. J. Schmitz, *Die Bussbücher und das kanonische Bussverfahren* (1898; reprint, Graz: Akademische Druck–U. Verlagsanstalt, 1958), 275–300. On the text and its manuscript traditions, see Raymond Kottje, *Die Bussbücher Halitgars von Cambrai und des Hrabanus Maurus,* Beiträge zur Geschichte und Quellenkunde des Mittelalters, 8 (Berlin: Walter de Gruyter, 1980), 111–16.

40. These include Oxford, Bodleian Library, Bodley 311, a tenth-century manuscript associated with Exeter; Bodley 718, written in Exeter in the tenth century and later at Worcester; London, British Library, Royal E.xiii, a ninth-century manuscript from Brittany in England in the tenth century; Cambridge, Corpus Christi College 320, from the second half of the tenth century, with tenth- or eleventh-century Old English additions; and Cambridge, Corpus Christi College 190, a mid-eleventh-century Exeter manuscript. See Frantzen, *Literature of Penance,* 129–32, for further information.

41. Payer, *Sex and the Penitentials,* 20–21.

42. *Penitential* of Theodore, 1.7.1, *CED* 3:182. For a summary of Theodore's penances for adultery, see Payer, *Sex and the Penitentials,* 133. The canon numbers in *CED* generally but not always correspond to those used in the translation by McNeill and Gamer, *MHP* 182–215.

43. Translation based on *MHP* 209 note 12.

44. Josef Raith, ed., *Die altenglische Version des Halitgar'schen Bussbuches (sog. Poenitentiale Pseudo-Ecgberti),* Bibliothek der Angelsächsischen Prosa 13, 2d ed. (1933; reprint, Darmstadt: Wissenschaftliche Buchgesellschaft, 1964). This edition is cited hereafter as *DAV*.

45. Fowler, "Late Old English Handbook."

46. Franz Joseph Mone, ed., *Quellen und Forschungen zur Geschichte der teutschen Literatur und Sprache* (Aachen and Leipzig: Verlag von Jacob Anton Mayer, 1830), 514–28. This edition is hereafter cited as Mone. Benjamin Thorpe edited the text in two forms. He printed an extract found only in Cambridge, Corpus Christi College 190, part B, pp. 416–18, a mid-eleventh-century Exeter manuscript (date and provenance taken from Ker, *Catalogue,* no. 45B). He joined to this text canons selected from two

other manuscripts (not indicating omissions). They are Oxford, Bodleian Library, Laud Misc. 482 (see note 7 above) and Brussels, Bibliothèque royale, 8558–63, 146v–53v, an eleventh-century southeastern manuscript (Ker, *Catalogue*, no. 10). The Brussels and Oxford versions of the text are very similar, but the Oxford manuscript is missing a leaf containing material on sexual offenses. The Cambridge manuscript version contains only a fraction of the canons found in the other two manuscripts; below I refer to the Cambridge text as the *Canons of Theodore, Supplement (CTHS)*. See Benjamin Thorpe, ed., *Ancient Laws and Institutes of England,* 2 vols. (London: Commissioners on the Public Records, 1840; also published in one volume in 1840), 2:228–31, 232–39 (volume 2 hereafter cited as *ALI*). The enumeration and Latin translation are Thorpe's; there is no manuscript evidence for the latter. Thorpe confusingly prints all this material (2:228–39) as part of the fourth book of the *Old English Penitential.*

47. For the sources of the *Scriftboc,* see *DAB* 23–91. On the relation of the *Scriftboc* to the *Old English Penitential,* see *DAV* xxiii, and on the dependence of the *Old English Handbook* on the *Old English Penitential,* see Fowler, "Late Old English Handbook," 8–9.

48. Spindler prints a penance of twelve years but notes that all three manuscripts specify ten years. See *DAB* 177, note to line 121, and 28, note to 6c.

49. Spindler discusses the mistranslation of the Latin (Theodore 2.12.10); the translator, he says, "meint es mit der Ehebrecherin gar zu gut" (19zσ, *DAB* 57).

50. *Canons of Theodore (CTH)* 147 (Mone 521). See also *CTHS* 68.14 (*ALI* 2:230). The source is the *Penitential* of Theodore 1.2.19 (*CED* 3:179). See also Egbert's *Penitential* 4.4 (daughter or sister, twelve years) and 4.5 (brother, fifteen years; *CED* 3:420).

51. This unusual canon is not found in the text's chapters devoted to marriage but in a catchall concluding chapter that concerns purification and animals and miscellaneous subjects. For the source, see the *Penitential* of "Bede" 3.1–3 (*CED* 3:327).

52. Payer, *Sex and the Penitentials,* 37, 39–40, concerning "ambiguous canons" against illicit heterosexual relations. There are few such canons, and none makes a strong claim to authority.

53. Compare these divisions to those outlined by Payer, *Sex and the Penitentials,* 135–36.

54. Bernadette J. Brooten, *Love between Women: Early Christian Responses to Female Homoeroticism* (Chicago: University of Chicago Press, 1996), 49.

55. *Penitential* of Theodore 1.14.15. The version printed by Haddan and Stubbs reads, "Mulier quæ se more fornicationis adulterio conjunxerit III annos peniteat sicut fornicator" (*CED* 3:188). For "adulterio" some manuscripts read "ad alteram" ("with another [woman]"). See Theodore 1.14.15 in Wasserschleben, *Die Bussordnungen der abendländischen Kirche,* 199; and *MHP* 196.

56. Payer suggests that the "machina" is an "artificial phallus" (*Sex and the Penitentials,* 43; see also 138).

57. Although two manuscripts of the *Scriftboc* specify ten years, the Latin source and Spindler's base manuscript say three; see *DAB* 185, note to line 289.

58. Spindler has three years, but all manuscripts read "two years"; see *DAB* 185, note to line 290.

59. Vern L. Bullough, "The Sin against Nature and Homosexuality," in *Sexual Practices,* ed. Bullough and Brundage, 58–59.

60. Brooten, *Love between Women,* 324–25.

61. Vito Russo, *The Celluloid Closet: Homosexuality in the Movies,* rev. ed. (New York: Harper and Row, 1987), 55.

62. Mark D. Jordan, *The Invention of Sodomy in Christian Theology* (Chicago: University of Chicago Press, 1997), 42.

63. "Sodomiticum" appears in a list of sins that includes "luxuria, adulterium, fornicationem, sodomiticum, pollutio, libido," in an Anglo-Saxon manuscript, Cambridge, Trinity College O.2.30 (Canterbury, St. Augustine's, from the middle of the tenth century, 129v; the list is partly printed by M. R. James, *The Western Manuscripts in the Library of Trinity College, Cambridge: A Description Catalogue,* 4 vols. (Cambridge: Cambridge University Press, 1900–1904), 3:126–29. My thanks to Thomas N. Hall for this reference.

64. See commentary on references to sodomy in Egbert's *Penitential* in Bailey, *Homosexuality and the Western Christian Tradition,* 104.

65. Oxford, Bodleian Library, Bodley 718, 5b, an Exeter manuscript from the tenth century. See Frantzen, *Literature of Penance,* 131. This variant is reported by Haddan and Stubbs, *CED* 3:419 note 14. See also Bailey, *Homosexuality and the Western Christian Tradition,* 104 note 2.

66. Compare Bailey's translation: "If a man commits sodomy often, or if one doing so is in orders, some hold that he must do penance for ten years; others say, for seven years; others again, for one year if he has taken the passive role (molles); others, for one hundred days if the offender is a boy" (*Homosexuality and the Western Christian Tradition,* 104).

67. This canon has been compared to the Council of Ancyra (AD 314), canon 16, but unlike the Old English canon this one does not mention same-sex intercourse. See Henry R. Percival, ed., *The Seven Ecumenical Councils of the Undivided Church,* Select Library of Nicene and Post-Nicene Fathers, 14 (New York: Scribner's, 1900), 70.

68. Joseph Bosworth and T. Northcote Toller, eds., *An Anglo-Saxon Dictionary* (1898; reprint, Oxford: Oxford University Press, 1991), 314; see also T. Northcote Toller and Alistair Campbell, eds., *An Anglo-Saxon Dictionary: Supplement* (1921; reprint, Oxford: Oxford University Press, 1992), 248.

69. For discussion of sexual relations between boys and men in ancient Greece, see Michel Foucault, *The Use of Pleasure,* trans. Robert Hurley (New York: Vintage, 1986), 187–246, and David M. Halperin, *One Hundred Years of Homosexuality: And Other Essays on Greek Love* (New York: Routledge, 1990), 15–40. See also Bullough, "The Sin against Nature and Homosexuality," in *Sexual Practices,* ed. Bullough and Brundage, 62.

70. Rob Meens, "Children and Confession in the Early Middle Ages," in *The Church and Childhood,* ed. Diana Wood, Studies in Church History 31 (Oxford: Blackwell, 1994), 53–55.

71. *Penitential* of Cummean, in *The Irish Penitentials,* ed. Ludwig Bieler, Scriptores Latini Hiberniae 5 (hereafter abbreviated *IP;* Dublin: Institute for Advanced Studies, 1963), "Ponamus nunc de ludis puerilibus priorum statuta patrum nostrorum," 126–29.

72. "Be unrihtum dædum geongra manna"; *DAB* 177, reports this heading in Cambridge, Corpus Christi College 190. For Cummean's heading, see *IP* 127.

73. Spindler's edition reads "fæste VII niht," but all three manuscripts say five days, as his apparatus shows; see *DAB* 177, note to line 131.

74. Payer raises the possibility of classroom use of the handbooks. See *Sex and the Penitentials,* 42.

75. On violence and pedagogy, see Walter J. Ong, "Latin Language Study as a Renaissance Puberty Rite," in *Rhetoric, Romance, and Technlogy: Studies in the Interaction of Expression and Culture* (Ithaca: Cornell University Press, 1971), 133–41; and Jody Enders, "Rhetoric, Coercion, and the Memory of Violence," in *Criticism and Dissent in the Middle Ages,* ed. Rita Copland (Cambridge: Cambridge University Press, 1996), 14–55.

76. Greenberg, *Construction of Homosexuality,* 284.

77. Michael Goodich, *The Unmentionable Vice: Homosexuality in the Later Medieval Period* (Santa Barbara: ABC-Clio, 1979), 27. For Regino's text, see J. P. Migne, ed., *Patrologiae cursus completus, Series Latina,* 221 vols. (Paris: J. P. Migne, 1844–55), vol. 132, cols. 333–34, canons 257–58.

78. John Boswell, "Revolutions, Universals, and Sexual Categories," in *Hidden from History: Reclaiming the Gay and Lesbian Past,* ed. Martin Duberman, Martha Vicinus, and George Chauncey, Jr. (New York: Penguin, 1989), 28–29.

79. George Norman Garmonsway, "The Development of the Colloquy," in *The Anglo-Saxons: Studies in Some Aspects of Their History and Culture Presented to Bruce Dickins,* ed. Peter Clemoes (London: Bowes and Bowes, 1959), 248–61. See the summaries, 255–57, especially 256, par. 10. See further Scott Gwara, ed., *Latin Colloquies* (Toronto: University of Toronto Press, 1995).

80. G. N. Garmonsway, ed., *Ælfric's Colloquy* (London: Methuen, 1939).

81. Peter L. Allen, *The Art of Love: Amatory Fiction from Ovid to the Romance of the Rose* (Philadelphia: University of Pennsylvania Press, 1992), 40.

82. Marjorie Woods, "Rape and the Pedagogical Rhetoric of Sexual Violence," in *Criticism and Dissent in the Middle Ages,* ed. Copland, 69. See also works by Ong and Enders, n. 75 above.

83. "Visitatio sepulchri," in *Regularis concordia,* ed. Thomas Symons (London: Thomas Nelson and Sons, 1953), 5.51, p. 50. The text is printed in David Bevington, ed., *Medieval Drama* (Boston: Houghton Mifflin, 1975), 27–28.

84. Woods, "Rape and the Pedagogical Rhetoric," 73.

85. Woods, "Rape and the Pedagogical Rhetoric," 66.

86. Bosworth and Toller, *Anglo-Saxon Dictionary,* 66.

87. "Bædling," in *Dictionary of Old English,* fasc. B, ed. Ashley Crandell Amos, Antonette diPaolo Healey, Joan Holland, Christine Franzen, David McDougall, Ian McDougall, Nancy Speirs, and Pauline Thompson (Toronto: Pontifical Institute of Mediaeval Studies, 1994), 73.

88. Hans Kurath and Sherman M. Kuhn, eds., *Middle English Dictionary,* fasc. B, part 1 (Ann Arbor: University of Michigan Press, 1957), 602. "Bæddel" is one term for "hermaphrodite" given in *A Thesaurus of Old English,* ed. Jane Roberts and Christian Kay with Lynne Grundy, 2 vols. (London: King's College Centre for Late Antique and Medieval Studies, 1995), entry 02.01.03.03.06, "Sex, kind," 1:28. "Bædling" occurs under "unnatural sexual behavior," offered as a definition of "a sodomite" (entry 12.08.08.01.02.02.03, 1:591).

89. Wayne Dynes's comments were offered in an exchange of letters in the *Times Literary Supplement* about the word "gay." See Bruce R. Smith, *Homosexual Desire in Shakespeare's England: A Cultural Poetics* (Chicago: University of Chicago Press, 1991),

275 note 29, who notes that in modern usage "bad" has come to mean "good," another word—like "gay" and "queer"—turned against its hostile sense. The source, Zupitza, has become "Zupicka" in Smith's notes.

90. Greenberg, *Construction of Homosexuality*, 249.

91. I wish to thank Joseph Harris for his thoughts on this topic. Scott Gwara has pointed out to me that "bædling" has a short stressed vowel in the dictionaries. Adding diminutive suffix "-el" would create I-mutation, giving spellings of bad/bed.

92. Boswell, *Christianity, Social Tolerance*, 106–7.

93. Halperin, *One Hundred Years*, 22–24.

94. Payer, *Sex and the Penitentials*, 40–41.

95. Some translations: "fornicators, idolaters, adulterers, male prostitutes, sodomites" (New Revised Standard Version); "no fornicator or idolater, no adulterer or sexual pervert" (Revised English Bible); "neither fornicators nor idolaters nor adulterers nor boy prostitutes nor practicing homosexuals" (New American Bible); "the sexually immoral, idolaters, adulterers, the self-indulgent, sodomites" (New Jerusalem Bible, quoted from *The Complete Parallel Bible* [New York: Oxford University Press, 1993], 3020–21). The passage is mentioned by Payer, *Sex and the Penitentials*, 40. Boswell discusses these terms in *Christianity, Social Tolerance*, appendix 1, 335–53.

96. *Penitential* of Pseudo-Theodore, chap. 13, canon 28, "De sodomitis et mollibus, et immundis pollutionibus," in Wasserschleben, *Die Bussordnungen der abendländischen Kirche*, 598; also edited by Thorpe, *ALI* 2:35. The manuscript is Cambridge, Corpus Christi College 190. The accepted date is 830–47; see Payer, *Sex and the Penitentials*, 61, 180 note 40.

97. Payer, *Sex and the Penitentials*, 52–53. On the proportion of sex canons in later penitentials, which rose as high as 50 percent, see Pierre J. Payer, "Sex and Confession in the Thirteenth Century," in *Sex in the Middle Ages*, ed. Joyce E. Salisbury (New York: Garland, 1991), 128–29.

98. *Scriftboc* 19h, *DAB* 184: "A woman who mixes a man's seed in her food and then eats it so she shall be more agreeable to the male is to fast for three years" ("Wif seo ðe mencgð weres sæd in hire mete and ðone þigeð þæt heo þam wæpnedmen sy ðe leofre, fæste III winter"). See Theodore 1.14.15 (*CED* 3:188): "Sic et illa [mulier] quæ semen viri sui in cibo miscens ut inde plus amoris accipiat peniteat."

99. One cannot argue that such statistics are overly reliable or significant, for what constitutes a canon, as opposed to one canon in two parts, is sometimes debatable (some of the canons are long and complex, and editors divide and enumerate them differently). I have not calculated frequency ratios or attempted other forms of statistical analysis on these data. For an example of such analysis, see James A. Brundage, "Sex and Canon Law: A Statistical Analysis of Samples of Canon and Civil Law," in *Sexual Practices*, ed. Bullough and Brundage, 89–101.

100. Greenberg, *Construction of Homosexuality*, 262 (no evidence is offered for this claim).

101. Payer does not report any penitential with no reference to homosexual acts, and there is only one: the *Penitential of Finnian*, ed. and trans. Bieler, *IP* 74–95; the homosexual acts mentioned at the start of the text (74–75) do not, as Bieler notes, belong to the original text but rather to the *Penitential* of Cummean (17, 242).

102. These figures are reasonably close to those compiled by Bailey, *Homosexuality and the Western Christian Tradition*, 101: Theodore, 3.5 percent; Bede, 8 percent; Egbert,

4.5 percent. Bullough comments on Bailey's statistics in *Sexual Variance in Society and History,* 360–61.

103. Surveying eight Irish handbooks, Payer (*Sex and the Penitentials,* 137) lists twenty-three canons in censuring homosexual acts; I count six references to Sodom among them. Some of these texts ("Synod of North Britain," "Grove of Victory") are better called protopenitentials than handbooks of penance. As Payer's table shows, most of the Irish references are contained in two major texts, the *Penitential* of Columbanus and the *Penitential* of Cummean.

104. The *Old Irish Penitential* is not a "typical" Irish penitential, since it seems to be part of an eighth-century reaction against the lax standards of certain monastic communities. See the commentary by D. A. Binchy, "Penitential Texts in Old Irish," in *IP* 47–48.

105. For example, one of two texts, either the *Scriftboc* or *CTH,* was appended to the fourth book of the *Old English Penitential* in four manuscripts of the Anglo-Saxon penitentials. I discuss the manuscript arrangement of the vernacular penitentials in "The Tradition of Penitentials in Anglo-Saxon England," *Anglo-Saxon England* 11 (1983): 23–56.

106. See the *Penitential* of Theodore 1.2.19, *CED* 3:179. See also Egbert's *Penitential* 4.4 (sister, twelve years) and 4.5 (brother, fifteen years), *CED* 3:420. See also *CTH* 147, Mone 521; and *CTHS* 68.14, *ALI* 2:230.

107. Bailey, *Homosexuality and the Western Christian Tradition,* 106.

108. Alan Bray, *Homosexuality in Renaissance England* (1982; reprint, New York: Columbia University Press, 1995), 17.

109. David M. Halperin, "Is There a History of Sexuality?" *History and Theory* 28 (1989): 273, quoted in Pierre J. Payer, *The Bridling of Desire: Views of Sex in the Later Middle Ages* (Toronto: University of Toronto Press, 1993), 15.

110. Simon Keynes and Michael Lapidge, eds. and trans., *Alfred the Great: Asser's "Life of King Alfred" and Other Contemporary Sources* (Harmondsworth, Middlesex: Penguin, 1983), 35. Alfred established a school as part of his household "for the education not only of his own children but also of the sons of his leading men and others of lesser birth." For a discussion of the circumstances limiting Alfred's schools, see Alfred P. Smyth, *King Alfred the Great* (Oxford: Oxford University Press, 1995), 559–61.

111. Payer (*Sex and the Penitentials,* 31) notes that incest appears in detailed form first in the *Penitential* of Theodore and associated texts, including relations with one's mother, sister, and brothers, as well as sex acts between mothers and small boys.

NOTES TO CHAPTER FIVE

1. Wulfstan, "Sermo Lupi ad Anglos," in *The Homilies of Wulfstan,* ed. Dorothy Bethurum (Oxford: Clarendon, 1957), 272, line 138, 273, line 164. I have emended "folegene" to "forlegene."

2. Paul Hallam, *The Book of Sodom* (London: Verso, 1993), 15.

3. For an illuminating introduction to the literary culture of these authors, see Martin Irvine, *The Making of Textual Culture: "Grammatica" and Literary Theory, 350–1100* (Cambridge: Cambridge University Press, 1994), 272–333; Irvine situates these authors in both English and Continental contexts.

4. London, British Library, Cotton Claudius B.iv, edited in *The Old English Version*

of the Heptateuch: Ælfric's Treatise on the Old and New Testaments and His Preface to Genesis, ed. S. J. Crawford, EETS, OS, 160 (1922; reprint, London: Oxford University Press, 1969). References to the Old English text are from Crawford and are given in the text by page and verse number. Crawford does not reproduce the illustrations. For them, see C. R. Dodwell and Peter Clemoes, eds., *The Old English Illustrated Heptateuch: British Museum Cotton Claudius B. iv,* Early English Manuscripts in Facsimile 18 (Copenhagen: Rosenkilde and Bagger, 1974). Several of the illustrations are reproduced by M. R. Godden, "The Trouble with Sodom: Literary Responses to Biblical Sexuality," *Bulletin of the John Rylands University Library of Manchester University* 77 (1996): 105–8.

5. See Derrick Sherwin Bailey, *Homosexuality and the Western Christian Tradition* (1955; reprint, Hamden, Conn.: Archon, 1975), 9–28.

6. John Boswell, *Christianity, Social Tolerance, and Homosexuality: Gay People in Western Europe from the Beginning of the Christian Era to the Fourteenth Century* (Chicago: University of Chicago Press, 1980), 98.

7. Godden, "Trouble with Sodom," 98.

8. Mark D. Jordan, *The Invention of Sodomy in Christian Theology* (Chicago: University of Chicago Press, 1997), 37, 35. Jordan surveys the analysis of Sodom in patristic authorities, 33–40.

9. Jordan, *Invention of Sodomy,* 39, citing Gregory the Great, *Moralia in Job,* book 26, chap. 17, par. 29, ed. Marc Adriaen, Corpus Christianorum Series Latina, vols. 143–143B (Turnhout, Belgium: Brepols, 1979–85), 143B:1287.

10. Jordan, *Invention of Sodomy,* 42.

11. Richard Kay, *Dante's Swift and Strong: Essays on* Inferno *XV* (Lawrence: Regents Press of Kansas, 1978), 211.

12. I quote the New Revised Standard Version from *The Complete Parallel Bible* (New York: Oxford University Press, 1993) by chapter and verse in the text.

13. Kay, *Dante's Swift and Strong,* 229.

14. See Kurt Weitzmann and Herbert L. Kessler, eds., *The Cotton Genesis: British Library Codex Cotton Otho B. VI* (Princeton: Princeton University Press, 1986), 80, citing illustrations on folios 30v and 31v.

15. Alberto Culunga and Larentio Turrado, eds., *Biblia sacra* (Madrid: Biblioteca de Autores Cristianos, 1959), 15.

16. Compare Weitzmann and Kessler, *Cotton Genesis,* fig. 219 and color plate VII, 19, which shows Lot greeting winged angels in Sodom; see commentary, 80.

17. The Middle English poem known as *Cleanness* is an excellent example. The poet carefully describes the angels entering Sodom: "Bolde burneȝ wer þay boþe, with berdles chynneȝ, / Royl rollande fax to raw sylk lyke, / Of ble as þe brere-flour where-so þe bare scheweed" (Noble men were they both, with beardless chins, regal, rolling hair like raw silk, of the color of the briar-rose where the bare skin showed; my translation, text quoted from J. J. Anderson, ed., *Cleanness* [Manchester: Manchester University Press, 1977], 789–91). I discuss the episode in "The Disclosure of Sodomy in the Middle English *Cleanness,*" *PMLA* 111 (1996): 451–64.

18. As Godden notes, Lot's actions at this point and his subsequent incest with his daughters are rarely examined in discussions of the destruction of Sodom. See "Trouble with Sodom," 97–119.

19. Weitzmann and Kessler, *Cotton Genesis,* figs. 223–24 and color plate VIII, 22;

see 81. This illustration also shows two Sodomites struck down, anticipating the angels' attack that follows Lot's speech.

20. Fertility and survival are pressing concerns throughout Genesis, according to J. P. Fokkelman, "Genesis," in *The Literary Guide to the Bible,* ed. Robert Alter and Frank Kermode (Cambridge: Harvard University Press, 1987), 42–43. See also Robert Alter, "Sodom as Nexus: The Web of Design in Biblical Narrative," in *Reclaiming Sodom,* ed. Jonathan Goldberg (New York: Routledge, 1994), 34–36.

21. For an introduction to Bede's exegetical method, see George Hardin Brown, *Bede the Venerable* (Boston: Twayne, 1987), 42–61. Bede addressed *In principium Genesis* to Bishop Acca of Hexham and described his commentaries, according to Brown, as "popular recensions for his age" (43).

22. Kay, *Dante's Swift and Strong,* 230.

23. "Quibus autem peccatis Sodomitae fuerint subiugati, excepto illo infando quod in sequentibus scriptura commemorat. Iezechiel propheta sufficienter exponit, loquens ad Hierusalem, 'Ecce haec . . . coram me.' A quibus omnibus immunem fuisse beatum Loth, et textus sacrae historiae testatur. Quem angelos hospitio recepisse, ac per eos a pereuntibus impiis ereptum esse declarat" (Bede, *In Genesiam,* in *Bedae Venerabilis opera,* ed. Ch. W. Jones, Corpus Christianorum Series Latina, 118A [Turnhout, Belgium: Brepols, 1967], 179, quoted in Kay, *Dante's Swift and Strong,* 384 note 49, 229–30). On the date of this work, see Jones, *Bedae Venerabilis opera,* viii–ix.

24. "'Peccatum' quipe 'suum' sicut sodoma 'praedicauerunt nec absconderunt,' cum absque respectu pudoris alicuius omnes a puerili aetate usque ad ultimam senectutem masculi in masculos turpitudinem operari solebant, adeo ut ne hospitibus quidem ac peregrinis sua scelera abscondere, sed et hos uim inferendo suis similes facere sceleribus atque suis facinoribus implicare contenderent" (Bede, *In Genesiam,* 19:4–5, in *Bedae Venerabilis opera,* 222, quoted in Kay, *Dante's Swift and Strong,* 384–85 note 53, paraphrased by Kay, 231).

25. Bede, *In Genesiam,* 18:20, in *Bedae Venerabilis opera,* 220.

26. Kay, *Dante's Swift and Strong,* 231.

27. Gildas, *The Ruin of Britain and Other Documents,* ed. and trans. Michael Winterbottom (London: Phillimore, 1978). See Nicholas Howe, *Migration and Myth-Making in Anglo-Saxon England* (New Haven: Yale University Press, 1989), 33–71, for a discussion of Gildas, Bede, and the pattern of prophetic history.

28. Bertram Colgrave and R. A. B. Mynors, eds. and trans., *Bede's Ecclesiastical History of the English People* (Oxford: Oxford University Press, 1969), book 1, chap. 14, pp. 48–49.

29. Colgrave and Mynors, *Bede's Ecclesiastical History,* book 1, chap. 22, pp. 68–69.

30. N. J. Higham, *The English Conquest: Gildas and Britain in the Fifth Century* (Manchester: Manchester University Press, 1994), 204. See earlier comments, 43–44.

31. Gildas, *Ruin of Britain,* chap. 28, pp. 29–30.

32. For a complete list of Gildas's references to Sodom, see Higham, *English Conquest,* 61 note 48.

33. "This unspeakable sin is not unknown to Constantine, tyrant whelp of the filthy lioness of Dumnonia" ("Cuius tam nefandi piaculi non ignarus est inmundae leaenae Damnoniae tyrannicus catulus Constantinus"; Gildas, *Ruin of Britain,* chap. 28, p. 29).

34. *Aldhelm: The Poetic Works,* trans. Michael Lapidge and James L. Rosier (Cam-

bridge: D. S. Brewer, 1985), 158, line 2515. The *Carmen de virginitate* is translated by Rosier, 97–167.

35. Aldhelm, *Carmen de virginitate,* line 2518. The Latin text is edited by Rudolf Ehwald, *Aldhelmi opera,* Monumenta Germaniae Historica, Auctores Antiquissimi 15 (Berlin: Weidmann, 1915), 11–32.

36. On the career of Boniface, see Wilhelm Levison, *England and the Continent in the Eighth Century* (Oxford: Clarendon, 1946), 70–93.

37. For the letter, see Arthur West Haddan and William Stubbs, eds., *Councils and Ecclesiastical Documents Relating to Great Britain and Ireland,* 3 vols. (1871; reprint, Oxford: Clarendon, 1964), 3:354. The translation is quoted from Ephraim Emerton, *The Letters of Saint Boniface* (New York: Norton, 1976), 128. For commentaries, see David F. Greenberg, *The Construction of Homosexuality* (Chicago: University of Chicago Press, 1988), 250; and Bailey, *Homosexuality and the Western Christian Tradition,* 110.

38. Boswell, *Christianity, Social Tolerance,* 202–3; Boswell quotes the letter and provides a translation. Boswell cites this correspondence to support his untenable view that "[t]he thrust of the relatively rare theological objections to homosexual acts in the early Middle Ages could not therefore be traced to a concept of 'nature'" but rather that they dealt with the release of semen for purposes other than reproduction (202). Godden reaches the same conclusion as Boswell, "Trouble with Sodom," 99.

39. Bailey, *Homosexuality and the Western Christian Tradition,* 110–11.

40. Greenberg, *Construction of Homosexuality,* 250.

41. Boswell, *Christianity, Social Tolerance,* 191, in reference to letter 294 in E. Dümmler, ed., *Monumenta Germaniae historica: Epistolae* (Berlin: Weidmann, 1895), 2: 451–52. The letter is partly translated by Stephen Allott, *Alcuin of York* (York: William Sessions, 1974), no. 127, pp. 133–34.

42. Quoted from Allott's translation, *Alcuin of York,* 134; the reference to Sodom, translated from the Latin, is omitted in Allott's excerpt.

43. See C. Stephen Jaeger, "L'Amour des rois: Structure sociale d'une forme de sensibilité aristocratique," *Annales: Économies Sociétes Civilisations* 46 (1991): 548–49, 566 note 10 (where letter 294 is incorrectly listed as letter 249), for a refutation of Boswell's position on Alcuin, Anselm, and other authors of passionate correspondence. "Alcuin pouvait déclarer son amour pour Charlemagne et pour Arn de Salzbourg de manière aussi directe précisément parce que plus le ton de l'expression était passionné, plus la relation était innocente. Loin de le stigmatiser comme sodomite, l'amour du roi en faisait un homme de la vertu la plus élevée" (557).

44. I cite the edition with the Anglo-Saxon translation, George E. MacLean, ed., "Ælfric's Version of *Alcuini interrogationes Sigeuulfi in Genesin,*" *Anglia* 6 (1883): 425–73, and 7 (1884): 1–59. For the quotation see *Anglia* 7 (1884): 49. On Alcuin's use of Bede's commentaries, see 49 note to par. 191 (67). See further comments by Godden, "Trouble with Sodom," 99–101.

45. See Bailey, *Homosexuality and the Western Christian Tradition,* 82–85, and Jordan, *Invention of Sodomy,* 29–40, for surveys of the patristic tradition.

46. Some of the following material appeared in shorter form in "Sodom and Gomorrah in Prose Works from Alfred's Reign," in *Alfred the Wise: Studies in Honour of Janet Bately,* ed. Jane Roberts and Janet L. Nelson with Malcolm Godden (Cambridge: D. S. Brewer, 1997), 25–33. For general background on these texts, see Allen J. Frantzen, *King Alfred* (Boston: G. K. Hall, 1986).

47. Henry Sweet, ed., *King Alfred's West-Saxon Version of Gregory's "Pastoral Care,"* 2 vols., EETS, OS, 45, 50 (1871–72; reprint, London: Oxford University Press, 1958), 2:393, lines 20–21. References to page and line number are given in the text.

48. This list corresponds to Gregory's Latin, Alfred's source: "Neque fornicatores, neque idolis servientes, neque adulteri, neque molles, neque masculorum concubitores, neque fures" (Neither fornicators, nor idolaters, nor adulterers, nor the effeminate, nor liers with mankind, nor thieves; *Regulae Pastoralis Liber,* in *Patrologiae cursus completus, Series Latina,* 221 vols., ed. J. P. Migne [Paris: J. P. Migne, 1844–55], 77:104). See the discussion of this passage from Paul in chapter 4, note 95.

49. Gregory the Great, *Moralia in Job,* cited by Jordan, *Invention of Sodomy,* 38 note 43.

50. Gabriel Rotello, *Sexual Ecology: AIDS and the Destiny of Gay Men* (New York: Dutton, 1997), 63.

51. Hans Hecht, ed., *Bischof Wærferths von Worcester Übersetzung der Dialoge Gregors des Grossen* (1900–1907; reprint, Darmstadt: Wissenschaftliche Buchgesellschaft, 1965), 323, lines 16–22. The traditional attribution of this translation to Bishop Wærferth has recently been challenged by Alfred P. Smyth, *King Alfred the Great* (Oxford: Oxford University Press, 1995), 545. For a study of the work's manuscript history, see Malcolm Godden, "Wærferth and King Alfred: The Fate of the Old English *Dialogues,"* in *Alfred the Wise,* ed. Roberts and Nelson, 35–51.

52. Janet M. Bately, ed., *The Old English Orosius,* EETS, ES, 6 (London: Oxford University Press, 1980), book 1, chap. 3, p. 1, lines 6–7.

53. Jordan, *Invention of Sodomy,* 39. See 35–40 for additional references to Sodom in Gregory's work; most of these references are sexual, but none is explicitly a reference to same-sex acts.

54. "Dominica sexta in quadragesima," in *The Blickling Homilies of the Tenth Century,* ed. Richard Morris, EETS, OS, 58, 63, 73 (1874–80; reprint, London: Oxford University Press, 1967), 79, lines 7–10. On the date of the collection, see D. G. Scragg, "The Homilies of the Blickling Manuscript," in *Learning and Literature in Anglo-Saxon England,* ed. Michael Lapidge and Helmut Gneuss (Cambridge: Cambridge University Press, 1985), 299–316; and Scragg, "The Corpus of Vernacular Homilies and Prose Saints' Lives before Ælfric," *Anglo-Saxon England* 8 (1979): 233–35.

55. See Michael W. Twomey, "Sodom and Gomorrah," in *A Dictionary of Biblical Tradition in English Literature,* ed. David Lyle Jeffrey (Grand Rapids, Mich.: William B. Erdmans, 1992), 720–21.

56. "Assumptio S. Mariæ Virginis," in *Blickling Homilies,* ed. Morris, 153, lines 26–30. Another anonymous homily, found in Cambridge, Corpus Christi College 162, pp. 382–91, includes the destruction of Sodom and Gomorrah on the sixth day of creation (the same "day" on which Adam was made and fell, and Cain killed Abel). *Homily for Easter Sunday* is cited from a transcript made for the *Dictionary of Old English* (250, lines 19–21) and made available to me through the generosity of the editors.

57. D. G. Scragg, ed., *The Vercelli Homilies,* EETS, OS, 300 (Oxford: Oxford University Press, 1992). The quotation from Matthew 7:14 is identified on 138 note 31–4 and that from Ezekiel on 138 note 41. For the date of this collection, see xxxviii–xxxix.

58. "Sermo ad populum dominicis diebus," in *Wulfstan: Sammlung der ihm zugeschriebenen Homilien nebst Untersuchungen über ihre Echtheit,* ed. Arthur S. Napier (Berlin: Weidmann, 1883), 295, lines 21–26.

59. MacLean, "Ælfric's Version of *Alcuini interrogationes Sigeuulfi in Genesin,*" *Anglia* 6 (1883): 426. Quotations are taken from MacLean's text, *Anglia* 7 (1884): 1–59, and page and line number are given in the text. Peter Clemoes suggested that Ælfric translated this text to supply commentary missing in his translation of Genesis. See "The Chronology of Ælfric's Works," in *The Anglo-Saxons: Studies in Some Aspects of Their History and Culture Presented to Bruce Dickins,* ed. Peter Clemoes (London: Bowes and Bowes, 1959), 224–25.

60. MacLean, "Ælfric's Anglo-Saxon Version," 49.

61. Ælfric, "On the Old and New Testament," in *Old English Version of the Heptateuch,* ed. Crawford, 25, lines 231–38. See Jonathan Wilcox, ed., *Ælfric's Prefaces,* Durham Medieval Texts 9 (Durham: Durham Medieval Texts, 1994), 40–41, for further commentary.

62. "De oratione Moysi: In medio quadragesima," in *Ælfric's Lives of Saints,* ed. Walter W. Skeat, EETS, OS, 76, 82, 94, 114 (London: Oxford University Press, 1966), 1:4, lines 43–44. References to page and line number are given in the text. On the date, see Wilcox, *Ælfric's Prefaces,* 44.

63. Ælfric, "Sermo de die iudici," in *Homilies of Ælfric: A Supplementary Collection,* ed. John C. Pope, EETS, OS, 259–60 (Oxford: Oxford University Press, 1968), 2:591. References to page and line number are given in the text.

64. Ælfric, "In Letania Maiore," in *The Homilies of the Anglo-Saxon Church: The First Part, Containing the Sermones catholici, or Homilies of Ælfric,* ed. Benjamin Thorpe (London, 1844–46; reprint, New York: Johnson Reprint, 1971), 1:246–47.

65. See Wilcox, *Ælfric's Prefaces,* 38 note 125. Ælfric's translation of Genesis 1:1–24:22 is found in Cambridge, University Library, Ii.1.33; the version in the *Old English Heptateuch* is augmented by another author. On authorship, see C. R. Dodwell and Peter Clemoes, "The Composition of the Old English Text," in *Old English Illustrated Heptateuch,* ed. Dodwell and Clemoes, 42–58. The passage about the Sodomites' demand (which replaces Genesis 19:4–11) is also found in the Cambridge manuscript, as Crawford's variant readings make clear (Crawford, *Old English Version of the Heptateuch,* 132, textual apparatus).

66. Godden, "Trouble with Sodom," 103. He quotes and translates the passage, 102 note 18.

67. A. N. Doane, ed., *Genesis A: A New Edition* (Madison: University of Wisconsin Press, 1978), 301–2 note 2147.

68. Wilcox, *Ælfric's Prefaces,* 65.

69. See Wilcox, *Ælfric's Prefaces,* 26–27, and Ælfric's homily, "Kalendas Ianuarii octabas et circumcisio Domini," in *Ælfric's Catholic Homilies: The First Series,* ed. Peter Clemoes, EETS, SS, 17 (Oxford: Oxford University Press, 1997), 226–27, where Ælfric comments that Christian men do not practice circumcision, a comment he inserted parenthetically into his translation of Genesis 17:27 (Crawford, *Old English Version of the Heptateuch,* 127).

70. Roger Fowler, "A Late Old English Handbook for the Use of a Confessor," *Anglia* 83 (1965): 17, lines 38–39. The manuscripts are Cambridge, Corpus Christi College 201, mid–eleventh century, and London, British Library, Cotton Tiberius A.iii, a mid-eleventh-century manuscript from Canterbury. See Fowler, "Late Old English Handbook," 2.

71. H. Logeman, "Anglo-Saxonica Minora," *Anglia* 11 (1889): 97–98, an eleventh-century confessional prayer found in London, British Library, Cotton Vespasian D.xx,

and London, British Library, Cotton Tiberius C.i (which reads "sodomitiscre" instead of "sodomiscre").

72. A. B. Kuypers, ed., *The Prayer Book of Aedeluald the Bishop, Commonly Called the Book of Cerne* (Cambridge: Cambridge University Press, 1902), prayer 8, pp. 92–95. For useful discussions of this prayer book, see Kathleen Hughes, "Some Aspects of Irish Influence on Early English Private Prayer," *Studia Celtica* 5 (1970): 48–61; and Michelle P. Brown, *The Book of Cerne: Prayer, Patronage, and Power in Ninth-Century England* (Toronto: University of Toronto Press, 1996).

73. The decoration of Junius 11 is complete only up to Abraham's approach to Egypt, folio 88 (Genesis 12), but spaces were left for illustrations throughout the whole of Genesis. The manuscript is from the second quarter of the eleventh century. According to Barbara Raw, along with Cotton Claudius B.iv (of Canterbury provenance), Junius 11 has "the distinction of being an extensively illustrated vernacular text." Most illustrated manuscripts are Latin service books. See Barbara C. Raw, "The Probable Derivation of Most of the Illustrations in Junius 11 from an Illustrated Old Saxon *Genesis,*" *Anglo-Saxon England* 5 (1976): 135. See further Raw, "The Construction of Oxford, Bodleian Library, Junius 11," *Anglo-Saxon England* 13 (1984): 187–207.

74. On the manuscript and the text, see Doane, *Genesis A,* 3–48. For analysis of the poet's vocabulary and style in relation to other Old English poems, including *Beowulf,* see M. S. Griffith, "Poetic Language and the Paris Psalter: The Decay of the Old English Tradition," *Anglo-Saxon England* 20 (1991): 167–86.

75. For the probable circumstances of the interpolation, see A. N. Doane, *The Saxon Genesis: An Edition of the West Saxon Genesis B and the Old Saxon Vatican Genesis* (Madison: University of Wisconsin Press, 1991), 41–42.

76. For an analysis of the poem's structure, see Nancy Mohr McKinley, "Poetry vs. Paraphrase: The Artistry of *Genesis A,*" diss., Harvard University, 1991. In his review of McKinley's work, J. R. Hall points out other dissertations on the poem, including his own. The poem's critical tradition remains remarkably impoverished (J. R. Hall, "Individual Poems," in *Year's Work in Old English Studies* 27 [1994]: 33–34).

77. Doane, *Genesis A,* 49. References to line numbers are to this edition.

78. Doane, *Genesis A,* 301 note 2147, citing similar forms in lines 971 and 2608.

79. Patrick Sims-Williams, "Thought, Word, and Deed: An Irish Triad," *Eriu* 29 (1978): 78–111.

80. Doane, *Genesis A,* 197, 10–11; the page was cut out, Doane has suggested, because someone was interested in the Old English for 50, 45, 30, 20, and 10, numbers used in Abraham's bargaining with God for the Sodomites.

81. For the semantic range of "hæman," see *A Thesaurus of Old English,* ed. Jane Roberts and Christian Kay with Lynne Grundy, 2 vols. (London: King's College Centre for Late Antique and Medieval Studies, 1995), 2:1039.

82. Doane, *Genesis A,* 60, 198 (where he gives the Latin sources); Paul G. Remley, "The Latin Textual Basis of *Genesis A,*" *Anglo-Saxon England* 17 (1988): 163–89. See also Richard Marsden, *The Text of the Old Testament in Anglo-Saxon England* (Cambridge: Cambridge University Press, 1995), 442–43.

83. See Doane, *Genesis A,* 44 and notes 28–30 for examples; and Godden, "Trouble with Sodom," 111.

84. Noah forgot to cover his genitals because he was drunk and therefore without shame. His son Ham saw him and, unashamed, told his brothers. They, however, were embarrassed for their father, and walking backwards with a cloak, did not look on

Noah as they covered his nakedness with it. When Noah awoke and learned what Ham had done, he cursed him (Genesis 9:20–24). This intramale encounter between father and son connects sexual knowledge to shame and uses that knowledge to juxtapose fathers and sons. It is worth a closer look.

85. Doane, *Genesis A,* 357, "gesceap," and 278 note 1573b.

86. Doane, *Genesis A,* 314 note 2608a. See "willgebroðor," *Genesis A,* line 971. Doane laconically remarked that the expression is used "ironically where the family relationship is somewhat amiss" (246 note 971b).

87. Kay, *Dante's Swift and Strong,* 219.

88. Boswell, *Christianity, Social Tolerance,* 34–36, 208–9. Boswell's thesis links the growth of cities to tolerance for same-sex relations but argues that intolerance became marked in the thirteenth century. There was, however, a continued growth of urban centers in this century, and, as James A. Brundage notes, "Boswell's hypothetical linkage of tolerance to urbanization and intolerance to ruralization is rather seriously jeopardized." See Brundage's review of Boswell's book in *Catholic Historical Review* 68 (1982): 63–64.

89. Hugh Magennis, *Images of Community in Old English Poetry* (Cambridge: Cambridge University Press, 1996), 144, and, in Augustine and Bede, 157.

90. Alan Bray, *Homosexuality in Renaissance England* (1982; reprint, New York: Columbia University Press, 1995), 68.

91. Warner of Rouen, *Moriuht,* ed. and trans. Christopher J. McDonough (Toronto: Pontifical Institute of Mediaeval Studies, 1995); see 5–7 for the date and provenance of the work. References to line number are given in the text, using McDonough's translation.

92. See McDonough, *Moriuht,* 136 note 79, which identifies Ravola as a "lubricious character" from one of Juvenal's satires, noted for both homosexual and heterosexual adventures.

NOTES TO CHAPTER SIX

1. Clare A. Simmons, *Reversing the Conquest: History and Myth in Nineteenth-Century British Literature* (New Brunswick: Rutgers University Press, 1990), 14.

2. As I note in chapter 3, Chaucer's Parson does not use the word; for this and other examples, see chapter 3, note 26.

3. Bernhard Fehr, ed., *Die Hirtenbriefe Ælfrics in altenglischer und lateinischer Fassung* (1914; reprint, Darmstadt: Wissenschaftliche Buchgesellschaft, 1966), with a supplement by Peter Clemoes; see letter 1, chaps. 3, 15–27, pp. 2, 4–7, and letter 2, chaps. 86–95, pp. 45–47.

4. Theodore H. Leinbaugh, "Ælfric's *Sermo de sacrificio in die Pascae:* Anglican Polemic in the Sixteenth and Seventeenth Centuries," in *Anglo-Saxon Scholarship: The First Three Centuries,* ed. Carl T. Berkhout and Milton McC. Gatch (Boston: G. K. Hall, 1982), 51–68.

5. Peter Damian, *Book of Gomorrah: An Eleventh-Century Treatise against Clerical Homosexual Practices,* trans. Pierre J. Payer (Waterloo, Ontario: Wilfrid Laurier University Press, 1982), 22. For a recent analysis, see Mark D. Jordan, *The Invention of Sodomy in Christian Theology* (Chicago: University of Chicago Press, 1997), 45–66.

6. Frank Barlow, *The Norman Conquest and Beyond* (London: Hambledon Press, 1983), 154–55. For more recent work concentrating on English life after the Conquest,

see Ann Williams, *The English and the Norman Conquest* (Woodbridge, Suffolk: Boydell, 1995).

7. Frank Barlow, *William Rufus* (Berkeley: University of California Press, 1983), 99–155, a detailed portrait of William as a "bachelor king."

8. A. L. Poole, *From Domesday Book to Magna Carta, 1087–1216,* 2d ed. (Oxford: Oxford University Press, 1955), 119–21.

9. Nancy F. Partner, *Serious Entertainments: The Writing of History in Twelfth-Century England* (Chicago: University of Chicago Press, 1977), 5. For a general overview of English sources on the Conquest, see Antonia Gransden, *Historical Writing in England, c. 550–1307* (Ithaca: Cornell University Press, 1974), 92–104.

10. James Campbell, "Some Twelfth-Century Views of the Anglo-Saxon Past," in *Essays in Anglo-Saxon History* (London: Hambledon Press, 1986), 209.

11. R. W. Southern, "Aspects of the European Tradition of Historical Writing: 4, The Sense of the Past," *Transactions of the Royal Historical Society,* ser. 5, vol. 23 (1973): 246. See also Gransden, *Historical Writing in England,* 105–35.

12. Campbell, "Some Twelfth-Century Views," 211. Campbell particularly stresses a new, critical attitude toward evidence that took Henry of Huntingdon, John of Worcester, and William of Malmesbury beyond the synthesis of Bede's *Ecclesiastical History* and the *Anglo-Saxon Chronicle* that constituted the historical record for Henry's predecessors; see 212–15.

13. William of Malmesbury, *De Gestis regum Anglorum,* ed. William Stubbs, Rolls Series (London: Eyre and Spottiswoode, 1887), 2:496–98. For Ordericus's account of the episode, see Marjorie Chibnall, ed. and trans., *Orderici Vitalis historia æcclesiastica,* 6 vols. (Oxford: Oxford University Press, 1969–80), book 12, chap. 26, 6:294–307.

14. On Ordericus's writing, see Gransden, *Historical Writing in England,* 151–65. See also Marjorie Chibnall, *The World of Orderic Vitalis* (Woodbridge, Suffolk: Boydell, 1984), 169–80.

15. Chibnall, *Orderici Vitalis historia æcclesiastica,* book 12, chap. 26, 6:302–3.

16. Thomas Forester, ed. and trans., *The Ecclesiastical History of England and Normandy of Ordericus Vitalis,* 4 vols. (London: Henry G. Bohn, 1856), 4:38 note 1.

17. Chibnall, *Orderici Vitalis historia æcclesiastica,* book 12, chap. 26, 6:296–97.

18. John Boswell, *Christianity, Social Tolerance, and Homosexuality: Gay People in Western Europe from the Beginning of the Christian Era to the Fourteenth Century* (Chicago: University of Chicago Press, 1980), 52.

19. On Anselm's relations with William Rufus, see Poole, *From Domesday Book to Magna Carta,* 167–82.

20. *The Life of St. Anselm by Eadmer,* ed. and trans. R. W. Southern (Oxford: Clarendon, 1962), 64. Southern says that the passage "refers, without doubt, to the homosexual vices of Rufus's court" (64 note 1). This meeting is also discussed by William of Malmesbury, *De gestis pontificum Anglorum,* ed. N. E. S. A. Hamilton, Rolls Series (London: Longman, 1870), 79.

21. Barlow, *William Rufus,* 103, referring to Eadmer, *Historia novarum in Anglia,* ed. M. Rule, Roll Series (London: Longman, 1884), 47–49.

22. J. S. P. Tatlock, *The Legendary History of Britain: Geoffrey of Monmouth's "Historia regum Britanniae" and Its Early Vernacular Versions* (Berkeley and Los Angeles: University of California Press, 1950), 353.

23. Barlow, *William Rufus,* 109 and note 49.

24. See Council of London, *Sacrorum conciliorum nova et amplissima collectio,* ed. J. D. Mansi, 31 vols. (Florence and Venice: Expensis Antonii Zatta Veneti, 1759), vol. 20, col. 1151, chap. 28. The Latin text is quoted by Boswell, *Christianity, Social Tolerance,* 215 note 25, and is translated by Derrick Sherwin Bailey, in *Homosexuality and the Western Christian Tradition* (1955; reprint, Hamden, Conn.: Archon, 1975), 124.

25. Barlow, *William Rufus,* 106, quoting F. S. Schmitt, ed., *S. Anselmi Cantuariensis archiepiscopi opera omnia,* 6 vols. (Edinburgh: Thomas Nelson, 1946–52), letter 365, 5: 308–9.

26. Bailey, *Homosexuality and the Western Christian Tradition,* 125, countered by Boswell, *Christianity, Social Tolerance,* 216 note 29.

27. Boswell, *Christianity, Social Tolerance,* 215. Anselm's letter is quoted in Bailey, *Homosexuality and the Western Christian Tradition,* 125.

28. See Bailey, *Homosexuality and the Western Christian Tradition,* 124. Promulgation of the canon about proclaiming the new statute was delayed, according to Anselm, because it needed redrafting.

29. On other decrees propagated by the Council of London of 1102, see Poole, *From Domesday Book to Magna Carta,* 40; and Marjorie Chibnall, *Anglo-Norman England, 1066–1166* (Oxford: Basil Blackwell, 1986), 188.

30. Henry of Huntingdon, *Historia Anglorum,* ed. Thomas Arnold, Rolls Series, 74 (London: Longman and Co., 1879), 234, quoted in translation from Partner, *Serious Entertainments,* 41.

31. Poole, *From Domesday Book to Magna Carta,* 183.

32. Bailey, *Homosexuality and the Western Christian Tradition,* 125.

33. Chibnall, *Orderici Vitalis historia ecclesiastica,* book 4, 2:246–47. See also Williams, *The English and the Norman Conquest,* 175–76.

34. Chibnall, *Orderici Vitalis historia ecclesiastica,* book 8, chap. 4, 4:146–47, a passage cited by Bailey, *Homosexuality and the Western Christian Tradition,* 123.

35. Burning was used to punish sodomites in the Levant during the Crusades and in Italy in the late thirteenth century (in Bologna in 1288) and after. For municipal statutes requiring that sodomites be burned, see James A. Brundage, *Law, Sex, and Christian Society in Medieval Europe* (Chicago: University of Chicago Press, 1987), 473, 533–34.

36. Barlow, *William Rufus,* 409, citing Hugh of Flavigny. Gerard was one of two chancery clerks sent by William Rufus to Pope Urban in an attempt to depose Anselm. See Poole, *From Domesday Book to Magna Carta,* 174–75.

37. E. A. Freeman, *The History of the Norman Conquest of England: Its Causes and Its Results,* 3d ed., 6 vols. (Oxford: Clarendon, 1873–79), 3:503–4. For a discussion of Freeman's work, see Simmons, *Reversing the Conquest,* 145–55.

38. E. A. Freeman, *Comparative Politics* (London: Macmillan, 1873), 25, quoted in Hugh A. MacDougall, *Racial Myth in English History: Trojans, Teutons, and Anglo-Saxon* (Hanover, N.H.: University Press of New England, 1982), 100.

39. Simmons, *Reversing the Conquest,* 61–65, surveys Palgrave's work.

40. MacDougall, *Racial Myth in English History,* 89–103.

41. Francis Palgrave, *A History of Normandy and of England,* 4 vols. (London: John Parker, 1851–64); the prefatory letter addressed to Anna Gurney is quoted by Simmons, *Reversing the Conquest,* 63.

42. Carlyle's *Chartism* is quoted by Simmons, *Reversing the Conquest,* 95.

43. Quoted in M. T. Clanchy, *England and Its Rulers* (New York: Barnes and Noble, 1983), 51.

44. Kingsley's lecture notes are quoted by Reginald Horsman, *Race and Manifest Destiny: The Origins of American Racial Anglo-Saxonism* (Cambridge: Harvard University Press, 1981), 76.

45. Simmons comments on Edward's failure to leave an heir (*Reversing the Conquest*, 145). Freeman's discussion of Edward is laced with backhanded compliments. "Vice of every kind, injustice, wanton cruelty, were hateful to him. But in all kingly qualities he was utterly lacking" (*Norman Conquest*, 2:23).

46. Simmons, *Reversing the Conquest*, 146.

47. Frank Stenton, *Anglo-Saxon England*, 3d ed. (Oxford: Oxford University Press, 1971), 425.

48. Edward A. Freeman, *The Reign of William Rufus*, 2 vols. (Oxford: Clarendon, 1882), 1:159.

49. See the summary in Tatlock, *Legendary History of Britain*, 351–52. Some of these references are also found in Barlow, *William Rufus*, 106.

50. "By their long beards they make themselves like goats, whose filthy lasciviousness is shamefully imitated by fornicators and sodomites" (Chibnall, *Orderici Vitalis historia ecclesiastica*, book 11, chap. 11, 3:362.

51. The knight who dreamed that he strangled in his hair promptly had his locks shorn. See William of Malmesbury, *Historia novella*, trans. K. R. Potter (London: Thomas Nelson, 1955), 5–6. For general comments on effeminate dress, see William of Malmesbury, *De Gestis regum Anglorum*, 2:369–70. These episodes are discussed by Tatlock, *Legendary History of Britain*, 352.

52. Tatlock, *Legendary History of Britain*, 352.

53. Barlow, *William Rufus*, 106.

54. Hair was society's most visible marker of who was free and who was not. See John Thrupp, *The Anglo-Saxon Home: History of the Domestic Institutions and Customs of England, from the Fifth to the Eleventh Century* (London: Longman, Green, 1862), 173–77. Recent work by Robert Bartlett has confirmed the importance of hair and haircutting; see "Symbolic Meanings of Hair in the Middle Ages," *Transactions of the Royal Historical Society*, ser. 6, no. 4 (1994): 43–60.

55. Havelock Ellis, *Sexual Inversion*, vol. 1, part 4 of *Studies in the Psychology of Sex*, 2 vols. (1905; reprint, New York: Random House, 1936), 9, 40.

56. G. Rattray Taylor, *Sex in History* (New York: Vanguard Press, 1954), 34.

57. Freeman, *William Rufus*, 1:157–59, 2:502–3; Freeman collects all the denunciations of William in vol. 2, appendix G.

58. Bailey, *Homosexuality and the Western Christian Tradition*, 123, citing Freeman and Taylor.

59. Tatlock, *Legendary History of Britain*, 353.

60. Christopher Brooke, *The Saxon and Norman Kings* (London: Batsford, 1963), 162.

61. Poole, *From Domesday Book to Magna Carta*, 99. For a summary of similar views, see Michael Goodich, *The Unmentionable Vice: Homosexuality in the Later Medieval Period* (Santa Barbara: ABC-Clio, 1979), 4–5.

62. Jack Lindsay, *The Normans and Their World* (London: Hart-Davis, MacGibbon, 1974), 14.

63. Barlow, *William Rufus*, 109–10.

64. Barlow, *Norman Conquest and Beyond,* 167.

65. Alan Bray, *Homosexuality in Renaissance England* (1982; reprint, New York: Columbia University Press, 1995), 7.

66. Bailey, *Homosexuality and the Western Christian Tradition,* 122–23, 127.

67. Boswell, *Christianity, Social Tolerance,* 230.

68. Boswell, *Christianity, Social Tolerance,* 230.

69. George Chauncey, *Gay New York: Gender, Urban Culture, and the Making of the Gay Male World, 1890–1940* (New York: Basic Books, 1994), 55.

70. On the eleventh- and twelfth-century tradition of Ælfric's works, see Malcolm Godden, "Ælfric and the Vernacular Prose Tradition," in *The Old English Homily and Its Backgrounds,* ed. Paul E. Szarmach and Bernard F. Huppé (Albany: State University of New York Press, 1978), 110–11.

71. On the dating and provenance of the manuscripts, see N. R. Ker, *Catalogue of Manuscripts Containing Anglo-Saxon* (Oxford: Clarendon, 1957): Oxford, Bodleian Library, Junius 121, third quarter, eleventh century, Worcester (Ker no. 338); Cambridge, Corpus Christi College 190, part B, mid–eleventh century, Exeter (Ker no. 45B); Oxford, Bodleian Library, Laud Misc. 482, mid–eleventh century, Worcester (Ker no. 343); Brussels, Bibliothèque royale, 8558-63, eleventh century, southeastern (Ker no. 10); London, British Library, Cotton Tiberius A.iii, mid–eleventh century, Canterbury (Ker no. 186).

72. See Gransden, *Historical Writing in England,* 157–58.

73. Chibnall, *Orderici Vitalis historia æcclesiastica,* book 4, 2:240–41 (on Alfred's virtue). Ordericus compares the generosity of English kings to the poor to the avaricious character of Normans, especially *William Rufus,* book 8, chap. 8, 174–75. Bede is cited as one of Ordericus's models (preface; 1:130–31). See Chibnall's comments on Bede's influence, 1:56–57, 84–85.

74. There is a good assessment in Horsman, *Race and Manifest Destiny,* 10–12. See also MacDougall, *Racial Myth in English History,* 7–27.

75. Valerie I. J. Flint, "The *Historia regum Britanniae* of Geoffrey of Monmouth: Parody and Its Purpose: A Suggestion," *Speculum* 54 (1979): 447–68. See the earlier suggestion by Robert Hanning, *The Vision of History in Early Britain* (New York: Columbia University Press, 1966), 124.

76. Geoffrey of Monmouth, *History of the Kings of Britain,* trans. Sebastian Evans, rev. Charles W. Dunn (New York: Dutton, 1958), see book 2, chap. 6, pp. 32–33 for Mempricius, and book 11, chap. 7, pp. 238–39 for Malgo. The Latin is taken from Acton Griscom, *The "Historia regum Britanniae" of Geoffrey of Monmouth* (New York: Longman, Green, 1929).

77. See chapter 5, notes 32–33.

78. Tatlock, *Legendary History of Britain,* 353.

79. For an introduction to the text, see Edward Donald Kennedy, "Chronicles and Other Historical Writing," in *A Manual of the Writings in Middle English, 1050–1500,* ed. Albert E. Hartung (New Haven: Connecticut Academy of Arts and Sciences, 1989), 8:2611–17.

80. I. J. Kirby has suggested that Laȝamon did not follow his source and did not repeat a story told against his own origins but rather that he distinguished Angles from Saxons and upheld the honor of the former against the latter. See "Angles and Saxons in Laȝamon's *Brut,*" *Studia Neophilologica* 36 (1964): 51–62. But Neil Wright argues that Laȝamon does not make such a distinction and that he follows the political lines

laid down by Wace, who got them from Geoffrey of Monmouth. See "Angles and Saxons in La3amon's *Brut:* A Reassessment," in *The Text and Tradition of La3amon's "Brut,"* ed. Françoise H. M. Le Saux (Cambridge: D. S. Brewer, 1994), 161–70.

81. I quote the Caligula text, *La3amon: "Brut,"* ed. G. L. Brook and R. F. Leslie (London: Oxford University Press, 1963, 1978), 1:3; references to volume, page number, and line are given in the text; the translation is mine. For recent work on the poem, see Françoise H. M. Le Saux, *La3amon's "Brut": The Poem and Its Sources* (Cambridge: D. S. Brewer, 1989).

82. Thomas Miller, ed. and trans., *The Old English Version of Bede's Ecclesiastical History of the English People,* EETS, OS, 95, 96, 110, 111 (London: Oxford University Press, 1890–98; reprint, 1959–63). The manuscript is Cambridge, University Library Kk. 3.18, written at Worcester in the second half of the eleventh century; see Ker, *Catalogue,* no. 23.

83. Chibnall, *Orderici Vitalis historia ecclesiastica,* 2:241.

84. O. Arngart, ed., *The Proverbs of Alfred,* 2 vols. (Lund: C. W. K. Gleerup, 1942–55). On the use of the Proverbs in La3amon, see Tatlock, *Legendary History of Britain,* 497.

85. See Emma Mason, *St Wulfstan of Worcester, c. 1008–1095* (Oxford: Basil Blackwell, 1990), on Wulfstan and his achievement.

86. Quoted in Southern, "Aspects of the European Tradition of Historical Writing," 249–50.

87. Christine Franzen, *The Tremulous Hand: A Study of Old English in the Thirteenth Century* (Oxford: Clarendon, 1991), 184.

88. See Sir Frederick Pollock and Frederic William Maitland, *The History of English Law before the Time of Edward I,* 2 vols., 2d ed. (1895; reprint, Cambridge: Cambridge University Press, 1968), 1:97; on the Norman law books, see 1:98–110. See also Mary P. Richards, "The Manuscript Contexts of the Old English Laws: Tradition and Innovation," in *Studies in Earlier Old English Prose,* ed. Paul E. Szarmach (Albany: State University of New York Press, 1986), 171–92. On the continuity between Anglo-Saxon law and the laws collected as *Leges Henrici Primi,* see L. J. Downer, ed. and trans., *Leges Henrici Primi* (Oxford: Clarendon, 1972), 2–7.

89. See Mary P. Richards, *Texts and Their Traditions in the Medieval Library of Rochester Cathedral Priory* (Philadelphia: American Philosophical Society, 1988), 46–52.

90. Wendy E. J. Collier, "'Englishness' and the Worcester Tremulous Hand," *Leeds Studies in English* 26 (1995): 43.

91. Douglas Moffat, ed., *The Soul's Address to the Body: The Worcester Fragments* (East Lansing, Mich.: Colleagues Press, 1987); see 1–6 for a description of the manuscript. See also Franzen, *Tremulous Hand,* 12–14, 70–71.

92. *Sanctus Beda,* ed. Bruce Dickins and R. M. Wilson, in *Early Middle English Texts* (Cambridge: Bowes and Bowes, 1951). For a recent examination of texts indicating knowledge of Anglo-Saxon after the Old English period, see Hans Sauer, "Knowledge of Old English in the Middle English Period?" in *Trends in Linguistics: Language History and Linguistic Modelling,* ed. Raymond Hickey and Stanisław Puppel (Berlin: Walter de Gruyter, 1997), 791–814.

93. "Cuthbert's Letter on the Death of Bede," in *Bede's Ecclesiastical History of the English People,* ed. and trans. Bertram Colgrave and R. A. B. Mynors (Oxford: Oxford University Press, 1969), 582–83.

94. Franzen, *Tremulous Hand,* 59.

95. Franzen, *Tremulous Hand,* 54–59.

96. Franzen, *Tremulous Hand,* 102, explains that he might have realized either that the task was too difficult or that it was not the best way to make the texts available.

97. I thank Wendy E. J. Collier for permission to quote from her unpublished Ph.D. thesis, "The Tremulous Worcester Scribe and His Milieu: A Study of His Annotations," University of Sheffield, 1992, 46–49.

98. Collier, "Tremulous Worcester Scribe," 240; the gloss is noted by Josef Raith, ed., *Die altenglische Version des Halitgar'schen Bussbuches (sog. Poenitentiale Pseudo-Ecgberti,* Bibliothek der Angelsächsischen Prosa 13, 2d ed. (1933; reprint, Darmstadt: Wissenschaftliche Buchgesellschaft, 1964), 18, note to canon 6.

99. Raith, *Die altenglische Version des Halitgar'schen Bussbuches,* book 4, canon 10, p. 52; gloss noted in Raith's apparatus.

100. The manuscript is Oxford, Bodleian Library, Junius 121; see Collier, "Tremulous Worcester Scribe," 240–43.

101. Collier, "Tremulous Worcester Scribe," 44, citing Oxford, Bodleian Library, Hatton 115, folios 23–25. See Ker, *Catalogue,* no. 332, art. 4.

102. Pierre J. Payer, *Sex and the Penitentials: The Development of a Sexual Code, 550–1150* (Toronto: University of Toronto Press, 1984), 82.

103. Cambridge, Corpus Christi College 265 is a Worcester manuscript, a predominantly Latin collection that, significantly, has a thirteenth-century table of contents. This manuscript does not contain Halitgar's *Penitential,* but it does hold a number of other Latin handbooks, including those attributed to Egbert and Theodore, both prominent English authorities. In this manuscript, the *Penitential* of Egbert is found on pp. 37–50 and excerpts from the *Penitential* of Pseudo-Theodore are found on pp. 50–51, 58–59, 66, 95–95. See M. R. James, *Catalogue of Manuscripts of Corpus Christi College, Cambridge,* 2 vols. (Cambridge: Cambridge University Press, 1912), 2:14–21.

104. Joscelyn (or a contemporary) compared two versions of the passage from the *Old English Penitential* quoted above. He corrected a reading in one of them. Junius 121 reads "geonglicum besmiteð," which Joscelyn corrected to "geonglingum besmiteð," basing his correction on Laud Misc. 482. This correction is noted by Raith, *Die altenglische Version des Halitgar'schen Bussbuches,* 18, note to canon 6. On Joscelyn's work, see M. Sue Hetherington, "The Recovery of the Anglo-Saxon Lexicon," in *Anglo-Saxon Scholarship,* ed. Berkhout and Gatch, 79–89.

105. H. G. Richardson and G. O. Sayles, ed. and trans., *Fleta* (London: Bernard Quaritch, 1955), chap. 35, "Of Arson" ("De combustione domorum"), 2:90.

106. Pollock and Maitland, *History of English Law,* 1:206.

107. Bailey, *Homosexuality and the Western Christian Tradition* 145–46. See also Pollock and Maitland, *History of English Law,* 2:556.

108. Pollock and Maitland, *History of English Law,* 1:210. Boswell exaggerates the significance of *Fleta,* noting that the text juxtaposed bestiality and sodomy and translating the text's reference to "sodomites" as "persons of their own gender." There is no reason to believe that "sodomite" would have been defined in that way in the mid–thirteenth century, however. The Tremulous Hand, as I have shown, glossed bestiality as sodomy at about the same time. See Boswell, *Christianity, Social Tolerance,* 292 notes 69–70.

109. Pollock and Maitland, *History of English Law,* 2:556–57; see also 1:130.

110. Douglas Moffat, "Sin, Conquest, Servitude: English Self-Image in the Chron-

icles of the Early Fourteenth Century," in *The Work of Work: Servitude, Slavery, and Labor in Medieval England,* ed. Allen J. Frantzen and Moffat (Glasgow: Cruithne, 1994), 146–47.

111. Moffat, "Sin, Conquest, Servitude," 153.

112. Moffat, "Sin, Conquest, Servitude," 157.

113. Angus F. Cameron, "Middle English in Old English Manuscripts," in *Chaucer and Middle English Studies in Honour of Rossell Hope Robbins,* ed. Beryl Rowland (Kent, Ohio: Kent State University Press, 1974), 218–29.

114. Anne Hudson, *The Premature Reformation: Wycliffite Texts and Lollard History* (Oxford: Clarendon, 1988); see especially chap. 9, "The Context of Vernacular Wycliffism," 390–445. The fourteenth-century movement was "premature" because England lacked a system of secular education, printing, and widespread lay literacy. These characteristics were essential to the success of the Reformation a century and a half later. An earlier and seminal study is Margaret Deanesly, *The Lollard Bible and Other Medieval Biblical Versions* (Cambridge: Cambridge University Press, 1920).

115. Nicholas Watson, "Censorship and Cultural Change in Late-Medieval England: Vernacular Theology, the Oxford Translation Debate, and Arundel's Constitutions of 1409," *Speculum* 70 (1995): 822–64. See Watson's list of works of "vernacular theology," 860–64.

116. Hudson, *Premature Reformation,* 237–38, 243–47.

117. Josiah Forchall and Sir Frederic Madden, *The Holy Bible, Containing the Old and New Testaments, with the Apocryphal Books, Made from the Latin by John Wycliffe and His Followers,* 4 vols. (Oxford: Oxford University Press, 1850), 1:59. Also printed in Anne Hudson, ed., *Selections from English Wycliffite Writings* (Cambridge: Cambridge University Press, 1978), 71.

118. Curt F. Bühler, ed., "A Lollard Tract: On Translating the Bible into English," *Medium Aevum* 7 (1938): 174, lines 131–40. I am much indebted to Andrew Cole for sharing his unpublished work on Lollards.

119. Bühler, "Lollard Tract," 174, lines 146–51.

120. See James Wilson Bright and Robert Lee Ramsay, eds., *Liber Psalmorum: The West-Saxon Psalms, Being the Prose Portion, or the "First Fifty," of the So-Called Paris Psalter* (Boston: D. C. Heath and Co., 1907); and Patrick P. O'Neill, "The Old English Introductions to the Prose Psalms of the Paris Psalter: Sources, Structure, and Composition," in *Eight Anglo-Saxon Studies,* ed. Joseph Wittig (Chapel Hill: University of North Carolina Press, 1981), 20–38.

121. See James Parker, *The Early History of Oxford* (Oxford: Oxford University Press, 1885), 39–52. For some other references to Alfred in the Middle English period, see Simon Keynes and Michael Lapidge, eds. and trans., *Alfred the Great: Asser's "Life of King Alfred" and Other Contemporary Sources* (Harmondsworth, Middlesex: Penguin, 1983), 44–48.

122. Sauer, "Knowledge of Old English," 799. The author of *Seinte Marherete* refers to "ald English." See N. R. Ker, ed., *Facsimile of MS. Bodley 34: St. Katherine, St. Margaret, St. Juliana, Hali Meiðhad, Sawles Warde,* EETS, OS, 247 (London: Oxford University Press, 1960), 36r.

123. See chapter 3, notes 25–28.

124. Hudson, *Selections from English Wycliffite Writings,* 25.

125. Bühler, "Lollard Tract," 167.

126. Hudson, *Premature Reformation,* 392. See Andrew W. Cole, "The 'Grand

Translateur' and 'Trewe and Hool Translacioun': Chaucer's Wycliffite Translation Theory in the Prologue to the Treatise on the Astrolabe," forthcoming.

127. Geoffrey Chaucer, *The Riverside Chaucer,* ed. Larry D. Benson, 3d ed. (Boston: Houghton Mifflin, 1987), 87. References to line number are given in the text. Chaucer makes a passing reference to Anglo-Saxon history in *The Nun's Priest's Tale* when Chauntecleer cites the dream of Cenhelm (Kenelm), son of Cenwulf, king of Mercia (d. 821), p. 257, lines 3110–14. See *Riverside Chaucer,* 938, note to lines 3110–12.

128. Chaucer, *Riverside Chaucer,* 812, note to lines 323–24. Paul A. Olson regards the claim as ironic; see *The Canterbury Tales and the Good Society* (Princeton: Princeton University Press, 1986), 91.

129. Margaret Schlauch, "The Man of Law's Tale," in *Sources and Analogues of Chaucer's "Canterbury Tales,"* ed. W. F. Bryan and Germaine Dempster (1941; reprint, New York: Humanities Press, 1958), 155–206. Schlauch prints excerpts from Trivet's *Les Chroniques ecrites pour Marie d'Angleterre, fille d'Edward I,* 165–81 and from the Middle English version of the story of Custance by Chaucer's contemporary, John Gower, 181–206 (*Confessio amantis,* 2:587–1612).

130. Schlauch, "The Man of Law's Tale," 156. The still-standard comparison of Chaucer's version to Trivet is Edward A. Block, "Originality, Controlling Purpose, and Craftsmanship in Chaucer's *Man of Law's Tale,*" *PMLA* 68 (1953): 572–616.

131. Sauer, "Knowledge of Old English," 802–4.

132. Colgrave and Mynors, *Bede's Ecclesiastical History,* book 2, chap. 1, p. 135.

133. Quoted from Schlauch, "Man of Law's Tale," 184, line 723.

134. Quoted from Schlauch, "Man of Law's Tale," 168.

135. Olson, *Canterbury Tales,* 94, comparing Chaucer's Northumbria to that of Bede, Trivet, and Gower.

136. See Block, "Originality, Controlling Purpose," 580–81, for the evidence of Chaucer's simplification of narrative detail; and David Raybin, "Custance and History: Woman as Outsider in Chaucer's *Man of Law's Tale,*" *Studies in the Age of Chaucer* 12 (1990): 65–84.

137. Forchall and Madden, *Holy Bible,* 1:59.

138. Margaret Schlauch, *Chaucer's Custance and the Accused Queens* (New York: New York University Press, 1927); see further Derek Pearsall, *The Canterbury Tales* (London: George Allen and Unwin, 1985), 260.

139. Trivet, *Les Chroniques,* quoted in Schlauch, "Man of Law's Tale," 171. In Chaucer's text, the book would seem to be a Latin copy of the Gospels.

140. Trivet, *Les Chroniques,* 171. Gower notes that the two women are in one bed; Hermengyld goes to bed, "[w]her that this maiden [Custance] with hire lay" (823); cited in Schlauch, "Man of Law's Tale," 187.

141. See D. Michael Quinn, *Same-Sex Dynamics among Nineteenth-Century Americans: A Mormon Example* (Urbana: University of Illinois Press, 1996), 1, 39–40, 86–91.

142. *The Reeve's Tale,* lines 4262–67, in *Riverside Chaucer,* 83.

143. Schlauch, "Man of Law's Tale," 158. See also Olson, *Canterbury Tales,* 95, where he points out that Custance was the name of the daughter of the Roman emperor Tiberius II (reigned 578–82) and that she married one of his generals, Mauritius, who succeeded Tiberius (582–602). Maurice is the name Trivet and Chaucer give to the son of Alla and Custance. For the story of Hermengyld in Old English, see Hans Hecht, ed., *Bischof Wærferths von Worcester Übersetzung der Dialoge Gregors des Grossen* (1900–1907; Darmstadt: Wissenschaftliche Buchgesellschaft, 1965), book 3, chap. 31, 237–40.

There are brief comments by Malcolm Godden, "Wærferth and King Alfred: The Fate of the Old English *Dialogues,*" in *Alfred the Wise,* ed. Jane Roberts and Janet L. Nelson with Malcolm Godden (Cambridge: D. S. Brewer, 1997), 45–46.

144. P. M. Kean, *Chaucer and English Poetry,* 2 vols. (London: Routledge and Kegan Paul, 1972), 2:192. See Carleton Brown, ed., *Religious Lyrics of the Fifteenth Century* (Oxford: Oxford University Press, 1939), "She Sang, Dear Son, Lullay," 7–8; in *Riverside Chaucer,* see 862, note to lines 848–49.

NOTES TO CHAPTER SEVEN

1. See Robert P. Miller, ed., *Chaucer: Sources and Backgrounds* (New York: Oxford University Press, 1977), 484. On the narrator's many apostrophes, see the explanatory notes by Patricia J. Eberle in Geoffrey Chaucer, *The Riverside Chaucer,* ed. Larry D. Benson, 3d ed. (Boston: Houghton Mifflin, 1987), 856–58. Innocent's treatise was addressed to a deposed cardinal; Chaucer reported that he had translated this work himself. See the G Prologue to the *Legend of Good Women,* lines 414–15, in Benson, *Riverside Chaucer,* 600.

2. References to *The Man of Law's Tale* are given by line number from *Riverside Chaucer,* 89–103.

3. For an analysis of hagiographical tropes in *The Man of Law's Tale,* see Melissa M. Furrow, "The Man of Law's St. Custance: Sex and the Saeculum," *Chaucer Review* 24 (1990): 223–35.

4. Æthelburh was allowed to marry Edwin because he promised to allow her to worship as she wished and agreed to consider accepting her faith as his own. Eventually he did so, but only after letters to him and his wife from Pope Boniface and persuasions of other forms, including victory over his assailants, a vision, and the sage counsel of his wise men. See Bertram Colgrave and R. A. B. Mynors, eds. and trans., *Bede's Ecclesiastical History of the English People* (Oxford: Oxford University Press, 1969), book 2, where the saga of Edwin's conversion occupies chaps. 9–14, pp. 162–89.

5. Colgrave and Mynors, *Bede's Ecclesiastical History,* book 2, chap. 9, pp. 162–63.

6. Some of the Anglo-Saxon evidence discussed in this chapter appears in my essay "Bede and Bawdy Bale: Gregory the Great, Angels, and the 'Angli,'" in *Anglo-Saxonism and the Construction of Social Identity,* ed. Allen J. Frantzen and John D. Niles (Gainesville: University of Florida Press, 1997), 17–39.

7. Colgrave and Mynors, *Bede's Ecclesiastical History,* book 2, chap. 1, pp. 132–35. Gregory's puns were not original with Bede; a version of the story is found the anonymous Whitby *Life of St. Gregory,* probably written between 704 and 714 but unknown to Bede when he finished the *Ecclesiastical History* in 731. See Bertram Colgrave, ed. and trans., *The Earliest Life of Gregory the Great* (Cambridge: Cambridge University Press, 1985), 49, 144–45.

8. Gildas, *The Ruin of Britain and Other Documents,* ed. and trans. Michael Winterbottom (London: Phillimore, 1978). See Nicholas Howe, *Migration and Myth-Making in Anglo-Saxon England* (New Haven: Yale University Press, 1989), 33–49, for a discussion of Gildas and the pattern of prophetic history.

9. Colgrave, *Earliest Life,* 144–45 note 42. See "Angles" and variants in the index to Colgrave and Mynors, *Bede's Ecclesiastical History,* 596. Recent studies on the meaning of "angli" in Bede's *Ecclesiastical History* do not discuss Gregory's role in choosing the name, presumably because it is seen as merely symbolic. See D. P. Kirby, *The Earliest English Kings* (London: Unwin Hyman, 1991), 13–15; and H. E. J. Cowdrey, "Bede

and the 'English People,'" *Journal of Religious History* 11 (1981): 501–23. See also Patrick Wormald, "Bede, the *Bretwaldas,* and the Origins of the *Gens Anglorum,*" in *Ideal and Reality in Frankish and Anglo-Saxon Society,* ed. Patrick Wormald with Donald Bullough and Roger Collins (Oxford: Basil Blackwell, 1983), 121–24.

10. Colgrave and Mynors, *Bede's Ecclesiastical History,* book 1, chap. 15, p. 51. For an analysis of the ethnography operating in Bede's analysis, see John Hines, "The Becoming of the English: Identity, Material Culture, and Language in Early Anglo-Saxon England," *Anglo-Saxon Studies in Archaeology and History* 7 (1994): 49–59.

11. Colgrave and Mynors, *Bede's Ecclesiastical History,* book 5, chap. 24, pp. 566–67. Although Bede clearly wished to present the Angles (the angels) as the primary group in the migration, there was never a consensus about which group, the Angles or the Saxons, was primary, or even about where in England they settled. D. P. Kirby notes that Gregory believed that the Saxons settled in the north and the Angles in the south, reversing the usual assumptions about the pattern of distribution and pointing to its arbitrary nature. The *Life* of Wilfrid, who came from York, describes him as a Saxon bishop. See Kirby, *Earliest English Kings,* 12–13.

12. Colgrave and Mynors, *Bede's Ecclesiastical History,* preface, 2–3.

13. Peter Hunter Blair, *The World of Bede* (Cambridge: Cambridge University Press, 1970), 45. See also Hunter Blair, *An Introduction to Anglo-Saxon England* (Cambridge: Cambridge University Press, 1956), 116–17.

14. Colgrave and Mynors, *Bede's Ecclesiastical History,* 72 note 1; the letter is found in Arthur West Haddan and William Stubbs, eds., *Councils and Ecclesiastical Documents Relating to Great Britain and Ireland,* 3 vols. (Oxford: Clarendon, 1871), 3:5 (quoted here), and is translated in Dorothy Whitelock, ed., *English Historical Documents, c. 500–1042* (London: Eyre Methuen, 1979), no. 161, p. 790.

15. David Pelteret, "Slave Raiding and Slave Trading in Early England," *Anglo-Saxon England* 9 (1981): 104. See also Pelteret, *Slavery in Early Mediaeval England: From the Reign of Alfred until the Twelfth Century* (Woodbridge, Suffolk: Boydell Press, 1995).

16. Colgrave, *Earliest Life,* 145 note 43.

17. Dorothy Whitelock, *The Beginnings of English Society* (Harmondsworth, Middlesex: Penguin, 1952), 111. The church allowed penitents to free or manumit slaves as a form of penance or as an act of mercy.

18. On the Council of London of 1102, dominated by Anselm, see the discussion in chapter 6. On the question of selling women who were wives of the clergy into slavery, see A. L. Poole, *From Domesday Book to Magna Carta, 1087–1216,* 2d ed. (Oxford: Oxford University Press, 1955), 40. The Normans' decrees did not affect the status of those who were already slaves, and it continued to be possible for individuals to voluntarily surrender their freedom when compelled by necessity to do so; see Marjorie Chibnall, *Anglo-Norman England, 1066–1166* (Oxford: Basil Blackwell, 1986), 188.

19. Ruth Mazo Karras comments on prostitution and female slaves in "Desire, Descendants, and Dominance: Slavery, the Exchange of Women, and Masculine Power," in *The Work of Work: Servitude, Slavery, and Labor in Medieval England,* ed. Allen J. Frantzen and Douglas Moffat (Glasgow: Cruithne, 1994), 16–29. See also Elizabeth Stevens Girsch, "Metaphorical Usage, Sexual Exploitation, and Divergence in the Old English Terminology for Male and Female Slaves," in *Work of Work,* 30–54. I raise the possibility that the Anglian boys were intended for sexual purposes in *Desire for Origins: New Language, Old English, and Teaching the Tradition* (New Brunswick: Rutgers University Press, 1990), 47.

20. G. L. Brook and R. F. Leslie, eds., *Laʒamon: "Brut,"* 2 vols., EETS, OS, 250, 277 (London: Oxford University Press, 1963, 1978), 2:770. For commentary on versions of the anecdote by Wace and Geoffrey of Monmouth, see Lawman, *Brut,* trans. Rosamond Allen (London: Dent, 1992), 463, notes to lines 14695–923.

21. John Boswell, *Christianity, Social Tolerance, and Homosexuality: Gay People in Western Europe from the Beginning of the Christian Era to the Fourteenth Century* (Chicago: University of Chicago Press, 1980), 144.

22. For an informative survey of Bale's achievement, see Leslie P. Fairfield, *John Bale: Mythmaker for the English Reformation* (West Lafayette, Ind.: Purdue University Press, 1976). See also Hugh A. MacDougall, *Racial Myth in English History: Trojans, Teutons, and Anglo-Saxon* (Hanover, N.H.: University Press of New England, 1982), 33–37. On Bale's Anglo-Saxon manuscripts, see David Dumville, "John Bale, Owner of St. Dunstan's Benedictional," *Notes and Queries* 41 (1994): 291–95.

23. John N. King, *English Reformation Literature: The Tudor Origins of the Protestant Tradition* (Princeton: Princeton University Press, 1982), 56. For recent commentary on Bale in the context of Renaissance humanism, see Alan Stewart, *Close Readers: Humanism and Sodomy in Early Modern England* (Princeton: Princeton University Press, 1997), 38–83.

24. See Fairfield, *John Bale,* 55–56, 121.

25. John Bale, *The Actes of Englysh Votaryes* (London, 1548), 22a–22b. Stewart comments briefly on this episode, *Close Readers*, 42.

26. Contemporary sources invite wordplay on "Angles" and "Ingles." In the sixteenth century "Ingles" meant both "English" and "a boy-favourite (in bad sense): a catamite" *(OED)*, and was used to pun both on "angle" and on "angel." "Ingle" was also a term of abuse for boys who played women on the stage. See Patricia Parker, *Shakespeare from the Margins: Language, Culture, Context* (Chicago: University of Chicago Press, 1996), 143–46.

27. John Bale, *The Image of Bothe Churches* (Antwerp, 1545 or 1546). For Foxe's views, see William Haller, *The Elect Nation: The Meaning and Relevance of Foxe's "Book of Martyrs"* (New York: Harper and Row, 1963).

28. Ultimately these stories derive from Geoffrey of Monmouth, *History of the Kings of Britain,* trans. Sebastian Evans, revised by Charles W. Dunn (New York: Dutton, 1958), book 11, chap. 7, p. 238, for Malgo. Bale indicates a variety of sources, ranging from Gildas to Geoffrey of Monmouth, "Florence" (John) of Worcester, and others, including William Tyndale (22a). Bale's immediate source is probably the *Nova legenda Angliae* of John Capgrave, whose narratives of saints' lives he grossly distorted. See Fairfield, *John Bale,* 114, 121–22.

29. John Bale, *Apology against a Rank Papist* (London, 1550), xxvii, xii (v).

30. John Bale, *The Pageant of Popes* (London, 1574), 36.

31. Bale cites Gregory's "Epistle to Nicolas" *(Pageant of Popes,* 34v–35r).

32. Bale, *Pageant of Popes,* 32.

33. Fairfield, *John Bale,* 17–18, 42–43.

34. This summary is based on Fairfield's analysis, *John Bale,* 31–49.

35. Donald N. Mager, "John Bale and Early Tudor Sodomy Discourse," in *Queering the Renaissance,* ed. Jonathan Goldberg (Durham: Duke University Press, 1994), 141–61. See also Stewart, *Close Readers,* 52–62.

36. John Bale, *A Comedy concernynge Thre Lawes, of Nature, Moses, & Christ, Corrupted by the Sodomytes, Pharysees, and Papystes,* ed. Peter Happé, in *The Complete Plays*

of John Bale, 2 vols. (Cambridge: D. S. Brewer, 1986), 2:65–121. References to act and line number are for quotations from this text. On the attire for Sodomismus, see 121.

37. See Happé, *Complete Plays of John Bale,* 165, note to line 575.

38. Bale, *King Johan,* lines 368–70, in Happé, *Complete Plays of John Bale,* 1:39.

39. Thomas Stapleton, *The History of the Church of England Compiled by Venerable Bede, Englishman* (1565; reprint, Menston, England: Scolar, 1973), 3b. Stapleton's translation is used in the Loeb Classical Library, *Baedae opera historica,* ed. J. E. King (New York: Putnam, 1930).

40. John Bale, *Scriptorum illustrium Maioris Brytanniae* ("Ipswich," but really Wesel, 1548). For a list of Bede's works, including an English translation of the Gospel of John ("in patriam transtulit linguam"), see 50v–52r; for Chaucer's, see 198, unhelpfully alphabetized under *G* for "Galfridus Chaucer").

41. David Savran, "Ambivalence, Utopia, and a Queer Sort of Materialism: How *Angels in America* Reconstructs the Nation," *Theatre Journal* 47 (1995): 218. Some of the following material appears in my essay "Prior to the Normans: The Anglo-Saxons in *Angels in America,*" in *Approaching the Millennium: Essays on Tony Kushner's Angels in America,* ed. Deborah A. Geis and Steven F. Kruger (Ann Arbor: University of Michigan Press, 1997), 134–50.

42. Manifest Destiny had its roots in a theory of natural rights for a particular race that translates into nationalism and then imperialism. See Albert K. Weinberg, *Manifest Destiny* (1935; reprint, Chicago: Quadrangle, 1963), 8 (for the quote), 41.

43. Reginald Horsman, *Race and Manifest Destiny: The Origins of American Racial Anglo-Saxonism* (Cambridge: Harvard University Press, 1981); the phrase "Manifest Destiny" was not coined until 1845; see 219. On Anglo-Saxonism, see Frantzen, *Desire for Origins,* 15–18, and 27–61, where I comment on the phenomenon as a force in Anglo-Saxon studies from the Renaissance to the present.

44. Tony Kushner, "The Secrets of 'Angels,'" *New York Times,* 27 March 1994, H5.

45. Tony Kushner, *Angels in America: A Gay Fantasia on National Themes,* part 1, *Millennium Approaches* (New York: Theatre Communications Group, 1993); part 2, *Perestroika* (New York: Theatre Communications Group, 1994). References to volume and page number are given in the text (vol. 1 for *Millennium Approaches* and vol. 2 for *Perestroika*).

46. Savran, "Ambivalence," 212 note 14.

47. For an excellent summary of this issue, see Clare A. Simmons, *Reversing the Conquest: History and Myth in Nineteenth-Century British Literature* (New Brunswick: Rutgers University Press, 1990), 13–41.

48. The earl Harold was elected king of England at the death of Edward the Confessor in 1066; he was said to have given an oath of allegiance to William, duke of Normandy, and betrayed that oath when he claimed the throne of England. Harold was defeated at the Battle of Hastings by William the Conqueror. See Frank Stenton, *Anglo-Saxon England,* 3d ed. (Oxford: Oxford University Press, 1971), 576–80.

49. According to Savran, "The opposite of nearly everything you say about *Angels in America* will also hold true" ("Ambivalence," 208; see also 222).

50. David J. Bernstein, *The Mystery of the Bayeux Tapestry* (Chicago: University of Chicago Press, 1986), reports that Hitler, like Napoleon, studied the tapestry when he contemplated an invasion of England, 28–30.

51. Bernstein, *Mystery of the Bayeux Tapestry,* 8, 14.

52. Bernstein, *Mystery of the Bayeux Tapestry*, 30.

53. The term was originally used to describe American Protestantism. See E. Digby Baltzell, *The Protestant Establishment: Aristocracy and Caste in America* (New Haven: Yale University Press, 1964). Kushner's elaborate genealogy for Prior Walter attaches a far more ambitious historical and international sense to the term.

54. May McKisack, *The Fourteenth Century, 1307–1399* (Oxford: Oxford University Press, 1959), 219.

55. See Savran, "Ambivalence," 223–24, for an analysis of Kushner's treatment of identity politics and race in this scene.

56. Weinberg, *Manifest Destiny,* 8.

57. Savran, "Ambivalence," 213.

58. Kushner, "Secrets of 'Angels,'" H5.

59. Several reviewers have commented on the identification of Louis with Kushner's own views. See, for example, John Simon, "Angelic Geometry," *New York,* 6 December 1993, 130. Savran says that Louis is "constructed as the most empathetic character in the play" ("Ambivalence," 223).

60. Susan Reynolds, "What Do We Mean by 'Anglo-Saxon' and 'Anglo-Saxons'?" *Journal of British Studies* 24 (1985): 397–98.

61. Reynolds, "What Do We Mean by 'Anglo-Saxon'?" 402–3.

62. On the need for narratives that reverse the usual trajectory of the experience of AIDS, see Steven F. Kruger, *AIDS Narratives: Gender and Sexuality, Fiction and Science* (New York: Garland, 1996), 73–81.

63. Savran, "Ambivalence," 222–23.

64. D. Michael Quinn, *Same-Sex Dynamics among Nineteenth-Century Americans: A Mormon Example* (Urbana: University of Illinois Press, 1996), 2.

NOTES TO THE AFTERWORD

1. George Chauncey, *Gay New York: Gender, Urban Culture, and the Making of the Gay Male World, 1890–1940* (New York: Basic Books, 1994), 6.

2. John D'Emilio, *Sexual Politics, Sexual Communities: The Making of a Homosexual Minority in the United States, 1940–1970* (Chicago: University of Chicago Press, 1983), 33–37.

3. Allan Bérubé, *Coming Out under Fire: Gay Men and Women in World War Two* (New York: Penguin, 1991).

4. D. Michael Quinn, *Same-Sex Dynamics among Nineteenth-Century Americans: A Mormon Example* (Urbana: University of Illinois Press, 1996).

5. Will Fellows, ed., *Farm Boys: Lives of Gay Men from the Rural Midwest* (Madison: University of Wisconsin Press, 1996); Richard Rutt, *Korean Works and Days: Notes from the Diary of a Country Priest* (Rutland, Vt.: Tuttle, 1964), 122–13.

6. Steven Preston recounts that he and his brothers had sex with their uncle after the uncle's marriage (Fellows, *Farm Boys,* 263). For the penitentials, see chapter 4, table 2.

7. On crackdowns against gay men and women in the late 1940s and 1950s, see Bérubé, *Coming Out under Fire,* 257–60. See also D'Emilio, *Sexual Politics,* 49–53.

8. William of Newburgh, *Historia rerum Anglicarum,* quoted in Nancy F. Partner, *Serious Entertainments: The Writing of History in Twelfth-Century England* (Chicago: University of Chicago Press, 1977), 105.

9. Mike Johnson and Sam Jackson are not the real names of these men.

10. Henning Bech, *When Men Meet: Homosexuality and Modernity,* trans. Teresa Mesquit and Tim Davies (Chicago: University of Chicago Press, 1997), 22.

11. Robert Storey and Geoff Crowther, *Korea: A Lonely Planet Travel Survival Kit,* rev. ed. (Hawthorn, Victoria, Australia: Lonely Planet Publications, 1996), 162.

12. See, for example, *Boys like Us: Gay Writers Tell Their Coming Out Stories,* ed. Patrick Merla (New York: Avon, 1996), nearly thirty coming-out stories, most of them by men who grew up in cities and suburbs.

Index

Page numbers in italics refer to figures and captions.